Designing a Secure Microsoft Windows 2000 Network

Designing a Secure Microsoft Windows 2000 Network

iUniverse.com, Inc.

San Jose   New York   Lincoln   Shanghai

Designing a Secure Microsoft Windows 2000 Network

Published by iUniverse.com, Inc.

For information address:
iUniverse.com, Inc.
5220 S 16th, Ste. 200
Lincoln, NE 68512
www.iuniverse.com

Cover Creation by Shay Jones

Graphic Production by Matt Bromley, Associate Consultant
Domhnall CGN Adams, Corporation Sole-http://www.dcgna.com
5721-10405 Jasper Avenue
Edmonton, Alberta, Canada T5J 3S2
(780) 416-2967-dcgna@yahoo.com

CD-ROM Duplication by Paragon Media, Seattle, Washington

ISBN: 0-595-14817-4

Printed in the United States of America

Acknowledgments

We are pleased to acknowledge the following professionals for their important contributions in the creation of this study guide.

Technical Writer and Layout Review—Barbara Kowalik, BFA

Technical Writer—Joseph H. Rawlings III, BSCS, BSCE, ASM, ASEET

Technical Writer and Content Review—Paul Brodeur, BA, D.E.C.

Supplemental Technical Writers—Anthony Iannone, BA; Barb Young, BA, MCSE; Kim Kerr; Terry Beckett; Elizabeth LeReverend

Technical Reviewer—Joseph H. Rawlings III, BSCS, BSCE, ASM, ASEET

Indexer—Loral Pritchett

Cover Creation, Text Conversion and Proofing—Shay Jones, AA, MCSE, MCP

Graphic Designer—Matt Bromley

V.P. Publishing and Courseware Development— Candace Sinclair

Course Prerequisites

The Designing a Secure Microsoft Windows 2000 Network study guide targets individuals who have the following skills:

• Working knowledge of Windows 2000 Directory Services

• Ability to upgrade Microsoft Windows NT 4.0 to Microsoft Windows 2000

• General knowledge of implementing and administering Windows 2000 Directory Services

The Designing a Secure Microsoft Windows 2000 Network exam tests an individual's knowledge and skills for designing a security framework for small, medium, and enterprise networks using Microsoft Windows 2000 technologies.

In addition, we recommend that you have a working knowledge of the English language, so that you are able to understand the technical words and concepts this study guide presents.

To feel confident about using this study guide, you should have the following knowledge or ability:

• The desire and drive to become an MCSE certified technician through our instructions, terminology, activities, quizzes, and study guide content

• Basic computer skills, which include using a mouse, keyboard, and viewing a monitor

• Basic networking knowledge including the fundamentals of working with Internet browsers, e-mail functionality, and search engines

• IP, remote connectivity and security

Hardware and Software Requirements

To apply the knowledge presented in this study guide, you will need the following minimum hardware:

- For Windows 2000 Professional, we recommend 64 megabytes of RAM (32 megabytes as a minimum) and a 1-gigabyte (GB) hard disk space.

- For Windows 2000 Server, we recommend a Pentium II or better processor, 128 megabytes of RAM (64 megabytes minimum), and a 2-GB hard drive. If you want to install Remote Installation Server with Windows 2000 Server, you should have at least two additional gigabytes of hard disk space available.

- CD-ROM drive

- Mouse

- VGA monitor and graphics card

- Internet connectivity

To apply the knowledge presented in this study guide, you will need the following minimum software installed on your computer:

- Microsoft Windows 2000

- Microsoft Internet Explorer or Netscape Communicator

Symbols Used in This Study Guide

To call your attention to various facts within our study guide content, we've included the following three symbols to help you prepare for the Designing a Secure Windows 2000 Network exam.

Tip: The Tip identifies important information that you might see referenced in the certification exam.

Note: The Note enhances your understanding of the topic content.

Warning: The Warning describes circumstances that could be harmful to you and your computer system or network.

How to Use This Study Guide

Although you will develop and implement your own personal style of studying and preparing for the MCSE exam, we've taken the strategy of presenting the exam information in an easy-to-follow, ten-lesson format. Each lesson conforms to Microsoft's model for exam content preparation.

At the beginning of each lesson, we summarize the information that will be covered. At the end of each lesson we round out your studying experience by providing the following four ways to test and challenge what you've learned.

Vocabulary—Helps you review all the important terms discussed in the lesson.

In Brief—Reinforces your knowledge by presenting you with a problem and a possible solution.

Activities—Further tests what you have learned in the lesson by presenting ten activities that often require you to do more reading or research to understand the activity. In addition, we have provided the answers to each activity.

Lesson Quiz—To round out the knowledge you will gain after completing each lesson in this study guide, we have included ten sample exam questions and answers. This allows you to test your knowledge, and it gives you the reasons why the "answers" were either correct or incorrect. This, in itself, enhances your power to pass the exam.

You can also refer to the Glossary at the back of the book to review terminology. Furthermore, you can view the Index to find more content for individual terms and concepts.

Introduction to MCSE Certification

The Microsoft Certified Systems Engineer (MCSE) credential is the highest-ranked certification for professionals who analyze business requirements for system architecture, design solutions, deployment, installation, and configuration of architecture components, as well as troubleshooting system problems.

When you receive your MCSE certification, it proves your competence by having earned a nationally-recognized credential as an information technology professional who works in a typically complex computing environment of medium to large organizations. It is recommended that a Windows 2000 MCSE candidate should have at least one year of experience implementing and administering a network operating system environment.

To help you bridge the gap between needing the knowledge and knowing the facts, this study guide presents concepts and procedures for designing a secure Microsoft Windows 2000 network environment that will help you pass this exam.

The MCSE exams cover a vast range of vendor-independent hardware and software technologies, as well as basic Internet and Windows 2000 design knowledge, technical skills and best practice scenarios.

 Note: This study guide presents technical content that should enable you to pass the Designing a Secure Microsoft Windows 2000 Network certification exam on the first try.

Designing a Secure Microsoft Windows 2000 Network Study Guide Objectives

Successful completion of this study guide is realized when you can competently design a secure network for small, medium, and enterprise-wide organizations using Microsoft Windows 2000 technologies.

You must fully comprehend each of the following objectives and their related tasks to prepare for this certification exam:

- Identify the security risks associated with managing resource access and network data flow

- Describe how key technologies within Windows 2000 can secure a network and its resources

- Create a Windows 2000 administrative structure with permissions assigned only to appropriate users

- Design an Active Directory directory service structure that employs secure and verifiable user account creation and administration

- Define the minimum security requirements for a Windows 2000-based domain controller, application server, file and print server, and workstations

- Plan for securing local data storage of, and providing secure network access to, file and print resources

- Design end-to-end security for data transmission between hosts on a network

- Create a strategy for securing access to non-Microsoft clients within a Windows 2000-based network

- Secure an organization's local resources accessed by remote users using dial-in or Virtual Private Network (VPN) technologies

- Create a plan for securing local resources accessed by remote offices within a wide area network (WAN) environment

- Protect private network resources from public network users

- Design a secure private network that allows user access to public networks

- Design a structure for authenticating trusted users over public networks

- Design a plan for securing data and application access for a private network that can be accessed by trusted partners

- Implement an E-commerce site between your organization and external business partners that allows business communication

- Design a structured methodology for securing a Windows 2000 network

Figures

List of Tables

Table of Contents

Lesson 1

Windows 2000 Security Features and Risk Assessment

Implementing a well-planned and carefully thought-out security system in your computing environment provides important benefits. A good security system design provides the functionality to keep unauthorized outsiders out of your system. It supports your administrative security goals by preventing access or modification of data by legitimate users. A good security system design makes the task of security maintenance in your environment simple and efficient.

By implementing a security system tailored for your specific organizational needs, you can shield the information and resources from unauthorized access, theft, and damage, while enabling your users to access information and resources they need.

Windows 2000 provides new scalable, flexible security processes applicable to both small companies and large international corporations. Most of the new features of Windows 2000 target Internet-based enterprises, however. Windows 2000 Active Directory is used to secure large organizations. Internet public key certificates and logon using Smart Cards provide integrated authentication for network security.

Windows 2000 Active Directory supports a multilevel tree of domains structured as per a new domain model. Two-way transitive trusts (Kerberos trusts) in the domain tree enact trust relationships between domains. Efficient scalability is achieved from the combination of Windows 2000 domain tree structure and Kerberos trusts.

After completing this lesson, you should have a better understanding of the following topics:

*   Security Features Overview
*   Security Risk Assessment

Security Features Overview

Windows 2000 provides security features and tools to implement a security system tailored for your specific organizational needs. Your network and the information within it can not only be protected from outsiders, but protected from the unintentional mishaps of legitimate network users as well. A well-designed security system for your network provides the following functions and features:

Keeps unauthorized outsiders out—By verifying the identity of anyone who attempts to access your organization's computer resources, a well designed security system denies intruders access to system resources, protecting confidential data and your computer programs from theft or damage.

Prevents legitimate users from accessing or modifying specific data—For example, you can ensure that only authorized officers have access to employee payroll information.

Makes it simple and efficient for you to maintain the security in your environment—For example, you can set up password policies that all users within your environment must follow.

Windows 2000 along with its directory service structure of the Active Directory, provides numerous features that enhance the security of your network. Windows 2000 provides the following security features:

- Central storage of security policy and account information

- Automatic updating and synchronization of all security policy and account information across all or specified domain controllers

- Per-property access control for objects

- Transitive trust relationships among domains

- Multiple authentication mechanisms for authenticating both internal and external users, including Windows NT Version 4 users

- Common administrative tools to manage access control and account information

- Smart card support for secure storage of user credentials

- Encryption for data transmitted over the network or stored on disk

Understanding Active Directory

Active Directory for Windows 2000 Server is a directory service that inventories the users and the objects on the network. It uses a structured data store to create a hierarchy for directory information and enables authorized users to access this information.

Windows 2000 Server security integrates with Active Directory to control access to objects in the directory, and provide logon authentication that enables administrators or authorized network users to log on only once and yet be able to manage or navigate the entire network.

Windows 2000 Server security allows even the most complex network to be more easily managed with the policy-based administration.

 Note: A directory merely stores information about objects in a hierarchical structure on a network. Active Directory does far more. It provides methods for storing and making data available to network users, and it stores information about user accounts and enables authorized users to access the data.

Active Directory implements the Internet standard directory and naming protocols. The Active Directory database engine provides transactional support and supports various application programming interface standards.

Windows 2000 and Windows NT have the following different namespaces:

Windows 2000 Active Directory hierarchical namespace for user, group, and computer account information—Accounts are grouped by Organizational Units (OUs). OUs inherit security policies from higher level OUs, and inheritance is either blocked or enforced. Active Directory stores domain security policy information, provides replication for Domain Controllers (DCs), and facilitates remote administration.

Windows NT 4.0 flat namespace—Windows NT 4.0 domain namespaces have no hierarchy— everything is at the same level. Therefore, the Windows NT 4.0 domain namespace is often called a flat namespace. The flat domain namespace consists of user, global group, local group and computer accounts (Figure 1.1).

Figure 1.1 Windows 2000 Active Directory Versus Windows NT

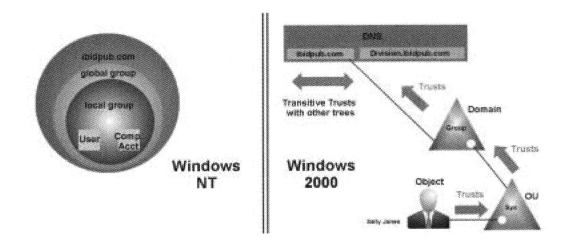

Understanding Access Control Lists (ACLs)

Access control is the process of granting or denying users and groups authorization to access objects on the network.

The following controls access to the Active Directory objects and Windows 2000 resources:

- Discretionary ACLs
- Permission inheritance
- Logon process
- Access tokens

Windows 2000 opens only those resources you have permission to use. You must log on with a set of verifiable security credentials. These credentials are compared against a set of permissions assigned to

Active Directory objects and network resources, such as shared folders and the New Technology File System (NT File System) files.

 Note: NT File System and File Allocation Table (FAT) are Windows NT file systems. NT File System features, such as transaction logs to help disk failure recoveries, improve reliability. To control access to files, permissions are set for directories or individual files.

You can use all the network resources for which you have permissions as soon as Windows 2000 and Active Directory authenticate your identity.

Defining Discretionary Access Control Lists (DACLs)

Windows 2000 Discretionary Access Control Lists (DACLs) are lists of security groups and user accounts, and their associated permissions. DACLs impose resource security for each entry in the list, and are used in the following ways:

• DACLs define user access levels and object permissions

• DACLs are attached to all resources in a Windows 2000 network

• DACLs store the type of resource access, either granted or denied, for a resource

Access Control Entries (ACEs), the entries in the DACL, identify permissions for a group or user object.

 Tip: Resource access is usually granted to groups containing users, not often to individual user accounts. Therefore, DACL entries (ACEs) are usually group objects.

Windows 2000 network resources have DACLs for the following objects:

Files and folders on NTFS volumes—DACLs for these objects define permissible file or folder user actions.

Active Directory objects—DACLs for these objects define permissible administrator or user actions on objects, such as attribute modification for a user account.

Printer objects—DACLs for these objects define permissible user actions on printers, such as print authorization and queue management (Figure 1.2).

Figure 1.2 DACLs

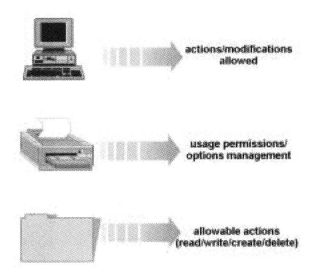

Note: Every Windows 2000 user must have a user account. When a user or group is granted a particular type of access permission, the permission data is added to the DACL. When a user requests access to an object, the system checks the Security Identifier (SID) and group memberships against the DACL before allowing the request.

Object Ownership

Every Windows 2000 object (whether in Active Directory or in an NTFS volume) has an owner. By default, Windows 2000 assigns the creator as the object's owner. The owner controls how permissions are set on objects and to whom permissions are granted.

Administrators create and own most objects in Active Directory and on network servers. For example, when they install programs on the server administrators own the object. Users create and own data files, some of which are network servers.

You can transfer object ownership according to the following guidelines:

Take-ownership permission—The current owner can grant other users the take-ownership permission that allows those users to take ownership at any time.

Administrative control—An administrator can take ownership of any object through administrative control. For example, if an employee leaves the company, the administrator can take ownership of the ex-employee's files.

Administrative no transfer—An administrator cannot transfer ownership to others. This restriction makes administrators accountable for their actions.

Permissions Attached to Objects

Permissions, or access rights, are attached to objects as the primary means for controlling access control to those objects. Permissions allow or deny users or groups particular user or group actions. For example, a Read permission can be attached to a file. Permissions are primarily realized by security descriptors, which also define auditing and ownership.

Object-type permissions define the types of objects that a user or group is entitled to create or delete. An object-type permission entry has the following syntax:

Group: Permission: Object-type

For example, permissions for a file could look as follows:

Everyone: create; delete: file.

You cannot manage this permission type through the Properties dialog box.

Active Directory Object Permissions

Active Directory Object permissions control access to Active Directory objects. Each type of object can be only attached to certain types of permissions. The way in which you can attach these permissions delegates administrative responsibility for Active Directory objects (Figure 1.3).

You can attach the following permissions to Active Directory objects:

- Create Child (specific to the type of object or general for any object under the container)
- Delete Child (specific to the type of object or general for any object under the container)
- Read Property (specific to an individual property of the object or general for all attributes of the object)
- Write Property (specific to an individual property of the object or general for all attributes of the object)
- List Contents
- Write Self
- Delete Tree
- List Object
- Control Access (specific to an individual control operation or general for all control operations)

Figure 1.3 Objects With Permissions

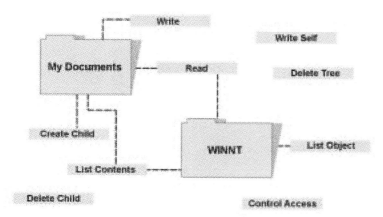

Inheritance of Permissions

Inheritance is a Windows 2000 feature reserved to administrators, whereby objects at one level inherit the permissions of the level immediately above. For example, the files in a folder inherit the folder's permissions (Figure 1.4).

Figure 1.4 Inheritance

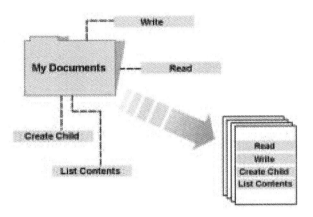

Inheritance File and Folder Permissions

By default, once you set permissions on a parent folder, all new files and subfolders that you create in the folder inherit these permissions.

To prevent all of them from inheriting permissions, select **This folder only** in **Apply onto** when you assign special permissions for the parent folder.

To prevent certain files or subfolders from inheriting permissions, follow these steps:

From **This folder only**, right-click the file or subfolder, choose **Properties**, and then select **Security** (Figure 1.5).

Figure 1.5 The Security Property Page

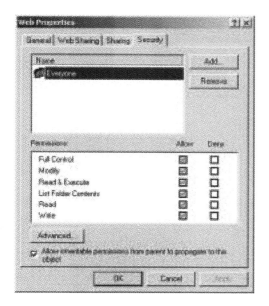

Clear the **Allow inheritable permissions from the parent to propagate to this object** check box and select **OK.**

From the **Security** popup (Figure 1.6), choose **Remove**.

Figure 1.6 The Security Popup

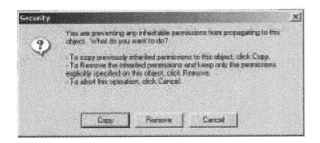

If the **Permissions** check boxes appear shaded on the **Security** page, the file or folder has inherited permissions from the parent folder. You can change inherited permissions by one of the following methods:

• Change the permissions for the parent folder, and then the child file or folder inherits the changes to the permissions

• Choose the opposite permission option (Allow or Deny) to override the inherited permission (Figure 1.7)

Figure 1.7 Inheritance Override

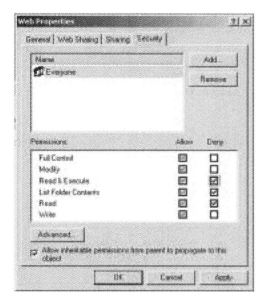

Neither Allow nor Deny is selected for a permission (Figure 1.8) on the **Security** page when one of the following situations has occurred:

- The group or user has obtained the permission through group membership

- The group or user is implicitly denied the permission

To explicitly allow or deny a permission, choose the appropriate check box.

Figure 1.8 Blank Permissions Check Boxes

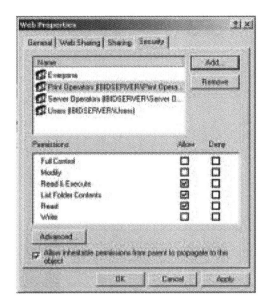

Object Managers

To change permissions for an individual object, start the appropriate tool and change the properties for that object.

For example, to change permissions for a file, from Windows Explorer, right-click the filename, and then choose **Properties** (Figure 1.9).

Figure 1.9 Properties

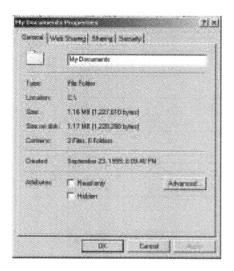

In the dialog box that appears, change permissions for the file. There are five object types, and five object managers. For each object type, there corresponds one object manager. Table 1.1 lists the object types, their object managers, and the tools you can use to manage objects.

Table 1.1 Object Manager

Object Type	Object Manager	Management Tool
Files and folders	NTFS	Windows Explorer
Shares	Server service	Windows Explorer
Active Directory objects	Active Directory	Active Directory Users and Computers
Registry keys	The Registry	REGEDIT32 command
Printer	Print spooler	Start menu

Using Security Configuration Tools

The expression, security configuration, is interchangeable with the expression, security settings. Security settings include security policies such as account and local policies, and access control policies such as services, files, and Registry. You can set security policies for event log, group membership such as restricted groups, Internet Protocol Security, security policies, and public key policies.

Windows 2000 fulfills the most stringent security requirements provided security is deployed after a careful planning assessment and with effective security guidelines.

 Note: The Windows 2000 security configuration tools enable central security configuration and enterprise-level security analysis.

Through **Active Directory Users and Computers**, you can configure various security features as follows:

• View or set the permissions for an Active Directory object

- View the users or groups to which these permissions are granted.

- View or set the auditing events for an object, and the object's owner (Figure 1.10).

Figure 1.10 Active Directory Users and Computers

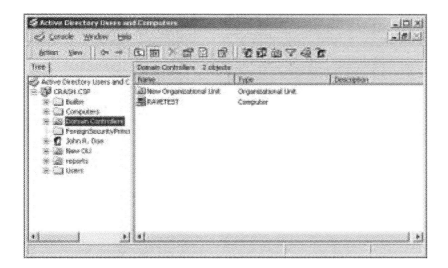

 Note: A security template is a file that stores a group of security settings. Each security template in Windows 2000 lists security settings based on a computer's role, ranging from low security domain clients to highly secure domain controllers.

To configure and analyze security settings, you can use the **Security Template** and **Security Configuration and Analysis** snap-ins found in MMC, and the **SECEDIT** command-line utility. The tools allow you to load, combine, and edit the security templates to configure local security, and to export security templates to other computers on a network.

More specifically, to define and control security templates, use the **Security Template** snap-in from MMC (Figure 1.11), and to configure and analyze security locally, use the **Security Configuration and Analysis** snap-in, also from MMC (Figure 1.12).

Figure 1.11 Security Templates

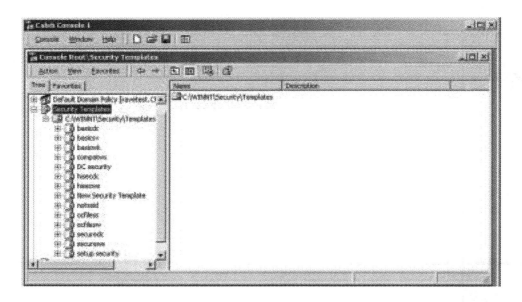

Figure 1.12 Security Configuration and Analysis

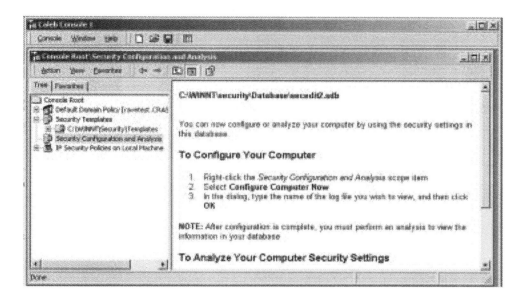

To configure security in Active Directory, use the **Group Policy** snap-in from MMC (Figure 1.13).

Figure 1.13 Group Policy

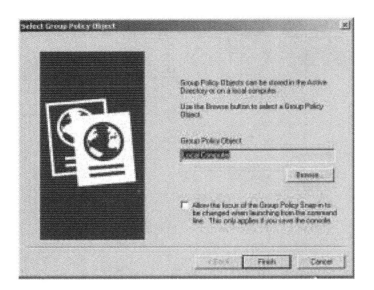

Note: When you import a security template into a group policy object, **Group Policy** implements the template's changes in all members of that group policy object, whether users or computers.

Security settings define how the system behaves with regard to security. Administrators use Group Policy objects to apply the appropriate security levels to protect enterprise systems.

The organizational and functional character of the OU is crucial in determining security settings for a Group Policy object that contains several or many computers. For example, the security level necessary for an OU of sales department computers is significantly different from an OU of payroll department computers.

Understanding Encryption

Windows 2000 uses several encryption methods to authenticate digital signatures: Signed ActiveX controls and Java classes for Internet Explorer, and digital signatures for integrity in various programs.

The Windows 2000 Encryption File System (EFS) enables you to encrypt entire folders or individual files and to read the data in plaintext without explicitly having to decrypt it. Once you have edited a file, it automatically re-encrypts. EFS combines the speed of secret key encryption with the greater security of public key encryption.

Secret Key Encryption

Secret key encryption, also called symmetric encryption, is a fast but less secure encryption method that uses the same key to encrypt and to decrypt. For example, when encrypting a file, EFS randomly generates a key and uses it for fast encryption. To render its encryption more secure, EFS then uses public encryption to encrypt the key itself.

Public Key Encryption

Public key encryption, also called asymmetric encryption, is a very secure but slower encryption method that uses two keys: a public key to encrypt messages or other data and a private key to decrypt them. The private key is kept confidential. The public key is freely given out to all potential correspondents or, in the case of EFS, is used to encrypt the secret key that EFS used to encrypt the data.

Understanding Certificates

A public key certificate is a digitally signed statement certifying that a public key indeed belongs to the person, device, or service that holds the corresponding private key. Certificates are issued for various functions such as Web user or server authentication, secure e-mail (S/MIME), IP security, Transaction Layer Security (TLS), and code signing. In an organization that uses the Windows 2000 enterprise certification, certificates can aid in the log on to Windows 2000 domains.

Most certificates are based on the X.509 standard, a fundamental technology of Windows 2000. Certificates normally contain the following information:

• Subject public key value

- Subject identifier information (name and e-mail address)

- Validity period (the length of time that the certificate is valid)

- Issuer identifier information

- The issuer's name, which testifies that the correspondence or binding between the subject public key and the subject identifier information is valid

A certificate is valid only for the period of time defined by the certificate's **Valid From** and **Valid To** dates. After the validity period expires, the subject of the expired certificate must request a new one. The issuer can revoke a certificate. Each issuer maintains a Certificate Revocation List (CRL) that programs can use to check the validity of any given certificate.

 Note: A great advantage of public key certificates is that hosts require authentication for network access do not need to maintain a set of passwords. Instead, they merely establish trust in a certificate issuer.

When a secure Web server or other host trusts that the issuer has verified the identity of the certificate subject, it designates the issuer as a trusted root authority. It places the issuer's self-signed certificate that contains the issuer's public key into the host computer's trusted root CA. Intermediate or subordinate CAs are trusted only if they are certified by a trusted root CA.

Certificate-Based Authentication

With a certificate-based authentication, an administrator can support authentication of external users that have secure access to company data. For example, an external consultant may need to upload contract work to a server.

To authenticate users external to your system, the following factors are necessary:

- The external user must have a certificate

- A user account must be established for each external user

- The external user's certificate must be issued by a CA trusted by the site, domain, or OU in which the user has the account

- Name mapping must be established between the external user certificate and the Active Directory account set up for authenticated access.

Any external user with a mapped certificate can then access permitted locations in your organization.

The authentication process is transparent to the external user.

 Note: Ensure that the external users' rights and permissions meet their work needs as well as your organization's security policy.

The Certificates Snap-In

The Certificates snap-in enables administrators to perform many certificate management tasks in their personal certificate store and the certificate stores for any user, computer, or service within their influence.

Both administrators and users can use the Certificates snap-in to request new certificates from Windows 2000 enterprise certification authorities.

Users can find, view, import, and export certificates from within certificate stores. Users usually do not need to manage their own certificates and certificate stores. Administrators do so by means of policy settings and programs that use certificates.

Understanding Security Protocols

Authentication based on Internet standard security protocols is another aspect of Windows security. Kerberos Version 5 is the default protocol. Windows NT LAN Manager (NTLM) is supported to provide backward-compatibility. The Transport Layer Security (TLS) protocol, based on Secure Sockets Layer Version 3 (SSL3/TLS), supports client authentication by mapping user public key certificates to existing Windows NT accounts. These processes give Windows 2000 fuller support for public key protocols. Whether using shared secret authentication or public key security, common administration tools are used to manage account information and access control.

Understanding Trust Relationships

Windows 2000 supports two types of trusts: Certificate Authority (CA) trust and Domain trust. CA trust allows the user to trust certificates issued by another certificate authority. Domain trust enables a user to authenticate another domain's resources and an administrator to administer user rights for the other domain's users.

Domain Trust

When a domain joins an existing forest or domain tree, a transitive trust is automatically set up. This is the standard type of trust relationship.

Trust relationships build on one another. For example, if Domain A trusts Domain B and Domain B trusts Domain C, then Domain A trusts Domain C (Figure 1.14).

Figure 1.14 Domain Trusts

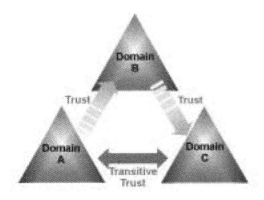

Transitive trusts are always two-way relationships used for the purposes of authentication.

Windows 2000 lets you also establish an inter-domain logical relationship to allow pass-through authentication. In this relationship, the trusting domain honors the trusted domain's logon authentications.

A trusting domain can give rights and permissions to user accounts and global groups defined in a trusted domain, even though the user accounts or groups do not exist in the trusting domain's directory.

Understanding Smart Cards

Smart Cards, though they look like automatic teller machine bankcards, hold many times more information. Portable and tamper-resistant, they securely store public and private keys, passwords, and other types of personal information. To use a Smart Card, a Smart Card reader must be attached to the computer and the user must have a Personal Identification Number (PIN).

Smart Cards provide security solutions for client authentication, interactive logging on to a Windows 2000 domain, code signing, and securing e-mail. Windows 2000 also supports cryptographic Smart Cards.

Smart Cards have the following features:

• Tamper-resistant storage for protecting private keys and other forms of personal information

• Isolation of security-critical authentication computations

• Isolation from key exchange with other parts of the organization that do not need to know

• Portability of credentials and other private information between computers

A Smart Card uses cryptography-based identification and proof of possession when it authenticates you to a domain.

Smart Cards are safer than password-based authentication. Upon merely obtaining a user's password and assuming the user's identity, an impostor could simply use the password to access the network and wreak havoc. Some users even choose easy-to-guess passwords, which facilitate password theft. Smart Cards, however, force a would-be intruder to obtain both the Smart Card and the user's PIN to impersonate the authorized user. This requirement makes it much more difficult to fraudulently use a Smart Card. Furthermore, a Smart Card locks after a few consecutive incorrect PIN entries.

Understanding IP Security

In planning an effective security implementation, follow these guidelines:

Evaluate the type of information sent over your network—Since some departments may require a higher level of security than others, find out what kind of data they exchange: sensitive financial data, proprietary information, electronic mail, and so forth.

Determine where your information is stored—Know how the information routes through the network, and from what computers information is accessed. Obtaining a profile of the speed, capacity, and utilization of the network prior to implementation facilitates performance optimization.

Evaluate your network's vulnerability to attacks—Determine if you have implemented a secure network. Test it for potential weaknesses.

Design and document an enterprise-wide network security plan—Take into account the security framework of Windows 2000, particularly the Active Directory model and how security is applied to Group Policy (Figure 1.15).

Figure 1.15 Effective Planning—Guidelines

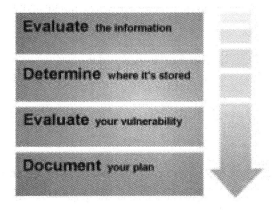

Consider these issues and concerns as you plan and design network security:

What do you want to secure?—Should it be traffic between some or all computers, or only certain protocols or ports?

How should you secure it?—Should you secure the traffic with integrity or confidentiality and at what strength?

Where should you secure it?—Should you secure it just over remote access connections, or also through the Local Area Network (LAN)?

Who will manage policy?—Should domain administrators, server administrators, or local computer administrators manage the policy?

Will export requirements need to be met?—Will data be accessed by both computers running domestic and export versions of Windows 2000? (Figure 1.16).

Figure 1.16 Effective Planning—Issues to Consider

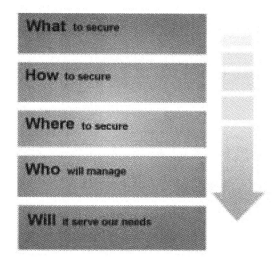

You should also consider the following issues as you plan a secure network:

Design, create, and test the IPSec policies—Clarify and refine what policies and policy structures are truly necessary. For realistic results as you test deployment scenarios, run normal workloads on applications. To view packet contents with Network Monitor or a sniffer, you cannot use the High security method level or ESP. Use the Medium security method level or set your custom security method to AH.

Reduce administrative overhead spent on policy—Whenever possible, use the predefined policies, rules, and filter actions that you can activate, modify, or use as a template for defining your own.

Extensive use of the Internet, intranets, branch offices, and remote access results in a constant data flow between networks. Administrators and other network professionals must safeguard the data from these following potential dangers:

- Modification while en route

- Interception, viewing, or copying

- Access by unauthenticated persons

To guard against these security breaches, Windows 2000 Server implements the IP Security Protocol (IPSec) as specified by the Internet Engineering Task Force (IETF). Since IPSec operates below the transport level, applications transparently inherit its security services. Microsoft Windows IP Security uses industry-standard encryption algorithms to provide secure TCP/IP communications on both sides of a firewall. As a result, Windows 2000 security defends against both external and internal attacks.

IPSec Security Negotiation

Before two computers can exchange secured data, they must establish a contract, which is called a Security Association (SA). In an SA, the computers reach an agreement on how to exchange and protect data. Data transfers only after the security contract negotiates.

Security Associations (SA)

An SA combines a policy and keys, and defines the common security services, mechanisms, and keys that protect communication. The SA contains a Security Parameters Index (SPI), a unique value the receiving computer uses to distinguish the multiple SAs it receives. This is the case, for example, when a file server simultaneously and securely serves multiple clients. In this situation, the receiving computer uses the SPI to determine which SA will process the incoming packets.

Note: Only your system resources limit the potential number of SAs you can form.

A contract is built between two computers by an IETF-established standard method of SA and key exchange resolution. This method harnesses both the Internet SA and Key Management Protocol (ISAKMP) and the Oakley key-generation protocol. ISAKMP centralizes SA management, reducing connection time. Oakley generates and manages the keys that secure the data.

The ISAKMP/Oakley process protects computer-to-computer communication, including the following scenarios:

- A remote computer requests secure access to a network

- A security router or other proxy server negotiates on behalf of the final destination (endpoint) computer

In the latter scenario, referred to as ISAKMP client mode, the endpoints identities are hidden for further protection.

ISAKMP/Oakley operates through two distinct phases: the key-exchange phase and the data protection phase. Confidentiality and authentication are ensured during each phase by the use of negotiated encryption and authentication algorithms agreed upon by both computers. As the duties are split between two phases, keying, when required, can be accomplished with great speed.

The Key Exchange Phase

During the key-exchange phase, the two computers establish the first SA, called the ISAKMP SA to differentiate it from the SA used in the data protection phase. During the key-exchange phase, Oakley provides identity protection and total privacy, which helps ward off common types of network attacks revolving around hijacking identities.

During the key-exchange phase, the security negotiation process includes policy negotiation to determine the following:

- The encryption algorithm: DES, 3DES, 40-bit DES, or none

- The integrity algorithm: MD5 or SHA

- The authentication method: Public Key Certificate, preshared key, or Kerberos Version 5 (the default in Windows 2000)

- The Diffie-Hellman algorithm

An authentication based on certificates or pre-shared keys protects the computer identity throughout the process. The default Windows 2000 method, however, requires the computer identity to be unencrypted until the entire identity payload is encrypted during the key information exchange authentication process.

After the key information exchange, both computers have the necessary data to generate the shared, secret key for the ISAKMP SA. They do not exchange the actual keys—they exchange only the public information required by Diffie-Hellman to generate the shared, secret key. As for the master key that protects authentication, it is generated by the Oakley service on each computer.

The computers strive to authenticate the key information exchange. They use the master key together with the algorithms negotiated earlier, and they protect the identity payload from both modification and interception.

The initiating computer (or peer) sends the responding peers an offer list of potential security levels. The responder must not modify the offer. If the offer is modified, the initiator rejects the responder's message. The responder replies, either accepting the offer or stating no offer was chosen, in which case, the process begins again.

The Data Protection Phase

The computers automatically resend the negotiation messages five times and, after three seconds, establish a soft SA if the active policies permit insecure communications with non-IPSec capable peers. If an ISAKMP response is received before the cycle times out, the soft SA deletes and the standard SA negotiation begins (Figure 1.17).

Figure 1.17 ISKAMP SA Response

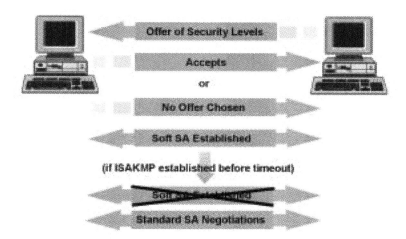

When a pair of SAs negotiate on behalf of the IPSec service, they are called IPSec SAs. Keying material is refreshed or new keys generate if Perfect Forward Secrecy (PFS) or key lifetimes are enabled, and the ISAKMP SA has expired. PFS prevents session keys or keying material from being used to generate other keys.

The security negotiation process now includes policy negotiation that determines the following:

- The IPSec protocol: AH, ESP
- The integrity algorithm: MD5, SHA
- The encryption algorithm: DES, 3DES, 40bitDES, or none

When agreement is reached, two SAs are set up, one for inbound communications and the other for outbound communications. Oakley refreshes the keying material and generates new, shared, secret keys to authenticate and encrypt the packets (Figure 1.18).

Figure 1.18 Inbound/Outbound SAs

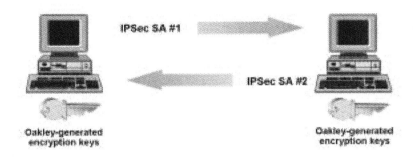

If a new key is needed, a second Diffie-Hellman exchange occurs. Unless a key or SA has expired, Oakley refreshes the keying material from the Diffie-Hellman exchange that took place during the key exchange.

The SAs and keys and SPI pass to the IPSec driver. The negotiation is protected throughout by the ISAKMP SA. All the message packets encrypt, except for the ISAKMP header on the packets, and an integrity signature after the ISAKMP header authenticates the message. Oakley prevents negotiation message replays.

The automatic message retry process is almost identical to the process in the key exchange negotiation with the following exception: if this process reaches a time-out for any reason during or after the second negotiation of the same ISAKMP SA, a renegotiation of the ISAKMP SA is attempted. If a message for the data protection phase is received without establishing an ISAKMP SA, it is rejected.

The security negotiation process is extremely fast, thanks to the ability to use a single ISAKMP SA for multiple IPSec SA negotiations. As long as the ISAKMP SA does not expire, renegotiation and re-authentication are not required. The active IPSec policy determines how often this occurs.

SA Lifetimes

Lifetime settings determine when a new key generates. Whenever a key lifetime expires, the associated SA renegotiates. The generation of new keys at intervals is called dynamic re-keying or key regeneration. Lifetimes allow you to force the generation of a new key (regeneration) after a specific period of time.

For example, if the communication takes 49 minutes and you specify the key lifetime as 7 minutes, 7 keys generate, one every 7 minutes during the exchange.

 Warning: Setting very different key lifetimes can be dangerous because they also determine the SA's lifetime. For example, establishing a master key lifetime of 7 hours (420 minutes), and a session key lifetime (set within a Filter Action) of 2 hours may cause an IPSec SA to stay in place for almost 2 hours after the ISAKMP Sac's expiration. This can occur if the new IPSec SA generates right before the ISAKMP SA's expiration.

The use of multiple keys guarantees that if an intruder gains the key to one part of a communication, the rest of the communication is not compromised. Automatic key regeneration is provided by default. Experts may override the default, specifying a master key lifetime in minutes, by session key, or Perfect Forward Secrecy (PFC).

Warning: Repeated re-keying from the same master key may end up compromising the key.

For example, if User A on Computer A sends a message to User B on Computer B, and then a few minutes later sends User B another message, the same master key material may be re-used since an SA was recently set up with Computer B (Figure 1.19).

Figure 1.19 Key Reuse

To limit how often reuse occurs, consult an expert who can specify a session key limit.

 Note: If you enable Perfect Forward Secrecy (PFS) for the master key, the Session key limit is ignored and PFS forces key regeneration each time. Enabling master key PFS is the same as specifying a session key limit of one.

If you specify both a master key lifetime in minutes and a session key limit, the interval reached first triggers a new key.

PFS determines how a new key generates. Enabling PFS ensures that no one can use a key that protects a transmission to generate other keys. PFS also protects the keying material for that key from being used to generate any new keys.

 Warning: Master key PFS requires re-authentication, which may increase the overhead for any domain controllers in your network. You do not need to enable PFS on both computers.

When a key lifetime expires for the master or session key, the associated SA renegotiates. Oakley transmits a Delete message to the responding computer, which requests the responder to expire the ISAKMP SA. This prevents the formation of fraudulent IPSec SAs from an old SA. Oakley expires ISAKMP SAs, and the IPSec driver expires IPSec SAs.

When the IPSec Policy Agent retrieves policy updates, it updates the IP filter list stored in the IPSec driver. Any SAs associated with old filters that no longer exist in the policy are deleted, as well as the old filters in the IPSec driver cache.

If the Windows 2000 power-saving features put the computer to sleep or hibernation, and the SA expires during this time, the SA automatically renegotiates when the computer reactivates. If Windows 2000 is shut down on one of the computers, Oakley deletes any remaining SAs. New SAs renegotiate when the computers attempt to communicate again. If Windows 2000 is abnormally terminated, Oakley does not transmit its Delete message. In this case, the old SAs might remain in place until they time out. If this occurs, you must manually delete them.

Working With Virtual Private Networks (VPNs)

A Virtual Private Network (VPN) enables a user to tunnel through the Internet or another public network to a private network, while maintaining the security level of the private network. To a user, VPN looks like a point-to-point connection with the private server. A VPN must comply with the following requirements:

*   It must allow roaming or remote clients to connect to authentication resources

*   The user's private address, name, and password must be kept private

- Data must be encrypted

- Encryption keys for both the client and server must generate and refresh

- It must support common protocols used in the public network

Windows 2000 currently supports VPN solutions based on Point-To-Point Tunneling Protocol (PPTP) and the recently developed Layer Two Tunneling Protocol (L2TP). IPSec also supports VPNs, but does not commonly meet all the requirements.

Second-Layer Authentication Methods

Layer 2 protocols inherit authentication from Point-to-Point Protocol (PPP), including methods such as Password Authentication Protocol (PSP), Challenge Handshake Authentication Protocol (CHAP), and Microsoft Challenge Handshake Authentication Protocol (MS-CHAP). Microsoft's implementation of PPTP and L2TP also uses Extensible Authentication Protocol (EAP), and, in particular, Extensible Authentication Protocol-Transport Level Security (EAP-TLS).

The following second-layer authentication methods are available for Windows 2000 VPNs:

- PAP

- CHAP

- MS-CHAP

- MS-CHAP Version 2

- SPAP (Shiva PAP)

- EAP-TLS

Password Authentication Protocol (PAP)—PAP is an unsecured clear-text authentication scheme. If the user's password is compromised, PAP provides no protection against replay attacks or remote client impersonation.

Challenge Handshake Authentication Protocol (CHAP)—CHAP is an encrypted authentication mechanism. To protect against replay attacks, it uses an arbitrary challenge string for each authentication attempt. To protect against remote-client impersonation, CHAP sends repeated, unpredictable challenges to the remote client through the entire connection.

Microsoft-CHAP—MS-CHAP is an encrypted authentication mechanism similar to CHAP. MS-CHAP has one layer of security and enables the server to store hashed passwords instead of clear-text. MS-CHAP is required for MPPE-based data encryption.

MS-CHAP Version 2—MS-CHAP Version 2 is just like MS-CHAP, except that it runs only on Windows 2000 computers.

SPAP (Shiva PAP)—SPAP supports clients using Shiva LAN Rover software.

EAP-TLS—EAP-TLS is a strong, public-key certificate-based authentication scheme. The client and dial-in server exchange certificates. The client's user certificate authenticates the user to the server. The server certificate proves that the user has reached the correct server. The user's certificate is kept on the dial-up client computer or on a Smart Card.

Authentication for VPN Connections

Authentication for VPN connections takes the following three formats:

User-level authentication by using PPP authentication—To establish the VPN connection, the VPN server uses a Point-to-Point Protocol (PPP) user-level authentication method to authenticates the VPN client who is attempting the connection. The server also verifies that the VPN client has the required permissions. If mutual authentication is used, the VPN client authenticates the VPN server, which protects against masquerading VPN servers.

Computer-level authentication by using ISAKMP—To establish an IPSec SA, both the VPN client and VPN server use machine certificates, ISAKMP, and Oakley.

Data authentication and integrity—To verify that the data transmitted on the VPN connection did originate at the other endpoint and was not modified in transit, the data includes a cryptographic checksum based on an encryption key that only the sender and the receiver know. Data authentication and integrity are available only for L2TP over IPSec connections.

Data Encryption

To ensure data confidentiality as it tunnels through the shared or public internetwork, the data is sender-encrypted and receiver-decrypted. The encryption and decryption processes depend on the use of a common encryption key by both the sender and receiver.

Encryption key length is an important security parameter. To ensure data confidentiality, use the largest possible key size. However, the larger the encryption key, the more computing power and computational time is required.

Security Risk Assessment

The state of a computer's operating system and applications is dynamic and needs to be monitored for security purposes. For example, you may need to temporarily lower the security levels to resolve an administration or network issue, but if you forget to restore the security levels, a computer may constitute a gaping security hole that compromises the security of the entire network.

Regular analysis enables an administrator to track the security level of each computer and ensure it is adequate as part of an enterprise risk management program. Security Configuration and Analysis is a tool that provides a highly specified analysis of all the security-related aspects of your network. An administrator can detect any security flaws that develop in the system and fine-tune the security levels.

Security Configuration and Analysis presents recommendations alongside current system settings, and icons or remarks highlight any areas where the current settings fall below the proposed security level. Security Configuration and Analysis also provides the ability to resolve any discrepancies revealed by analysis.

 Note: If you frequently need to analyze a large number of computers, as in a domain-based infrastructure, use the SECEDIT.EXE command-line tool for batch analysis. However, you must still view analysis results with Security Configuration and Analysis.

Avoiding Potential Network Threats

You must secure data in transit in and out of your site and data within your site. The appropriate methodology includes encryption, protocols, and firewall protection.

Network Data Security

To secure data in transit, you need cryptographic methods and a supporting protocol. IPSec and the Router Service provides this service. To secure data at the network interface, you need both a firewall to control proxy services and mediate connections between the internal network (LAN) and external network (Internet).

To protect data within your local network and subnets, use the authentication protocol. For a higher security level, encrypt network data. With IPSec, you can encrypt all network communication for specific clients, or for all of a domain's clients.

To secure network data that passes in and out of your site across intranets, extranets, or an Internet gateway, use these utilities for specific purposes, as follows:

• IPSec encrypts all TCP/IP communication for a client

• Routing and Remote Access configures remote-access protocols and routing

• Proxy Server provides a firewall and proxy server for a site

Other programs such as Microsoft Exchange, Microsoft Outlook, and Microsoft Internet Explorer provide public key encryption of both messages and transactions, either within a site or across networks (Figure 1.20).

Figure 1.20 Secure I/O for Network Data

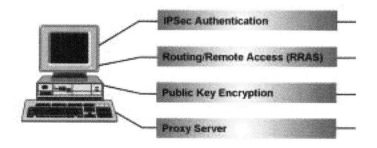

Internet Protocol Security

IPSec is a framework of open standards that ensures secure private communications over Internet Protocol networks that use cryptographic security services. IPSec is based on an end-to-end security model. This means that only the sending and receiving computers need to know that IPSec is being used. Standards developed by the Internet Engineering Task Force (IETF) IPSec working group form the basis of the Windows 2000 implementation of IPSec.

Router Service

The Windows 2000 Router Service provides routing services in the LAN and WAN environments, and over the Internet using PPTP- and L2TP-based VPN connections.

Use Router Service only if you are a system administrator already familiar with routing protocols and routing services. To view and manage both routers and dial-up servers, use the Routing and Remote access feature.

Proxy Server

You can jeopardize LAN security with unregulated Internet connections. Proxy servers help reduce this threat because they regulate LAN-Internet traffic to maximize the security and efficiency of intranet applications. Proxy servers provide firewall-class security. They act as as a gateway between the network and the Internet.

A proxy server acts as a secure switchboard between programs on one network and servers on another. When a client program makes a request, the proxy server translates the request and passes it to the Internet. When a computer on the Internet responds, the proxy server passes the response to the client program that made the original request. The proxy server computer has two network interfaces: one connected to the LAN and the other, to the Internet.

Following are the primary security features of a proxy server:

- It blocks inbound connections
- LAN clients can initiate connections to Internet servers, but Internet clients cannot initiate connections to LAN servers
- It restricts outbound connections

LAN client authentication uses the client's standard security credentials. Proxy server can restrict outbound connections in several ways: by user, program protocol, TCP/IP port number, time of day, and destination domain name or IP address.

Programs need to be reconfigured or to have replacement drivers when using a proxy server. Web browsers must usually be reconfigured, but require no additional software. Other WinSock programs require no reconfiguration, but the client system needs a replacement WinSock driver.

Determining Common Security Threats

You need to be aware of events that can pose serious threats to your organization. Once you are aware of possible problems, you can minimize the risk of security threats by incorporating various auditing steps.

Security Configuration and Analysis

Security Configuration and Analysis analyzes the security of a system by comparing the current state of system security against a base configuration. The base configuration is a security template that contains the preferred or recommended security settings for that system.

Security Configuration and Analysis looks up all the security areas in the base configuration and queries the system's security settings for each one of them. Values found are compared with the base configuration values. Values that match are assumed to be correct on the system. Values that do not match display as potential problems in need of investigation.

You can import and merge multiple analysis templates into one composite template in a database. If the imported templates conflict, the last one imported takes precedence. Once you have imported the templates to the selected database, you can analyze or configure the system.

Table 1.2 lists various events that you should audit as well as the specific security threat monitored by the audit event.

Table 1.2 Security Threats

Audit Event	Potential Threat
Failure audit for logon/logoff	Random password hack
Success audit for logon/logoff	Stolen password break-in
Success audit for user rights, user and group management, security change policies, restart, shutdown, and system events	Misuse of privileges
Success and failure audit for file-access and object-access events. File Manager success and failure audit of read/write access by suspect users or groups for sensitive files	Improper access to sensitive files
Success and failure audit for file-access printers and object-access events. Print Manager success and failure audit of print access by suspect users or groups for the printers	Improper access to printers
Success and failure write access auditing for program files (.EXE and .DLL extensions). Success and failure auditing for process tracking. Run suspect programs; examine security log for unexpected attempts to modify program files or create unexpected processes. Run only when actively monitoring the system log	Virus outbreak

Security Configuration

The security configuration tools directly configure local system security. With a personal database, you can import security templates created with the Security Templates snap-in, and apply these templates to the Group Policy object for the local computer. This immediately configures the system security with the levels specified in the template.

Securing Enterprise Networks

Enterprise security extensively relies on the flexible use of various security mechanisms and protocols like those described in this lesson. Enterprise computing presents far-sweeping security challenges in the form of wide ranges of remote file servers and print servers, data warehousing and transaction processing environments, Internet, and intranet communications that all require robust and proactive security strategies. Windows 2000 supports multiple network security protocols, empowering administrators to meet large-enterprise-level security needs with an array of powerful tools introduced in this lesson.

Vocabulary

Review the following terms in preparation for the certification exam.

Term	Description
ACEs	Access Control Entries are entries in a Discretionary Access Control List (DACL) that identify security groups or individual user accounts, and their permissions.
Active Directory	A directory service based on central policies that manages authorization and authentication services, remote network administration and security features.
authentication	A screening process during access to a network resource where a person's identity is verified with a username and password.
container object	An object that contains other objects, such as a folder that holds files.
DACL	Discretionary Access Control Lists define security groups, user accounts, and associated permissions, and enforces resource security and access levels for each list member.
domain	A group of computers on a network that share a common directory database, with a unique name, organized in levels, and administered as a unit with common rules and procedures.
domain controller	A Windows 2000 Server that stores user and computer accounts, Access Control Lists (ACLs), and Active Directory data about a domain.
Group Policy	Group Policy allows administrative settings and applies management policies to Active Directory OUs.
object	An entity such as a file, folder, shared folder, printer, in the Active Directory object.

Term	Description
object permission	Authorization or restriction assignment made by the network system administrator to a user or user group regarding access to functions or resources.
OU	An Organizational Unit is an entity or entity group logically organized by the system administrator according to business or system functions or policies.
permission inheritance	When objects within a container or OU automatically inherit that container's permissions.
SID	A Security Identifier enables the operating system to uniquely identify each group and each user who is logged on to the system.
TCO	Total Cost of Ownership in networked systems is the cost to an organization for all the phases of setup and maintenance of computer systems.

In Brief

If you want to...	Then do this...
Change access rights for an Active directory object	Use Active Directory Users and Computers to change access rights or permissions.
Specify settings and apply management policies to Active Directory OUs	Use Group Policy to define and set policies for individuals or computers only once, and let the operating system continuously enforce them.
Provide a tamper-resistant, portable security and authentication system	Use Smart Cards. Portable and tamper-resistant, they provide security solutions for client authentication, logging on to a Windows 2000 domain, code signing, and securing e-mail.
Prevent interception, modification, or unauthorized access to data while en route	Use IPSec. IP Security uses industry-standard encryption algorithms to provide secure TCP/IP communications on both sides of a firewall. As a result, Windows 2000 security defends against both external and internal attacks.
Support Virtual Private Networks	A VPN must allow roaming or remote clients to connect to authentication resources. The user's private address, name and password must be kept private. Data must be encrypted. Encryption keys for both the client and the server must be generated and refreshed. The common protocols used in the public network must be supported.

If you want to...	Then do this...
Protect networks from potential threats	Use a combination of security protective measures, including: IPSec security protocols, VPN tunneling connections and Proxy Servers.
Detect security threats	Schedule regular security analysis that yields highly specified data on all security-related system aspects. This enables administrators to detect any security flaws that develop in the system, and to fine-tune the security levels.

Lesson 1 Activities

Complete the following activities to better prepare you for the certification exam.

1. Describe Active Directory and its relationship to the Internet.

2. Explain how users are authenticated using Access Control Lists.

3. Describe how Windows 2000 sets up security configurations.

4. List the methods Windows 2000 uses for encryption.

5. Describe the default and legacy-compatible security protocols in Windows 2000.

6. Explain the meaning of domain trust.

7. Describe the security features of Smart Cards.

8. Describe the main advantage of Virtual Private Networks.

9. Explain how a proxy server works.

10. Describe security analysis.

Answers to Lesson 1 Activities

1. Active Directory implements the Internet standard directory and naming protocols. Its database engine provides transactional support and supports various application programming interface standards.

2. Users are authenticated with Access Control Lists. Users must log on to Windows 2000 with a set of verifiable security credentials. These are compared against a set of permissions assigned to Active Directory objects and network resources, such as shared folders and the NT File System files.

3. Windows 2000 provides the Security Template and Security Configuration and Analysis snap-ins found in MMC, and the SECEDIT command-line utility. The tools allow you to load, combine, and edit the security templates to configure local security, and to export security templates to other computers on a network

4. Windows 2000 uses the following methods for encryption: Public Key Encryption, Certificates, and Certificate-based Authentication.

5. The default and legacy-compatible security protocols in Windows 2000 security includes authentication based on Internet standard security protocols. Kerberos Version 5 is the default protocol. Windows NT LAN Manager (NTLM) is also supported to provide backward-compatibility.

6. A domain trust enables a user to authenticate another domain's resources, and an administrator to administer user rights for the other domain's users.

7. Following are security features of a Smart Card: An attempt to misuse a Smart Card involves obtaining both the user's Smart Card and the Personal Identification Number (PIN) to impersonate the user. Also, a Smart Card is "locked" after a few consecutive unsuccessful PIN inputs, making a dictionary attack against a Smart Card extremely unlikely to succeed.

8. A Virtual Private Network (VPN) enables a user to tunnel through the Internet or another public network to a private network, while maintaining the security level of the private network.

9. A proxy server acts as a secure switchboard between programs on one network and servers on another. When a client program makes a request, the proxy server translates the request and passes it to the Internet. When a computer on the Internet responds, the proxy server passes the response to the client program that made the original request. The proxy server computer has two network interfaces: one connected to the LAN and the other, to the Internet.

10. Security analysis is a highly specified analysis of all the security-related aspects of your network. An administrator can detect any security flaws that develop in the system and fine-tune the security levels.

Lesson 1 Quiz

These questions test your knowledge of features, vocabulary, procedures, and syntax.

1. Which Windows 2000 feature is a service that stores information about objects on a network, makes it available to individuals, and delegates group network administrators?
    A. Active Directory

    B. Group Policy

    C. TCO

    D. OUs

2. Which Active Directory method controls user access and permissions over resources in a Windows 2000 network?
    A. Permission inheritance

    B. Logon process

    C. Access tokens

    D. Discretionary Access Lists (DACLs)

3. What are the encryption methods supported by Windows 2000?
    A. Public key encryption

    B. Certificates

    C. Certificate-based authentication

    D. Certificates snap-in

4. What is the default security protocol for Windows 2000?
    A. Windows NT LAN Manager

    B. Kerberos Version 5

    C. TLS

    D. ISO 9000

5. What types of trust relationships does Windows 2000 support?
    A. Security Associations

    B. Domain trust

C. Smart Card

D. CA trust

6.   What are the major advantages of Smart Cards? (Choose all that apply.)
A. Tamper resistance

B. Isolation

C. Portability

D. Time-limited

7.   What policies are determined during the IPSec SA security negotiations?
A. AH, ESP

B. MD5, SHA

C. DES, 3DES, 40-bit DES

D. Diffie-Hellman

8.   What are the authentication methods used for VPNs?
A. PPP

B. ISKAMP

C. Oakley

D. L2TP

9.   Describe the purpose of using a proxy server? (Choose all that apply.)
A. Block inbound connections

B. Prevent Internet clients from accessing the LAN

C. Monitor proxies for shareholder meetings

D. Restrict outbound connections

10.   Which tools should be used to monitor security levels in an enterprise system?
A. SECEDIT.EXE

B. Security Configuration and Analysis

C. Security Templates snap-in

D. Group Policy

Answers to Lesson 1 Quiz

1. Answer A is correct. Active Directory is a Windows 2000 directory service that stores information about objects and makes the information available to individuals and delegated group network administrators.

    Answer B is incorrect. The Group Policy feature enables you to specify settings and apply management policies to Active Directory OUs.

    Answer C is incorrect. TCO means Total Cost of Ownership

    Answer D is incorrect. OUs are objects in the Active Directory.

2. D is correct. Windows 2000 uses lists of security groups, user accounts and associated permissions called DACLs to define existing object permissions and to enforce resource security.

    Answers A, B, and C are incorrect. Permission inheritance, logons and access tokens are means of establishing security access. Once established, the permissions are controlled by the DACLs.

3. Answers A, B, and C are correct. Public Key Encryption, Certificates and Certificate-based authentication are all methods of ensuring secure communications.

    D is incorrect. Certificates snap-in is a management tool, not a method.

4. B is correct. Kerberos Version 5 is the default security protocol for Windows 2000.

    Answer A is incorrect. Windows NT LAN Manager is supported to ensure backwards compatibility with Windows NT systems.

    Answer C is incorrect. The Transport Layer Security (TLS) protocol supports client authentication by mapping user public key certificates to existing Windows NT accounts.

    Answer D is incorrect. ISO 9000 is an internationally recognized quality management standard.

5. Answers B and D are correct. Windows 2000 supports transitive trust relationships. These include domain trust and Certificate Authority (CA) trust.

    Answer A is incorrect. Security Associations combine a policy and keys that protect communications from end to end.

    Answer C is incorrect. Smart Cards are devices that securely store public and private keys, passwords, and other types of personal information.

6.   Answers A, B, and C are correct. Smart Cards provide tamper-resistant storage for protecting passwords and other forms of personal information, isolation of security-critical authentication computations, and portability of credentials and other private information between computers.

Answer D is incorrect. While Smart Cards can be limited by changing the database information, this is not an inherent advantage.

7.   Answers A, B, and C are correct. AH and ESP are IPSec protocols. MD5 and SHA are integrity algorithms and DES, 3DES, and 40bitDES are encryption algorithms.

Answer D is incorrect. The Diffie-Hellman exchange generates the shared, secret key in a separate operation.

8.   Answers A, B, C, and D are correct. Point-to-Point Protocol (PPP) verifies that the VPN client has the appropriate permissions. Internet Security Association and Key Management Protocol (ISAKMP) and Oakley are used for key generation. Data authentication and integrity is only available for L2TP over IPSec connections.

9.   Answers A, B, and D are correct. Proxy servers can block inbound connections. LAN clients are authenticated using their standard security credentials. Proxy servers can restrict outbound connections in several ways, including by user, program protocol, TCP/IP port number, time of day, and destination domain name or IP address.

Answer C is incorrect. Monitoring shareholders is not within the purview of Windows 2000.

10.   Answer B is correct. Security Configuration and Analysis presents recommendations alongside current system settings, and icons or remarks highlight any areas where the current settings fall below the proposed security level. Regular analysis enables an administrator to track the security level of each computer and ensure it is adequate, as part of an enterprise risk management program.

Answer A is incorrect. The SECEDIT.EXE command-line tool can be used as a method for batch analysis. However, analysis results must still be viewed using Security Configuration and Analysis.

Answer C is incorrect. The Security Templates snap-in is used to import and edit security templates.

Answer D is incorrect. Group Policy sets policies and inheritance for Group Policy objects.

Active Directory and the Access Control List (ACL)

Descriptors that control object access are used for security with Windows 2000 Active Directory. A list of entries that grants or denies access to individuals and groups is called the Access Control List (ACL).

After completing this lesson, you should have a better understanding of the following topics:

• Active Directory Structure

• Access Control List

• Scalability Factors

Active Directory Structure

The Active Directory structure includes these features:

Data store, or directory—Stores information about Active Directory objects. These objects include shared resources such as servers, files, printers, the network user, and computer accounts.

Set of rules, or schema—Defines the classes of objects and attributes in the directory, the limits on instances of these objects, and the format of their names.

Global catalog—Stores information about each object in the directory. This allows users and administrators to find directory information no matter which directory domain contains the data.

Query and index mechanism—Provides network users or applications with the means to find published objects, and check their properties.

Replication service—Distributes directory data across a network. Changes to directory data are replicated to all domain controllers in that domain. All domain controllers in a domain take part in replication, and each domain controller contains a complete copy of all directory information for its domain.

Integration with the security subsystem—Offers a secure logon process to a network, and controls access to directory data queries and data changes.

Computers running Active Directory client software gain the full benefit of Active Directory. On a computer without Active Directory client software, the directory looks like a Windows NT directory.

Organizational Units (OUs)

An Organizational Unit (OU) is a type of directory object within a domain. OUs are Active Directory containers for users, groups, computers, and other OUs. An OU cannot contain objects from other domains.

OUs help minimize the number of domains required by the network because OUs can contain other OUs. Within a domain, you can extend the hierarchy of containers as often as necessary, to model the organization's hierarchy.

You can use OUs to create an administrative model that scales to any size. You can grant a user administrative authority for all OUs in a domain, or authority for a single OU.

To add an OU, follow these steps:

1. From the Start menu, choose Programs, Administrative Tools, and then select Active Directory Users and Computers. The Active Directory Users and Computers window displays (Figure 2.1).

Figure 2.1 MMC Active Directory Users and Computers

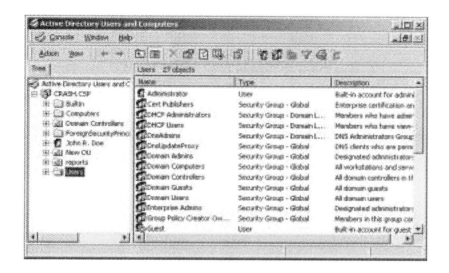

2.   Choose New, and then select Organizational Unit (Figure 2.2).

Figure 2.2 Organizational Unit

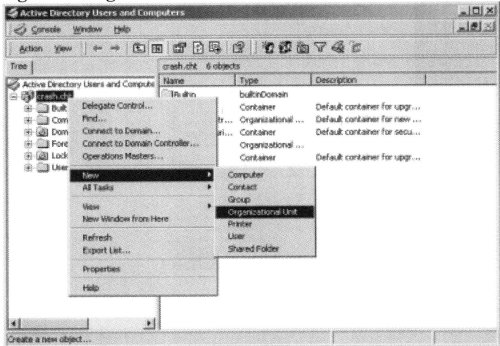

3.   Type the name of the OU (Figure 2.3).

Figure 2.3 Organization Unit Name

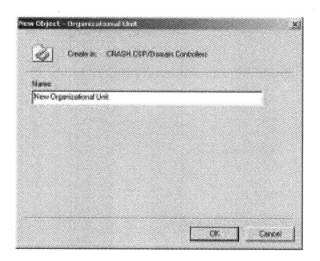

To delegate control of an OU, follow these steps:

1. Choose **Active Directory Users and Computers**.

2. From the console tree, double-click the domain node (Figure 2.4).

Figure 2.4 Domain Node

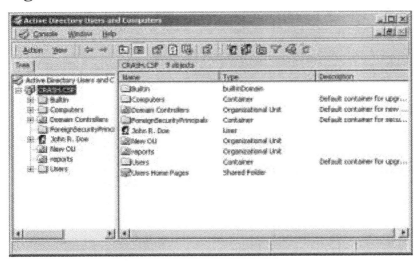

3. From the **Details** pane, right-click the **Organizational Unit** (OU), and then choose **Delegate control** to start the **Delegation of Control Wizard** (Figure 2.5).

Figure 2.5 Delegate Control

4.   Follow the instructions in the Delegation of Control Wizard.

To delete an OU, follow these steps:

1.   Choose **Active Directory Users and Computers**.

2.   From the console tree, double-click the domain node (Figure 2.6).

Figure 2.6 Domain Node

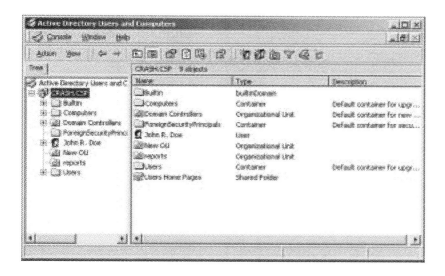

3.   From the Details pane, right-click the organizational unit, and then choose **Delete** (Figure 2.7).

Figure 2.7 Delete Control

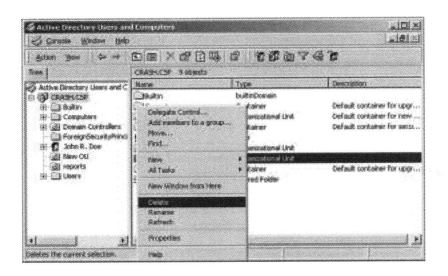

 Warning: When you delete an OU that contains objects, you are asked if you want to delete the OU and the objects it contains. If you answer yes, all objects are deleted, along with the OU.

To find an OU, follow these steps:

1. Choose **Active Directory Users and Computers**.

2. From the console tree, right-click the domain node, and then choose **Find**. (Figure 2.8).

3. From the Find list, choose **Organizational Units.**

Figure 2.8 Domain Node

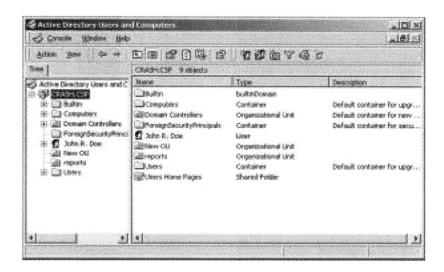

4.   Type the name of the organizational unit you want to find, and then choose **Find Now** (Figure 2.9).

Figure 2.9 Find Dialog Box

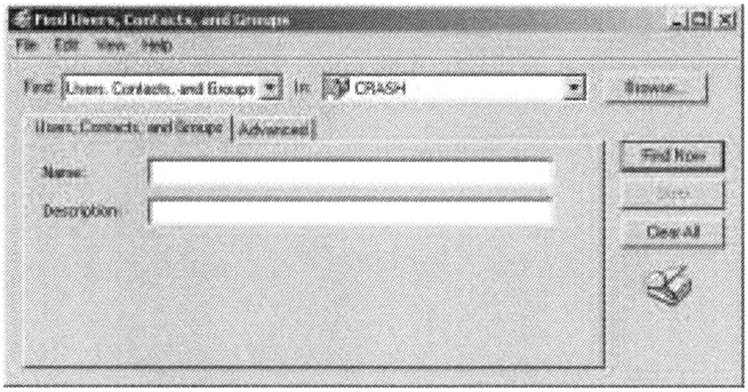

To modify OU properties, follow these steps:

1. Choose **Active Directory Users and Computers.**

2. From the console tree, double-click the domain node (Figure 2.10).

Figure 2.10 Domain Node

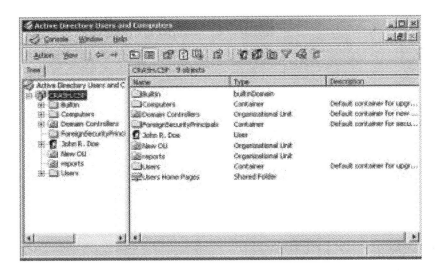

3. From the Details pane, right-click the Organizational Unit folder, and then choose **Properties** (Figure 2.11).

Figure 2.11 Properties Dialog Box

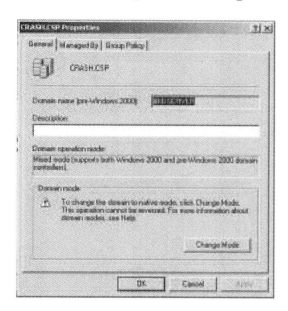

To move an OU, follow these steps:

1. Choose **Active Directory Users and Computers**.

2. From the console tree, choose the domain node (Figure 2.12).

Figure 2.12 Domain Node

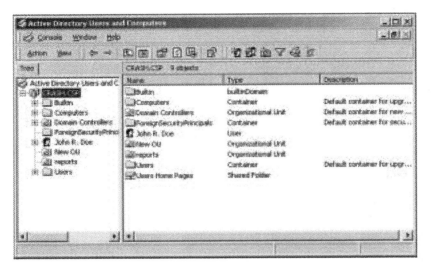

3. From the Details pane, right-click the Organizational Unit, and then choose **Move**.

4. From the **Move** dialog box, choose the folder to which you want to move the OU (Figure 2.13).

Figure 2.13 Move Dialog Box

Tip: Active Directory Users and Computers can only move OUs within the same domain. To move OUs between domains, use Movetree.

To rename an OU, follow these steps:

1.   Choose **Active Directory Users and Computers**.

2.   From the console tree, double-click the domain node (Figure 2.14).

Figure 2.14 Domain Node

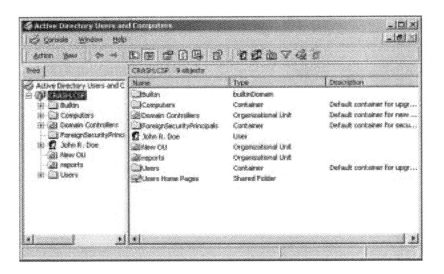

3.   From the Details pane, right-click the OU you want to rename.

4.   Choose **Rename**, and then type the new name (Figure 2.15).

Figure 2.15 Rename Dialog Box

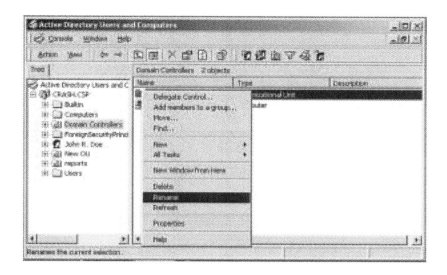

Namespace Planning for DNS

Active Directory domains in Windows 2000 have DNS names. The Active Directory structure must be available before a DNS domain namespace can be properly implemented in Windows 2000. Therefore, use the your Active Directory to support the DNS namespace.

Before you use the Domain Name System (DNS) on the network, decide on a plan for the DNS domain namespace. A namespace plan design involves decisions about how you intend to use DNS naming and how the design supports your goals.

Ask yourself the following questions as you develop a namespace plan:

- Is this a registered DNS domain name in use on the Internet?

- Will the DNS servers be available on a private network or on the Internet?

- Will the DNS support Active Directory?

- What naming requirements should we follow when choosing DNS domain names for computers?

Choosing a DNS Domain Name

Before you decide on a parent DNS domain name for your organization to use on the Internet, perform a search to see if the name is already registered to another organization or person. The Internet DNS namespace is currently managed by the Internet Network Information Center (InterNIC). In the future, other domain name registrars might also be available.

First choose and register a unique parent DNS domain name to use for hosting your organization on the Internet. For example, **microsoft.com**, is a second-level domain within the .com top-level domain on the Internet.

Once you have chosen your parent domain name, combine this name with a location or organizational name to form other sub domain names. For example, you can add a sub domain, such as the **itg.example.microsoft.com** domain tree, for resources used by the information technology group at your organization. You can form additional sub domain names with this name. For example, a group working on Electronic Data Interchange (EDI) in this division could have a sub domain named, **edi.itg.example.widget.com**.

DNS Namespace Planning for Active Directory

With Active Directory, you must develop a namespace plan. Before a DNS domain namespace can be properly implemented in Windows 2000, the Active Directory structure must be available. Begin with the Active Directory design and support it with the appropriate DNS namespace. You can revise your plans later, if there are unforeseen conflicts or difficulties.

In Windows 2000, Active Directory domains are assigned DNS names. When choosing DNS names for your Active Directory domains, begin with the registered DNS domain name suffix that your organization has reserved for use on the Internet. An example might be **widget.com**. By combining this name with attributes for divisions and departments in your organization, you can devise full names for your Active Directory domains.

For a small organization that uses a single domain or a small multidomain model, planning can be straightforward. Larger organizations, with more complex domain models can refer to additional Microsoft resources, such as the Windows 2000 Server Resource Kit Deployment Planning Guide. It provides more advanced planning information for Active Directory namespace design.

Note: Use a different set of distinguished names that do not overlap as the basis for your internal and external DNS use, as you plan DNS and Active Directory namespaces.

Keep your internal and external namespaces separate and distinct, so that you can easily maintain configurations such as Domain Name Filter or exclusion lists. For example, assume your organization's parent domain name is **example.widget.com**. For internal DNS names usage, you could use a name such as **.example.widget.com**. For external DNS names, you could use a name such as **external.example.widget.com**.

Choosing Names

It is best to use only characters that are part of the Internet standard character set permitted for use in DNS host names. These allowed characters are defined in RFC1123 as follows: all uppercase letters (A-Z), lowercase letters (a-z), numbers (0-9), and the hyphen (-).

For organizations that invest in Microsoft NetBIOS technology, existing computer names might conform to the NetBIOS naming standard. Those organizations can consider computer name revision to comply with the Internet DNS standard.

To ease the transition from Windows NT 4.0 NetBIOS names to Windows 2000 DNS domain names, the DNS service includes support for extended ASCII and Unicode characters. However, this additional character support is only possible in a pure Windows 2000 network environment. This is because most other DNS resolution client software is based on RFC1123, the specification that standardizes Internet host naming requirements.

If a nonstandard DNS domain name is entered during Windows 2000 setup, a warning message appears.

A NetBIOS name identifies a Windows computer on the network in Windows NT 4.0 and earlier versions. Windows 2000 identifies a computer by any of the following ways:

A NetBIOS computer name—An optional name used for interoperability with earlier Windows systems.

The full computer name—A Fully Qualified Domain Name (FQDN) for the computer that is its main, or default, name.

A FQDN— A computer can also be identified by an FQDN that includes the computer (or host) name and a connection-specific domain name. The computer must be configured and applied for a specific network connection.

This full computer name combines both the computer name and the DNS domain name for the computer. The computer's DNS domain name is part of the System properties for the computer. It is not related to any specific installed networking components. However, computers that run Windows 2000 and do not use either networking or TCP/IP do not have a DNS domain name.

The NetBIOS computer name was introduced to ensure interoperability between NetBIOS and DNS naming in Windows 2000. This parameter derives from the first 15 octets of the DNS full computer name. It is not a requirement in an exclusive Windows 2000 environment.

The transition from a NetBIOS namespace to a DNS namespace is easier when the full computer name is a combination of the computer name and the DNS domain name for the computer. Users can continue to enter the short computer name. A name that is 15 characters or less can duplicate the NetBIOS computer name. The administrator then assigns a DNS domain name to each computer. The administrator may choose to do this with remote administration tools.

You can make the following settings to the System Properties page, on the Network Identification page or its related dialog boxes:

- Computer name longer than 15 characters-name

- NetBIOS computer name longer than 15 characters

- Primary DNS suffix for this computer is **example.widget.com**

 Note: Windows 2000 provides connection-specific DNS naming, in addition to the primary DNS domain name for a computer.

Configuring Multiple Names

Many networks require support for resolving external DNS names like those used on the Internet in addition to support for the internal DNS namespace used by Windows 2000 and Active Directory. The DNS service offers ways to integrate and manage disjointed namespaces when both external and internal DNS names are resolved on your network.

Before you decide how to integrate namespaces, determine which of the following scenarios most closely resembles your network DNS namespace requirements:

- An internal DNS namespace used only on our own network

- An internal DNS namespace with referral and access to an external namespace, such as forwarding to a DNS server on the Internet

- An external DNS namespace used only on a public network, such as the Internet

There are no restrictions on how you can design or implement the limits you decide to place on the use of a DNS name service. For example, you can choose any DNS naming standard, configure your DNS servers to be valid root servers for your network's DNS-distributed design, or create a self-contained DNS domain tree structure and hierarchy.

It is important, however, to consider the compatibility issues between private and external namespaces. Make sure your resolve compatibility issues before you provide a referral to an external DNS namespace or a full DNS service on the Internet. Keep in mind that Internet service requires your organization to register parent domain names.

 Note: The first time you add and connect to a Windows 2000 DNS server with the DNS console, the root file (CACHE.DNS) is automatically primed for use on your network.

If you are connected to the Internet, you can either edit or update the CACHE.DNS root file upon update and release of the file NAMED.ROOT. For a current copy of this file, use anonymous FTP to access the following site: ftp://rs.internic.net/domain/named.root.

The default resource records in the CACHE.DNS root file can be removed even if you are not connected to the Internet. Remove the default resource records, and replace them with DNS and resource records for the DNS authoritative servers at the root domain of your site.

You can safely remove this file on your private network root domain servers. At that level, servers do not use a root file cache.

You must take an additional step if you delete the CACHE.DNS file for a private root domain server, and you used the Boot From File method to configure the DNS service. Remove the cache directive from the server boot file before restarting the DNS service.

Transitive Two-Way Trusts

In earlier versions of Windows, trusts were restricted to two domains with a one-way trust relationship.

With Windows 2000, the trust relationship is a two-way, or transitive trust relationship. When a domain joins an existing forest or domain tree, a transitive trust is automatically established.

This series of trusts between parent and child domains in a domain tree and between root domains of domain trees in a forest, allows all domains in a forest to trust each other for authentication purposes. For example, if Domain A trusts Domain B and Domain B trusts Domain C, then Domain A trusts Domain C.

Domain Trusts

A domain trust is a relationship between two domains. It allows users in one domain to be authenticated by a domain controller in another domain. Domain trust relationships have only two domains in the relationship: the trusting domain and the trusted domain.

 Note: Authentication of a user by a domain controller does not confer access to resources in that domain. Authentication is determined solely by the rights and permissions granted to the user account by the domain administrator of the trusting domain.

Explicit Domain Trusts

In addition to trusts that are automatically created during installation of a domain controller, you can create trust relationships. These are called explicit trusts. You create and manage explicit trusts with Active Directory Domains and Trusts.

You can create two kinds of explicit trusts: external trusts and shortcut trusts. External trusts enable user authentication to a domain outside of a forest. Shortcut trusts are useful for creating a straight-forward trust path within a complex forest.

External Trusts

External trusts enable trust relationships to domains outside the forest, even if the path is not encompassed by the trust paths of that forest. External trusts are always one-way, non-transitive trusts, but you can combine two one-way trusts to create a two-way trust relationship.

Shortcut Trusts

To compute and complete a trust path between two domains in a complex forest can be a lengthy process. Before an account is granted access to resources by a domain controller of another domain, Windows 2000 determines whether the target domain and the source domain have a trust relationship. The target domain contains the desired resources, and the source domain is where the account resides. Shortcut trusts reduce the time this security process takes.

Shortcut trusts are two-way transitive trusts that let you shorten the path in a complex forest. You create shortcut trusts between Windows 2000 domains in the same forest. The most effective use of shortcut trusts is between two domain trees in a forest.

 Note: If necessary, you can create multiple shortcut trusts between domains in a forest.

Explicit Trusts

Before you can create an explicit trust, you need to have the following items of information: the domain names and a user account with permission to create trusts in each domain, and the trust password of each domain in the relationship. The administrators of each domain in the relationship must know the passwords for both domains.

Learning to Delegate Administration Tasks

Administrative control can be delegated to any level of a domain tree. You do this by creating OUs within a domain, and delegating administrative control for specific OUs to particular users or groups.

When you decide what OUs to create, and which OUs should contain accounts or shared resources, consider the structure of your organization. For example, you may want to create an OU that enables you to grant to a user the administrative control for all user and computer accounts in all branches of a department, such as Human Resources. You may choose to limit that user's administrative control to only some of the resources within a department, such as computer accounts alone, or to the Human Resources OU, but not to any OUs contained within the Human Resources OU.

Delegating administrative responsibilities lets you eliminate the need for multiple administrative accounts that have broad authority, such as over an entire domain. You can still use the predefined Domain Admins group for administration of the entire domain, and limit the accounts included in the Domain Admins group to highly trusted administrative users.

Windows 2000 features help to define appropriate administrative scopes and limit administrative control. These can apply to a particular person, an entire domain, all OUs within a domain, or even a single OU. With a combination of OUs, groups and permissions, you can define appropriate scope scenarios.

The Delegation of Control Wizard allows you to grant administrative control to a user or group. The Delegation of Control Wizard allows selection of the user or group to which you want to delegate control. You can also select the OUs and objects you want those users to be able to control, and the permissions to access and modify objects. For example, you could give a user the right to modify the Owner Of Accounts property, but not the right to delete accounts in that OU.

Application Programming Interfaces (APIs)

Windows 2000 supports APIs that let you write applications that are consistent with the operating system. When you use API, you ensure a common interface for all programs, as well as simplified user and administrator needs. The following topics present a variety of APIs and their features.

ADSI

Active Directory Service Interfaces (ADSI) offers a simple, powerful, object-oriented interface to Active Directory. By using ADSI, programmers and administrators can easily create directory programs. ADSI allows the use of high-level tools such as Visual Basic, Java, C, or C++, without having to worry about the underlying differences between namespaces.

ADSI lets you build programs that provide a single point of access to multiple directories in the network environment, even if those directories are based on a protocol other than LDAP. ADSI is fully scriptable, so administrators can easily use it.

MAPI

Messaging Application Programming Interface (MAPI) is supported by Active Directory, so legacy MAPI programs continue to work with Active Directory. Active Directory provides support for backward compatibility with Microsoft Exchange applications. New applications should use Active Directory Service Interfaces to access Active Directory.

LDAP

Lightweight Directory Access Protocol (LDAP) Version 3 is the primary access protocol for Active Directory. LDAP is defined by a set of Proposed Standard documents in Internet Engineering Task Force (IETF) RFC2251.

LDAP is a communication protocol specifically designed for TCP/IP networks. This API defines the way a directory client can access a server, as well as how the client can perform directory operations and share directory data. LDAP standards are determined by working groups of the Internet Engineering Task Force (IETF). Active Directory uses the LDAP attribute draft specifications and the IETF standards for LDAP Versions 2 and 3.

LDAP is a simple and efficient way to access directory services. It defines which operations are performed to query and modify information in a directory, and how information in a directory can be securely accessed. Use LDAP to find or enumerate directory objects and to query or administer Active Directory.

LDAP and Interoperability

LDAP is an open Internet standard that lets Active Directory enable interoperability with other vendors' directory services. Active Directory support for LDAP includes an LDAP provider-object within the Active Directory Service Interfaces (ADSI). ADSI supports the C-binding application programming interfaces for LDAP that are defined by Internet standard RFC1823. With ADSI and LDAP, other directory service applications are modifiable for access to information in Active Directory.

CAPI

CryptoAPI, also known as CAPI, is an Application Programming Interface (API) in Microsoft Windows. It includes a set of functions that give applications the ability to encrypt or digitally sign data, and provide protection for users' sensitive key data. The cryptographic operations are performed by independent modules called Cryptographic Service Providers (CSPs).

Novell Network Directory Services (NDS)

NDS is a distributed database that maintains information about every resource on the network. It provides access to and control of those resources. NDS is the directory service on networks that run Novell NetWare 4.0.

Access Control List (ACL) Functionality

Distributed security simplifies the assignment work for rights and permissions. These rights and permissions assignments can affect groups, users, computers, a container tree, a hierarchy of containers, and other resource objects.

To take the best advantage of distributed security, apply the following general principles:

- Rely on rights from group assignments, rather than the less efficient direct user account assignment and maintenance method

- Assign rights to objects as high in the container tree as possible, to accommodate the majority of the security principals

- Apply inheritance to extend rights through the container tree, and apply access control settings to all child objects of parent objects

- Delegate container administration to those who manage the computers where the containers reside, to decentralize administrative operations

Understanding Access Rights

Access control authorizes users and groups to access objects on the network.

Key concepts of access control include the following:

- Object ownership
- Permissions attached to objects
- Inheritance of permissions
- Object managers
- Object auditing

Object Ownership

When an object is created, Windows 2000 assigns an owner to it. By default, the owner is the creator.

Permissions Attached to Objects

The primary means of access control is to attach permissions or access rights to objects. These permissions are the control for accesses to users and groups. Permissions are usually implemented with security descriptors, which also define permissions for auditing and ownership. An example of a permission that is attached to an object is the Read permission on a file.

Inheritance of Permissions

Inheritance is a Windows 2000 feature that allows administrators to easily assign and manage permissions. When a file is created in a folder, for example, it inherits the permissions of the folder, or container, where it resides. This process is called inheritance.

Object Managers

If you need to change the permissions on an individual object, start the appropriate tool and change the properties for that object. For example, to change the permissions on a file from Windows Explorer, right-click on the username, and then select **Properties**. Make permission changes to a file on the property pages.

Object Auditing

Windows 2000 provides the ability to audit users' activities, including accesses to objects. With Event Viewer, you can view security-related events in the Security log.

Active Directory Services

Windows 2000 utilizes Active Directory to publish information that makes the service more accessible to clients, and more manageable for administrators. Domain controllers usually publish directory information and respond to service requests. But Windows 2000 also uses Active Directory to publish configurations or bindings.

Applications obtain information from the directory and use the information to access services provided on network servers. You can extend the default set of services published in the directory to meet the needs of your network environment.

Among the benefits of publishing services to the directory are the following:

Resource availability—Because it is service-centric, accessibility to distributed network services is easy for clients. The services publish to the directory, so clients do not need to store the resource's location. Any published service could be accessed from any computer running Windows 2000.

Administration—Publishing services allows you to modify bindings or resolve configuration issues centrally, rather than from individual computers. This means that all services use the latest configuration information.

The Active Directory Sites and Services feature does not display the Services node by default. However, you have the option to display it.

Default Security Settings

Upon domain controller installation, several default groups install in the built-in folders and the Users folders of the Active Directory Users and Computers console. These are security groups. The built-ins represent common sets of rights and permissions. You can grant certain roles, rights, and permissions to accounts and groups you place in these default groups.

The built-in folder contains default groups with domain local scope. Predefined global-scope groups are in the Users folder. You can move the built-in and predefined groups to other group or OU folders within the same domain, but you cannot move them to other domains.

Built-In Groups

The default built-in groups placed in the built-in folder for Active Directory Users and Computers are as follows:

- Account Operators
- Administrators
- Backup Operators
- Guests
- Print Operators
- Replicator
- Server Operators
- Users

Table 2.1 shows the default rights held by built-in groups.

Table 2.1 Built-In Group Default Rights

User Right	Allowable Action	Groups Assigned This Right by Default
Access this computer from the network	Connect to the computer over the network.	Administrators, Everyone, Power Users
Back up files and file folders	This right supersedes file and folder permissions.	Administrators, Backup Operators
Bypass traverse checking	Move between folders to access files, even if the user has no permission to access the parent file folders.	Everyone
Change the system time	Set the time for the internal clock of the computer.	Administrators, Power Users
Create a pagefile	This right has no effect.	Administrators
Debug programs	Debug various low-level objects, such as threads.	Administrators
Force shut down from a remote system	Shut down a remote computer.	Administrators
Increase scheduling priority	Boost the execution priority of a process.	Administrators, Power Users
Load and unload device drivers	Install and remove device drivers.	Administrators
Log on locally	Log on at the computer from the computer keyboard.	Administrators, Backup Operators, Everyone, Guests, Power Users, and Users

User Right	Allowable Action	Groups Assigned This Right by Default
Manage auditing and Security log	Specify the types of resource access (such as file access) that are to be audited, and view and clear the Security log. This right does not allow a user to set system auditing policy. Members of the Administrators group can always view and clear the Security log.	Administrators
Modify firmware environment variables	Modify system environment variables stored in nonvolatile RAM on computers that support this type of configuration.	Administrators
Profile single process	Perform profiling (performance sampling) on a process.	Administrators, Power Users
Profile system performance	Perform profiling (performance sampling) on the computer.	Administrators
Restore files and file folders	Restore backed-up files and file folders. This right supersedes file and directory permissions.	Administrators, Backup Operators
Shut down the system	Shut down Windows 2000.	Administrators, Backup Operators, Everyone, Power Users, and Users
Take ownership of files or other objects	Take ownership of files, folders, printers, and other objects on (or attached to) the computer. This right supersedes permissions protecting objects.	

Predefined Groups

The predefined groups placed in the Users folder for Active Directory Users and Computers are as follows:

- Group name
- Cert Publishers
- Domain Admins
- Domain Computers
- Domain Controllers
- Domain Guests
- Domain Users
- Enterprise Admins
- Group Policy Admins
- Schema Admins

Tip: You can use predefined groups with global scope to collect into groups the various types of user accounts in that domain. User accounts include regular users, administrators, and guests into groups. You can then place these groups in groups with domain local scope, in that domain and others.

Any user account you create in a domain adds by default to the Domain Users group. Any computer account you create automatically adds to the Domain Computers group. You can use the Domain Users and Domain Computers groups to govern all the accounts created in the domain. For example, if you want all the users in this domain to have access to a printer, assign permissions for the printer to the Domain Users group. Alternatively, you could put the Domain Users group into a domain local group that has permissions for the printer. The Domain Users group in a domain is, by default, a member of the Users group in the same domain.

The Domain Admins group can represent all the users who have broad administrative rights in a domain. Windows 2000 Server does not automatically place accounts in this group. However, you can add the accounts that require sweeping administrative rights in one or more domains to the Domain Admins group. Windows 2000 Server supports delegation of authority, so broad administrative rights should be limited.

By default, the Domain Admins group in a domain belongs to the Administrators group in the same domain.

By default, the Domain Guests group belongs to the Guests group in the same domain. The Guest user account is automatically a member of the Domain Guests default group.

User Default Access Control Settings

Windows 2000 security is based on two concepts: authentication and authorization. Access control is the means for implementing authorization. When a user account receives authentication and accesses an object, the type of access granted depends on either the user rights assigned to the user, or the permissions that are attached to the object.

Within a domain, the object manager for that object type enforces access control. For example, the Registry manager enforces access control on Registry keys.

Every object controlled by an object manager has an owner, a set of permissions that apply to specific users or groups, and auditing. The owner of the object controls which users and groups on the network are allowed to access the object by setting the permissions on an object. Permission settings also define what type of access is allowed, such as Read permission for a file. Auditing defines which users or groups are audited when they attempt to access that object.

Administrator Default Settings

Table 2.2 shows the default permissions on Group Policy objects.

Table 2.2 Group Policy Objects Default Permissions

Security Group	Default Permissions
Authenticated users	Read, Apply Group Policy (AGP)
Local system	Full Control (includes AGP)
Domain administrators	Read, Write, Create Child, Delete Child, AGP
Administrators	Read, Write, Create Child, AGP

Default Domain Policy

Group Policy objects contain settings necessary for the domain. To prevent the accidental deletion, Group Policy objects cannot be deleted by any administrator. If you truly need to delete it—for example, because the policies have been set in other Group Policy objects—return the Delete Access Control Entry (ACE) to the appropriate group.

Understanding Group Membership

The groups to which a user account belongs are called group membership. Permissions and rights granted to a group are also afforded to its members. In most cases, the actions a user can perform in Windows 2000 are determined by the group memberships of the user account to which the user has logged on.

Scalability Factors

The Windows 2000 Server family covers a gamut of deployments from small workgroups to enterprise data centers. The family includes products that support up to 32 processors and advanced Input/Output (I/O). It integrates network load balancing and new multiprocessor optimizations for your business applications.

Hardware Scalability

You can take advantage of the growing number of competitively priced 2-, 4-, 16-, and 32-way multiprocessor computers, by choosing from products in the Windows 2000 Server family. These products use the ever-faster Alpha and Intel technology.

I2O Support

The new I2O architecture, also called Intelligent Input/Output architecture, brings higher I/O performance to your servers. It offloads certain I/O operations to a secondary processor. I2O improves I/O performance in high-bandwidth applications such as networked video, groupware, and client/server processing.

Network Load Balancing

Network Load Balancing is available on Windows 2000 Advanced Server. Previously known as WLBS, Network Load Balancing distributes incoming TCP/IP traffic among multiple servers. With Network Load Balancing, your servers, especially Web servers, perform better when demand is high.

Planning Solutions for Small and Large Businesses

When you make decisions about customization, keep in mind that your decisions affect Connection Manager implementation methods. Consider the impact of a service profile plan on the following factors:

- The number of service profiles to be developed

- The distribution methods to be used

- Streamlining installation with additional components

- Integrating your Connection Manager Service Profile with an Internet Explorer installation package

- The size of the service profile

- Phone book support to be implemented

- Maintenance and update requirements for the service profile, including all files included in the profile

The following topics answer some frequently asked questions about how the customization of your service profile affects its implementation.

How many service profiles do you need?

Create additional service profiles to support special needs for specific groups or personnel. For example, if you support multiple geographic locations, you might want to create separate profiles for the specific locations, with a unique local phone book in each. Or, you might want to create separate profiles for each operating system your service supports.

When users install more than one service profile, each profile installs into a separate folder. Each profile shares the same copy of Connection Manager Version 1.2 software.

To provide support for another national language, run the CMAK Wizard. It must run on a computer with operating systems that have been localized for the appropriate national language.

What distribution methods are appropriate?

Your service profile can be distributed by CD-ROM or by a downloadable file over a private network or on the Internet. Take into account the size of your customized profile, including all files that you add to it, when you determine which distribution method to use. Remember that download time significantly affects users; especially those using relatively slow modems.

If you use the Internet Explorer Administration Kit 5 (IEAK 5) to distribute Internet Explorer 5, include a Connection Manager profile in an Internet Explorer installation package. This will make installation easier for users. With this integrated installation package, users install and use Internet Explorer and Connection Manager in one procedure. They use the same username as the one they select in the signup process. Files in the Internet Explorer installation package should not be repeated in the Connection Manager profile.

What is the size of your service profile?

The size of your service profile must be compatible with your distribution method. Consider the features you want, and whether you plan to distribute the profile by CD-ROM or through a download from the Internet.

If you distribute through an Internet download, for example, consider how the download time affects users. In some cases you might decide to offer users more than one distribution method. The Connection Manager Administration Kit (CMAK) Wizard does not support profiles that span multiple disks. It does not prompt you if the profile does not fit on one disk.

If a service profile includes Connection Manager, it will use about 800 kilobytes (KB) of disk space. Without Connection Manager, the profile uses as little as about 200 KB. The total size of a service profile depends on customization options, the method you use to provide phone books, and whether you include connect actions or other optional programs and graphics.

 Note: If disk space allows, include Connection Manager in the service profile to ensure that your users always have the latest version.

How can you streamline installation for your users?

One way to simplify installation and updates for your users is to incorporate programs and files that automatically install and configure as part of the Connection Manager installation package. However, you should tailor these features to the individual needs of specific user groups. This will control the size of the service profile that you distribute, and promote the effective use of your service.

For example, if you support a corporate account with marketing and accounting departments, you might provide separate profiles for each department. You could provide the marketing department with a phone book covering the entire sales area, and offer the accounting department with a phone book containing only the numbers of the local access points.

How can you integrate your service profile with an Internet Explorer installation package?

Decide on your delivery method before creating a service profile, to foresee the impact of integration. Some of your planning decisions will depend on whether you are integrating Connection Manager and your custom service profile with Internet Explorer installation, or another implementation package.

For example, if you decide to integrate your Connection Manager service profile with an installation package created with the IEAK, you could coordinate the graphics included in your profile with those you include in the installation package.

If you decide to deliver your Connection Manager service profile with an Internet Explorer installation package, create both using the IEAK 5 Wizard. The Connection Manager Administration Kit Wizard works in tandem with the IEAK 5 Wizard.

After you build your service profile, check the information to determine whether you need additional customization to integrate your service profile with other packages.

What phone book support is required?

You can offer a single phone number for user connection, or additional support for roaming access, by providing a phone book of access numbers. Connection Point Services allow you to provide phone book support that includes automatic updates. You create the initial phone books and decide how to implement phone book support before running the CMAK Wizard.

What is required to maintain and use existing service profiles?

Many types of files can be incorporated into a service profile. You can edit or merge other profiles, include program files to support connect actions and auto-applications, provide user documentation, and incorporate many other types of files to customize Connection Manager for your users.

To maintain these service profiles so that the appropriate version of an incorporated file is available, you need to understand how the CMAK Wizard incorporates and uses such files.

When you edit a service profile that contains a merged service profile, the CMAK Wizard tries to use the latest version of the merged profile. If the CMAK Wizard cannot find the merged profile in the appropriate \Program Files\CMAK\Profiles\ServiceProfileFileName folder, it defaults to the current version of the merged profile that was stored with the profile.

Plan your profiles, especially those with incorporated files, so that the information and elements can be maintained and updated easily.

Domain Trees and Forests

Each domain in a directory is identified by a DNS domain name and requires one or more domain controllers. You can easily create new domains if your network requires more than one.

A forest comprises one or more domains sharing a common schema and global catalog. If multiple domains in the forest have contiguous DNS domain names, that structure is called a domain tree. If multiple domains have noncontiguous DNS domain names, then they form separate domain trees within the forest. A forest contains one or more domain trees. The forest root domain is the first domain in a forest.

A domain creates when you install the first domain controller for a domain. During installation of the first domain controller, the Active Directory Installation Wizard uses the information you give to install the domain controller. It creates the domain within the existing context of relationships to other domains and any existing domain controllers. A domain can be created in the relationship context of the first domain in a new forest, of the first domain in a new domain tree, or as a child domain of an existing domain tree.

For fault-tolerance and high availability of the directory, install additional domain controllers in an existing domain after you install the first domain controller for a domain.

Domain Naming

Domains that form a single domain tree share a contiguous namespace or naming hierarchy. Following DNS standards, the Fully Qualified Domain Name for a domain that is part of a contiguous namespace is the name of that domain appended to the names of the parent and root domains. It uses the dot (.) character format.

For example, a domain with a NetBIOS name of grandchild, and a parent domain named **parent.widget.com**, has a fully qualified DNS domain name of **grandchild.parent.widget.com**.

Domain trees associated in a forest share the same directory configuration and replication information. But they do not share a contiguous DNS domain namespace.

The combination of domain trees and forests provides flexible domain naming options. You can use both contiguous and noncontiguous DNS namespaces in your directory.

Trust Relationships

For Windows 2000 computers, account authentication between domains enables two-way, transitive trusts based on the Kerberos Version 5 security program.

Trust relationships are created automatically for adjacent, or parent-child domains, when a domain is created in a domain tree.

In a forest, a trust relationship is automatically created between the forest root domain and the root domain of each domain tree added to the forest. Because these trust relationships are transitive, users and computers can be authenticated among all domains in the domain tree or forest.

When you upgrade a Windows pre-Windows 2000 domain to Windows 2000, the existing one-way trust relationships between that domain and any other domains are maintained. This includes all trusts in pre-Windows 2000 domains. If you install a new Windows 2000 domain and want trust relationships with any pre-Windows 2000 domains, create external trusts with those domains.

A Distributed Security Model

Distributed security makes domain administration easier and more effective at the following levels:

- Authentication of users and computers distributes across the enterprise

- Security credentials for users and computers store in Active Directory and computers authenticate upon startup

The default transitive trust is a trust relationship where all other domains in the domain tree accept the security credentials of one domain as valid. This means that users authenticated for one domain are also authenticated in any other domain within the domain tree. However, you can define explicit trust relationships among domains where appropriate.

A distributed security model includes the following characteristics:

- Users have a secure single sign-on to the enterprise because security credentials store in Active Directory

- All Active Directory objects replicate to every domain controller in a domain

- Accounts, policies, and resources are managed and accessed at the nearest domain controller

- All Active Directory objects inherit properties from their parent object

- Account and policy properties create at the group level and apply to all new and existing members

In a secure distributed security model, administrative responsibilities are delegated to specific users or groups. By applying inheritance to the assignment of rights and permissions, administration of accounts is distributed across enterprise management, policies, and resources. The administrative component of your security policy can effectively parallel an organizational chart: a tree of administrators with a successively limited scope of authority.

Certificate-based authentication is used within the enterprise for connections through intranet or the Internet, and for logon with smart cards. Smart card users have a single sign-on to the domain. Servers have the ability to authenticate on behalf of clients. Servers transparently impersonate clients when authenticating to other servers in a client transaction requiring multiple servers, and when acting on behalf of local (client) system services.

The Group Policy Object (GPO)

Group Policy Objects define access, configuration, and usage settings for grouped accounts and resources. You can assign IPSec policies to the Group Policy object of a computer account, site, domains, or organizational unit. When the IPSec policy is applied to the Group Policy object for the Active Directory object, the IPSec policy propagates to any computer accounts affected by that Group Policy object.

Keep the following factors in mind when you assign an IPSec policy:

• IPSec policies applied to domain policy override the local, active IPSec policy when that computer is connected to the domain

• IPSec policies assigned to OUs in Active Directory override domain-level policy for any members of that OU

• The lowest level OU IPSec policy overrides IPSec policy for higher level OUs for any members of that OU, and do not merge with them

• Assigning policies at the highest possible level provides the best effect with the least administrative effort

The IPSec Policy Agent only checks Active Directory for updates to the active or assigned policy. If new policies are created in Active Directory, or a policy is changed and assigned to a computer, restart the computer, so that the new policy or policy changes transfer from Active Directory.

Local Computer Policy

Local computer policy applies to computers you administer locally or remotely, and are not usually connected to a domain. Similar to domain members, you can have only one currently active policy. If the computer connects to a domain that has a local policy assigned to it, the Active Directory policy for that computer overrides the local, active policy.

A Security Configuration Within a GPO

With the Security Template snap-in, Windows 2000 provides a centralized method for defining security. It is a single point of entry from which to view the full range of the system security as it applies to a local computer, or is imported to a Group Policy object. Security Templates does not introduce new security parameters. It simply organizes all existing security attributes into one place, to ease security administration. You can also use security templates as base configurations for security analysis, when used with the Security Configuration and Analysis snap-in.

The following are examples of security templates and their functions:

Security Policies—Security-relevant behavior of the system.

Account Policies—Security for passwords, account lockouts, and Kerberos policies.

Local Policies—User rights, and logging for security events.

Restricted Groups—Local group membership administration.

Registry—Security for local registry keys.

File System—Security for the local file system.

System Services—Security and startup mode for local services.

You can import a security template to a Group Policy object. Any computer or user accounts in the site, domain, or OU to which the Group Policy object is applied receive the security template settings. Local Group Policy is a special Group Policy object. It cannot override domain-based policy; only local and account policies are part of the local security template settings.

Importing a security template to a Group Policy object makes domain administration easier. It configures security for multiple computers at once. The Group Policy object defines access, configuration, and usage settings for accounts and resources.

Each template is saved as a text-based .INF file. This means you can copy, paste, import, or export some or all of the template attributes. With the exceptions of IP Security and public key policies, all security attributes are contained in a security template.

The initial template applied to a computer is called the Local Computer Policy. To preserve initial system security settings, the Local Computer Policy can be exported to a security template file. This will enable restoration of the initial security template at any later point. The only possible exceptions to this rule are legacy systems that are being upgraded to Windows 2000.

For example, if a Windows NT 4.0-based computer uses a customized security template that must not be overwritten, the new Local Computer Policy does not apply during the upgrade. In this case, you can configure and apply security after the installation.

ACL Editor

The Security ACL Editor for a GPO is in the Properties form of that GPO. To access the ACL Editor, right-click the root node of a GPO in the MMC Group Policy snap-in, choose Properties, and then select Security. The Security properties page sets permissions on a selected GPO. These permissions control the access to the GPO by specified groups.

From the Start menu, choose Run, and type mmc. Then perform the following procedures:

1.   Choose the **MMC Console** menu item.

2.   Choose the **Add/Remove Snap-in. The Add/Remove Snap-in** dialog box displays (Figure 2.16).

Figure 2.16 Add/Remove Snap-In Dialog Box

3.   Choose **Add**. The **Add Standalone Snap-in** dialog box displays (Figure 2.17).

Figure 2.17 Add Standalone Snap-In Dialog Box

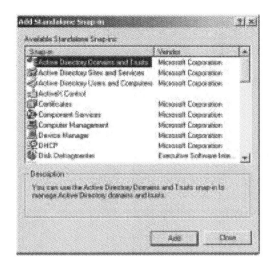

4.   From the **Available Standalone Snap-in** list box, choose **Group Policy**, and then select **Add** (Figure 2.18).

Figure 2.18 Group Policy Dialog Box

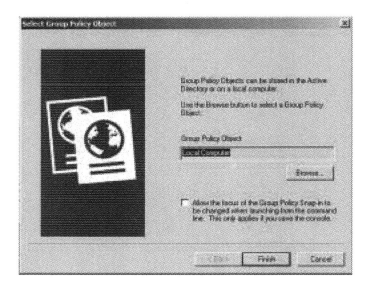

5.   Choose **Browse,** and select the **Domain Controllers** container. Select **OK.**

6.   Right-click **Default Domain Controllers Policy**. Choose **Properties**. (Figure 2.19).

Figure 2.19 Default Domain Controllers Policy Dialog Box

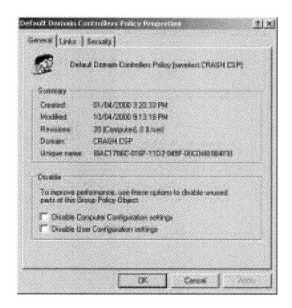

7. From the **Default Domain Controller Policy Properties** page, choose **Security**. This is the ACL Editor. The dialog box title does not tell you that you are using the ACL Editor. Instead it tells you what you are editing (Figure 2.20).

Figure 2.20 The ACL Editor

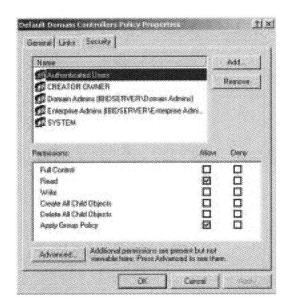

8.   From the **Security** property page, note the available options. Explore the advanced options and select the **Advanced** button (Figure 2.21).

Figure 2.21 Advanced Dialog Box

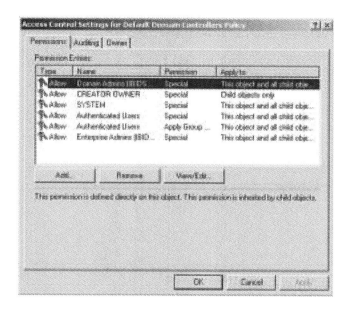

9. Choose **OK** on each of the dialog boxes, and select **Finish** on the **Select Group Policy Object** page. Close the **Add Standalone Snap-in** dialog box, and select **OK** to exit from the snap-in.

Members of the Domain Administrators group also have the ability to use the ACL Editor to determine which administrator groups are able to modify policies in GPOs. The network administrator defines groups of administrators (for example, Accounting Administrators) and then gives them Read/Write access to selected GPOs, thus delegating control of the GPO policies. Granting Read/Write access to a GPO allows administrators to control all aspects of the GPO.TK

Vocabulary

Review the following terms in preparation for the certification exam.

Term	Description
ACE	An Access Control Entry identifies permissions for a group or user object.
ACL	Access Control List is a list of entries in the Active Directory object's security descriptor. It grants or denies access rights to individuals or groups.
ADSI	Active Directory Service Interfaces is a simple, powerful, object-oriented interface to Active Directory.
CAPI	Crypto Application Programming Interface, also known as CryptoAPI, provides functions that allow applications to encrypt or digitally sign data, and provide protection for sensitive private key data.
DACL	Discretionary Access Control Lists define object permissions and impose resource security for each list entry. DACLs are security group, user account, and associated permissions lists.
DNS	Domain Name Service is a network server service that translates domain names into IP addresses.
domain	In Active Directory, a collection of computers defined by the administrator of a Windows 2000 Server network that share a common directory database.
explicit domain trusts	Trust relationships manually created by the administrator.
external trusts	Trusts relationships to domains outside the forest.
forest	A collection of one or more Windows 2000 domains that share a common schema, configuration, and global catalog and are linked with two-way transitive trusts.

Term	Description
FQDN	The Fully Qualified Domain Name for the computer is its primary (or default) name.
GPO	A Group Policy Object defines access, configuration and usage settings for accounts and resources.
I2O	Intelligent Input/Output architecture allows for higher I/O performance on servers by offloading certain I/O operations to a secondary processor.
IEAK 5	The Internet Explorer Administration Kit 5.
IPSec	IPSec Security protocols provide data and identity protection for each IP packet. Windows 2000 IPSec uses the Authentication Header and Encapsulating Security Payload to provide these services.
LDAP	Lightweight Directory Access Protocol, a communications protocol designed for use on TCP/IP networks, defines how a directory client accesses directory servers, performs directory operations and shares directory data.
MAPI	Messaging Application Programming Interface is used by Active Directory to support backward compatibility with Microsoft Exchange applications.
NDS	Novell Network Directory Services is a distributed database that maintains information about every resource on the network and provides access to, and control of, these resources.
OUs	Organizational Units are Active Directory containers for users, groups, computers, and other OUs. An OU cannot contain objects from other domains.
Security Templates	Security Templates do not introduce new security parameters, but organize existing security attributes into one place to ease security administration.

Term	Description
shortcut trusts	Shortcut trusts are Windows 2000-computed trust paths between the domain controllers for two domains in a forest.
transitive trusts	Transitive trusts are two-way relationships. They are a series of trusts between parent and child domains in a domain tree, and among root domains of domain trees in a forest. They allow all domains in a forest to trust each other for authentication purposes.

In Brief

If you want to...	Then do this...
To add an organizational unit	Choose the domain node or folder in which you want to add the OU, and then select the toolbar.
To choose a DNS domain name for Active Directory domains	Start with the registered DNS domain name suffix that the organization has reserved on the Internet. Combine this name with either geographical or divisional names used in the organization, to form full names.
To delegate administration tasks	Create an OU that enables you to grant to a user administrative control for all user and computer accounts in all branches of a single organizational department. Or Grant a user administrative control only to some resources within a department, for example, computer accounts. Or Grant a user administrative control for the Human Relations organizational unit, but not to any OUs contained within the Human Relations organizational unit.
Create a Domain	Install the first domain controller for a domain.
Upgrade a pre-Windows 2000 domain to Windows 2000	Maintain existing one-way trust relationships between the domain and any other pre-Windows 2000 domains, or create external trusts with those domains.
Preserve initial system security settings.	Export the Local Computer Policy to a security template file to preserve initial system security settings.

Lesson 2 Activities

Complete the following activities to better prepare you for the certification exam.

1. List the features of Active Directory.

2. Describe an Organizational Unit.

3. Explain the prerequisites for using DNS on the network.

4. List the types of trusts.

5. Describe the advantages of delegating administrative responsibilities.

6. Name the default security groups installed with a domain controller.

7. Describe the areas to be considered when planning a service profile for a business or enterprise.

8. Explain the relationship between domain trees and forests.

9. Describe four things to keep in mind when assigning IPSec policies.

10. Explain how GPO policies are controlled.

Answers to Lesson 2 Activities

1. The features of Active Directory include a data store or directory, a schema defining classes of objects and attributes, a global catalog, a query and index, a replication service, and integration with security subsystems.

2. An OU is the smallest unit that can be assigned Group Policy settings or have administrative authority. OUs create containers in a domain representing the hierarchical, logical structures of an organization. OUs can also contain other OUs. The hierarchy of containers can be extended as long as necessary to model the organization's hierarchy within a domain.

3. The prerequisites for DNS implementation on a network include planning procedures. First, determine whether there is a registered DNS domain name for use on the Internet. Then determine whether the DNS servers will be set up on a private network or on the Internet, and if the DNS will support the Active Directory. Determine what naming requirements will be followed when choosing DNS domain names for the computers.

4. Types of trusts include the following: Domain Trusts, Explicit domain trusts, External trusts, and Shortcut trusts.

5. Delegating administrative responsibilities lets you eliminate the need for multiple administrative accounts that have broad authority, such as over an entire domain. You can still use the predefined Domain Admins group for administration of the entire domain, and limit the accounts included in the Domain Admins group to highly trusted administrative users.

6. The default security groups that install with the domain controller are: Account Operators, Administrators, Backup Operators, Guests, Print Operators, Replicator, Server Operators and Users.

7. When planning a security profile for a business or enterprise, consider the number of service profiles to be developed and the distribution methods to be used. It's important to consider streamlining installation with additional components, and integrating your Connection Manager Service Profile with an Internet Explorer installation package. Plan the size of the service profile, and the Phone book support that could be implemented. Finally, maintenance and update requirements for the service profile, including all files included in the profile, should be considered when planning a business or enterprise security profile.

8. A forest comprises one or more domains sharing a common schema and global catalog. If multiple domains in the forest have contiguous DNS domain names, that structure is called a domain

tree. If multiple domains have noncontiguous DNS domain names, then they form separate domain trees within the forest. A forest contains one or more domain trees. The forest root domain is the first domain in a forest.

9.   Four things to keep in mind when assigning IPSec policies follow:

IPSec policies that are applied to domain policy will override the local, active IPSec policy when that computer is connected to the domain.

IPSec policies that are assigned to OUs in Active Directory will override domain level policy for any members of that OU, and the lowest level OU IPSec policy overrides IPSec policy for higher level OUs for any members of that OU, not merge with them.

Assigning policies at the highest possible level provides the greatest breadth of effect with the least amount of administrative effort.

IPSec policy remains active even after the Group Policy object to which it is assigned is deleted. You must unassign the IPSec policy before you delete the policy object. If you delete the policy objects and keep the policy assigned, the IPSec Policy Agent assumes it simply cannot find the policy and uses a cached copy.

10.   GPO policies are controlled as follows: Members of the Domain Administrators group can also use the ACL Editor to determine which administrator groups are able to modify policies in GPOs. The network administrator defines groups of administrators, Accounting Administrators, for example, and gives them Read/Write access to selected GPOs. This delegates control of the GPO policies. Granting Read/Write access to a GPO allows administrators to control all aspects of the GPO.

Lesson 2 Quiz

These questions test your knowledge of features, vocabulary, procedures, and syntax.

1.   What is the Active Directory Structure?
     A. A data store

     B. A set of rules

     C. A global catalog

     D. A replication service

2.   What are the required identification features when using the DNS in Windows 2000?
     A. Domain name

     B. NetBIOS

     C. FQDN

     D. CAPI

3.   What is the best way to connect two domain trees in the same forest?
     A. External trusts

     B. Shortcut trusts

     C. Domain trusts

     D. Explicit domain trusts

4.   What are the APIs commonly used by Windows 2000 Active Directory?
     A. MAPI

     B. NDS

     C. DNS

     D. ADSI

5.   What are appropriate ways to assign rights across a tree?
     A. Use group assignment rights

     B. Assign rights high in the tree

     C. Use inheritance

     D. Delegate administration

6.   Which groups are default built-in groups?
     A. Administrators

     B. Replicator

     C. Cert Publishers

     D. Group Policy Admins

7.   What are the critical factors involved in scalability?
     A. Domain tree and forest hierarchy

     B. I2O support

     C. Hardware scalability

     D. Network Load Balancing

8.   What are some of the factors involved in customization planning?
     A. The number of service profiles to be developed

     B. The size of the internet site

     C. The distribution methods to be used

     D. The size of the service profile

9.   What are some advantages of the Distributed Security Model?
     A. Distributed Authentication

     B. Stored Security Credentials

     C. Transitive trust

     D. Single sign-on

10. What IPSec policy parameters affect Group Policy Objects?
     A. Override

     B. High-level assignment

     C. Unassigning IPSec

     D. IPSec policy Agent

Answers to Lesson 2 Quiz

1. Answer A is correct, the Active Directory is a data store, also known as the directory, which stores information about Active Directory objects.

    Answer B is correct. Active Directory is a set of rules, the schema, that defines the classes of objects and attributes contained in the directory,

    Answer C is correct. Active Directory is a global catalog that contains information about every object in the directory,

    Answer D is correct. The Active Directory acts as a replication service that distributes directory data across a network.

2. Answer A is correct. In Windows 2000, Active Directory domains are assigned DNS names. When choosing DNS names for your Active Directory domains, begin with the registered DNS domain name suffix that your organization has reserved for use on the Internet.

    Answer C is correct. Fully Qualified Domain Names are a requirement for identification when using the DNS in Windows 2000.

    Answers B and D are incorrect. NetBIOS is necessary for migration of Windows NT computers, but is optional for Windows 2000 systems. The Crypto Application Programming Interface is not necessary for identification in DNS.

3. Answer B is correct. Shortcut trusts are two-way transitive trusts, which let you shorten the path in a complex forest. You create shortcut trusts between Windows 2000 domains in the same forest. The most effective use of shortcut trusts is between two domain trees in a forest.

    Answers A, C, and D are incorrect. External trusts create trust relationships to domains outside the forest. A domain trust is a relationship established between two domains that enable users in one domain to be authenticated by a domain controller in another domain. This basic trust contains but is not specifically a shortcut trust between two domains.

4. Answers A and D are correct. Active Directory provides support for Messaging Application Programming Interface (MAPI), so legacy MAPI programs will continue to work with Active Directory. Active Directory Service Interfaces (ADSI) provides a simple, powerful, object-oriented interface to Active Directory.

Answers B is incorrect. NDS is a directory service on networks running Novell NetWare 4.0. It is a distributed database that maintains information about every resource on the network and provides access to and control of these resources.

Answer C is incorrect. Domain Name Space (DNS) is a set of domain naming protocols, not an API.

5.   Answer A is correct. An appropriate way to assign rights across a tree includes using group assignment rights. You can rely on rights from group assignments because this method is more efficient than maintaining user accounts directly, and assigning rights on a user basis.

Answer B is correct. Another appropriate method for assigning rights across a tree is to assign rights as high in the container tree as possible. This method accommodates the majority of the security principals.

Answer C is correct. Apply inheritance to extend rights through the container tree, and apply access control settings to all children of a parent object.

Answer D is correct. An appropriate method to assign rights across a tree is to delegate the administration of containers to the administrators who manage the computers where those containers reside. It decentralizes administrative operations.

6.   Answers A and B are correct. The Administrators and Replicator groups are default built-in groups. The Administrators group in a domain has a broad set of administrative authority over all accounts and resources in the domain. Replicators have control over local replication functionality.

Answers C and D are incorrect. Cert Publishers and Group Policy Admins are not default built-in groups. Certificate Publishers and Group Policy Admins have responsibilities that cover cross-domain issues and are not a purely local function. The system administrator can use these groups with global scope to collect the various types of user accounts in that domain (regular users, administrators, and guests) into groups. These groups can then be placed in groups with domain local scope in that domain and others.

7.   Answer B is correct. New I2O, also called Intelligent Input/Output, architecture brings higher I/O performance to your servers. It offloads certain I/O operations to a secondary processor. I2O improves I/O performance in high-bandwidth applications such as networked video, groupware, and client/server processing.

Answer C is correct. The Windows 2000 Server family covers a gamut of deployments, from small workgroups to enterprise data centers. The family includes products that support up to 32 processors and advanced Input/Output (I/O). It integrates network load balancing and new multiprocessor optimizations for your business applications.

Answer D is correct. Network Load Balancing distributes incoming TCP/IP traffic between multiple servers. These servers, especially Web servers, can perform better when demand is high.

Answer A is incorrect. Domain tree and forest hierarchy is an efficient way to establish and maintain control over the network, however large it may become.

8.   Answer A is correct. The administrator can create additional service profiles to support specialized needs of specific groups or personnel.

Answer C is correct. The administrator can distribute service profiles by CD-ROM or downloadable file (over a private network or the Internet).

Answer D is correct. A service profile that includes Connection Manager uses about 800 kilobytes (KB) of disk space. A profile without Connection Manager can use as little about 200 KB. The total size of your service profile depends on your customization options, such as the method you use to provide phone books, whether you include connect actions or other optional programs, and which graphics you incorporate.

Answer B is incorrect. The Website size can expand or contract independently of the size of the service profile.

9.   Answers A, B, C, and D are correct. Advantages of the Distributed Security Model include distributed authentication, stored security credentials, transitive trusts, and single sign-on.

Authentication of users and computers is distributed across the enterprise. Security credentials for users and computers are stored in Active Directory. Computers are authenticated when started.

Transitive trust, in which all other domains in the domain tree accept security credentials valid for one domain, is the default. This means that users authenticated for one domain are also authenticated in other domains within the domain tree. You can limit explicit trust relationships between domains.

10.   Answers A, B, and C are correct. IPSec policies assigned to OUs in Active Directory override domain-level policy for any members of that OU. The lowest level OU IPSec policy overrides IPSec policy for higher level OUs for any members of that OU, and do not merge with them.

IPSec policy remains active even after the Group Policy object to which it is assigned is deleted. You must unassign the IPSec policy before you delete the policy object. If you delete the policy objects and keep the policy assigned, the IPSec Policy Agent assumes it simply cannot find the policy and uses a cached copy.

Answer D is incorrect. The IPSec Policy Agent only checks Active Directory for updates to the active or assigned policy. If new policies have been created in Active Directory, or a policy has been changed and assigned to a computer, it must be restarted for the new policy or policy changes to be transferred from Active Directory.

Lesson 3

Security Configuration Tools

It is easy to administer Windows 2000 security using the various built-in configuration tools. The user configures and analyzes security settings based on templates that load, combine, and edit local security settings. In addition, the user has the ability to configure security by editing the Access Control List (ACL) and editing Group Policy Objects (GPOs) in Activity Directory by using the Group Policy snap-in for the Microsoft Management Console (MMC).

After completing this lesson, you should have a better understanding of the following topics:

• Security Templates

• Security Configuration and Analysis Snap-In

• The SECEDIT Analysis Tool

• Predefined Security Templates

Security Templates

Windows 2000 presents a centralized approach for defining security with the Security Templates snap-in. The Security Templates snap-in provides a single point of entry where the full range of system security can be viewed, adjusted, and applied to a local computer or imported to a Group Policy object. New security restrictions are not introduced. The Security Templates snap-in organizes all the existing security attributes into one place making security administration easier. Security Templates can also be used as base configurations for security analysis, and then used with the Security Configuration and Analysis snap-in.

Understanding Security Templates

Windows 2000 provides a number of MMC snap-ins and a command-line utility for dealing with security. You use these tools to configure and analyze security settings based on a series of standard templates. You can use them to load, combine, edit and to configure local security. These tools analyze security settings by comparing them with defaults, and allow users to export custom security templates to other machines on a network. These security templates enable users to configure security at the local machine level, or to revise a specific template that can be applied to every machine of that type (workstation, member server, and so on) in the network.

These tools are as follows:

Security Template snap-in—Allows the creation of a text-based template file that contains security settings for all security areas. With the snap-in you can view, adjust, and apply the template to a local computer or to a GPO. This tool does not create new security parameters, but brings all of the existing security attributes into one place to facilitate security administration. You can also use security templates with the Security Configuration and Analysis snap-in to use as base configurations for security analysis.

The Security Configuration and Analysis snap-in—Configures or analyzes Windows 2000 operating system security. Its functionality is based on the contents of a security template created using the Security Templates snap-in. This tool allows a quick review of security analysis results and provides recommendations together with current system settings. You can also use it to resolve discrepancies discovered by analysis, and to configure local system security. The Security Configuration and Analysis snap-in imports security templates and applies them to the GPO for the local computer and configures the local system security correctly.

SECEDIT.EXE—Provides a command-line form of the Security Configuration and Analysis snap-in which you can perform security configuration and analysis without a Graphical User Interface (GUI).

Account Policies

Optionally, you can apply the following policies to user accounts:

Password—Establishes the settings, such as enforcement and lifetimes, for passwords for domain and local user accounts.

Account lockout—Establishes the specific account and the time the account is to be locked out of the system for domain and local user accounts.

Kerberos—Establishes the Kerberos-related settings, such as ticket lifetimes and enforcement for domain user accounts.

 Note: You do not need to configure account policies for OUs that do not contain any computers. OUs that contain only users always receive account policy from the domain.

Default Domain Upgrade Policies

Account and password policies take precedence over local policy on domain controllers, servers, and workstations in the Windows 2000 domain when you upgrade to Windows 2000 Professional.

Local Policies

Each computer has its own rights and local policies. The following are the security area element policies:

Audit—Establishes the security events, such as successful attempts, failed attempts or both, to record into the Security log.

User rights assignment—Establishes the users or the groups that have logon or task privileges.

Security options—Enables or disables the security settings, such as Administrator and Guest account names, digital signatures on data, hard drive and CD-ROM access, device driver installation, and the logon prompts for the specific computer.

Local policies relate to a specific computer. When these settings are imported to a Group Policy Object (GPO) in Active Directory, they affect the security settings of all computer accounts to which the GPO is applied. In both cases, user account rights do not apply if a local policy setting overrides those privileges.

Event Log

The security area of the Event log defines the features of the Application, Security, and System event logs. This includes the maximum log size, access rights for each log, and the retention settings and methods.

You should match the event log size and log wrapping to match business and security requirements. You should implement the Event log settings at the site, domain, or OU level, to take advantage of your group policy settings.

File or Folder Sharing

You can configure the attributes for existing files and folders in the local file system. This includes the existing Registry keys on the local system and the existing system services on the local computer.

These attributes include the following:

Inherit—Any child object inherits the parent object's security, if the child object has not been protected from inheritance.

Overwrite—No matter what the child object's protection setting, the parent object's security overrides any security set on the child object.

Ignore—When placed on an object, it prevents the configuring or analyzing security for the object or any of its child objects.

The user has the capability of editing the Security properties of an object.

Directory Security

Windows 2000 Active Directory uses access control on objects and credentials to deliver protected storage of user account and group information. Active Directory stores user credentials and access control information. This means users logging on to the network get authentication and authorization to access system resources.

For example, a user logs on to the network and Windows 2000 security authenticates the user with information from the Active Directory. Each time the user tries to access a service on the network, the system checks the properties defined in the Discretionary Access Control List (DACL) for that service.

System security runs more effectively as Active Directory allows administrators to create group accounts. Access to objects in Active Directory can be based on group membership. For example, by adjusting a file's properties, an administrator can permit all of the users in a group to read that file.

Preset Configurations

For common security scenarios, a set of predefined security templates is provided in Windows 2000. You can assign these to a computer or change them to fit particular security requirements.

The following preset configurations are available:

- Default workstation (BASIEWK.INF)

- Default server (BASICSV.INF)

- Default domain controller (BASIEDC.INF)

- Compatible workstation or server (COMPATWS.INF)

- Secure workstation or server (SECUREWS.INF)

- Highly Secure workstation or server (HISDCWS.INF0

- Dedicated domain controller (DEDICADC.INF)

- Secure domain controller (SECUREDC.INF)

- Highly Secure domain controller (HISECDC.INF)

By default, these templates are stored in \%systemroot%\security\templates.

Restricted Groups

Restricted Groups are an important security feature for Windows 2000 as they automatically provide security memberships to groups that have predefined capabilities—such as Administrators, Power Users, Print Operators, Server Operators and Domain Admins. Restricted Groups act as an administrator for group membership. You can add groups that you consider sensitive or privileged to the Restricted Groups security list.

The following example explains how you can use Restricted Groups to your benefit. The Power Users group is automatically part of Restricted Groups as it is a default Windows 2000 group. In our example, it has two users, Alice and Bob. Through the Active Directory Users and Computers snap-in, Bob adds Charles to cover for him while he is on vacation. When Bob returns, no one remembers to remove Charles from the group.

Over time, these situations can add up. Extra members, who should no longer have these rights, are still full members of the group. When you configure security through Restricted Groups, these situations can be prevented.

If only Alice and Bob are listed in the Restricted Groups node for Power Users, when Group Policy settings are applied, Charles will be removed from the group.

File System

When you load the security template into the Security Configuration and Analysis tool, you can browse the local directory and specify security settings for any file or folder. The template list treats all of the volumes on a system as part of a single tree. The first level nodes will appear as the root directory of each volume.

System Services

There is a wide range of system services, including network services, file and print services, telephony and fax services, and Internet/intranet services. Security templates back each of the system services general settings. These settings include the service startup mode (automatic, manual, or disabled), and security on the service.

Registry

The templates enable the user to manage the Registry by placing a security descriptor on the Registry key objects. The Registry list contains the full Registry key path and security descriptor. You can manage Registry security settings by right-clicking any Registry key in a template loaded into the Security Configuration and Analysis tool.

Editing a Template

You can directly edit the security templates. Once you have edited and tested a security template, you can export the new security policy to the Security Templates container and use it on other computers. You can also alter a predefined template and apply it to all the appropriate computers on your network. This will alter each of their default settings. The Security Templates MMC snap-in provides copy-and-paste editing facilities, which allows you to simultaneously amend all the policies in one template container.

 Note: Amendments made to predefined or custom policy configurations in the security templates do not alter any policies on computers until the new policy template is applied.

Importing/Exporting Security Templates

With Security Configuration and Analysis, you can import and export security templates either into or from a working database. You can also merge several different templates into one composite template by importing each template into a working database. You can then use it for analysis or configuration of a system. If you chose to overwrite, the templates do not merge into a composite template (stored configuration). Once you have created a composite configuration, you can save it for future analysis or configuration of other systems.

With the export feature, you can save the stored configuration as a new template file. You can then import this template into other databases, use it to analyze or configure a system, or redefine with the Security Templates snap-in.

Security Configuration and Analysis Snap-In

Security Configuration and Analysis uses a database to carry out analysis and configuration functions. The Windows 2000 database architecture allows the use of personal databases, importing and exporting security templates, and combining multiple base security templates into one composite security template to be used for analysis or configuration.

The Security Configuration and Analysis database is a computer-specific data store. You can incrementally add new security templates to the database and create or overwrite a composite security template. You can also create personal databases for storing your own customized security templates.

You use security settings to define the security-relevant behavior of the system. By using Group Policy objects in the Active Directory, administrators can apply the security levels required to protect enterprise systems centrally.

When you determine the settings for a Group Policy object containing multiple computers, you must consider the organizational and functional character of that given site, domain, or OU. For example, the security levels needed for an OU of the computers in a Sales department would be very different from that for an OU containing Finance Department computers.

Security Settings

The term *security settings* is interchangeable with security configuration. Security settings include Security Policies (account and local policies), access control (to services, files, and the Registry), Event log, group membership (restricted groups), Internet Protocol security (IPSec) policies, and public key policies.

To set the security settings Advanced Restore options, follow these steps:

1.   Open Backup (Figure 3.1). To do so, from the **Start Menu**, choose **Programs, Accessories**, select **System Tools**, and then select **Backup**.

2.   Choose **Restore** and select the files and folders you want to restore.

Figure 3.1 Open Backup

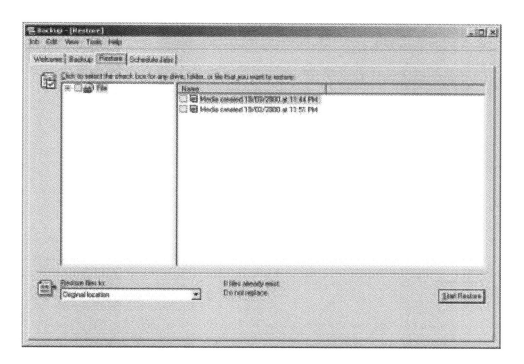

3.   Choose **Start Restore**.

4.   On the **Confirm Restore** dialog box, choose **Advanced** (Figure 3.2).

5.   Set the advanced restore options you want, and then choose **OK**.

Figure 3.2 Advanced

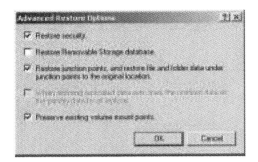

The following paragraphs provide a description for each restore option:

Choosing **Restore security** restores the security settings for each file and folder. These security settings include permissions, audit entries, and ownership. You have this option only if you have backed up data from an NTFS volume in Windows 2000 and you are restoring it to an NTFS volume in Windows 2000.

Choosing **Restore removable storage database** restores the Removable Storage database. This database is stored in Systemroot\System32\Ntmsdata. If you do not use Removable Storage for managing storage media, you do not need to select this option. Using this option deletes your existing Removable Storage database.

Choosing **Restore junction points, and restore file and folder data under junction points to the original location** restores the junction points on your hard disk and the data the junction points to. If you do not select this check box, the junction points are restored, but the data to your junction points may not be accessible. If you are restoring a mounted drive and want to restore the data mounted on the drive, you must select this check box. If you do not select this check box, you restore only the folder containing the mounted drive.

Choosing **When restoring replicated data sets, mark the restored data as the primary data for all replicas** ensures that the restored File Replication Service (FRS) data replicates to your other servers. If you are restoring FRS data, choose this option. If you do not select this option, FRS data may not replicate to other servers because the restored data appears older than the data already on the servers. This can cause the other servers to overwrite the restored data, preventing you from restoring the FRS data.

Choosing **Preserve existing volume mount points** prevents the restore operation from overwriting any volume mount points you have created on the partition or volume to where you are restoring data. You would use this option when you are restoring data to an entire drive or partition. For example, if you are restoring data to a replacement drive, and you have partitioned and formatted the drive and restored volume mount points, you would select this option so your volume mount points do not restore. If you are restoring data to a partition or drive that you have just reformatted and you want to restore the old volume mount points, do not select this option.

Security Templates

A *security template* is a physical representation of a security configuration: a file containing a group of security settings. Windows 2000 includes a set of security templates, each based on the role of a computer from security settings for low security domain clients to highly secure domain controllers. You can use these templates as provided, modify them, or use them as a basis for creating custom security templates.

Security Configuration Tools

As an administrator, you have the option of using security configuration tools that help use, analyze, and configure security templates. The following three tools are helpful in this process:

Security Templates snap-in—Facilitates defining and using security templates.

Security Configuration and Analysis snap-in—Facilitates configuring and analyzing security locally.

Group Policy snap-in—Facilitates configuring security centrally in Active Directory.

To start Security Templates, follow these steps:

Decide whether to add Security Templates to an existing console or create a new console.

To create a new console, From the **Start Menu**, choose **Run**, type **mmc**, then select **OK**.

To add Security Templates to an existing console, open the console, then go to the next step.

On the **Console** menu, choose **Add/Remove Snap-in**, then select **Add** (Figure 3.3).

Figure 3.3 Add/Remove Snap-In

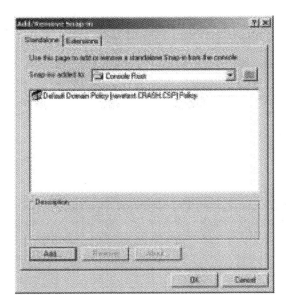

Choose **Security Templates, Add, Close,** then select **OK.** (Figure 3.4).

Figure 3.4 Security Templates

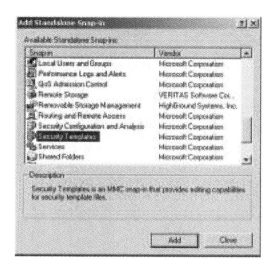

From the **Console** menu, choose **Save**.

Enter the name to assign to this console and choose **Save**.

 Note: If you save the console in **My Documents**, it is accessible from either on the desktop or from the **Start** menu.

To customize a predefined security template, follow these steps:

1. In the Security Templates snap-in, double-click **Security Templates**.

2. Double-click the default path folder (*Systemroot*\Security\Templates), and right-click the predefined template you want to modify (Figure 3.5).

Figure 3.5 Security Templates

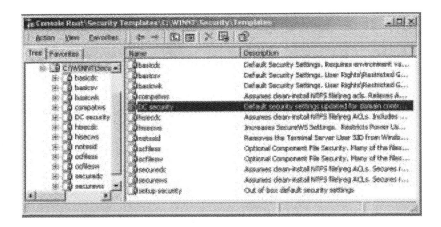

3.   Choose **Save As** and specify a filename for the security template.

4.   Double-click the new security template to display the security policies (such as Account Policies) and double-click the security policy you want to modify (Figure 3.6).

Figure 3.6 Account Policies

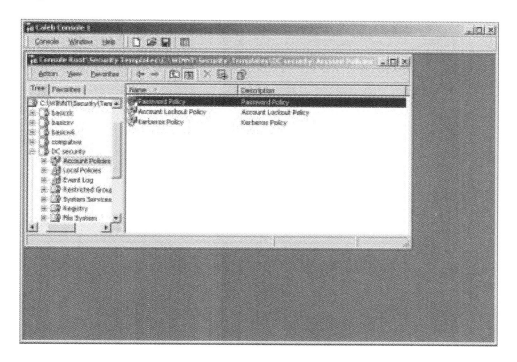

5. Choose the security area you want to customize, such as Password Policy, thenand then double-click the security attribute to modify, such as Minimum Password Length (Figure 3.7).

Figure 3.7 Minimum Password

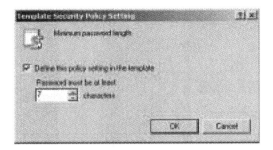

6.   Confirm that the **Exclude this setting in analysis** check box is cleared to allow configuration (Figure 3.8).

Figure 3.8 Exclude This Setting in Analysis Check Box

To define a security template, follow these steps:

1.   In the Security Templates snap-in, double-click **Security Templates**.

2.   Right-click the template path folder where you want to store the new template and choose **New Template** (Figure 3.9).

Figure 3.9 New Template

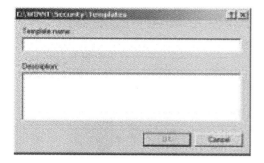

3. Enter the name and description for your new security template. The new template then displays in the console tree (Figure 3.10).

Figure 3.10 Display New Template

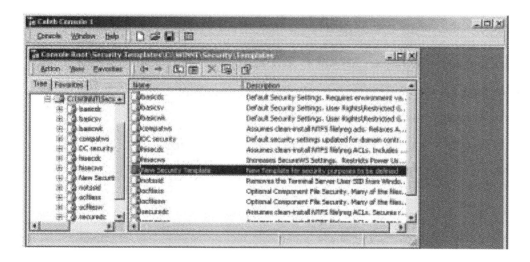

4. Double-click the new security template to display the security areas.

5. Double-click the security policy, such as Account Policies, that you want to customize, thenand then choose the security area, such as Password Policy (Figure 3.11)

Figure 3.11 Account Policies

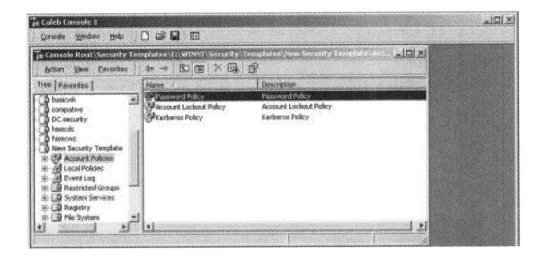

6. Double-click the security attribute you want to configure (such as Minimum Password Length).

7. Confirm that the **Exclude this setting in analysis** check box is cleared, in order to allow editing.

To delete a security template, follow these steps:

1. In the Security Templates snap-in, double-click **Security Templates**.

2. Double-click the template path folder where the security templates are stored and right-click the security template you want to delete.

3. Choose **Delete**.

To refresh the security template list, follow these steps:

1. In the Security Templates snap-in, double-click **Security Templates**.

2.   Double-click the template path folder where the security templates are stored.

3.   Choose **Refresh**. The console tree displays any new additions or deletions.

To set a description for a security template, follow these steps:

1.   In the Security Templates snap-in, double-click **Security Templates**.

2.   Right-click any of the following: Security Templates, the security template path folder, or a security template.

3.   Choose **Set Description**.

To apply a security template to a local computer, follow these steps:

1.   In the Security Configuration and Analysis snap-in, right-click **Security Configuration and Analysis** (Figure 3.12).

Figure 3.12 Security Configuration and Analysis

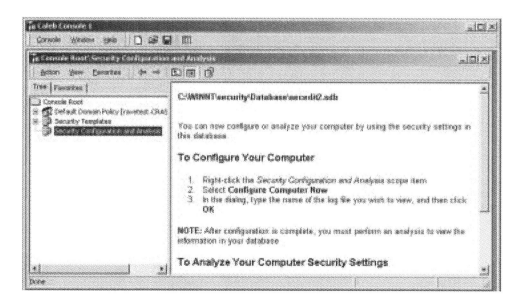

2.   If a working database is not already set, choose **Open Database** to set a working database.

If no database is available, you have to create one.

To create a new database, follow these steps:

1.   Right-click the **Security Configuration and Analysis** scope item.

2.   Choose **Open Database**.

3.   Type a new database name, and then choose **Open**.

4.   Choose a security template to import, and then select **Open** (Figure 3.13).

Figure 3.13 Open Database

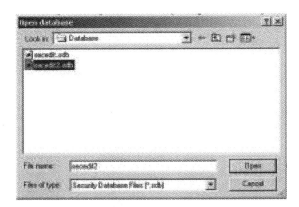

5.   Choose **Import Template** (Figure 3.14).

Figure 3.14 Import Template

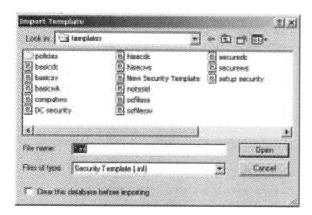

6. Choose a security template file and select **Open**.

7. Repeat the previous step for each template you want to merge into the database.

8. Right-click **Security Configuration and Analysis**, and choose **Configure System Now** (Figure 3.15).

Figure 3.15 Security Configuration and Analysis

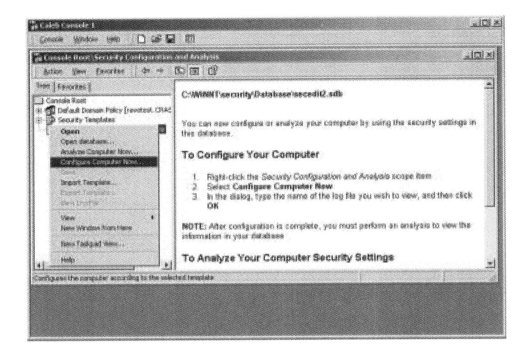

 Note: The security settings you configure take effect immediately.

To import a security template to a Group Policy object, follow these steps:

1. In a console from which you manage Group Policy settings, choose the Group Policy Object to which you want to import the security template.

2. In the console tree, right-click **Security Settings** (Figure 3.16).

Figure 3.16 Security Settings

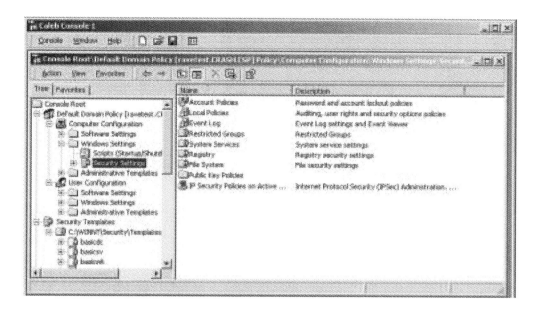

3.   Choose **Import Policy** (Figure 3.17).

Figure 3.17 Import Policy

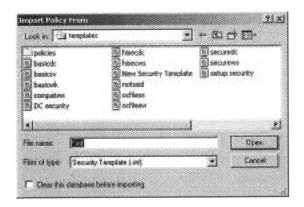

4.   Choose the security template you want to import.

   Note: The security settings apply when the computer starts or as the Group Policy settings dictate.

To view effective security settings, follow these steps:

1.   In the console from which you manage Group Policy, double-click the Group Policy Object which you want to view.

2.   In the console tree, choose **Security Settings**.

3.   Double-click a security policy node (such as Account Policies) and choose a security area (such as Password Policy).

4.   Double-click the security attribute you want to view (such as Minimum Password Length).

Note: Security settings reflect both local policy and the policy in effect on the system. These may not be the same if the computer inherits Group Policy settings.

The SECEDIT Analysis Tool

SECEDIT.EXE is a tool you can activate from the command line, a batch file, or an automatic task scheduler. You use this tool for analyzing system security or for creating and applying templates. It is extremely convenient to analyze or configure multiple computers during off-hours.

Understanding the Command-Line SECEDIT Tool

The command-line SECEDIT.EXE interface helps you perform batch network security analysis. The basic tools and command lines are listed in the next sections.

Analyze System Security

The following command analyzes system security:

```
secedit /analyze
```

Syntax

secedit /analyze [/DB filename] [/CFG filename] [/log logpath] [/verbose] [/quiet]

Parameters

/DB filename—This provides the path to a database that contains the stored configuration against which the analysis is to be performed. This is a required argument. If **filename** specifies a new database, you must also specify the CFG argument.

/CFG filename—This argument is only valid when used with the **/DB parameter**, and is the path to the security template to be imported into the database for analysis. If you do not specify this argument, the analysis performs against any configuration already stored in the database.

/log logpath—This is the path to the log file for the process. If you do not provide this, the default file is used.

/verbose—Requests more detailed progress information during the analysis.

/quiet—Suppresses screen and log output. You will still be able to view analysis results using Security Configuration and Analysis.

Configure System Security

secedit /configure—This command configures system security by applying a stored template.

Syntax

secedit /configure [/DB *filename* **] [/CFG** *filename* **] [/over-write][/areas** *area1 area2...***] [/log** *logpath***] [/verbose] [/quiet]**

Parameters

/DB filename—Provides the path to a database that contains the security template that should be applied. This is a required argument.

/CFG filename—This argument is only valid when used with the **/DB** parameter. It is the path to the security template to be imported into the database and applied to the system. If you do not specify this argument, the template already stored in the database applies.

/overwrite—This argument is only valid when the **/CFG** argument is also used. This specifies whether the security template in the **/CFG** argument should overwrite any template or composite template stored in the database instead of appending the results to the stored template. If this is not specified, the template in the **/CFG** argument appends to the stored template.

/area area1 area2—Specifies the security areas to be applied to the system. The default is "all areas." Separate each area by a space.

Table 3.1 Security Configuration Settings

Area Name	Description
SECURITYPOLICY	Local policy and domain policy for the system, including account policies, audit policies, and others.
GROUP_MGMT	Restricted group settings for any groups specified in the security template.
USER_RIGHTS	User logon rights and granting of privileges.
REGKEYS	Security on local Registry keys.
FILESTORE	Security on local file storage.
SERVICES	Security for all defined services.

/log *logpath*—Path to the log file for the process. If not specified, the default is used.

/verbose—Specifies more detailed progress information.

/quiet—Suppresses screen and log output.

Refresh Security Settings

secedit /refreshpolicy—This command refreshes system security by reapplying the security settings to the Group Policy object.

Syntax

secedit /refreshpolicy {machine_policy | user_policy}[/enforce]

Parameters

machine_policy—Refreshes security settings for the local computer.

user_policy—Refreshes security settings for the local user account currently logged on to the computer.

/enforce—Refreshes security settings even if there have been no changes to the Group Policy object settings.

When you set up a security policy for a large number of computers within an organization, the SECEDIT tool configures and analyzes security and then allows you to view the analysis results in a text editor. In addition, you can view analysis results with the Security Configuration and Analysis Tool.

Configuring and Analyzing System Security

The Security Configuration and Analysis tool is part of the Security Configuration and Analysis console. With this tool, you have the ability to configure or analyze security, view results and rectify any inconsistencies that are discovered during analysis. Administrators can use Security Configuration and Analysis in adjusting security policy and to detect security flaws that develop in the system.

Security Analysis

A computer's applications and operating system are dynamic. You may need to change security levels temporarily to resolve administration and network issues. These quick changes can be easily forgotten. Over time, that computer may not meet your enterprise security requirements.

With regular analysis, and as part of an enterprise risk program, an administrator can make sure that each computer meets the security level standards. All aspects of the system security can be highly specified in your analysis results. With these results, you cane fine-tune security levels and detect any security flaws early.

By using the Security and Analysis console, you can quickly perform security analysis. During analysis, the results display beside the current system settings as icons or remarks that highlight the areas where the current settings do not match your planned level. At the same time, you can resolve any differences that appear through your analysis.

By performing regular analysis, you can track and ensure an acceptable level of security on each computer. If you frequently need to analyze a large number of computers, such as in a domain, you can use SECEDIT.EXE for batch analysis. You can still use the Security and Configuration Analysis console to view the results.

Security Configuration

With the Security Configuration tool, you can configure local security. When you have created security templates using the Security Templates snap-in and a personal database, you can import the security templates and apply them to the Group Policy object for the local computer. You have to configure the system security so that it is supplied in the template.

The Security Configuration and Analysis console displays analysis results and organizes the security area. Flags indicate problems. For each security attribute in the security areas, the current system and base configuration settings display.

The following are the indicators of how your current settings do not match the base settings:

- A red X indicates a difference

- A green check mark indicates consistency

- No icon indicates that security attribute was not part of your template, and therefore not analyzed

If you choose to accept current settings, the corresponding value in the base configuration modifies to match. If you change the system setting to match the base configuration, the change reflects when you configure the system with Security Configuration and Analysis.

To avoid continued flagging of settings that you have already investigated and determined reasonable, you can modify the base configuration. The changes are made to a copy of the template.

Validating Security Configuration Files

secedit /validate—This command validates the syntax of a security template the user wants to import into a database for analysis or application to a system.

Syntax

```
secedit /validate filename
```

Parameters

filename—The filename of the security template you have created with Security Templates.

Exporting Security Configuration Settings

With Security Configuration and Analysis, you can import and export security templates into or out of a working database. You can merge several different templates into a composite template, through importing each template into a working database. Unless overwritten, they merge into a composite template or a stored configuration. You can then use this composite template for analysis or configuration of a system.

Once you have created a composite configuration, you can save it to use on other systems. With the export feature, you have the ability to save the stored configuration as a new template file that can be imported into other databases used as is to analyze or configure a system, or even redefined with the Security Templates snap-in.

Export Security Settings

secedit /export—This command exports a stored template from a security database to a security template file.

Syntax

secedit /export [/mergedPolicy] [/DB *filename*] [/CFG *filename*] [/areas *area1 area 2*...] [/log *logPath*] [/verbose] [/quiet]

Parameters

/MergedPolicy—Merges and exports domain and local policy security settings.

/DB filename—Provides the path to a database that contains the template to be exported. If you do not provide a database, the system policy database is used.

/CFG filename—Provides the path and name of a file where the template should be saved.

/area area1 area2—Specifies the security areas to be exported to a template. The default is "all areas." Separate each area by a space.

Table 3.2 Export Security Settings

Area Name	Description
SECURITYPOLICY	Local policy and domain policy for the system, including account policies, audit policies, and so on.
GROUP_MGMT	Restricted group settings for any groups specified in the security template.
USER_RIGHTS	User logon rights and granting of privileges.
REGKEYS	Security on local Registry keys.
FILESTORE	Security on local file storage.
SERVICES	Security for all defined services.

`log logpath`—Provides the path to the log file for the process. If not specified, the default is used.

`/verbose`—Specifies more detailed progress information.

`/quiet`—Suppresses screen and log output.

Predefined Security Templates

Windows 2000 contains a set of security templates that you can use for common security settings. You can assign these templates exactly the way they are to a computer, or you can modify them for specific security requirements. These predefined security templates should not be applied to production systems without first testing to make sure the right level of application functionality is maintained for your network and system architecture.

The predefined security templates are as follows:

• Default workstation (BASICWK.INF)

- Default server (BASICSV.INF)

- Default domain controller (BASICDC.INF)

- Compatible workstation or server (COMPATWS.INF)

- Secure workstation or server (SECUREWS.INF)

- Highly secure workstation or server (HISECWS.INF)

- Dedicated domain controller (DEDICADC.INF)

- Secure domain controller (SECUREDC.INF)

- Highly secure domain controller (HISECDC.INF)

By default, these templates are stored in the *systemroot*\security\templates folder.

Understanding the Five Template Categories

The templates cover the following five common requirements for security:

Basic

Basic (basic*.inf)—The basic configuration templates are used to reverse the application of a different security configuration. Using the basic configurations applies the Windows 2000 default security settings to all security areas, except those associated with user rights. User rights do not change in the basic templates because application setup programs commonly modify them for successful use of the application. It is not the intent of the basic configuration files to undo such modifications.

Compatible

Compatible (compat*.inf)—When Windows 2000 security is configured, the members of the local users group have ideal security settings. For example, the members of the local Power Users group have security settings compatible with Windows NT 4.0 users.

This default configuration allows the development of applications to a standard definition of a secure Windows environment, and still allows the existing applications to run under the less secure, Power User configuration. By default, all users that are authenticated by Windows 2000 are members of the

Power Users group. In some situations or environments, this is too unsecure. You may want to have users, by default, be only members of the Users group. You could then decrease the level of security on the Users group so applications run effectively. By lowering the security levels on specific files, folders, and registry keys commonly accessed by applications, the compatible templates allow most applications to run effectively. Windows 2000 assumes the administrator applying the compatible template does not want users to be Power Users and all members of the Power Users group are removed.

Secure

Secure (secure*.inf)—The secure templates implement recommended security settings for all security areas except files, folders, and Registry keys. These are not modified, as file system and Registry permissions are configured securely by default.

Highly Secure

Highly Secure (hisec*.inf)—The highly secure templates define the security settings for Windows 2000 network communications. The security areas are set to require maximum protection for network traffic and protocols used between computers running Windows 2000. Because of this, computers configured with a highly secure template can only communicate with other Windows 2000 computers. They are not able to communicate with computers running Windows 95 or 98 or Windows NT.

Dedicated Domain Controller

Dedicated Domain Controller (dedica*.inf)—The local user security on Windows 2000 domain controllers is not at the optimum level of security by default. You can run existing server-based applications on domain controllers in a backward- compatible method. However, this is not recommended. It is recommended that you do not run server based-applications on domain controllers. The default file system and Registry permissions for the local users group can be defined as the same as those defined by default for Windows 2000 workstations and stand-alone servers.

By implementing a dedicated security template, these security settings for local users on Windows 2000 domain controllers are applied.

Applying Predefined Security Templates

A set of security templates is provided for common security scenarios. These can be assigned directly to a computer as-is, or modified to suit unique security requirements. You should not apply predefined security templates to production systems without testing to ensure that the right level of application functionality is maintained for your network and system architecture.

To apply a security template to a local computer, follow these steps:

1. In the Security Configuration and Analysis snap-in, right-click **Security Configuration and Analysis** (Figure 3.18).

Figure 3.18 Security Configuration and Analysis

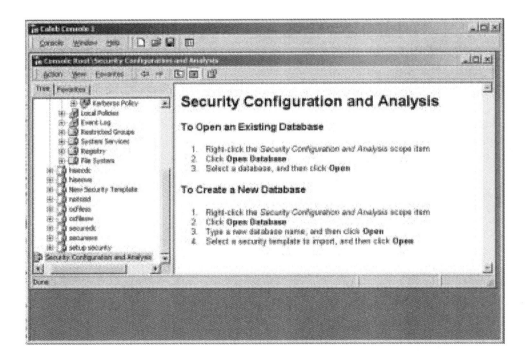

2. If a working database is not already set, choose **Open Database** to set a working database (Figure 3.19).

Figure 3.19 Open Database

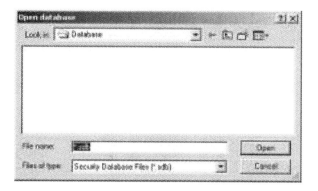

3. Choose **Import Template** (Figure 3.20).

Figure 3.20 Import Template

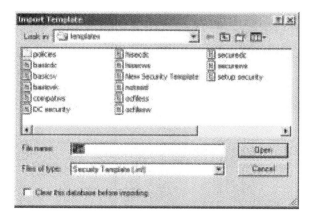

4. Choose a security template file and select **Open**.

5. Repeat the previous step for each template you want to merge into the database.

6.   Right-click **Security Configuration and Analysis**, and choose **Configure System Now** (Figure 3.21).

Figure 3. 21 Security Configuration and Analysis

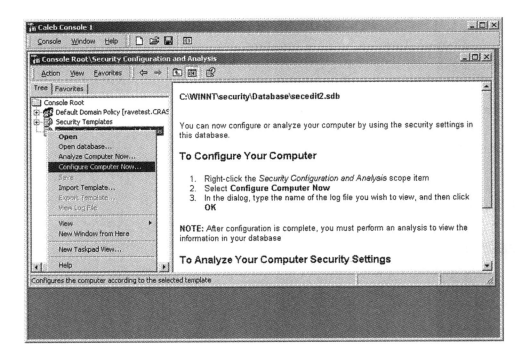

Note: The security settings take effect immediately.

The predefined security templates are as follows:

- Default workstation (BASICWK.INF)

- Default server (BASICSV.INF)

- Default domain controller (BASICDC.INF)

- Compatible workstation or server (COMPATWS.INF)

- Secure workstation or server (SECUREWS.INF)

- Highly secure workstation or server (HISECWS.INF)

- Dedicated domain controller (DEDICADC.INF)

- Secure domain controller (SECUREDC.INF)

- Highly secure domain controller (HISECDC.INF)

By default, these templates are stored in the *systemroot*\security\templates folder.

 Warning: Make sure you have set an appropriate security level before applying predefined security templates to maintain each template's functionality.

Vocabulary

Review the following terms in preparation for the certification exam.

Term	Description
account lockout policy	A Windows 2000 security feature that locks a user's account when a number of failed logon attempts have occurred in a specific period of time, based on policy settings. Locked accounts cannot log on.
audit policy	Determines which security events are reported to the administrator.
Event Log	Event Logs record audit entries when specific events happen. Events include services starting and stopping and users logging on, off, and accessing resources. The Event Viewer is used to review the events.
Kerberos	Kerberos is an authentication mechanism that verifies user or host identity. The policy determines the Kerberos-related settings.
password policy	Passwords restrict logon names to user accounts and computer systems and resources. The policy determines the settings for the passwords on a specific system.
predefined security templates	A physical representation of a security configuration, it is a file where a group of settings store, making it easier to administer.
Restricted Groups	A Windows 2000 security feature that acts as a governor for group membership. Restricted Groups automatically provide security membership for default groups that have pre-defined capabilities. This includes administrators, Power Users, and so forth. Any groups that are sensitive or privileged can be added to the Restricted Groups.
SECEDIT.EXE	A command-line form of the Security Configuration and Analysis snap-in that enables security configuration and analysis without a Graphical User Interface (GUI).

Term	Description
security options	Enables or disables security settings for the computer, such as digital signing of data, Administrator and Guest account names, floppy drive and CD-ROM access, driver installation, and logon prompts.
security settings	Defines the security-relevant behavior of the system. Through use of GPOs in the Active Directory, administrators can centrally apply the security levels required to protect enterprise systems.
Security Templates	A physical depiction of a security configuration, this is a file that contains a group of security settings. Windows 2000 includes a set of security templates, each based on the role of a computer, from low-security domain clients to highly-secure domain controllers. These templates can be used as provided, modified, or serve as a basis for creating custom security templates.
snap-in	Snap-ins are control modules that conform to and *snap-in* to the Microsoft Management Console (MMC) user interface.

In Brief

If you want to...	Then do this...
Administer Security Templates	Use the Security Template snap-in. This tool does not add any new security features, but collects all of the existing security attributes in one place. This facilitates the administration of security. You can also use security template as a basis for configuring security through the Security Configuration and Analysis snap-in.
View attributes concerning Application maximum log size, access rights for each log, and retention settings and methods.	The security area of the Event Log defines the features of the Application, Security, and System event logs. This includes the maximum log size, access rights for each log, and the retention settings and methods. You should match the event log size and log wrapping to match the business and security requirements. You should implement the Event log settings at the site, domain, or OU level to take advantage of your group policy settings.
Provide security memberships for groups with predefined capabilities, such as Administrators, Power Users, Print Operators, Server Operators, and Domain Admins.	Use Restricted Groups.
Configure security centrally in Active Directory.	Use the Security Configuration and Analysis snap-in.
Set up a security policy for a large number of computers.	Use **SECEDIT.EXE**. The SECEDIT tool configures and analyzes security and then allows you to view the analysis results in a text editor. In addition, you can view analysis results with the Security Configuration and Analysis Tool

If you want to...	Then do this...
Examine security analysis results.	Use Security Configuration and Analysis. This tool enables a quick review of security analysis results where recommendations are presented alongside current system settings, and icons or remarks are used to highlight areas where the current settings do not match the proposed level of security. Security Configuration and Analysis also offers the ability to resolve any discrepancies revealed by the analysis.
Import and export security templates into or from a working database.	Use Security Configuration and Analysis. You can merge several different templates into one composite template to use for analysis or configuration of a system by importing each template into a working database. Unless overwritten, they merge into a composite template (stored configuration).
Set default security settings that are compatible with Windows NT 4.0 users.	Use the Compatible Security Template. This default configuration enables development of applications to a standard definition of a secure Windows environment while still allowing existing applications to run successfully under the less secure, Power User configuration.
Apply a security template to a local computer.	Use the Security Configuration and Analysis snap-in by choosing Open Database and selecting Import Template. Right-click Security Configuration and Analysis, and choose Configure System Now.

Lesson 3 Activities

Complete the following activities to better prepare you for the certification exam.

1. List the tools used to configure Security Templates.

2. Describe the Local Policies security attributes.

3. Explain what happens when a user logs on to the network.

4. List the preset Security Templates.

5. Describe how to edit a template.

6. Explain how to configure and set security for multiple computers.

7. Explain how to validate the syntax of imported security templates.

8. List the five security categories.

9. Discuss the attributes of the Dedicated Domain Controller security level.

10. Describe in what circumstances security settings should be applied.

Answers to Lesson 3 Activities

1. The tools used to configure Security Templates are the Access Control List, the Group Policy MMC snap-in, the Security Template snap-in, the Security Configuration and Analysis snap-in, and Setup Security.

2. The Local Policies security attributes are as follows:

   The **Audit policy** determines which security events go into the Security log on the computer (successful attempts, failed attempts or both).

   The **User rights assignment** determines which users or groups have logon or task privileges on the computer.

   The **Security options** enable or disable security settings for the computer, such as digital signing of data, Administrator and Guest account names, floppy drive and CD-ROM access, driver installation, and logon prompts.

3. When a user logs on to the network, Windows 2000 security authenticates the user with information from the Active Directory. When the user attempts to access a service on the network, the system checks the properties defined in the discretionary Access Control List (DACL) for that service.

4. The preset Security Templates are:

   Default workstation

   Default server

   Default domain controller

   Compatible workstation or server

   Secure workstation or server

   Highly Secure workstation or server

   Dedicated domain controller

   Secure domain controller

   Highly Secure domain controller

5. Security Templates can be edited directly. Users can alter a predefined template and apply it to all the appropriate machines on the network to alter their default settings. In addition, the copy-and-paste editing facilities are provided by the Security Templates MMC snap-in and at the same time amend all the policies in one template container.

6. The SECEDIT.EXE command line tool, when called from a batch file or automatic task scheduler, creates and applies templates to analyze system security. SECEDIT.EXE also runs dynamically from a command line.

    This tool is useful for multiple computers on which security must be analyzed or configured, and when there is the need to perform these tasks off-hours.

7. Use **secedit /validate filename**. This command validates the syntax of a security template the user wants to import into a database for analysis or for application to a system.

8. The five security categories are: Basic, Compatible, Secure, Highly Secure, and Dedicated Domain Controller.

9. By default, local user security on domain controllers running Windows 2000 is not perfectly secure. The default file system and Registry permissions for the local users group are defined in the same way as those defined by default for Windows 2000 workstations and stand-alone servers. Through implementing a dedicated security template, these model security settings for local users on Windows 2000 domain controllers are applied. An administrator can also run existing server-based applications on domain controllers. However, this is not recommended. It is recommended that you do not run server based-applications on domain controllers.

10. You should not apply predefined security templates to your production system without first testing them to be sure application functionality is maintained for your network and system. When you apply security settings, they take effect immediately.

Lesson 3 Quiz

These questions test your knowledge of features, vocabulary, procedures, and syntax.

1. Which policies can be applied to user accounts?
    A. Password policy

    B. Audit policy?determinespolicy

    C. Account lockout policy?forpolicy

    D. Kerberos policy?forpolicy

2. What are the security options for files and folders?
    A. Inherit

    B. Overwrite

    C. Ignore

    D. Validate

3. Which of the following are predefined security templates for servers?
    A. Default server

    B. Compatible workstation or server

    C. Dedicated workstation or server

    D. Highly Secure domain controller

4. What are the advantages of Restricted Groups?
    A. Security memberships for groups that have predefined capabilities.

    B. Non-specified members, added over time.

    C. Reverse membership

    D. Sensitive groups

5. What are some areas affected by security templates?
    A. The file system

    B. System services

    C. The hard drive

    D. The Registry

6. Name some tools used to configure Security Templates.
    A. Security Templates snap-in.

    B. Security Configuration and Analysis snap-in

    C. Group Policy snap-in

    D. Logon dialog

7. What are some of the areas where Security Analysis is valuable?
    A. Regular analysis

    B. Security Configuration and Analysis

    C. Batch analysis

    D. System Analysis

8. Which security levels are not backward compatible?
    A. Compatible

    B. Secure

    C. Highly Secure

    D. Dedicated Domain Controller

9. Under what circumstances are Dedicated Domain Controllers backward compatible?
    A. Default set up

    B. Ideal set up

    C. Using a dedicated security template

    D. As a standalone Windows 2000 server.

10. What are some reasons for exporting Security Configuration Settings?
    A. Merge into a composite template to be used for analysis or configuration

    B. To save stored configurations

    C. Create new template files

    D. Used as is to analyze or configure a system

Answers to Lesson 3 Quiz

1. Answers A, C, and D are correct. Password policy is for domain or local user accounts. It determines the settings for passwords, such as enforcement, and lifetimes. The account lockout policy applies to domain or local user account. It determines when and for whom an account is locked out of the system. Kerberos policy is for domain user accounts; it decides the Kerberos-related settings, such as ticket lifetimes and enforcement.

    Answer B is incorrect. Audit policies are assigned to computers, not users.

2. Answers A, B, and C are correct. Inherit, Overwrite, and Ignore are valid settings.

    Answer D is incorrect. Validation is not a security option for files and folders.

3. Answers A, B, and D are correct. Default server, Compatible workstation or server, and Highly Secure domain controller are all default templates.

    Answer C is incorrect. Dedicated workstation or server is not a default template.

4. Answers A, C, and D are correct. The **Security membership** is for groups having predefined capabilities, such as Administrators, Power Users, Print Operators, Server Operators, and Domain Admins. **Reverse membership** makes sure each Restricted Group is a member of only those groups specified in the **Member Of** column. **Sensitive groups** You can add any groups considered sensitive or privileged to the Restricted Groups security list.

    Answer B is incorrect. Those members not on the Restricted Groups membership lists are removed when Group Policy settings are applied.

5. Answers A, B, and D are correct. The file system, system services, and the registry are all affected by security templates.

    Answer C is incorrect. The hard drive, per se, is unaffected by the Security Templates.

6. Answers A, B, and C are correct. The Security Templates snap-in, Security Configuration and Analysis snap-in, and Group Policy snap-in are all used to configure security templates.

    Answer D is incorrect. Logon dialog is not used to configure Security Templates.

7. Answers A, B, and C are correct. With regular analysis as part of an enterprise risk management program, you can track and ensure an adequate level of security on each computer. With Security Configuration and Analysis, you can get a quick review of security analysis results.

Recommendations are presented alongside the current system settings. In a domain-based infrastructure, you can use batch analysis particularly if frequent analysis of a large number of computers is required. The **SECEDIT.EXE** command line tool can be used for batch analysis. However, analysis results still must be viewed using Security Configuration and Analysis.

Answer D is incorrect. System Analysis does not play a specific part in Security Analysis.

8.   Answer C is correct. Computers configured with a highly secure template can only communicate with other Windows 2000 computers. They will not be able to communicate with computers running Windows 95 or 98 or Windows NT.

Answers A, B, and D are incorrect. Compatible, Secure and Dedicated Domain Controllers can all be made backwards compatible with Windows 95, 98, or Windows NT computers.

9.   Answer A is correct. The Default set up is backwards compatible.

Answers B, C, and D are incorrect. The Ideal set up, the default file system and Registry permissions for the local users group can be defined in the same ideal fashion as that defined by default for Windows 2000 workstations and standalone servers. By implementing a dedicated security template, these ideal security settings for local users on Windows 2000 domain controllers are applied.

10. Answers A, B, C, and D are all correct. The Security Configuration and Analysis tool provides you with the ability to import and export security templates into or out of a working database. You can merge several different templates into one composite template that can be used for analysis or configuration of a system. Unless overwritten, the templates will be merged into a composite template (stored configuration).

Once you have created a composite configuration, you can save it for future analysis or configuration of other systems. Export gives you the ability to save the stored configuration, as a new template file you can import into other databases, use to analyze or configure a system, or even redefined with the Security Templates snap-in.

Lesson 4

Internet Protocol Security (IPSec)

Internet Protocol Security (IPSec) is an easy-to-use feature of Windows 2000 that provides robust protection against attacks both internally from within a private network and externally through the Internet. Highlights of IPSec are as follows:

- Provides a comprehensive suite of protection services and security protocols based on variable-level encryption

- Supports end-to-end security. Only the sender and receiver ever know that IPSec is protecting their communication

- Provides secure communication between workgroups, Local Area Network (LAN) computers, domain clients and servers, remote-branch offices, extranets, and roving clients, and follows current trends for secure networking

The Windows 2000 implementation of IPSec is compatible with industry standards developed by the Internet Engineering Task Force (IETF) IPSec working group. It supports vintage standards such as Trivial File Transfer Protocol (TFTP) as well as newer ones like the Internet Group Management Protocol.

This lesson reviews the function and structure of IPSec protocols. It introduces the concept of security associations (SA) and ends with an explanation on how to effectively implement IPSec.

After completing this lesson, you should have a better understanding of the following topics:

- IPSec Functionality

- IPSec Security Protocols

- Security Associations (SA)

- IPSec Business Application

- Server Message Block (SMB) Security Solutions

IPSec Functionality

IPSec follows current trends towards ever more secure communication. It is a comprehensive suite of protection services and security protocols based on various levels of encryption. IPSec is easily deployed in existing networks because it requires no changes to applications or protocols. Central to IPSec's capabilities is that it provides computer-level authentication and data encryption for Virtual Private Network (VPN) connections that use the Layer 2 Tunneling Protocol (L2TP).

L2TP

Layer 2 Tunneling Protocol (L2TP) is an industry-standard Internet tunneling protocol. Unlike Point-to-Point Tunneling Protocol (PPTP) that requires IP connectivity between two hosts, L2TP only requires packet-oriented, point-to-point connectivity. L2TP provides the same functionality as PPTP, but is far more versatile in that you can use the protocol over diverse media such as ATM, Frame Relay, and X.25, running diverse protocols.

Based on Layer 2 Forwarding (L2F) and PPTP specifications, L2TP allows clients to set up secure communication channels across intervening networks. IPSec first determines authentication between the two hosts before an L2TP connection is established, securing both passwords and data. Standard point-to-point authentication protocols can be used, such as Extensible Authentication Protocol (EAP), Microsoft Challenge Handshake Authentication Protocol (MS-CHAP), Challenge Handshake Authentication Protocol (CHAP), SPAP (Shiva PAP), and Password Authentication Protocol (PAP) with IPSec.

The IPSec Security Association (SA) then defines the type of encryption. A security association is a combination of a destination address, a security protocol, and a unique identification value called a Security Parameters Index (SPI).

The following are the different levels of encryption available to support various security requirements:

- Data Encryption Standard (DES), which has a 40-bit key designed for international use that adheres to United States export laws

- DES with a 56-bit key which is designed for North American use

- Triple DES (3DES) which uses two 56-bit keys for North American environments requiring extra security measures

Supporting Industry Standards

The TCP/IP standards and other information are publicized through a series of documents called Requests for Comments (RFCs). These RFCs are a series of reports, proposals for protocols, and protocol standards that describe how the Internet, and in particular TCP/IP, function.

TCP/IP standards are always published as RFCs. However, not all RFCs specify standards. Individuals can write and submit a proposal for a new protocol or specification to the Internet Engineering Task Force (IETF) and other working groups. These drafts are reviewed by a technical expert, a task force, or an RFC editor before receiving an assigned status.

If a draft passes the review stage, it is assigned an RFC number circulated to the larger community for further review. If changes are made to the proposed specification, the revised draft is given a new RFC number higher than the original and is again circulated.

Table 4.1 shows the five six RFC status assignments in the standards process.

Table 4.1 Protocol Status

Status	Description
Standard protocol	An official standard Internet protocol.
Draft standard protocol	A protocol under active consideration and review to become a standard protocol.
Proposed standard protocol	A protocol that may in the future become a standard protocol.
Experimental protocol	A protocol designed for experimental purposes and not intended for operational use.
Informational protocol	A protocol developed by another standards organizations included for the convenience of the Internet community.
Historic protocol	A protocol that has been superseded or made obsolete by other protocols.

Table 4.2 lists the RFCs supported by the TCP/IP protocol in Windows 2000.

Table 4.2 RFC Protocols

RFC Number	Title
768	User Datagram Protocol (UDP)
783	Trivial File Transfer Protocol (TFTP)
791	Internet Protocol (IP)
792	Internet Control Message Protocol (ICMP)
793	Transmission Control Protocol (TCP)
816	Fault Isolation and Recovery
826	Address Resolution Protocol (ARP)
854	Telnet Protocol (TELNET)

RFC Number	Title
862	Echo Protocol (ECHO)
863	Discard Protocol (DISCARD)
864	Character Generator Protocol (CHARGEN)
865	Quote of the Day Protocol (QUOTE)
867	Daytime Protocol (DAYTIME)
894	IP over Ethernet
919	Broadcasting Internet Datagrams
922	Broadcasting Internet Datagrams in the Presence of Subnets
950	Internet Standard Subnetting Procedure
959	File Transfer Protocol (FTP)
1001	Protocol Standard for a NetBIOS Service on a TCP/UDP Transport: Concepts and Methods
1002	Protocol Standard for a NetBIOS Service on a TCP/UDP Transport: Detailed Specifications
1009	Requirements for Internet Gateways
1034	Domain Names–Concepts and Facilities
1035	Domain Names–Implementation and Specification
1042	IP over Token Ring
1112	Internet Group Management Protocol (IGMP)
1122	Requirements for Internet Hosts–Communication Layers
1123	Requirements for Internet Hosts–Application and Support
1157	Simple Network Management Protocol (SNMP)
1179	Line Printer Daemon Protocol
1188	IP Over FDDI
1191	Path MTU Discovery
1201	IP Over ARCNET
1256	ICMP Router Discovery Messages
1323	TCP Extensions for High Performance
1518	An Architecture for IP Address Allocation with CIDR
1519	Classless Inter-Domain Routing (CIDR): An Address Assignment and Aggregation Strategy
1812	Requirements for IP Version 4 Routers
1878	Variable Length Subnet Table for IPv4

RFC Number	Title
2018	TCP Selective Acknowledgment Options
2131	Dynamic Host Configuration Protocol (DHCP)
2136	Dynamic Updates in the Domain Name System (DNS UPDATE)
2236	Internet Group Management Protocol, Version 2

Obtaining RFCs

Members of the Information Sciences Institute (ISI) maintain a Web site that publishes a listing of all RFCs. RFCs are classified as approved Internet standard, proposed Internet standard (circulated in draft form for review), Internet best practices, or as a For Your Information (FYI) document.

 Note: You can obtain RFCs from the following Web site: http://www.rfc-editor.org/.

Hash Message Authentication Code (HMAC)

One developing IP standard is the Hash Message Authentication Code (HMAC). HMAC uses cryptographic hash functions to support message authentication. You can use HMAC with any iterative cryptographic hash function such as MD5 or SHA-1 in combination with a secret shared key. The cryptographic strength of HMAC depends on the properties of the underlying hash function.

Diffie-Hellman (DH) Technique

The Diffie-Hellman Technique is a method for generating secure keys prior to communication. The process involves two phases—key exchange and policy negotiation. You can set security methods and key properties for Phase I to ensure the appropriate level of security for your network. The same algorithms used for integrity and confidentiality in Phase I can also be used in Phase II. Details on these two phases can be found in the section on Using Internet Security Association and Key Management Protocol (ISAKMP).

Diffie-Hellman Groups

The Diffie-Hellman groups determine the length of the base prime number used during the key exchange, and hence security. Group 2 (medium) is stronger than Group 1 (low) because Group 2 protects 1,024 bits of keying material while Group 1 protects only 768 bits. Communication only occurs between two hosts using matched groups, which must stay consistent during the negotiation. The Diffie-Hellman group is configured as part of the key exchange settings, but it affects any new keys generated during the data protection phase.

Data Encryption Standard-Cipher Block Chaining (DES-CBC)

DES-CBC is a secret key algorithm that provides confidentiality. A random number generates and is used with the secret key to encrypt the data.

IPSec Security Protocols

Internet Protocol Security (IPSec) is an industry standard for encrypting TCP/IP traffic. It secures communications by creating secure Virtual Private Network (VPN) solutions across the Internet.

The communication requirements of a specific security method are defined by that security method. Communication can only occur between two computers using the same security method. By binding multiple security methods to computers, you can increase your chances that a common method of data exchange can be found between two computers. This is counterbalanced by the security risk involved in enabling multiple access points. The ISAKMP/Oakley service reads the list of security methods in descending order, and negotiates until a common method is found.

Predefined Security Methods

Predefined security methods are classified into the following two levels:

High level—Uses the Encapsulating Security Payload (ESP) to provide confidentiality (data encryption), authentication, anti-replay, and integrity. ESP does not provide integrity for the IP header (addressing). If data and addressing protection is required, the user can create a custom security method. If encryption is not required, use Medium level security.

Medium level—Uses the Authentication Header (AH) protocol to provide integrity, anti-replay, and authentication. AH provides integrity for both the IP header and data, but does not encrypt the data.

Custom Security Methods

Expert users can specify custom security methods where encryption, addressing integrity, stronger algorithms, or key lifetimes are required.

Security Protocols

If IP header integrity and data encryption are required, you can enable both AH and ESP using a custom security method. To enable both, do not specify a second integrity algorithm for ESP, the algorithm selected for AH will provide integrity.

Integrity

Integrity is provided by Message Digest 5 (MD5), which produces a 128-bit key. Secure Hash Algorithm (SHA) produces a 160-bit key. Longer key lengths provide greater security, making SHA stronger.

Confidentiality

3DES, the most secure of the DES combinations, has a somewhat slower performance because 3DES processes each block three times using a unique key each time. It is advisable to use ordinary DES when export requirements are an issue or when the high security and overhead of 3DES are not necessary. Ordinary DES uses 56 bits of keying material.

Key Lifetimes

The generation of a new key is determined by key lifetimes. A lifetime can be specified in Kbytes, seconds, or both. For example, if a communication takes 100,000 seconds and the key lifetime is 1,000 seconds, ten keys need to be generated to complete the transfer. This ensures that only segments of a communication can be intercepted, rather than the whole data exchange. You can configure automatic key regeneration.

Note: Any time a key lifetime is reached, the SA is also renegotiated in addition to the key refresh or regeneration.

Export Requirements

If export requirements are an issue, such as when data will be accessed by both computers running domestic and export versions of Windows 2000, or when data is exchanged outside of the United States, the list of security methods must include DES in order to ensure compliance with export regulations that limit key lengths. Otherwise, the computer with which you are trying to communicate may not be able to reach a common security agreement with your computer.

Using IP Encapsulating Security

Encapsulation is a process in which a packet is enveloped by the exterior structure of a new packet. This new packet provides the routing information needed for the packet to travel through intermediate networks without revealing the final destination hidden in the original packet header. The transit internetwork can be any internetwork, a private intranet, or the Internet. The exterior head removes once the encapsulated packets reach their destination so that the original packet header is used to route the packet to its endpoint. The entire process of encapsulation, routing, and de-encapsulation is called tunneling.

To each host, the tunnel appears to be a direct point-to-point connection. The hosts are not aware of intervening connections with routers, switches, proxy servers, or other security gateways. If the tunnel encrypts through the use of L2TP and EPSecs, it is called a Virtual Private Network (VPN). The encapsulated packets travel through the internetwork inside the tunnel. Different protocols and modes are available for tunneling.

L2TP and IPSec

IPSec and L2TP work together to ensure both tunneling and security for IP packets. While you can perform tunneling without L2TP using IPSec alone, this is only recommended when one of the computers does not support L2TP. The original packet header carries the ultimate source and destination addresses while the outer IP header usually contains only the address of the gateway. The PPP header identifies the protocol of the original packet, and the L2TP header routes the internal payload to the proper tunnel.

IPSec Tunneling

IPSec tunnels at the Network Layer level. IP packets encapsulate and secure for transport by an IPSec security protocol. Again, you would only use this transport method to allow for communication between computers that do not both support L2TP.

ESP Tunnel Mode

The original header of a packet is placed after the ESP header. An ESP trailer is then added prior to encryption. Because it is considered to be data, all information following the ESP header including the original header is encrypted, except for the ESP authentication trailer. The entire packet is then encapsulated, and the new IP header is used to route the packet.

AH Tunnel Mode

Packets are handled differently in the ESP and AH modes. In the AH tunnel mode the entire packet is signed to safeguard integrity, including the new tunnel header, but encryption is not provided. To guarantee integrity for the entire packet and confidentiality for data in the original packet, combine ESP and AH modes.

Using IP Authentication Header

ISAKMP provides support to security protocols during the two-phase negotiation for SAs.

Authentication Header (AH)

AH provides authentication, integrity, and anti-replay for the entire packet (both the IP header and the data carried in the packet). AH signs the entire packet, but does not encrypt the data, so it does not provide confidentiality. The data is readable, but protected from modification. AH uses HMAC algorithms to sign the packet. Integrity and authentication are provided by the placement of the AH header between the IP header and the transport protocol header (TCP or UDP).

Encapsulating Security Payload (ESP)

ESP provides confidentiality in addition to authentication, integrity, and anti-replay. ESP does not normally sign the entire packet unless it is being tunneled. Ordinarily, only the data is protected, not the IP header.

For example, User 1 on Computer A sends data to User 2 on Computer B. The data encrypts because ESP provides confidentiality. Upon receipt, after the verification process is complete, the data portion of the packet decrypts. User 1 can be certain User 2 really sent the data, the data is unmodified, and no one else was able to read it (Figure 4.1).

Figure 4.1 Encapsulated Payload

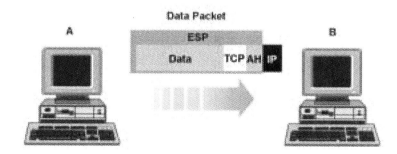

Security is provided by the placement of the ESP header between the IP header and the transport protocol header (Transmission Control Protocol (TCP) or User Datagram Protocol (UDP)). Expert users have the option to select which protocol to use for a communication by configuring security methods in the IPSec policy. The Windows 2000 implementation of IPSec uses the following security protocols:

- Internet Security Association and Key Management Protocol

- Oakley Key Determination

- IP Authentication Header

- IP Encapsulating Security Protocol

Using Oakley

Before secured data can be exchanged, a contract between the two computers must be established. This contract is called a security association (SA). In an SA, both computers agree on how to exchange and protect information. Oakley is a key determination protocol that uses the DH key exchange algorithm. Oakley supports Perfect Forward Secrecy (PFS), which ensures that if a single key is compromised, access is permitted only to data protected by that single key. A key (or that key's original keygeneration material) is never used to compute additional keys.

Security Associations

A security association (SA) is a combination of a policy and keys which defines the common security services, mechanisms, and keys used to protect the communication from end to end. The security parameters index (SPI) is a unique, identifying value in the SA used to distinguish among multiple security associations that exist at the receiving computer. For example, multiple associations may exist if a computer securely communicates with multiple computers simultaneously. This situation occurs mostly when the computer is a file server or a remote access server which serves multiple clients. However, one computer can have multiple SAs with a single computer. In these situations, the receiving computer uses the SPI to determine which SA will be used to process the incoming packets.

To build this contract between the two computers, the IETF has established a standard method of security association and key exchange resolution, which combines the Internet Security Association and Key Management Protocol (ISAKMP) and the Oakley key generation protocol. ISAKMP centralizes security association management, reducing connection time. Oakley generates and manages the authenticated keys used to secure the information.

This process protects not only computer-to-computer communications, but also protects remote computers requesting secure access to a corporate network or any situation in which the negotiation for the final destination computer (or endpoint) is actually performed by a security router or other proxy server. In the latter situation, referred to as *ISAKMP client mode*, the identities of the endpoints are hidden to further protect the communication.

To ensure successful, secure communication, ISAKMP/Oakley performs a two-phase operation. It assures confidentiality and authentication during each phase by the use of negotiated encryption and authentication algorithms that are agreed on by the two computers. With the duties split between two phases, keying can be accomplished with great speed when required.

Key Exchange

During the initial phase, the two computers establish the first SA, called the ISAKMP SA. (This SA is named in order to differentiate between the SAs established in each of the two phases.) Oakley provides identity protection during this exchange, enabling total privacy. This can help prevent common types of network attacks which focus on hijacking identities.

The security negotiation process during this phase includes:

Policy Negotiation

This determines:

The encryption algorithm: DES, 3DES, 40bitDES, or none.

The integrity algorithm: MD5 or SHA.

The authentication method: Public Key Certificate, preshared key, or Kerberos V5 (the Windows 2000 default).

The Diffie-Hellman group.

If certificates or preshared keys are being used for authentication, the computer identity is protected. However, if the default Windows 2000 method is used, the computer identity is unencrypted until the entire identity payload is encrypted during Step 3.

Key Information Exchange

This results in each computer having the necessary information to generate the shared, secret key—the master key—for the ISAKMP SA. Actual keys are never exchanged; only the public information needed by Diffie-Hellman to generate the shared, secret key. The Oakley service on each computer generates the master key used to protect authentication.

Authentication

The computers attempt to authenticate the key information exchange. Without successful authentication, communication cannot proceed. The master key is used, in conjunction with the algorithms negotiated in Step 1. Regardless of which authentication method is used, the identity payload is protected from both modification and interpretation.

The initiating peer sends an offer list of potential security levels to the responding peers. The responder cannot modify the offer. Should the offer be modified, the initiator will reject the responder's message. The responder sends a reply either accepting the offer, or it simply discards the offers and sends a message back indicating no offer was chosen. The process then begins again.

The negotiation messages that are exchanged are automatically resent five times.

After three seconds, a soft SA will be established, if the active policies allow unsecured communications with non-IPSec capable computers. If an ISAKMP response is received before the cycle times out, the soft SA will be deleted and standard SA negotiation begins. The potential number of SAs that are formed is only limited by system resources.

The ISAKMP SA is used to initiate the second phase of security negotiations.

Data Protection

A pair of SAs are negotiated on behalf of the IPSec service, and are referred to as IPSec SAs. Keying material is refreshed or new keys are generated if PFS or key lifetimes have been enabled, the ISAKMP SA has is marked as expired.

The security negotiation process during this second phase includes:

1.   Policy negotiation

• This determines:

• The IPSec protocol: AH, ESP.

• The integrity algorithm: MD5, SHA.

• The encryption algorithm: DES, 3DES, 40bitDES, or none.

   A common agreement is reached, and two SAs are established: one for inbound communications and one for outbound communications.

   Oakley refreshes the keying material and new, shared, secret keys are generated for authenticating and, possibly, encrypting the packets. If a new key is required, a second Diffie-Hellman exchange takes place. Unless a key or SA has expired, Oakley refreshes the keying material from the Diffie-Hellman exchange that was performed during the key exchange.

2.   The SAs and keys are passed to the IPSec driver, along with the SPI.

The entire negotiation is protected by the ISAKMP SA. Except for the ISAKMP header on the packets, all of the message packets are encrypted, and an integrity signature following the ISAKMP header authenticates the message. Oakley prevents replays of negotiation messages, providing anti-replay protection.

3.   The automatic message retry process is almost identical to the process discussed in the key exchange negotiation, with one exception: if this process reaches a time-out for any reason during the second or greater negotiation of the same ISAKMP SA, a re-negotiation of the ISAKMP SA is attempted. If a message for the data protection phase is received without establishing an ISAKMP SA, it is rejected.

The ability to use a single ISAKMP SA for multiple IPSec SA negotiations makes the security negotiation process extremely fast. As long as the ISAKMP SA does not expire, renegotiation and re-authentication are not necessary. The active IPSec policy determines the number of times this can occur.

SA Lifetimes

When a key lifetime is reached for the master or session key, the associated SA is re-negotiated. An Oakley "delete" message is sent to the responding peer which requests the responder to mark the ISAKMP SA as "expired." This prevents bogus IPSec SAs from being formed from an old SA. Oakley expires ISAKMP SAs, and the IPSec driver expires IPSec SAs.

When the IPSec Policy Agent retrieves policy updates, it will update the IP filter list stored in the IPSec driver. Any SAs associated with old filters which no longer exist in the policy will be deleted, along with the old filters in the IPSec driver cache.

If the power save features in Windows 2000 cause the computer to hibernate or sleep and the SA expires during this period, the SA will be automatically re-negotiated when the peer is re-activated. If Windows 2000 is shut down on one of the peers, the Oakley "delete" message cleans up any remaining SAs, and new SAs are re-negotiated when the peers attempt communication again. If Windows 2000 terminates abnormally, the Oakley "delete" message will not be sent. In this case, the old SAs might still be in place until the default time-out period is reached. If this occurs, the SAs must be manually deleted.

Using Internet Security Association and Key Management Protocol (ISAKMP)

ISAKMP supports in the negotiation of SAs for security protocols. The process of security negotiation has two phases that include policy negotiation and key exchange that are discussed in this section.

Key Exchange

During the initial negotiation phase between the two computers, the first SA or ISAKMP SA is created. To prevent network attacks involving the hijacking of identities, Oakley provides identity protection during this phase, thereby enabling total privacy.

The steps in the initial phase of the security negotiation for SAs are as follows:

1. Policy Negotiation determines the following:

1.   The encryption algorithm: DES, 3DES, 40bitDES, or none

2.   The integrity algorithm: MD5 or SHA

3.   The authentication method: Public Key Certificate, preshared key, or Kerberos Version 5 (the Windows 2000 default)

4.   The Diffie-Hellman group

The computer identity is protected if certificates or preshared keys are used for authentication. But if the default Windows 2000 Kerberos Version 5 method is used, the computer identity becomes transparent until the entire payload re-encrypts in Step 3.

2. Key Information Exchange occurs when each computer capable of creating the master key for the ISAKMP SA swaps information. Only the public information Diffie-Hellman needs to generate the shared, secret key is exchanged, not the key itself. The master key that protects authentication is eventually generated by the Oakley service itself (Figure 4.2).

Figure 4.2 Security Negotiation—Phase 1

3. Authentication occurs when computers try to authenticate the key information exchange. Communication stops without successful authentication, which involves using the master key along with the algorithms negotiated in Step 1. The identity payload is always protected from both modification and interpretation regardless of the authentication method used.

During authentication, the initiating computer offers a list of potential security levels to the responding computer. The responder cannot modify the offer. If the offer is modified, the initiator will reject the responder's message. The responding computer then either accepts the offer or discards it with a reply that no offer was chosen. If the first offer is discarded, up to four more offers can be made until one is accepted.

After three seconds of negotiation, a transient SA determines if system policies allow unsecured communications between computers that are incapable of supporting IPSec. The transient SA will be deleted and replaced by the standard SA negotiation process if an ISAKMP response is received before the cycle times out. Only system resources limit the potential number of SAs that may be created.

Policy negotiation, the second phase of security negotiations, is initiated by the ISAKMP SA. Two SAs, called IPSec SAs, negotiate on behalf of the IPSec service to protect data.

Policy negotiation determines the protocols and algorithms below:

- The IPSec protocol: AH, ESP

- The integrity algorithm: MD5, SHA

- The encryption algorithm: DES, 3DES, 40bitDES, or none

When a common agreement is reached, an SA for inbound communication and one for outbound communication is established.

Oakley then refreshes the keying material from the Diffie-Hellman exchange that was performed during the initial key exchange. New, shared, secret keys can be generated for authenticating and encrypting packets. If a new key is required, a second Diffie-Hellman exchange takes place (Figure 4.3).

Figure 4.3 Security Negotiation—Phase 2

The SAs and keys pass to the IPSec driver along with the Security Parameters Index (SPI).

The ISAKMP SA protects the entire negotiation. All parts of the packets encrypt except for the ISAKMP header, and an integrity signature following the ISAKMP header authenticates the message. As an additional measure of protection, Oakley prevents replays of negotiation messages.

The automatic message retry process is almost identical to the process discussed in the key exchange negotiation with one exception. If this process reaches a time-out for any reason during the second or greater negotiation of the same ISAKMP SA, a renegotiation of the ISAKMP SA attempts. If a message for the data protection phase is received without establishing an ISAKMP SA, it is rejected.

The ability to use a single ISAKMP SA for multiple IPSec SA negotiations makes the security negotiation process extremely fast. As long as the ISAKMP SA does not expire, renegotiation and re-authentication are not necessary. The active IPSec policy determines the number of times this can occur.

Security Associations (SA)

Two computers must establish a common understanding or contract before they can exchange secured data. This agreement on how to exchange and protect information is called a Security Association (SA). An SA ensures protected end-to-end communication through a combination of a policy and keys that defines the common security services, mechanisms, and keys. Multiple security associations can exist at the receiving computer, but the unique SPI value identifies a message originator.

One case in which multiple associations can exist is with a file or remote-access server supporting multiple clients simultaneously. A computer can also have multiple SAs with a single computer. When these events occur, the receiving computer uses the SPI to identify the particular SA to use to disassemble incoming packets (Figure 4.4).

Figure 4.4 Multiple Security Associations

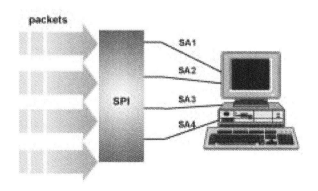

Both the ISAKMP and the Oakley key-generation protocol are used in a two-phase approach to generate the SA. The ISAKMP reduces connection time by centralizing security association management while the Oakley uses the DH key exchange algorithm to create authenticated keys and manage them. Confidentiality is ensured during each phase by the use of negotiated encryption and authentication algorithms. Keying can be done quickly because duties are divided.

The two-pronged process protects both direct computer-to-computer communications and remote computers requesting secure access to a corporate network through a security router or proxy server. The latter situation is referred to as ISAKMP client mode. Here, the identities of the final destination computers (endpoints) are masked to heighten security.

SA Lifetimes

When a key lifetime is reached for the master or session key, the associated SA is renegotiated. An Oakley delete message transmits to the responding peer that requests the responder to mark the ISAKMP SA as expired. This prevents bogus IPSec SAs from forming from an old SA. Oakley expires ISAKMP SAs, and the IPSec driver expires IPSec SAs.

When the IPSec Policy Agent retrieves policy updates, it updates the IP filter list stored in the IPSec driver. Any SAs associated with old filters that no longer exist in the policy are deleted, along with the old filters in the IPSec driver cache.

If the power-save features in Windows 2000 cause the computer to hibernate or sleep and the SA expires during this period, the SA automatically renegotiates when the peer re-activates. If Windows 2000 is shut down on one of the peers, the Oakley "delete" message cleans up any remaining SAs, and new SAs renegotiate when the peers attempt communication again. If Windows 2000 terminates abnormally, the Oakley "delete" message does not transmit. In this case, the old SAs might still be in place until the default time-out period is reached. If this occurs, you must manually delete SAs.

Security Services

The function of a given server within an organization, whether a domain controller, file server, database server, or Web server, determines to a large extent its security needs. Other considerations in designing a secure environment include the likelihood of your organization coming under attack and the significance of your data. You should incorporate a public key infrastructure into your overall security plan if your network consists of intranets, extranets, or Internet sites. In this situation, you may want to have one or more dedicated certification authorities for your organization.

Protection Keys

A Public Key Infrastructure (PKI) uses public key cryptography to enable a system of registration authorities to authenticate each party involved in an electronic transaction. As this area is fairly new, standards have not yet been widely accepted.

The following are some reasons why an organization would deploy a PKI using Windows 2000:

Strong security—The confidentiality of transmitted data on public networks is maintained through IP security, while the confidentiality of stored data is ensured through the use of the Encrypting File System (EFS). Administrators determine what certificates can be issued to particular users through security permissions.

Simplified administration—Many provisions exist to ensure easy administration of security measures across an enterprise in Windows 2000. These include scalability in managing trust relationships, and the capability of mapping certificates to user accounts in Active Directory or though Internet Information Services. Certificate Services integrate with Active Directory and Group Policy, and these revocable certificates are issued instead of passwords

New opportunities—Secure Sockets Layer (SSL) or TLS secures Web connections and Multipurpose Internet Mail Extensions (MIME) establishes secure e-mail connections.

The following features help the administrator to implement a public key infrastructure:

Certificates—A digital statement issued by an authority vouching for the identity of the certificate holder. It binds a public key to the person, computer, or service holding the corresponding private key. Certificates are used by a variety of public key security services and applications.

The standard certificate—Windows 2000 uses an X.509 Version 3 certificate that includes information about the holder of the certificate as well as the certificate itself, plus optional information about the certification authority. Extensions to Version 3 certificates can provide information on key identifiers, key usage, certificate policy, alternate names and attributes, certification path constraints, and certification revocation.

Certificate Services (CS)—Certification Authorities (CAs) are managed by the CS through the Certificates MMC console. A CA both vouches for the identity of certificate holders and revokes invalid certificates. It publishes the Certificate Revocation List (CRL) used by certificate verifiers. The simplest PKI design has only one root CA, but in larger organizations CAs are organized into trusted groups called certification hierarchies. CA Web enrollment pages are another component of CS. These Web pages allow certificate requesters to submit requests using a Web browser.

Examples of support for certificates in Windows 2000 include the following:

Smart Card—Certificates on Smart Cards can be used to log on to a network as well as authenticate Web sites and secure e-mail.

Public key policies—Group policies are used to automate a variety of tasks, including distributing certificates, establishing certificate trust lists and trusted CAs, and managing recovery policies for EFS.

SA Expiration

An SA is renegotiated when the associated master or session key expires. The old ISABIP SA is marked to prevent a bogus IPSec SA from being created through an old SA. Oakley is used to mark expired ISAKMP SAs while the IPSec driver is used for IPSec SAs.

The IP filter list is stored in the IPSec driver, and is updated by the IPSec Policy Agent. Any SAs associated with old filters that no longer exist in the policy are deleted, along with old filters in the IPSec driver cache. If a Windows 2000 computer hibernates to save power and the SA expires during this inactive period, the SA automatically regenerates when the computer reactivates. If Windows 2000 is shut down, Oakley deletes any remaining SAs; new SAs must go through the renegotiation process. And if Windows 2000 terminates abnormally, the old SAs might still be in place until the default time-out period is reached. You must then manually delete the SAs.

IPSec Business Application

The Internet Protocol Security (IPSec) protects communication between workgroups, LAN computers, domain clients and servers, branch offices which may be physically remote, extranets, roving clients, and remote administration of computers. The only computers that need to know about the IPSec protection are the sender and receiver. A suite of cryptography-based protection services and security protocols offers aggressive protection against private network and Internet attacks.

Note: The Windows 2000 implementation of IPSec is based on industry standards in development by the Internet Engineering Task Force (IETF) IPSec working group.

Understanding How IPSec Works

The IETF has established a standard method of security association and key exchange resolution, combining the Internet Security Association and Key Management Protocol (ISAKMP) and the Oakley key-generation protocol.

This process protects not only computer-to-computer communications, but also protects remote computers requesting secure access to a corporate network or any situation in which the negotiation for the final destination computer (or endpoint) is actually performed by a security router or other proxy server.

 Note: In the latter situation, referred to as ISAKMP client mode, the identities of the end-points are hidden to further protect the communication.

The Windows 2000 implementation of IPSec uses the following security protocols:

- Internet Security Association and Key Management Protocol

- Oakley Key Determination

- IP Authentication Header

- IP Encapsulating Security Protocol

Internet Security Association and Key Management Protocol (ISAKMP)—ISAKMP/Oakley performs a two-phase operation. It ensures confidentiality and authentication during each phase by the use of negotiated encryption and authentication algorithms that are agreed on by the two computers. With the duties split between two phases, keying is accomplished with great speed.

Oakley Key Determination—Generates and manages the authenticated keys used to secure the information. Before secured data can exchange, a contract between the two computers must be establish. This contract is called a Security Association (SA). In an SA, both computers agree on how to exchange and protect information. Oakley is a key determination protocol that uses the DH key exchange algorithm. Oakley supports Perfect Forward Secrecy (PFS), which ensures that if a single key is compromised, access is permitted only to data protected by that single key. A key (or that key's original key-generation material) is never used to compute additional keys.

Using IP Authentication Header—Provides data and identity protection by signing but not encrypting the data. The data is readable, but protected from modification. Integrity and authentication are provided by the placement of the AH header between the IP header and the transport protocol header (TCP or UDP).

Using IP Encapsulating Security—Hides the original packet inside a new packet. The new packet provides the necessary routing information, enabling the packet to travel without revealing the final destination that is stored in the original packet header. The transit internetwork can be any internetwork, a private intranet, or the Internet.

 Note: If the power save features in Windows 2000 causes the computer to hibernate or sleep and the SA expires during this period, the SA automatically renegotiates when the peer reactivates.

If Windows 2000 is shut down on one of the peers, the Oakley "delete" message cleans up any remaining SAs, and new SAs are renegotiated when the peers attempt communication again.

If Windows 2000 terminates abnormally, the Oakley "delete" message does not transmit. In this case, the old SAs might still be in place until the default time-out period is reached. If this occurs, the SAs must be manually deleted.

Oakley

Before secured data can exchange, a contract between the two computers must be established. This contract is called a Security Association (SA). In an SA, both computers agree on how to exchange and protect information. Oakley is a key determination protocol that uses the DH key exchange algorithm. Oakley supports Perfect Forward Secrecy (PFS), which ensures that if a single key is compromised, access is permitted only to data protected by that single key. A key (or that key's original key-generation material) is never used to compute additional keys.

Security Associations (SAs)

A security association (SA) is a combination of a policy and keys that defines the common security services, mechanisms, and keys used to protect the communication from end to end. The Security Parameters Index (SPI) is a unique, identifying value in the SA that distinguishes among multiple security associations that exist at the receiving computer. For example, multiple associations may exist if a computer securely communicates with multiple computers simultaneously. This situation occurs when the computer is a file server or a remote access server that serves multiple clients. However, one computer can have multiple SAs with a single computer. In these situations, the receiving computer uses SPI to determine which SA to use to process the incoming packets.

To build this contract between the two computers, the IETF has established a standard method of security association and key exchange resolution, which combines the Internet Security Association and Key Management Protocol (ISAKMP) and the Oakley key-generation protocol. ISAKMP centralizes security association management, reducing connection time. Oakley generates and manages the authenticated keys used to secure the information.

This process protects not only computer-to-computer communications, but also protects remote computers requesting secure access to a corporate network or any situation in which the negotiation for the final destination computer (or endpoint) is actually performed by a security router or other proxy server. In the latter situation, referred to as ISAKMP client mode, the identities of the endpoints are hidden to further protect the communication.

To ensure successful, secure communication, ISAKMP/Oakley performs a two-phase operation. It ensures confidentiality and authentication during each phase by the use of negotiated encryption and authentication algorithms that are agreed on by the two computers. With the duties split between two phases, keying is accomplished with great speed.

If the power save features in Windows 2000 cause the computer to hibernate or sleep and the SA expires during this period, the SA automatically renegotiates when the peer reactivates. If Windows 2000 is shut down on one of the peers, the Oakley delete message cleans up any remaining SAs, and new SAs are renegotiated when the peers attempt communication again. If Windows 2000 terminates abnormally, the Oakley delete message does not transmit. In this case, the old SAs might still be in place until the default time-out period is reached. If this occurs, the SAs must be manually deleted.Security protocols provide data and identity protection for each IP packet. Windows 2000 IPSec uses the Authentication Header and Encapsulating Security Payload to provide these services.

Authentication Header (AH)

AH provides authentication, integrity, and anti-replay for the entire packet (both the IP header and the data carried in the packet); AH signs the entire packet. It does not encrypt the data, so it does not provide confidentiality. The data is readable, but protected from modification. AH uses HMAC algorithms to sign the packet.

Integrity and authentication are provided by the placement of the AH header between the IP header and the transport protocol header (TCP or UDP).

Encapsulating Security Payload (ESP)

ESP provides confidentiality, in addition to authentication, integrity, and anti-replay.

ESP does not normally sign the entire packet unless it is being tunneled. Ordinarily, only the data is protected, not the IP header.

For example, Alice on Computer A sends data to Bob on Computer B. The data is encrypted because ESP provides confidentiality. Upon receipt, after the verification process is complete, the data portion of the packet is decrypted. Alice can be certain it was really Bob who sent the data, that the data is unmodified, and that no one else was able to read it.

Security is provided by by the placement of the ESP header between the IP header and the transport protocol header (TCP or UDP).

Expert users can select which protocol will be used for a communication by configuring security methods in the IPSec policy

Configuring IPSec Settings on a Single Computer

To start IP Security Policy Management, follow these steps:

1.   From **Start**, choose **Run**, type **MMC**, and then select **OK** (Figure 4.5).

Figure 4.5 IP MMC

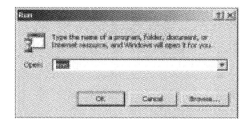

2. From **MMC**, choose **Console**, **Add/Remove Snap-in**, and then select **Add** (Figure 4.6).

Figure 4.6 IP Security Policy Management

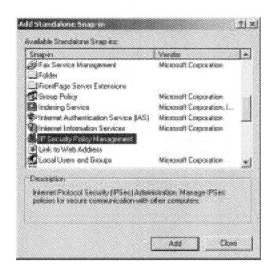

3. Choose **IP Security Policy Management**, and then select **Add**.

4. Choose the computer for which you want to manage IPSec policies (Figure 4.7).

Figure 4.7 IP Security Policy Selection

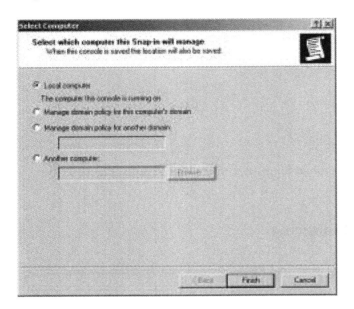

5.   Choose **Finish, Close,** and **OK,** and then select **Console** and then **Save** to save the console settings.

Table 4.3 Management Selections

To Do This...	Do This...
Only manage the computer on which this console is running	Choose Local Computer.
Manage IPSec policies for any domain members	Choose Manage domain policy for this computer's domain.
Manage IPSec policies for a domain of which the computer that is running this console is not a member	Choose Manage domain policy for another domain.
Manage a remote computer	Choose Another computer.

Note: Appropriate Administrator rights to Group Policy or membership in the local system Administrator's group is required in order to define IPSec policy.

To view the saved console, choose **Start**, select **Documents**, and then choose **My Documents**.

To revise your initial choice, start the Microsoft Management Console, add this snap-in again, and save the console again. (For a Multiple configuration save the file under a different name.)

Testing the IPSec Configuration

To test IPSec policy integrity, follow these steps:

1.   From **IP Security Policy Management**, choose the **IP Security Policies on** folder (Figure 4.8).

Figure 4.8 IP Security Policies on Folder

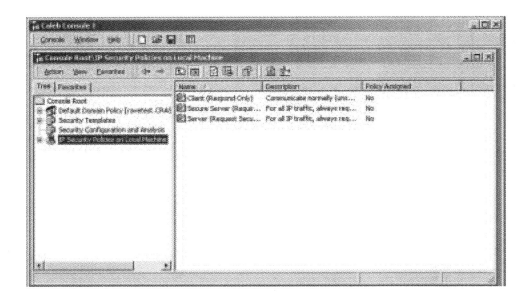

2.   Choose **Action, All Tasks,** and then select **Check Policy Integrity** (Figure 4.9.).

Figure 4.9 IP Check Policy Integrity

Note: To define IPSec policy for computers, you must have appropriate administrator rights to Group Policy or be a member of the local system Administrators group.

Configuring IPSec Settings on a Domain

To add or modify IPSec policies, follows these steps:

1. From **IP Security Policy Management**, choose whether to define a new policy or modify a current one.

Table 4.4 Policy Choices

To	Do This
Create a new policy	In the console tree, choose IP Security Policies on Description, then on the Action menu, select Create IP Security Policy. Complete the instructions in the IP Security Policy Wizard until the Properties dialog box for your new policy appears.
Edit an existing policy	Right-click the policy, and then select Properties.

2. Choose **General**, then in **Name**, enter a unique name (Figure 4.10)

Figure 4.10 Security Policy Name

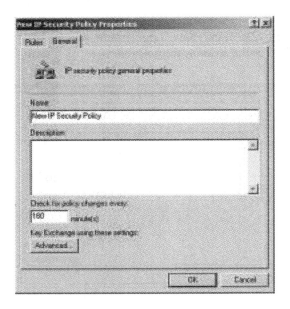

3.   From **Description**, type a description of the security policy, such as which groups or domains it affects.

4.   If this computer is part of a domain, type a value in **Check for policy changes every** *number* **minute(s)** (Figure 4.11) to specify how often the policy agent checks Group Policy for updates.

Figure 4.11 Check for Policy Changes

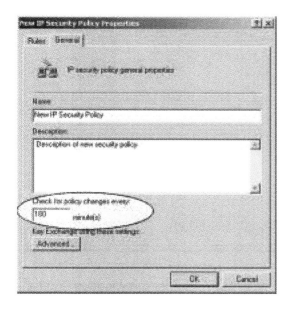

5.   Select **Advanced** (Figure 4.12) if you have special requirements for the security on the key exchange.

Figure 4.12 Advanced Rules

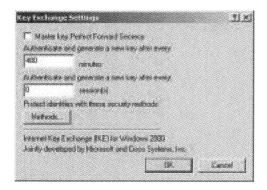

6.   Choose **Rules** and create any necessary rules for the policy.

 Note: IPSec, Internet Key Exchange (IKE) and related services for Windows 2000 are jointly developed by Microsoft Corporation and Cisco Systems, Inc. Negotiations fail if the Diffie-Hellman group on the sender and receiver are NOT the same.

Changing the Key Exchange Security Method

To modify key exchange methods, follow these steps.

1.   From **IP Security Policy Management**, right-click the policy you want to modify, and then select **Properties** (Figure 4.13).

Figure 4.13 IP Security Policy Property

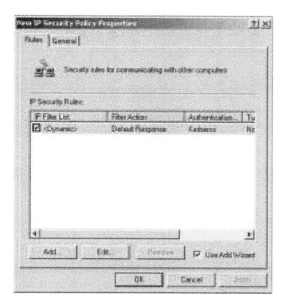

2.   Choose **General**, then select **Advanced**, and then choose **Methods**. (Figure 4.14)

Figure 4.14 IP Security Policy Method

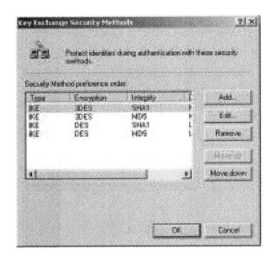

3.   Choose **Add**, or if you are reconfiguring an existing method, choose the security method, and then select **Edit**. (Figure 4.15).

Figure 4.15 IP Security Policies

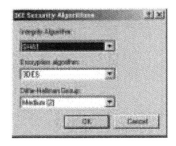

4.   Select an **Integrity Algorithm** (Figure 4.16).

Figure 4.16 Integrity Algorithm

5. Choose **MD5** to use a 128-bit value.

6. Choose **SHA** to use a 160-bit value (stronger).

7. Select a Confidentiality Algorithm (Figure 4.17).

Figure 4.17 Confidentiality Algorithm

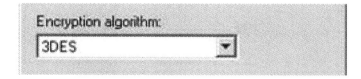

8. Choose **3DES** to use the highest security algorithm.

 Note: If compliance with export regulations is required, you must include DES in your list of security methods.

---

9. Select a **Diffie-Hellman Group** to set the length of base keying material used to generate the actual keys.

10. Choose **Low (1)** to use 768 bits as a basis. Choose **Medium (2)** to use 1,024 bits as a basis (stronger) (Figure 4.18);

Figure 4.18 Low and Medium Base Key Length

To define IPSec policy for computers, you must have appropriate administrator rights to Group Policy or be a member of the local system Administrators group.

IPSec, Internet Key Exchange (IKE), and related services for Windows 2000 are jointly developed by Microsoft Corporation and Cisco Systems, Inc.

The Diffie-Hellman group on the sender and receiver must be the same or negotiations will fail.

Tip: From **Key Exchange Security Methods**:

Choose **Remove** to delete the selected security method.

Choose **Move Up** to move the selected security method up one level. Repeat until the security method is at the desired preference level.

Choose **Move Down** to move the selected security method down one level. Repeat until the security method is at the desired preference level.

Using OUs and IPSec

To assign IPSec policy to Group Policy, follow these steps:

1. From the console in which you manage Group Policy, select the Group Policy object to which you want to assign an IPSec policy.

2. Double-click the **Computer Configuration**, then select **Windows Settings**, and choose **Security Settings** (Figure 4.19).

Figure 4.19 IP Windows Settings

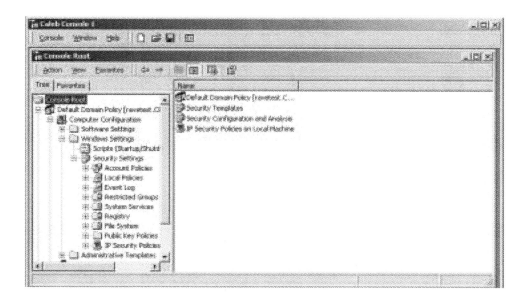

3. Choose the **IP Security Policies** folder.

4. Right-click the policy you want to assign, and then select **Assign** (Figure 4.20).

Figure 4.20 IP Security Policies

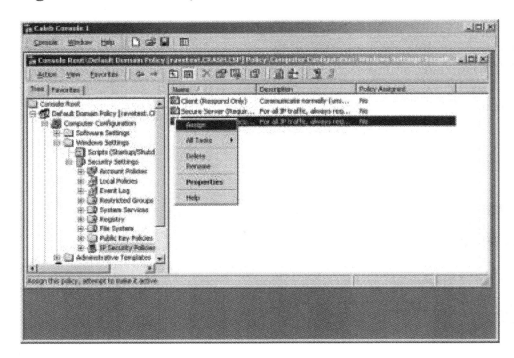

IPSec policy remains active even after the Group Policy object to which it is assigned has been deleted. It is necessary to unassign the IPSec policy before you delete the policy object. If you delete the policy objects and keep the policy assigned, the IPSec Policy Agent assumes it simply cannot find the policy and uses a cached copy.

Tip: To remove the IPSec policy assignment from the Group Policy, right-click the policy and select **Unassign**. If you need to disable IPSec only for a specific computer, you can disable the IPSec Policy Agent Service on that computer.

IPSec Policy Settings

Windows 2000 avoids the increased administrative overhead that cryptography- based security methods may create, using policies to configure IPSec. Network security administrators are able to configure IPSec policies ranging from those appropriate for a single computer to an Active Directory domain, site, or OU. Windows 2000 provides a central management console, IP Security Policy Management, for defining and managing IPSec policies. This allows administrators to configure the policies to provide variable levels of protection for most traffic types, in most existing networks.

Server Message Block (SMB) Security Solutions

The SMB protocol provides two levels of security when sharing files, serial ports, printers and secure communications between computers in a LAN, WAN, and enterprise environment:

User-level security—Allows the user to assign permissions and establish user-level security on any network file. To access the file, log on to the server and get authenticated. Once the server logon authenticates, a UID, transparent to the user, presents every time the user wants to access the server.

Share-level security—Protects files on a network drive based on assigned access permissions and rights. To access a network share, the administrator assigns a password and when the client types this password into the security dialog box, the client has access to all files on that network share.

Vocabulary

Review the following terms in preparation for the certification exam.

Term	Description
DES-CBC	Data Encryption Standard-Cipher Block Chaining is a secret key algorithm for confidentiality. A random number generates for use with the secret key to encrypt the data.
Diffie-Hellman	Diffie-Hellman groups determine the length of the base prime numbers for use during the key exchange.
ESP	IPSec's Encapsulated Security Payload protocol is referred to as a Virtual Private Network (VPN).
HMAC	Hash Message Authentication Code is a mechanism for message authentication using cryptographic hash functions.
IPSec	Internet Protocol Security is a suite of cryptography-based protection services and security protocols.
ISAKMP	Internet Security Association and Key Management Protocol (ISAKMP).
L2TP	Layer 2 Tunneling Protocol is an industry-standard Internet tunneling protocol that does not require IP connectivity between client workstations and servers.
Oakley	Oakley is a key determination protocol that uses the Diffie-Hellman key exchange algorithm.
PPP	Point-to-Point Protocol is a set of industry-standard framing and authentication protocols that is part of Windows 2000 remote access to ensure interoperability with other remote access software. PPP negotiates configuration parameters for networking protocols such as TCP/IP, IPX, and AppleTalk.

Term	Description
PPTP	Networking technology that supports multi-protocol VPNs, enabling remote users to access corporate networks securely across the Internet or other networks by dialing into an Internet service provider (ISP) or by connecting directly to the Internet. The Point-to-Point Tunneling Protocol (PPTP) tunnels, or encapsulates, IP, IPX, or NetBEUI traffic inside of IP packets. This means that users can remotely run applications that are dependent upon particular network protocols.
RFC	A Request for Comments is an evolving series of reports, proposals for protocols, and protocol standards that describe the internal workings of TCP/IP and the Internet.
SA	A Security Association is a combination of a policy and keys that defines the common security services, mechanisms, and keys used to protect the communication from end to end.
TCP/IP	Transmission Control Protocol/Internet Protocol is a set of networking protocols used on the Internet that provides communications across interconnected networks made up of computers with diverse hardware architectures and various operating systems. TCP/IP includes standards for how computers communicate and conventions for connecting networks and routing traffic.

In Brief

If you want to...	Then do this...
Change the Internet	Write and submit a draft proposal for a new protocol or specification to the Internet Engineering Task Force (IETF).
Establish an L2TP connection for a VPN	Use IPSec. IPSec provides machine-level authentication, as well as data encryption, for VPN connections that use the Layer 2 Tunneling Protocol (L2TP).
Ensure the highest level of security	Use 3DES, the most secure of the DES combinations.
Prevent network attacks	Use the ISKAMP SA to negotiate a connection between two computers.
Deploy strong, simple security	Use public-key infrastructure to verify and authenticate the validity of each party.
Store certificates used for Web authentication	Use Smart Cards.
Configure IPSec settings on a computer	Use IP Security Policy Management.
Secure communications between computers in a LAN or WAN	Use Server Message Block (SMB) security protocols.

Lesson 4 Activities

Complete the following activities to better prepare you for the certification exam.

1. List the features of IPSec.

2. Explain the significance of L2TP.

3. List the six status levels of Requests for Comments (RFCs)

4. Explain what Diffie-Hellman groups do.

5. Describe IP Encapsulating Security.

6. Explain AH tunnel mode

7. List the three steps involved in a security negotiation.

8. Describe Security Associations.

9. Explain PKI

10. Describe the SMB security solutions

Answers to Lesson 4 Activities

1. Following are features of IPSec:

   - IPSec is the preferred long-term direction for secure networking. IPSec is a suite of cryptography-based protection services, and security protocols.

   - IPSec supports end-to-end security, the only computers that need to know about IPSec protection are the sender and receiver in the communication.

   - IPSec can protect communication between workgroups, LAN computers, domain clients and servers, remote branch offices, extranets, roving clients, and remote administration of computers.

2. L2TP is an industry-standard Internet tunneling protocol. Unlike Point-to-Point Tunneling Protocol (PPTP), L2TP does not require IP connectivity between the client workstation and the server. L2TP only requires that the tunnel medium provide packet-oriented, point-to-point connectivity. The protocol can be used over diverse media such as ATM, Frame Relay, and X.25. L2TP provides the same functionality as PPTP, based on Layer 2 Forwarding (L2F) and PPTP specifications, L2TP allows clients to set up tunnels across intervening networks.

3. The six status levels for Request for Comments are:

   Standard protocol

   Draft standard protocol

   Proposed standard protocol

   Experimental protocol

   Informational protocol

   Historic protocol

4. Diffie-Hellman groups are used to determine the length of the base prime numbers used during the key exchange. The strength of any key-derived group depends in part on the strength of the Diffie-Hellman group the prime numbers are based on.

5. Encapsulation hides the original packet inside a new packet. This new packet provides the necessary routing information, enabling the packet to travel through transit internetworks without revealing the final destination that is stored in the original packet header. Once the encapsulated

packets reach their destination, the encapsulation header is removed and the original packet header is used to route the packet to its final destination.

6. In AH tunnel mode, the entire packet is signed for integrity, including the new tunnel header. However, encryption is not provided. ESP and AH can be combined to provide tunneling, which includes both integrity for the entire packet and confidentiality for the original IP packet.

7. The three steps involved in security negotiation are:

    Policy Negotiation

    Key Information Exchange

    Authentication

8. A Security Association (SA) is a combination of a policy and keys that defines the common security services, mechanisms, and keys used to protect the communication from end to end.

9. Public Key Infrastructure (PKI) is a system of digital, and other registration authorities that verify and authenticate the validity of each party involved in an electronic transaction through the use of public key cryptography.

10. SMB security solutions include User Level Security, where the user can assign permissions and establish user-level security on any network file.

    Share-Level Security protects files on a network drive based on assigned access permissions and rights.

Lesson 4 Quiz

These questions test your knowledge of features, vocabulary, procedures, and syntax.

1. Which of the following encryptions are available to the IPSec SA?
    A. 40-bit DES

    B. 56-bit DES

    C. 3DES

    D. 128-bit DES

2. Which of the following are industry-standard data encryption techniques?
    A. HMAC

    B. Diffie-Hellman

    C. DES-CBC

    D. RFC

3. Which of the following are pre-defined security methods?
    A. Encapsulating Security Payload

    B. Authentication Header

    C. Message Digest 5

    D. Secure Hash Algorithm

4. What qualities does Authentication Header provide for the packet?
    A. Integrity

    B. Confidentiality

    C. Anti-replay

    D. Authentication

5. What are the features of the ISKAMP SA?
    A. Key exchange

    B. Policy negotiation

    C. Key information exchange

    D. Authentication

6.   What are the attributes of Security Associations?
     A. SPI

     B. Gated communities

     C. ISAKMP

     D. Oakley key generation

7.   Which features encourage an administrator to implement a public-key infrastructure?
     A. Certificates

     B. Certificate Services

     C. Smart Card support

     D. MMC Console

8.   Which IPSec security protocols does Windows 2000 implement?
     A. Internet Security Association and Key Management Protocol

     B. Oakley Key Determination

     C. IP Authentication Header

     D. IP Encapsulating Security Protocol

9.   What is the Server Message Block Security protocol used for?
     A. Share serial ports

     B. Share printers

     C. User-level security

     D. Share-Level Security

10. Which of the following are reasons to use IPSec?
     A. Protection against private network and Internet attacks

     B. Ease of use

     C. The preferred long-term direction for secure networking

     D. Supports end-to-end security

Answers to Lesson 4 Quiz

1.   Answer A is correct. Data Encryption Standard (DES) with a 40-bit key is designed for international use and adheres to United States export encryption laws.

      Answer B is correct. DES with a 56-bit key is designed for North American use.

      Answer C is correct. Triple DES (3DES) uses two 56-bit keys and is designed for high-security environments in North America.

      Answer D is incorrect. 128-bit DES does not yet exist as an available encryption standard.

2.   Answers A, B, and C are correct. Hash Message Authentication Code (HMAC), Diffie-Hellman and Data Encryption Standard-Cipher Block Chaining (DES-CBC) are all encryption techniques.

      Answer D is incorrect. Requests for Comments (RFCs) are documents submitted to the IETF.

3.   Answers A, B, C and D are correct. Encapsulating Security Payload (EPS), Authentication Header (AH), Message Digest 5 (MD5), and Secure Hash Algorithm (SHA) are all pre-defined security methods.

4.   Answers A, C, and D are correct. AH provides authentication, integrity, and anti-replay for the entire packet (both the IP header and the data carried in the packet).

      Answer B is incorrect. AH signs the entire packet, but it does not encrypt the data, so it does not provide confidentiality.

5.   Answers A, B, C, and D are correct. The Key Exchange happens first, then the Policy Negotiation, followed by Key Information Exchange and Authentication.

6.   Answers A, C, and D are correct. The Security Parameters Index (SPI) is a unique, identifying value in the SA used to distinguish among multiple security associations that exist at the receiving computer.

      There is a standard method of security association and key exchange resolution that combines the Internet Security Association and Key Management Protocol (ISAKMP) and the Oakley key-generation protocol. ISAKMP centralizes security association management, reducing connection time. Oakley generates and manages the authenticated keys used to secure the information.

      Answer B is incorrect. At least in this document.

7.   Answers A, B, and C are correct. Certificates, Certificate Services, and Smart Card Support are all features that are supported by PKI.

Answer D is incorrect. Although the MMC Console is an important part of the Windows 2000 operating system, MMC does not, by itself, encourage the use of PKI.

8.   All answers are correct. Internet Security Association and Key Management Protocol, Oakley Key Determination, IP Authentication Header, IP Encapsulating Security Protocol are all implemented by Windows 2000 IPSec.

9.   Answers A, B, C, and D are correct. The SMB protocol Shares printers, serial ports, and is capable of both user-level and share-level file security.

10.   Answers A, B, C, and D are correct. IPSec provides both protection against private network and Internet attacks and ease of use. It is the preferred long-term direction for secure networking and supports end-to-end security.

Kerberos

Authentication is an important aspect of network security. It is the process of verifying the identity of a service or client. If you can verify a user, you can give that user rights in your network. With these rights, the user can proceed with business without further security checks. Kerberos is the security protocol for handling authentication of user or system identity included in Windows 2000. With Kerberos Version 5, passwords sent across network lines are not sent as plain text but are encrypted. Kerberos Version 5 is the primary security protocol for authentication within a domain that verifies both the identity of the user and the network services. This dual verification is known as mutual authentication.

Kerberos started as an MIT project called Athena, which ran during the 1980s and early 1990s. The purpose of this project was to establish a method to design and implement a distributed computing environment. Through this project, they improved authentication methods and developed an authentication method that was less susceptible to hackers. Instead of sending clear-text passwords over the wire, Kerberos uses encryption to authenticate users and grant access to resources on the network. Kerberos is also an Internet standard.

After completing this lesson, you should have a better understanding of the following topics:

- Kerberos Basics
- Benefits of Kerberos Authentication
- Overview of the Kerberos Protocol
- Kerberos Sub Protocols
- Kerberos Protocol Authentication
- Authentication Delegation
- Kerberos Domain Policy
- Security Support Provider Interface (SSPI)

By using Kerberos authentication for Windows 2000, Microsoft has increased the security capability of the operating system. NTLM (Windows NT Challenge/Response) provides for backward capability, but should be disabled as soon as all the users on the network are able to use Kerberos for authentication. As long as NTLM is available on the network, security is not at its maximum.

Kerberos Basics

Kerberos is an Internet security protocol for managing authentication of identities. Passwords that transmit across a network are not sent as plaintext but encrypted. Kerberos is the security protocol for authentication within a domain that verifies the identity of the user and the network services.

 Note: Kerberos is used by operating systems other than Windows 2000, including UNIX.

Version 5 is the default network authentication protocol for Windows 2000. Kerberos makes certain the network servers and services know the client requesting access is valid, and the client knows that the server to which it connects is also valid. Kerberos is based on tickets containing encrypted client credentials with shared keys.

The Kerberos security protocol uses the Data Encryption Standard (DES) shared secret-key concept for authentication. A secret-key can be either private, known to one party only, or shared, known to two or more parties. In Kerberos, both the client and the Kerberos service share the encrypted password as the session key. The Kerberos service issues a certificate, containing the user's identity, a session key, and the expiration time for the ticket. These tickets contain encrypted data, including an encrypted password that confirms the user's identity for use with the requested service. The user only needs to enter a password or use a Smart Card; the rest of the authentication process is invisible to the user.

Kerberos is the primary security protocol for authentication within a domain and verifies both the identity of the user and network services. This dual verification is known as mutual authentication.

Note: The Key Distribution Center (KDC) also functions with Kerberos Version 5. The KDC runs on the domain controller as part of Active Directory, storing passwords and other account information.

The following steps explain the Kerberos Version 5 authentication process:

1. The user client system authenticates to the KDC.

2. The KDC issues a Ticket-Granting Ticket (TGT). The client system uses this TGT to access the Ticket-Granting Service (TGS).

3. The TGS issues a service ticket to the client.

4. The client presents the service ticket to the network service it wants to access. The service ticket proves the user's identity and the service's identity (Figure 5.1).

Figure 5.1 Authentication Process

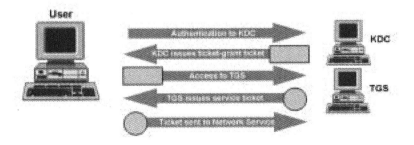

Kerberos services are installed on each domain controller, and a Kerberos client is installed on each Windows 2000 workstation and server. Each domain controller works as a KDC. The Windows 2000

system uses a Domain Name System (DNS) lookup to find the nearest available domain controller. That domain controller then operates as the preferred KDC for that particular user during their session. If the preferred KDC happens to be unavailable, the Windows 2000 system locates another KDC to provide authentication.

An administrator delegates authentication to a user or computer account. By default, only domain administrators have this privilege. This privilege must be assigned to trusted services.

Windows 2000 supports the following two types of Kerberos interoperability:

- Establishes a trust relationship between an MIT-based Kerberos realm and a domain. With this established, the client in a Kerberos realm authenticates to an Active Directory domain and can access network resources in that domain.

- Within a domain, UNIX Users and servers can have Active Directory accounts and obtain authentication from a domain controller.

 Note: The Group Policy editor is used to modify the Kerberos policy for individual user and group accounts. The Group Policy editor refers to the TGT as a user ticket.

Understanding Secret Key Cryptography

The Kerberos protocol name implies how it solves the difficulty of key distribution—Kerberos was the three-headed dog that guarded the gates of the Underworld in Greek mythology. Like the guard, Kerberos the protocol has three heads: a client, a server, and a trusted third party to mediate between them. The trusted intermediary is the Key Distribution Center (KDC). Secret key cryptography uses an encryption algorithm requiring the use of the same secret key for both encryption and decryption. Because of its speed, secret key encryption is also known as symmetric encryption. Secret key cryptography is used when a message sender needs to encrypt large amounts of data.

Authentication

Authentication is central to secure communication. Users need to be able to prove the identity of those with whom they communicate. Authenticating an identity on a network is complex because the communicating parties do not physically meet as they communicate. This allows an unethical party to intercept messages or to impersonate another person or entity.

The digital certificates are common credentials providing a means to verify identity. Certificates use cryptographic techniques to tackle the lack of physical contact between those communicating. These techniques limit the chance of an unethical person interrupting, changing, or forging communications. These techniques ensure certificates are difficult to change, making impersonation difficult.

Data in a certificate incorporates the public key from the certificate subject's public and private keys. Messages signed with the sender's private key are verified by the recipient who uses the sender's public key. This key is found on a copy of the sender's certificate. Confirming a signature with a public key from a certificate confirms the signature was created using the certificate subject's private key. If the sender has been cautious and has kept the private key secret, the receiver can be sure of the sender's identity.

The following are several ways you can use certificates to provide authentication:

- Authentication of a user to a secure Web site through the Transport Layer Security (TLS) or the Secure Sockets Layer (SSL) Protocol

- Authentication of a server to a user through TLS

- Logging on to a Windows 2000 domain

Exploring the Contents of a Kerberos Ticket

When configuring Kerberos policy, consider the following factors:

- The contents of a Kerberos ticket

- How expiration times are calculated

- How much of a ticket's content is known by the client

Ticket Contents

Table 5.1 describes the first three fields in a ticket. These fields are not encrypted, meaning the information is sent in plaintext for managing tickets in the cache.

Table 5.1 Plaintext Ticket Fields

Ticket Field	Content
Tkt-vno	The version number of the ticket format. In Kerberos Version 5, this is 5.
Realm	The name of the realm (domain) that issued the ticket. A KDC only issues tickets for servers in its own realm, so this is also the name of the server's realm (domain).
Sname	The name of the server.

The remaining fields encrypt with the server's secret key. These fields are listed in Table 5.2.

Table 5.2 Encrypted Ticket Fields

Key	Session Key
Crealm	The name of the client's realm (domain).
Cname	The client's name.
Transited	A list of the Kerberos realms that took part in authenticating the User who was issued the ticket.

Key	Session Key
Authtime	Time of the first authentication. The KDC puts a timestamp in the field when it issues a TGT. When the KDC issues tickets based on a TGT, the KDC Copies the authentication time of the TGT to the authentication time of the ticket.
Starttime	The time the ticket becomes valid.
Endtime	The time the ticket expires.
Renew-till	Tickets can have a maximum endtime set in a ticket with a RENEWABLE flag. (This field is optional)
Caddr	There are several addresses from which the ticket can be used. If this field is omitted, the ticket can be used from any address. (This field is optional).
Authorization-data	This field contains the privilege attributes for the client. Kerberos does not interpret anything entered into this field. The service does the interpretation.

In the flags field, options can be set by turning a particular bit on (1) or off (0). This field is 32 bits long and only a few of the ticket flags are of interest to administrators. These are listed in Table 5.3.

Table 5.3 Ticket Flags

Flag Field	Content
Forwardable	Informs the TGS that it can issue a new TGT with a different network address established on the presented TGT. TGT only.
Forwarded	Points out a TGT has been forwarded or a ticket was issued from a forwarded TGT.

Flag Field	Content
Proxiable	Tells the TGS that it can issue tickets with a different network address than the one in the TGT.
Proxy	Specifies the network address in the ticket is not the same as the one the TGT used to get the ticket.
Renewable	This field is used in combination with the Endtime and Renew-till fields so tickets with long life spans can be renewed from time to time at the KDC.
Initial	Points out this is a TGT.

Users must know some of the information contained in tickets and TGTs to manage their credentials cache. When the KDC returns a ticket and session key as the result of the information transfer, it wraps the user's copy of the session key in a data structure. This can include the information described in the tables. The entire structure encrypts in the client's key and returns with KRB_AS_REP or KRB_TGS_REP.

Using a Key Distribution Center (KDC)

The KDC is a service running on a physically secure server. It looks after a database with account information for all of the security principals in its realm (domain). Along with the security principle information, the KDC keeps a cryptographic key. This key is known only to KDC and the security principal. The key is known as a long-term key and is derived from a user's logon password.

To talk to a server, the client sends a request to the KDC. The KDC then shares out a unique, short-term session key to the parties to use when they authenticate each other. The server's copy of the session key encrypts in the server's long-term key. The client's copy of the session key encrypts in the client's long-term key.

The following steps show how the authentication process works:

1. The computer contacts the KDC for authentication to the network.

2. When the user is ready to access a resource for the first time, the computer contacts the KDC for a session ticket.

3. The KDC issues a special TGT to the client system.

4. The client system uses this TGT to access the TGS. This ticket proves both the user's identitiy to the service and the service's identity to the user.

5. On each subsequent attempt, the computer can contact the resource directly, using the same ticket, without having to go to a domain controller first. Unnecessary communication with the domain controller is eliminated   (Figure 5.2).

Figure 5.2 Kerberos Authentication

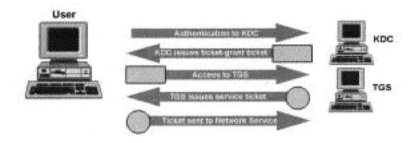

Benefits of Kerberos Authentication

Kerberos provides the following benefits that make it a better authentication choice than NTLM:

- **Kerberos is based on existing standards**—Kerberos makes it easier for Windows 2000 to interoperate with other networks that use Kerberos Version 5. NTLM cannot provide this functionality, as it is proprietary to Microsoft operating systems.

- **Connections to application and file servers are faster with Kerberos authentication**—The Kerberos server only needs to examine the credentials supplied by the client to determine whether access is allowed. These same credentials are used for the entire network logon session. When NTLM is used, the application and file servers must contact a domain controller to determine whether access is allowable.

- **Kerberos authenticates both the client and server**—NTLM only authenticates the client. NTLM users do not know that the server with which they are communicating is not a rogue server.

- **Kerberos is the basis for transitive domain trusts**—Windows 2000 uses transitive trusts by default with other Windows 2000 domains. The domains trust each other in a two-way trust because they both have a shared key.

Setting Standards by Using Kerberos Authentication

In May of 1983, engineers at the Massachusetts Institute of Technology (MIT) began working on Project Athena. In September of 1986, a prototype version of Kerberos was first used in Project Athena.

The goal of Project Athena was to develop the next generation of client/server-based distributed computing facilities. The first public release of the authentication protocol was Kerberos Version 4. Kerberos Version 5 has the following enhancements to that original version:

- Support for forwardable, renewable, and post-datable tickets

- Changing the key salt algorithm to use the entire principal's name

Refer to the following RFCs for more detailed information on Kerberos Version 5:

- RFC 1510, "The Kerberos Network Authentication Service (V5)," September 1993

- RFC 1964, "The Kerberos Version 5 GSS-API Mechanism," June 1996. (GSS-API stands for Generic Security Service-Application Program Interface.

The implementation of Kerberos in Windows 2000, according to Microsoft, closely adheres to the specifications outlined in both RFC 1510 for implementation of the protocol, and in RFC 1964 for the mechanism and format for passing security tokens in Kerberos messages.

Extensions to the Kerberos Protocol

In Windows 2000, Kerberos has been enhanced so the initial authentication of users can be done using public key certificates instead of shared secret keys (standard Kerberos procedure). Extending Kerberos in this way allows interactive logons using Smart Cards. The extensions implemented in Kerberos for Windows 2000 are based on the draft specification "Public Key Cryptography for Initial Authentication in Kerberos," proposed to the Internet Engineering Task Force (IETF) by several companies, including Digital Equipment Corporation (DEC), Novell, CyberSafe Corporation, and others.

Overview of the Kerberos Protocol

Kerberos protocol provides mutual authentication for both server-to-client connections and server-to-server connections. Other such protocols only authenticate the client. Kerberos assumes that the initial transaction between the client and server is done on an unsecured network. Unauthorized and possibly malicious parties may easily monitor unsecured networks.

Reviewing Basic Concepts

A shared secret is a secret that should only be shared with those who need to know the secret. The shared secret must be limited to the minimum number of agents necessary to accomplish the required task. Those who know the shared secret may verify the identity of others who also know the shared secret. To perform its authentication, Kerberos depends on shared secrets. Kerberos implements shared secrets by using secret key cryptography. For shared secrets, Kerberos uses symmetric encryption. Symmetric encryption uses a single key for both encryption and decryption. One agent encrypts the information, and another agent successfully decrypts the information. This constitutes proof of shared secret knowledge between the two agents (Figure 5.3).

Figure 5.3 Symmetric Encryption

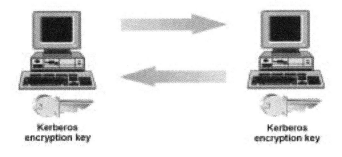

Kerberos
encryption key   Kerberos
                                  encryption key

Authenticators

An authenticator is the unique information encrypted in the shared secret. Kerberos uses timestamps so that the authenticator is always unique. Authenticators are valid for only one use. This minimizes the possibility of an attempt to use someone else's identity. An attempt to reuse an authenticator, called a replay, cannot be done in Kerberos. However, mutual authentication occurs only when the recipient of the authenticator performs the following tasks:

- Extracts a portion of the original authenticator

- Encrypts the portion in a new authenticator

- Sends the portion to the originator of the first authenticator

To prove the original authenticator has been successfully decrypted, a portion of the original authenticator is extracted. If the entire original authenticator were sent back unchanged, then the originator would not know whether it was sent by the intended recipient or an impersonator. Table 5.4 shows the contents of the authenticator fields as shown in Figure 5.4.

Figure 5.4 Authenticators

Table 5.4 Authenticator Field Contents

Name of Field	Contents of Field
Authenticator Version Number	5
Client Realm	The name of the client's realm.
Client Name	The name of the client.
Checksum	The checksum of data in message authenticator.
CUSEC	The millisecond portion of the client's time.
Client Time	The time on the client Key that specifies an alternate.
Subkey	A key to use instead of the session key.
Sequence Number	An optional application-specific number.
Authorization Data	An optional field used to include authorization data for specific applications.

Key Distribution Center (KDC)

The Kerberos authentication protocol has three parts, a client, a server, and a trusted authority. The trusted authority in Kerberos is the KDC, which maintains a database of all of the account information for principals in the Kerberos realm.

 Note: A principal is a uniquely named entity participating in the network. A realm is an organization that has a Kerberos server.

The system running KDC has to be physically secure because it contains a database with security information. The secret key shared between a principal and the KDC is a portion of the security information. Each principal has its own secret key. The key is also knows as the long-term key because it has a long lifetime. The long-term key is derived from the user's password when it is based on a human user's principal. The long-term key is symmetric.

A session key is another key that is also used with the KDC. A session key is issued when one principal wants to communicate with another principal. If a client wants to communicate with a server, for example, the following actions occur:

• The client sends a request to the KDC

• The KDC issues a session key

Now the client and the server can authenticate each other. The client's long-term key includes the client's copy of the session key. The server's long-term key includes the server's copy of the session key. Each respective portion of the session key encrypts in the long-term key both the client and server have. Session keys have a limited lifetime, meaning they are good for a single logon session. The session key is no longer valid after that logon session terminates. Then, the client has to go to the KDC for a new session key the next time the same client needs to contact the same server.

Kerberos Version 5 and Domain Controllers

The KDC is an Active Directory service located on every domain controller. The domain controller's Local Security Authority (LSA) automatically starts both Active Directory and KDC. You cannot stop either service. By allowing each domain to have several domain controllers, Windows 2000 ensures availability of these services. Any of the domain controllers can accept authentication requests and ticket-granting requests addressed to the domain's KDC. If the preferred KDC becomes unavailable, Windows 2000 finds another KDC to provide authentication.

Understanding Session Tickets

The KDC responds to user requests by sending the user both the server and the client session key copies. The key that the KDC shares with the client is used to encrypt the client copy of the session key. The server copy of the key and information about the client are embedded in a data structure called a session ticket. The session ticket then encrypts with the key that the server and the KDC share and send to the client. The client then contacts the server with the ticket.

The only task that the KDC does is to grant the ticket. However, if the KDC's messages fall into the wrong hands, security is not compromised because only the computer that knows the client's secret key can decrypt the client copy of the session key. Likewise, only the computer that knows the server's secret key can read inside the ticket.

Once the client receives the encrypted ticket from the KDC, it extracts both the ticket and the client's copy of the session key. These are placed in a secure cache in system memory. The ticket cache is not on disk. When the client connects to the server, it sends an authenticator and the ticket in a message to the server that is encrypted with the session key. At this point, the ticket is still encrypted with the server's secret key. The authenticator in combination with the session ticket forms the client's credentials to the server (Figure 5.5).

Figure 5.5 Session Key Authentication

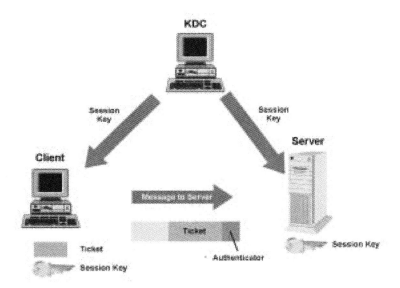

The server uses its secret key to decrypt the session ticket. The server extracts the session key and uses it to decrypt the client's authenticator. If the authenticator is valid, then the server knows that the client's credentials were issued by a trusted authority, the KD. In the case where mutual authentication is required, the server will use its copy of the session key to encrypt the client's authenticator timestamp and returns the encrypted timestamp to the client as the server's authenticator.

The server does not have to store the session key used in communicating with a client. The client holds the ticket for the server in its credentials cache and presents it to the server each time it wants to access it. When the server no longer needs the session key, it is discarded.

You can reuse session tickets until they expire. This means that the client does not need to go back to the KDC for a new session ticket each time it wants access to a particular server unless the current ticket has expired. Tickets usually expire after eight hours. How long the ticket remains valid depends on Kerberos policy for the domain.

 Note: When a user logs off the client computer, the client's credentials cache flushes, destroying all session tickets and session keys.

Understanding Ticket-Granting Tickets (TGT)

The Kerberos KDC uses TGT for securing network authentication in a domain. The time that the KDC issues a TGT is important to the Kerberos protocol. Using the Kerberos pre-authentication option works well because Windows 2000 uses other mechanisms to synchronize time.

In addition to session tickets, Kerberos uses a TGT. The KDC uses a TGT to verify that principals really are whom they claim. When a user logs on to a Kerberos realm, the user's password is run through a one-way hashing algorithm that results in a long-term key. The long-term key transmits to the KDC. When the client sends the long-term key, it also requests a session ticket and a session key so that it can communicate with the KDC during the logon session. When the KDC receives the long-term key, it also obtains a copy of the hash from its account database. The ticket that then returns to the client by the KDC is the TGT (Figure 5.6).

Figure 5.6 TGT

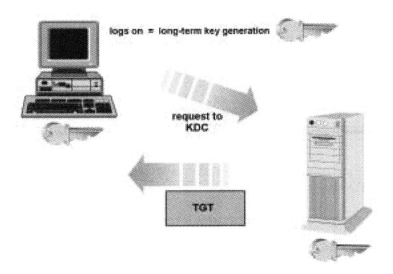

Both the KDC and the client have a long-term key. The KDC encrypts the TGT in its long-term key. The client's copy of the session key is encrypted in its long-term key. The client's long-term key is cached. The client uses its long-term key to decrypt the session key after it receives the reply message from the KDC. Once the session key decrypts, the long-term key flushes from the client's cache. The long-term key is no longer needed to communicate with the KDC until either the TGT expires or the logon session terminates. The session key is sometimes called the logon session key (Figure 5.7).

Figure 5.7 Logon Session Key

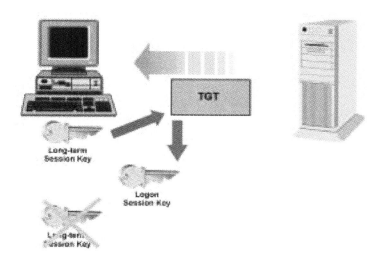

To communicate with another principal such as the server, a client principal contacts the KDC to retrieve the session ticket. The client uses the logon session key to set up an authenticator. The client then sends it to the KDC the authenticator, the TGT, and a request for a session ticket for the server it wants to access. When the KDC receives the message from the client, it uses the long-term key to extract the logon session key, decrypts the TGT, and uses that to verify the authenticator sent by the client. The client must send a new authenticator each time the client sends the TGT to the KDC (Figure 5.8).

Figure 5.8 TGT New Authenticator

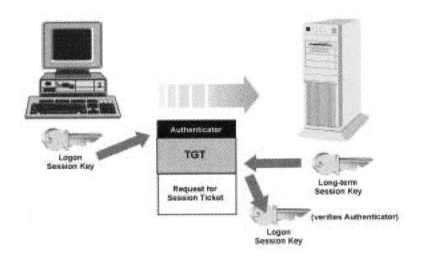

Working With KDC Domain Boundaries

The KDC is a service that runs on a physically secure server. It maintains a database with account information for all security principals in its realm, the Kerberos equivalent of a Windows 2000 domain.

Kerberos Sub Protocols

Kerberos contains the following three sub protocols:

Ticket-Granting Service (TGS) Exchange—Used when the KDC distributes a service session key and a session ticket for the service.

Authentication Service (AS) Exchange—Used when the KDC gives the client a logon session key and a TGT.

Client/Server (CS) Exchange—Used when the client presents the session ticket for admission to a service.

Working With the Ticket Granting Service (TGS) Exchange

The following is a summary of how the Kerberos Version 5 authentication process works:

1. The user on a client system, authenticates to the KDC using a password or a Smart Card. A special TGT is issued to the client by the KDC. The client system uses the TGT to access the TGS, part of the Kerberos Version 5 authentication mechanism.

2. A service ticket is issued to the client by the TGS.

3. The service ticket is presented to the requested network service by the client . Both the user's identity to the service and the service's identity to the user are proven by the service ticket (Figure 5.9).

Figure 5.9 TGS Exchange Process

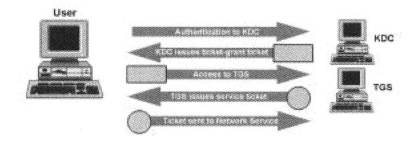

Using Authentication Server (AS) Exchange

The process for the Authentication Server information exchange is as follows:

1. User 1 logs on to the network. The Kerberos client on User 2's workstation converts the password to an encryption key, and saves the result in its credentials cache.

2. The Kerberos client sends the KDC authentication service a Kerberos Authentication Service Request (KRB AS_REQ). The first part of this message identifies User 1 and the name of the service needing credentials—the ticket-granting service. The second part of the message contains

preauthentication data that proves User 1 knows the password. This is usually a timestamp encrypted with User 1's long-term key.

3.   The KDC receives the KRB_AS_REQ.

4.   The KDC looks up User 1 in its database, gets the long-term key, decrypts the preauthentication data and evaluates the timestamp. If the timestamp is acceptable, the KDC is assured that the preauthentication data was encrypted with User 1's long-term key and that the client is genuine (Figure 5.10).

Figure 5.10 AS Exchange Process Authentication

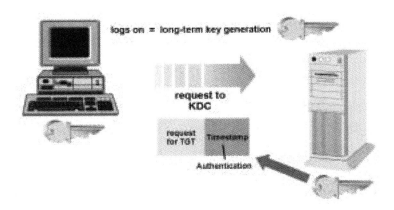

5.   The KDC creates credentials for the Kerberos client on User 1's workstation to present to the ticket-granting service.

• KDC creates a logon session key and encrypts a copy of it with User 1's long-term key.

• KDC embeds another copy of the logon session key in a TGT, along with other information about User 1, such as the authorization data.

• KDC encrypts the TGT with its own long-term key.

6.   KDC sends both the encrypted logon session key and the TGT back to the client in a Kerberos Authentication Service Reply (KRB_AS_REP).

7. When the client receives the message, it uses the key derived from User 1's password to decrypt the logon session key and then stores the key in its credentials cache. Next, it extracts the TGT from the message and stores that in its credentials cache, as well (Figure 5.11).

Figure 5.11 AS Exchange Process Credentials

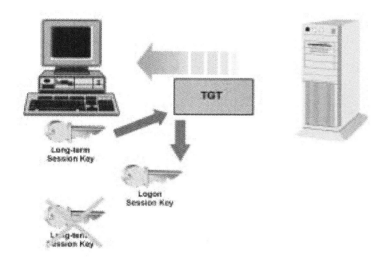

Using the Client/Server (CS) Exchange

The administrator should use CS Exchange once the TGS information exchange is complete. The CS information exchange proceeds as follows:

1. The Kerberos client on User 1's workstation requests service from User 2 by sending User 2 a Kerberos Application Request (KRB_AP_REQ). This message contains an authenticator encrypted with the session key for the service, the ticket obtained in the TGS information exchange, and a preconfigured flag indicating whether the client wants mutual authentication.

2. User 2 receives the KRB_AP REQ, decrypts the ticket, and extracts User 1's authorization data and the session key.

User 2 uses the session key to decrypt User 1's authenticator, and evaluates the timestamp inside.

If the authenticator is valid, User 2 looks for a mutual authentication flag in the client's request (Figure 5.12).

Figure 5.12 CS Exchange Process Mutual Authentication

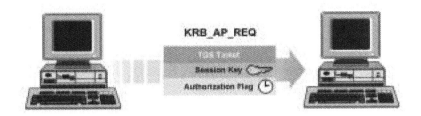

If the flag is set, the service uses the session key to encrypt the time from User 1's authenticator, and returns the result in a Kerberos Application Reply (KRB_AP_REP).

When the Kerberos client on User 1's workstation receives the KRB_AP_REP, it decrypts User 2's authenticator with the session key it shares with User 2, and compares the time returned by the service with the time in the client's original authenticator.

If the times match, the client knows that the service is genuine, and the connection proceeds. During the connection, the session key can be used to encrypt application data—or the client and server can share another key for this purpose (Figure 5.13).

Figure 5.13 CS Exchange Key Sharing

Kerberos Protocol Authentication

The Kerberos protocol is not for authorization but for authentication. It determines that security principals are who they say they are. Kerberos does not decide which files and other objects security principals may access or how they access them. These decisions are made by the access control mechanism available on the system. Kerberos assists by providing a field for authorization data in tickets, but it does not specify how the servers should use the data or its form.

Kerberos' authentication technique incorporates shared secrets. If only two people share a secret, then either person can verify the identity of the other by confirming that the other person knows that secret.

Suppose, for example, that User 1 often sends messages to User 2, who needs to be sure that a message from User 1 is genuine before acting on its information. They solve this problem by selecting a secret password that they do not to share with anyone else. If messages from User 1's show that User 1 knows the password, then User 2 will know that the sender is in fact User 1.

So, how will User 1 confirm knowledge of the password? User 1 could include it somewhere in the messages, such as in a signature block at the end. This is simple and efficient, but is secure only if Users 1 and 2 are certain that no one else is reading their mail. Unfortunately, their messages pass over a network used by a competitor, who has a network analyzer. User 1 can't prove that he knows the secret simply by saying it, and hence revealing it to the competition. To keep the password secret, User 1 must show that he knows the password without putting it in plain view on the network.

Kerberos solves this problem with secret key cryptography. Communication partners share a cryptographic key instead of sharing a password. They use this key to verify one another's identity. The shared key must be symmetric—a single key must be capable of both encryption and decryption. One party proves knowledge of the key by encrypting a piece of information, the other proves knowledge by decrypting that piece of information. Secret key authentication begins when a user presents an authenticator in the form of a piece of information that has been encrypted in the secret key. The information in the authenticator must be different each time the protocol executes. If the authenticator did not change, then an old authenticator can be reused by anyone who happens to overhear the communication and capture the authenticator. After receipt, an authenticator is decrypted by the recipient. If the decryption is successful, then the recipient knows that the person transmitting the authenticator has the correct key. Only two people can have the correct key—the recipient being one of them. Because the decryption worked, the person who presented the authenticator must be the other person with the correct key.

Where a trusted source downloads information, the key must ensure that the following is true:

- The source is whom it purports to be

- The information has not been tampered

This is a straightforward problem with limited parameters, and several solutions to the problem are available. When the communication is two-way, then mutual authentication is required. Mutual authentication presents a new set of problems regarding shared secrets. New techniques are available to solve these problems.

To provide mutual authentication, the recipient does the following:

- Extracts information from the original authenticator

- Encrypts it in a new authenticator

- Returns the new authenticator to the sender

The sender then decrypts the recipient's authenticator and compares it with the original. If there is a match, then the sender knows that the recipient was able to decrypt the original authenticator and therefore has the new key.

Suppose, for example, Users 1 and 2 decide to each share a secret key to verify the identity of the party at the other end of the connection before transferring any information. They agree on the following protocol:

User 1 sends User 2 a message containing User 1's name in plaintext and an authenticator encrypted in the secret key shared with User 1. In this protocol, the authenticator is a data structure with two fields. One field contains information about User 1—for example, "Smith." The second field contains the current time on User 1's workstation.

User 2 receives the message and uses the key he shares with User 1 to decrypt the authenticator. User 1 extracts and evaluates the field that contains the time on User 1's workstation.

Assume that both User 1 and User 2 use a network time mark to keep their clocks fairly close. User 2 can compare time from the authenticator with the current time on his clock. If the difference is outside a specified limit, User 1 rejects the authenticator (Figure 5.14).

Figure 5.14 Mutual Authentication Process 1

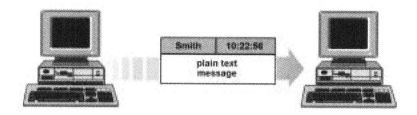

If the time is within allowable limits, the authenticator probably came from User 1. User 2 still does-n't have proof of this. It might be that the competition has been watching network traffic and is now replaying an earlier attempt by User 1 to establish a connection. If User 2 has recorded the times that authenticators were received from User 1, he can defeat these attempts to replay earlier messages by rejecting any message with a time that duplicates or is earlier than the time of the last authenticator.

User 2 uses the key he shares with User 1 to encrypt the time taken from User 1's message, and sends the result back to User 1. User 2 does not send back all the information taken from User 1's authenti-cator. If User 2 returned everything, User 1 has no way of knowing whether someone posing as User 2 simply copied the authenticator from the original message and sent it back. User 2 chooses the time because that is one piece of information that is certain to be unique in User 1's message to User 2.

User 1 receives User 2's reply, decrypts it, and compares the result with the time in the original authen-ticator. If the times match, User 1 is confident that the authenticator was received by someone who knows the secret key needed to decrypt the authenticator and extract the time. Remember that User 1 only shares that key with User 2, and, therefore, it must be User 2 who received the message and replied. Both the sender and the receiver can be confident in the connection (Figure 5.15).

Figure 5.15 Mutual Authentication Process 2

Tip: Remember the term *"replay attack"* because such attacks are a matter of concern to the security community

Understanding the Logon Process

When users log on to an account, they often assume they have access to the network, but this is not true. When logging on to a network using the Kerberos protocol, you get the authentication service. Specifically, you receive a TGT. You present this TGT for session tickets when requesting other services in the domain.

When you log on to a Windows 2000 domain, you need at least one session ticket for the computer to which you have logged on. Computers running Windows 2000 have their own accounts in the domain. Interactive users can access other resources in the Windows 2000 domain through submitting requests to the computer's workstation service. Remote users submit their requests to the server service. Before gaining admission to any service, you must present a session ticket for the computer (Figure 5.16). This process is as follows:

User 1 has a network account in the domain Widget and logs on to a computer.

1.   User 2 also has an account in Widget.

2.   User 1 starts with Ctrl+Alt+Delete—the Secure Attention Sequence (SAS).

User 2's WinLogon service switches to the logon desktop and accesses the Graphical Identification and Authentication (GINA) Dynamic Link Library (DLL), MSGINA.DLL. This DLL is responsible for the following services:

- Collecting logon data from the user

- Packaging it in a data structure

- Sending the package to the Local Security Authority (LSA) for verification

Figure 5.16 Logon Sequence 1

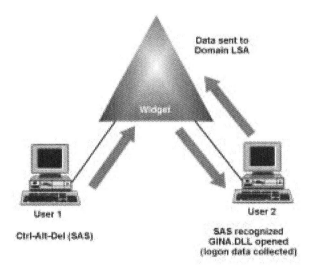

3. User 1 types in the username and password and selects Widget from the drop-down list of domains, then selects OK to end the dialog.

4. When User 1 selects OK, MSGINA.DLL returns the logon information to WinLogon, which then sends the information to the LSA for validation by calling the LsaLogonUser function (Figure 5.17).

Figure 5.17 Logon Sequence 2

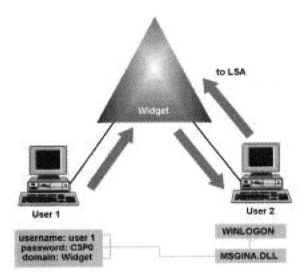

5.   When it receives the data structure with User 1's logon data, the LSA immediately passes it through a one-way hashing function to convert the clear-text password into a secret key.

6.   The resulting secret key is saved in the credentials cache. From the credentials cache, you can retrieve it when needed for either TGT renewal or for NTLM authentication to servers not capable of Kerberos authentication (Figure 5.18).

Figure 5.18 Logon Sequence 3

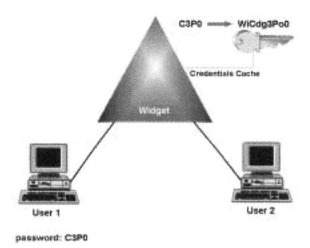

To validate User 1's logon information and set up the logon session on the computer, the LSA must obtain the following:

- A TGT that is good for admission to the ticket-granting service

- A session ticket good for admission to the computer

The LSA obtains these tickets by working through the Security Support Provider (SSP) that exchanges messages directly with the KDC in Widget.

The following is the message sequence:

1. The LSA sends a KRB_AS_REQ to the KDC in Widget. The message includes the following data:

- The user principal name: User 1

- The name of the account domain: Widget

- Pre-authentication data encrypted with the secret key derived from User 1's password

2. The KDC replies with a KRB_AS_REP if the client's preauthentication data is correct. The message includes the following:

- A session key for User 1 to share with the KDC

- A TGT for the KDC in Widget

The session key that User 1 shares with the KDC is encrypted with the secret key derived from User 1's password. The TGT for the KDC in Widget is encryped with the KDC's secret key. The TGT includes a session key for the KDC to share with User 1, and authorization data for User 1.

The authorization data contains the following data:

- A Security Identifier (SID) for User 1's account

- SIDs for security groups in the domain Widget that include User 1

- SIDs for universal groups in the enterprise that include either User 1 or one of the domain groups

3.   The LSA sends a KRB_TGS_REQ to the KDC in Widget. The message includes the following data:

- The name of the target computer, User 2

- The name of the target computer's domain: Widget

- User 1's TGT

- An authenticator encrypted with the session key User 1 shares with the KDC

4.   The KDC replies with a KRB_TGS_REP. The message includes the following data:

- A session key for User 1 to share with User 2 encrypted with the session key User 1 shares with the KDC

- User 1's session ticket to User 2, encrypted with the secret key User 2 shares with the KDC.

- The session ticket contains a session key for User 2 to share with User 1, and authorization data copied from User 1's TGT (Figure 5.19).

Figure 5.19 Message Sequences

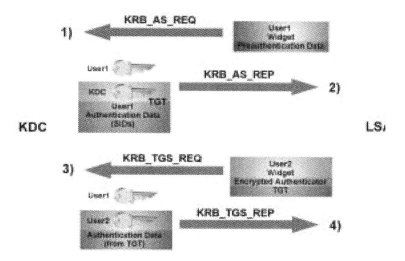

When it receives User 1's session ticket, the LSA decrypts it with the computer's secret key and extracts the authorization data.

LSA then queries the local Security Accounts Manager (SAM) database to discover whether User 1 is a member of any security groups local to the computer and whether User 1 has been given any special privileges on the local computer. The LSA adds any SIDs returned by this query to the list taken from the ticket's authorization data. The entire list is then used to build an access token. The handle to the token returns to WinLogon with an identifier for User 1's logon session, and confirmation that the logon information is valid.

WinLogon then creates a window station as well as several desktop objects for User 1. It then attaches the access token and starts the shell process that User 1 uses to interact with the computer. The access token is inherited by any application subsequent process that User 1 starts during the logon session.

Note: During the message sequencing, the same key was used for encryption and decryption. Shared secret keys used for password logon are symmetric.

Authentication Delegation

You can delegate authentication the following two ways:

Proxy tickets—The client gets a ticket for the back-end server and then gives it to the front-end server. Tickets obtained in this way—by a client for a proxy—are called proxy tickets. The major problem with a proxy tickets is the client must know the name of the back-end server.

Forwarded tickets—The client gives the front-end server a TGT it uses to request tickets as needed. Tickets acquired this way—with credentials forwarded by a client—are called forwarded tickets.

 Note: Whether the KDC allows clients to obtain proxy tickets or forwarded TGTs depends upon Kerberos policy.

Learning About Proxy Tickets

When the KDC issues a TGT to a client, it checks to see if the Kerberos policy allows proxy tickets. If it does, KDC sets the PROXIABLE flag in the TGT that it issues to the client. The following steps describe the Proxy process:

1. The client acquires a proxy ticket by presenting a TGT to the TGS and asks for a ticket to the back-end server.

2. This request includes a flag showing it wants a proxy ticket.

3. The name of the server that will represent the client is also included.

4. When the KDC receives the client's request, a ticket for the back-end server is created.

5. This process sets the PROXY flag in the ticket and the ticket transmits back to the client.

6. The client sends the ticket to the front-end server, which uses the ticket to access the back-end server (Figure 5.20).

Figure 5.20 Proxy Tickets

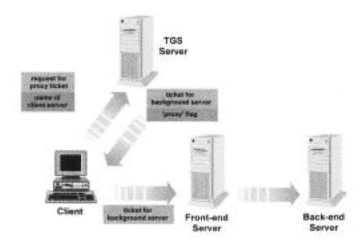

Understanding Forwarded Tickets

Clients ask the KDC for a forwarded TGT when they choose to delegate the task of acquiring tickets for back-end servers to a front-end server. The following steps describe the forward ticket process:

1. The process is accomplished through an AS Exchange request that tells the KDC the name of the server acting on its behalf.

2. The KDC creates a TGT for the front-end server to use in the client's name, if the Kerberos policy permits forwarding.

3.   The FORWARDABLE flag is set, and the TGT is sent back to the client.

4.   The client then forwards the TGT to the front-end server.

5.   When the front-end server requests a ticket to the back-end server, it presents the client's TGT to the KDC.

6.   When the KDC issues a ticket, it sees the FORWARDABLE flag in the TGT, and sets the FOR-WARDED flag in the ticket.

7.   The KDC then returns the ticket to the front-end server.

Kerberos Domain Policy

Kerberos policy is defined at the domain level and implemented by the domain KDCs in Windows 2000. The Kerberos policy is stored in Active Directory as a subset of the attributes of domain security policy. Only members of the Domain Administrators group can set policy options. Kerberos services are installed on each domain controller, and a Kerberos client is installed on each Windows 2000 workstation and server.

Setting Kerberos Domain Policies

Table 5.5 explains the elements of the Kerberos policy.

Table 5.5 Kerberos Policy

Name of Policy Option	Description	Default
Enforce user logon restrictions	When enabled, the KDC validates each request for a session ticket by examining the user rights policy on the target computer. Verifies that the user has the right either to log on locally or to access this computer from the network. Verification is optional, because the extra step takes time and may slow network access to services.	Enabled by default.
Maximum lifetime for service ticket	A service ticket is a session ticket. Settings are in minutes. The setting must be greater than 10 minutes and less or equal to the setting for maximum lifetime for user ticket.	600 minutes (10 hours).
Maximum lifetime for user ticket	A user ticket is a TGT. Settings are in hours.	600 minutes (10 hours).
Maximum lifetime for user ticket renewal	Settings are in days.	7 days.
Maximum tolerance for computer clock synchronization	Settings are in minutes.	5 minutes.

Security Support Provider Interface (SSPI)

Transport-level applications and system services access SSPs through the Security Support Provider Interface (SSPI). SSPI is a Win32 interface. You can enumerate the providers available on a system, choose one, and use it to obtain an authenticated connection.

SSPI methods are generic, black-box routines developers can use without knowing the details of a particular protocol.

Integrating Authentication, Message Integrity, and Privacy

Security Application Programmer Interfaces (APIs) for network authentication are defined by the Security Support Provider Interface. The SSPI is the architectural layer of Windows 2000 that provides a generic Win32 system API. This allows security providers to use various authentication services and account information stores.

A security provider is a DLL that performs the following services:

- Implements the Security Support Provider Interface

- Makes one or more security packages available to applications

- A security provider also maps the SSPI functions to an implementation of the security protocol specific to the package, such as NTLM, Kerberos, or SSL

The SSPI provides a common interface between transport-level applications and security providers. Examples of transport-level applications include the following:

- Microsoft RPC

- A file system redirector

- Security providers

A distributed application using SSPI can call one of several security providers to obtain an authenticated connection. The application can do this without knowledge of the details used by the security protocol.

Understanding the SSPI Interface Types

SSPI is the Win32 interface between network security service providers and transport-level applications. SSPI APIs integrate the following into distributed applications:

- Authentication

- Message integrity

- Privacy

You can access SSPI services from higher-level interfaces. Authenticated Remote Procedure Calls (RPCs) and the Distributed Component Object Model (DCOM) application framework use such access. You can also access the SSPI security services with an application-level interface like the interfaces integrated into both WinSock 2.0 and WinInet.

The SSPI is an abstraction layer between Application Level protocols and security protocols. You can use SSPI services in the following ways:

Traditional socket-based applications—Call SSPI routines directly and implement the application protocol carrying SSPI security-related data by using request and response messages.

DCOM—Applications use this to call security options to be implemented using authenticated RPC and SSPI APIs at lower levels. Applications do not call SSPI APIs directly.

WinSock 2.0—Extends the Windows Sockets interface to allow transport providers to expose security features. This integrates the SSPI security provider into the network stack and provides both security and transport services by means of a common interface.

WinInet—An application protocol interface designed to support Internet security protocols, such as Secure Sockets Layer (SSL). WinInet security support uses the SSPI interface to access the Secure Channel security provider.

Note: Scripting languages such as VBScript and JScript allow application developers to access the SSPI's APIs. A security administrator should be aware of the structure of the SSPI and the capabilities of scripting software.

The following are the four types of SSPI interfaces:

Credential-management interfaces— Provides access to credentials (password data, tickets, etc.) or to free up such access. The methods available include the following:

- **AcquireCredentialsHandle**—Acquires a handle to the reference credentials.

- **FreeCredentialsHandle**—Releases a credential handle and associated resources.

- **QueryCredentialAttributes**—Allows queries on various credential attributes such as associated name, domain name, and so forth.

Context management interfaces— Provides methods for creating and using security contexts. The security contexts are created on both the client and the server side of a communications link. These contexts are also used later with the message support interfaces. The following methods are available:

- **IntializeSecurityContext**—Initiates a security context, generating an opaque message (a security token) that can be passed to the server.

- **AcceptSecurityContext**—Creates a security context and uses the opaque message that was received from the client.

- **DeleteSecurityContext**—Frees up a security context and its associated resources.

- **QueryContextAttributes**—Allows queries on context attributes

- **ApplyControlToken**—Applies a supplemental security message to an existing security context.

- **CompleteAuthToken**—Completes an authentication token because some protocols, such as Distributed Computing Environment Remote Procedure Call (DCE-RPC), revise the security information once the transport has updated certain message fields and require this function.

- **ImpersonateSecurityContext**—Attaches the client's security context to the calling thread as an impersonation token.

- **RevertSecurityContext**—Ceases impersonation and defaults the Calling thread to its primary token.

Message-support interface—Provides communication integrity and security context based privacy services. The following methods are available:

- **MakeSignature**—Generates a secure signature based on a message and a security context.

- **VerifySignature**—Verifies that the signature matches a received message.

Package-management interfaces—Provides services for various security packages that the security provider supports. The following methods are available:

- **EnumerateSecurityPackage**—Lists available security packages and their capabilities.

- **QuerySecurityPackageInf**—Queries an individual security package for its capabilities.

A security provider is a DLL that implements the SSPI and makes one or more *security packages* available to applications. A security package SSP maps the SSPI functions to an iteration of the security protocol specific to that package, such as

NTLM, Kerberos or SSL. The name of the security package is used in initialization to identify a specific package.

The SSPI allows an application to use any of the available security packages on a system without changing the interface to use security services. The SSPI doesn't establish logon credentials because that is a privileged operation handled by the operating system.

An application can use package-management functions to list the security packages available and choose one to support its needs. The application then uses the credential-management functions to obtain a handle to the credentials of the user for whom they are executing. With this handle, the application can then use the context management functions to create a security context for a service. A security context is an opaque data structure that contains the security data relevant to a connection, such as a session key, the duration of the session, and so on. Finally, the application uses the security context with the message-support functions to ensure message integrity and privacy during the connection.

Vocabulary

Review the following terms in preparation for the certification exam.

Term	Description
API	Application Programming Interface is a set of routines that an application uses to request and carry out services performed by a computer's operating system. These routines are used for maintenance tasks such as managing files and displaying information.
AS Exchange	Authentication Service Exchange is used when the KDC gives the client a logon session key and a TGT.
CA	Certificate Authority is a trusted third-party organization or company that issues digital certificates that create digital signatures and public-private key pairs. The role of the CA in this process is to guarantee that the individual granted the unique certificate is, in fact, whom they claim to be. CAs are a significant component in data security because they guarantee that the two parties exchanging information are really who they claim to be.
Certificate Template	A Windows 2000 function that pre-specifies format and content for certificates based on their intended use. When requesting a certificate from a CA, certificate requestors are able to choose from a variety of certificate types based on certificate templates, such as "User" and "Secure Signing."
cryptography	The art and science of information security. There are four major information security functions: confidentiality, integrity, authentication, and non-repudiation.
CS Exchange	Client/Server Exchange is used when the client presents the session ticket for admission to a service.
DCE-RPC	Distributed Computing Environment Remote Procedure Call.

Term	Description
ESE	Extensible Storage Engine is the database engine for Active Directory. ESE (ESENT.DLL) is a better version of the Jet database used in Microsoft Exchange Server Versions 4.x and 5.5. The ESE uses log files to make sure committed transactions are safe (transacted database system).
GINA	Graphical Identification and Authentication is a Dynamic Link Library (DLL), MSGINA.DLL.
GPO	Group Policy Object is a virtual collection of policies. These policies are given unique names, such as a Globally Unique Identifier (GUID). GPOs store the policy settings in two locations: a Group Policy Container (GPC) and a Group Policy Template.
KDC	Key Distribution Center runs on each domain controller as part of Active Directory, storing all client passwords and other account information.
Kerberos	An authentication system developed at the Massachusetts Institute of Technology (MIT), Kerberos is designed so two parties can exchange private information across an open network. It works by assigning a unique key, called a ticket, to each user that logs on to the network. The ticket is embedded in messages to identify the sender of the message.
PKI	Public Key Infrastructure is a policy for establishing a secure method of exchanging information. PKI is an integrated set of services and administrative tools to create, deploy, and manage public-key-based applications. It includes the cryptographic methods, digital certificates, CAs, and the system for managing the process.
policy engine	The policy engine implements at decision points to perform policy selection, evaluate conditions, and decide what actions must be performed.

Term	Description
SIDs	Security Identifiers are part of Access Control Entry (ACE). Each ACE contains a SID that identifies the user or group to whom the ACE applies, and information on what type of access the ACE grants or denies.
SSPI	The Security Support Provider Interface defines the security APIs for network authentication
TGS Exchange	Ticket Granting Service Exchange is used when the KDC distributes a service session key and a session ticket for the service.
TGT	Ticket Granting Tickets is used by the Kerberos Key Distribution Center for securing network authentication in a domain.
WinInet	An application protocol interface designed to support Internet security protocols, such as Secure Sockets Layer (SSL).

In Brief

If you want to...	Then do this...
Store client passwords and other account information.	Use the Key Distribution Center (KDC). The KDC runs on each domain controller as part of Active Directory.
Authenticate a client	Use TGT for securing network authentication in a domain.
Send an encrypted message	Use Kerberos Protocol Authentication.
Get a proxy ticket	Obtains a proxy ticket by presenting a TGT to the TGS and asking for a ticket to the back-end server.
Create credentials for the Kerberos client	Use the Key Distribution Center (KDC).

Lesson 5 Activities

Complete the following activities to better prepare you for the certification exam.

1.   List some of the Encrypted Ticket Fields.

2.   Explain why security is preserved even if KDC messages fall into the wrong hands.

3.   List the Kerberos sub protocols.

4.   Describe the steps taken by the KDC to create credentials.

5.   Explain how either party can verify a shared secret.

6.   Describe the message sequence the LSA gets working through Kerberos Security Support Provide.

7.   Explain how to forward a ticket.

8.   List Kerberos domain policy settings.

9.   Describe the ways SSPI services are used.

10. List the types of SSPI interfaces.

Answers to Lesson 5 Activities

1. Some encrypted ticket fields are:

    Crealm—The name of the client's realm (domain),

    Starttime—The time after which the ticket is valid,

    Authorization-data—Privilege attributes for the client, Kerberos doesn't interpret the contents of this field.

2. Security is not compromised if the KDC's messages fall into the wrong hands because only the person who knows the client's secret key can decrypt the client copy of the session key, and only the person who knows the server's secret key can read inside the ticket.

3. The Kerberos sub protocols are:

    Authentication Service (AS) Exchange—Used when the KDC gives the client a logon session key and a TGT.

    Ticket-Granting Service (TGS) Exchange—Used when the KDC distributes a service session key and a session ticket for the service.

    Client/Server (CS) Exchange—Used when the client presents the session ticket for admission to a service

4. KDC creates a logon session key and encrypts a copy of it with User 1's long-term key KDC embeds another copy of the logon session key in a TGT, along with other information about User 1, such as the authorization data.

    KDC encrypts the TGT with its own long-term key.

    KDC sends both the encrypted logon session key and the TGT back to the client in a Kerberos Authentication Service Reply (KRB_AS_REP).

5. Kerberos uses an authentication technique involving shared secrets. If only two people know a secret, then either person can verify the identity of the other by confirming that the other person knows that secret.

6. The LSA sends a KRB_AS_REQ to the KDC

    If the client's pre-authentication data is correct, the KDC replies with a KRB_AS_REP.

The LSA sends a KRB_TGS_REQ to the KDC.

The KDC replies with a KRB_TGS_REP.

7. The client asks the KDC for a forwardable TGT through an AS Exchange request, indicating to the KDC the name of the server that will act on its behalf. If Kerberos policy permits forwarding, the KDC creates a TGT for the front-end server to use in the client's name, sets the FORWARDABLE flag, and sends the TGT back to the client. The client then forwards the TGT to the front-end server.

When the front-end server requests a ticket to the back-end server, it presents the client's TGT to the KDC. When the KDC issues a ticket, it sees the FORWARDABLE flag in the TGT, sets the FORWARDED flag in the ticket, and returns the ticket to the front-end server.

8. Kerberos Domain Policy settings include:

Enforce user logon restrictions

Maximum lifetime for service ticket

Maximum lifetime for user ticket

Maximum lifetime for user ticket renewal

Maximum tolerance for computer clock synchronization

9. Traditional socket-based applications can call SSPI routines directly and implement the application protocol carrying SSPI security-related data by using request and response messages.

Applications can use DCOM to call security options to be implemented using authenticated RPC and SSPI APIs at lower levels. Applications do not call SSPI APIs directly.

WinSock 2.0 extends the Windows Sockets interface to allow transport providers to expose security features. This integrates the SSPI security provider into the network stack and provides both security and transport services by means of a common interface.

WinInet is an application protocol interface designed to support Internet security protocols, such as Secure Sockets Layer (SSL). WinInet security support uses the SSPI interface to access the Secure Channel security provider.

10. SSPI interfaces include the following:

    Credential-management interfaces

    Context-management interfaces

    Message-support interfaces

    Package-management interfaces

Lesson 5 Quiz

These questions test your knowledge of features, vocabulary, procedures, and syntax.

1. Which of the following are Kerberos plaintext ticket fields?

    A. Realm

    B. Transited

    C. Starttime

    D. Endtime

2. Which of the following are related to the key distribution center authentication process?

    A. AS

    B. TGT

    C. DNS

    D. TGS

3. What are the three Kerberos sub protocols?

    A. Microsoft Exchange

    B. Authentication Service (AS) Exchange

    C. Ticket-Granting Service (TGS) Exchange

    D. Client/Server (CS) Exchange

4. In the Authentication Server information exchange process, identify some functions of the KDC.

    A. KDC creates a logon session key

    B. KDC encrypts the TGT with its own long-term key

    C. KDC embeds another copy of the logon session key in a TGT

    D. KDC sends both the encrypted logon session key and the TGT back

5. Kerberos Protocol Authentication depends on which of the following?

    A. User 1 knows a secret, User 2 does not

    B. User 2 knows a secret, User 1 does not

    C. Neither User 1 nor User 2 knows a secret, they depend upon third parties for security

    D. User 1 and User 2 share a secret between them

6. In the logon process which of the following steps is incorrect?

   A. The LSA sends a KRB_AS_REQ to the KDC in "Widget"

   B. If the client's pre-authentication data is correct, the KDC replies with a KRB_AS_REP

   C. The LSA sends a KRB_TGS_REQ to the KDC in "Widget"

   D. The KDC replies with a KRB_TGS_REP

7. Kerberos Domain Policy settings include

   A. Maximum lifetime for service ticket

   B. Enforce user logon restrictions

   C. Maximum lifetime for server ticket renewal

   D. Minimum tolerance for computer clock dysfunction

8. How may SSPI be accessed?

   A. Traditional socket-based applications can call SSPI routines

   B. Applications can use DCOM to call security options to be implemented

   C. WinSock 2.0 extends the Windows Sockets interface to allow transport providers to expose security features

   D. WinInet security support uses the SSPI interface to access the Secure Channel security provider.

9. What are the methods available to Credential-management interfaces for SSPI?

   A. AcquireCredentialsHandle

   B. FreeCredentialsHandle

   C. QueryCredentialAttributes

   D. AcceptSecurityContext

10. The following concepts are basic to the premise of Kerberos.

    A. Issued tickets

    B. Encrypted data

    C. Encrypted password

    D. Secret key

Answers to Lesson 5 Quiz

1. Answer A is correct. Of the four choices, only the name of the realm is transmitted in plaintext.

    Answers B, C, and D are incorrect. Transited, Starttime and Endtime are all encrypted ticket fields.

2. Answers B and D are correct. Ticket-Granting Tickets and Ticket-Granting Services are part of the KDC authentication process.

    Answers A and C are incorrect. Authentication Service and Domain Name Service are not directly related to the KDC.

3. Answers B, C, and D are correct. Authentication Service (AS) Exchange, Ticket-Granting Service (TGS) Exchange and Client/Server (CS) Exchange are sub-protocols.

    Answer A is incorrect. Microsoft Exchange is not concerned with these sub-protocols.

4. Answers A, B, C, and D are all correct. In the Authentication Server information exchange process, functions of the KDC include the following:

    KDC creates a logon session key

    KDC encrypts the TGT with its own long-term key

    KDC embeds another copy of the logon session key in a TGT

    KDC sends both the encrypted logon session key and the TGT back

5. Answer D is correct. The Kerberos protocol authentication depends on User 1 and User 2 sharing a secret between them.

    Answers A, B and C are incorrect. They are the wrong combinations.

6. Steps A, B, C and D are all correct. None of them are wrong.

    The LSA sends a KRB_AS_REQ to the KDC in "Widget".

    If the client's pre-authentication data is correct, the KDC replies with a KRB_AS_REP.

    The LSA sends a KRB_TGS_REQ to the KDC in "Widget"

    The KDC replies with a KRB_TGS_REP.

7. Answers A and B are correct. Both "Maximum lifetime for service ticket" and "Enforce user logon restrictions" are Kerberos settings.

    Answers C and D are incorrect. "Maximum lifetime for user ticket renewal" and "Maximum tolerance for computer clock synchronization" are the correct titles for those policies.

8. Answers A, B, C and D are all correct. Additionally, scripting languages such as VBScript and JScript allow application developers access to the SSPIs APIs.

9. Answers A, B, and C are correct. AcquireCredentialsHandle,

    FreeCredentialsHandle, and QueryCredentialAttributes are all SSPI Credential-management interfaces.

    Answer D is incorrect. AcceptSecurityContext is a Credential-management interfaces agent.

10. All answers are correct. All of these are basic concepts of Kerberos:

    Issued tickets

    Encrypted data

    Encrypted password

    Secret key

Public Key Infrastructure (PKI)

Microsoft Windows 2000 has combined services and administration tools called Public Key Infrastructure (PKI) to provide users with a consistent interface for more effective management of environments and applications with public key cryptography.

A decryption key is used to convert ciphertext (encrypted data) to plaintext using cryptographic algorithms. These same algorithms produce the encrypted data initially. If identical keys are used for encryption and decryption, it is referred to as symmetric key cryptography. Secret keys provide an added level of security because they are shared in a secure environment under symmetric key cryptography and shared before encrypted data exchange occurs.

The encryption and decryption keys are different and allow encryption in one direction only, such as plaintext to ciphertext conversion, in public key cryptography. To reverse the data back to plaintext, a different decryption key is required. Every user has a public and private key. It makes sense to distribute the public key to people with whom you want to share confidential information. Only when they use your public key with their private key are they able to interpret your data. In return, recipients use their private key to verify the origin of ciphertext as in the case of digital signatures.

The rules and regulations that make up PKI are necessary to regulate and manipulate certificates as well as public and private keys. The process of authenticating and validating individual parties engaged in electronic transactions requires that digital certificates, certification and other registration authorities be adhered to. PKI standards are an essential component for maintaining security in e-commerce. They will continue to evolve as the Internet becomes more interactive.

After completing this lesson, you should have a better understanding of the following topics:

- Public Key Cryptography

- Internet Security With PKI

- PKI Algorithm and Logons

Public Key Cryptography

Two different keys are used for Public Key Cryptography, often referred to as asymmetric cryptography: a public key to encrypt data, and a private key to decrypt data.

Understanding Digital Signatures

Security in a virtual environment like the Internet is challenging because users are communicating over a network and rarely meet face-to-face. They should rely heavily on user authentication techniques like digital signatures to verify the identity of others. Authentication is vital to safeguarding communications between users and protects them from unethical practices, interception of confidential information, and impersonation of identity.

Digital certificates verify identity. However, the absence of physical contact between parties who are communicating remains to be a challenge. Without visual contact, we should rely heavily on credentials like cryptographic certificates to confirm identification. Advanced cryptographic techniques make certificates difficult to modify and, therefore, deter users from engaging in unethical behavior like counterfeiting.

Both a private and public key is included in cryptographic certificates. Public keys are found on the sender's certificate. The data is verified through digital signatures between keys. For example, by signing your e-mail with your private key, the recipient would require your public key for authentication. Signatures produced with the private key are verified with a signature with a public key. By keeping the private key secret, the sender is able to let the recipient of his message know that his identity is valid.

The following are a few uses for authentication-providing certificates:

- User authentication to a secure Web site using the Transport Security Layer (TLS) or the Secure Sockets Layer (SSL) Protocol

- Server authentication to a user using Transport Layer Security (TLS)

- Logging on to a Windows 2000 domain

An algorithm combines the private key with the data to be signed, in order to form the basis of the digital signature.

The following are a few features and benefits of digital signatures:

- Only the owner of the private key could have created the digital signature

- Private keys verify ownership and origin of digital signatures

- Anyone with access to the corresponding public key may verify the signature

- Any modification of the signed data invalidates the signature

For example, when you receive a signed e-mail message from a friend that includes the signature and message text with everything you require to verify where the message originated and that the content has not been modified. Authentication is complete.

Authenticating Entity

Entity authentication is the receiver's guarantee that the data sender is the entity that the receiver thinks it is. For example, you send a challenge encrypted with your public key after receiving data from a friend. Your friend returns it to you after decoding the challenge, proving your friend has access to the private key that you associated the public key to initially in order to make the challenge.

In reverse, B receives a plaintext challenge from A and merges it with other digitally signed information. B's public key is used by A to verify the signature if B has the correct private key (Figure 6.1). This is called Proof-of-Possession Protocol Exchange. Users have to prove they have the proper key, which makes for a unique challenge, thereby preventing attacks by unauthorized third parties.

Figure 6.1 Authenticating Entity

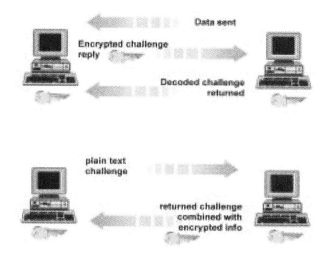

Comparing Public Key With Private or Secret Key Security

Every user has a public and private key, which make up a cryptographic key pair. Public keys use public key algorithms to confirm digital signatures, or encrypt a session key or data, which are converted with the matching private key. Private keys are the secret cryptographic of the pair used with public key algorithms to decrypt digitally signed data, symmetric session key or data that has been encrypted with the matching public key.

Secret Key Agreement With Public Key Cryptography

Public Key Cryptography allows two users to secure communications through non-secure public communication networks. Each user selects a random number that is half of the shared secret key. A sends the encrypted half to B with the public key. A decrypts the message received from B who decrypts the message received from A, extracting the secret half from the other and combine the two half to create the shared secret. A and B can use the shared secret to secure other communications (Figure 6.2) after the above initial process is complete.

Figure 6.2 Secret Key Agreement With Public Cryptography

 Tip: Nothing is 100% secure. Therefore do not assume that because a shared secret is secure that it will remain so forever. In a hostile environment, a 56-bit shared secret key may be secure for only a few hours. Only when two parties share the secret are shared secret keys secure.

Encrypting Mass Data Without Secrets

You can encrypt large volumes of data through public key cryptography without first establishing shared secrets. To create a random session key for encryption, select a key encryption algorithm. If User 1 is first to send the message then the session key is encrypted with user 2's public key. The ciphertext key that results is sent to User 2 with the encrypted data. User 2 recovers the session with the private key to decrypt the data (Figure 6.3).

Figure 6.3 Encrypting Mass Data Without Secrets

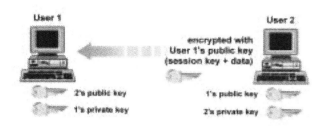

Guarding and Confidence in Cryptographic Keys

When users share a secret key cryptography they trust the secure manner by which it was created. It is wise to mutually agree to store the keys in safety to prevent unauthorized use. With public key cryptography, only the private key needs protection. They need only share their public keys.

Public keys are obtained through a non-secure public source. Users should not be concerned if public keys are shared in a secure manner, except where they are uncertain whether the other user really does have the corresponding public key. Certificates issued by a Certificate Authority (CA) are used for further identification.

Recovering Keys

All certificates eventually expire. A Certificates snap-in issues new certificates before and after expiration with the **Certificate Renewal Wizard** from Windows 2000 enterprise CA. You may renew a certificate with a new key set or use the same key set you initially used. You need to know about issuing certification authorities before renewal.

The Issuing Certification Authority (CA)

A Cryptographic Service Provider (CSP) is authorized to create new public and private key pairs for the certificate. You may renew certificates through Windows 2000 enterprise Certification Authorities and through Windows 2000 stand-alone with this service. You may renew certificates through Internet sites by pasting the PKCS No. 7 file, or renew with a new key and new certificate with the same key.

Establishing confidence in the relationship between the public key and the owner of private key is achieved with certificates. These digitally signed statements deal with a specific subject public key. The issuer, holding another pair of private and public keys, signs the certificate, which also contains other information related to the subject public key. Identification information for the recipient with permission to the corresponding key is included. The person who issues the certificate confirms the validity of the connection between the subject public key and the subject identity information.

The most common form of certificates is currently the Windows 2000 PKI that uses certificates based on the ITU-T X.509. This is not the only form of certificate. For example, Pretty Good Privacy (PGP), which secures e-mail, relies on a form of certificate unique to PGP.

Tip: You may reference the following Internet site for information about the Internet X. 509 Public Key standard in RFC2459 at located at http://www.ieff.org/rtc/rfcZ459.bft and the PGP homepage are at http://www.pgpi.org.

Certificates Authorities (CAs)

A service that issues certificates and acts as a guarantor of the correspondence (binding) between the subject public key and the subject identity information in the certificates issued by the CA is referred to as a Certificate Authority (CA). Other CAs may decide to verify the binding through alternate means. It is critical to understand the authority's policies and procedures prior to selecting that authority to vow for public keys. Microsoft Exchange Server and Windows 2000 Server may act as a CA. Additional authorities include commercial certificate authorities like VeriSign at http://www.verisign.com.

Validation and Trust

Users should decide to trust whether or not signatures are valid just by the signed messages they receive. They may confirm that signatures are mathematically valid by using corresponding known public keys. In other words, they should determine whether the public key used to verify the signature belongs to the person who claims to have created the signature in the first place. It is up to users to prove this to one another in order to bring confidence to recipients of their message.

If users may locate a certificate for the sender's public key that was issued by a trusted CA, then the recipient may trust that the public key really belongs to the sender. Users are more likely to trust that this is the case if the certificate has the following characteristics:

• A valid cryptographic signature has been provided by the sender

• The bond between the user and their public key are confirmed

• A trustworthy source issued the certificate

If the user finds such a certificate for the other users, public key authenticity may be confirmed by with the public key from the CA. How may the user be certain that the public key really belongs to the CA? The user needs to find a certificate that verifies the identity of the CA and the binding between the certificate authority and the CA public key.

Ideally the user would create a certificate chain leading from the other user and the other user's public key with a series of CAs that result in a certificate being issued to someone the sender trusts. It forms the root of a hierarchy of public keys and identity characteristics that the user may accept as being authentic. This certificate is referred to as a trusted root certificate. When you trust a particular trusted root certificate, you are trusting all certificates issued by that trusted root, in addition to all certificates issued by any subsidiary CA that is certified by the trusted root. The only information that you should acquire in a secure manner is the set of trusted root certificates. This certificate set verifies the users belief and trust in the PKI.

The PKI works with existing Windows domain trust-and-authorization mechanisms based on the Domain Controller (DC) and Kerberos Key Distribution CType (KDC), providing improved features that allow applications to address Internet and Extranet requirements. PKI addresses the requirement for authentication, integrity and distributed scalable identification and confidentiality.

Servers and workstations with Windows NT Version 4 and Windows 2000, and workstations running Windows 95 and 98 provide support for creating, deploying, and managing public key applications. Microsoft CryptoAPI provides a standard interface to cryptographic functionality from

Cryptographic Service Providers (CSPs) who may take advantage of cryptographic hardware devices or are software-based. CSPs shipping with Windows 2000 take advantage of the Microsoft Personal Computer Smart Card (PCSC), which is another term for compliant Smart Card infrastructure.

A set of certificate management services that support X.509 Version 3 standard certificates is provided with CryptoAPI. They provide constant storage, recording services and decoding support. Services for dealing with industry-standard message formats that support Internet Engineering Task Force (IETF) PKI X.509 (Public Key IX) and Public Key Cryptography Standards (Public Key CS), two evolving standards.

For additional functionality of application development, other services take advantage of CryptoAPI. Industry-standard Transport Layer Security (TLS) and Secure Sockets Layer (SSL) protocols are supported by Secure Channel, which supports network authentication and encryption. Obtained with Microsoft WinInet interface, these protocols are used with HTTP protocol (HTTPS) and other protocols of the Security Support Provider Interface (SSPI). Object signing and verification are supported through Authenticode that determines the origin and integrity of components downloaded over the Internet. Standard Smart Card interfaces are the foundation for Smart Card logon support.

Encrypting File System (EFS)

Transparent encryption and decryption of files stored on a disk is supported by EFS using the NTFS file system. Individual files and folders may be encrypted. Applications may not decrypt other user's encrypted files, but applications do have access to a user's encrypted files the same way they do with unencrypted files.

EFS supports bulk encryption without prior shared secrets with PKI. Each EFS user obtains an EFS certificate from an enterprise certificate authority and creates a public key pair. Where data sharing is not an issue, EFS creates a self-signed certificate for stand-alone operations. Where trusted recovery agents create an EFS recovery public key pair, Windows 2000 supports EFS recovery policy as well as EFS recovery certificates issued by the enterprise CA. Certificates of the EFS recovery agents are published to domain clients with Group Policy Object (GPO).

A random key is created for each file by EFS. The EFS public key encrypt this key and links it to the file. A copy of the secret key associates with the file, each encrypted with the recovery agent's EFS public key. No plaintext copy of the secret key is stored in the system.

EFS accesses the user's private key to unwrap the copy of the secret key encrypted with the user's public key when retrieving the file. During file read and write operations, the file is decrypted in real-time. A recovery agent may decrypt the file by accessing the secret key with the private key.

Smart Card Logon Protocol

As an alternative to passwords for domain authentication, Windows 2000 supports public key-based Smart Card logon. This relies on the RSA-capable Smart Cards for supporting CryptoAPI CSPs and PC/SC workgroup-compliant Smart Card infrastructure. To integrate public key-based authentication with Windows 2000 Kerberos access-control system, the authentication process applies the public key cryptography for initial authentication in the Kerberos protocol.

A Smart Card insertion is a substitute for the standard Ctrl+Alt+Delete attention sequence that initiates logon. Users are prompted for the Smart Card Personal Identification Number (PIN) code that controls access to operations with the private key that has been stored on the Smart Card. The Smart Card contains a copy of the user's certificate that is issued by an enterprise CA and, therefore, allows the user to roam within the domain.

IP Security (IPSec)

At the IP protocol layer, IPSec defines protocols for network encryption. It does not require public key-based technology. It uses shared secret keys that are securely exchanged through out-of-band mechanism points for encryption at the network end. Public key-based technology creates a scalable distributed-trust architecture whereby IPSec devices endorse each other and match encryption keys without reliance on preset secrets shared between users.

Microsoft and the IPSec community are actively working on developing standards for interoperable certificates and certificate enrollment and management protocols. Work is still required to ensure broad interoperability across IPSec devices and PKI implementations.

Enabling A Domain

A complete set of core services that support the development of interoperable public key-based applications is provided by Windows 2000. The most significant new features are policy models and integration with domain administration. Public key technology depends on the ability to develop and manage keys for public key algorithms. CryptoAPI supports key creation and management for a host of cryptographic algorithms and installable CSPs.

When a domain client enables for public key security, it obtains a security certificate from Exchange Key Manager, Windows 2000 Certificate Server, or a commercial provider like VeriSign. This is usually included in setup during the e-mail service configuration.

To set up the request for a user certificate, follow these steps:

1. From the browser, connect to **http://ServerName/CertSRV** where ServerName is the name of the certificate authority server (Figure 6.4).

Figure 6.4 CertSRV

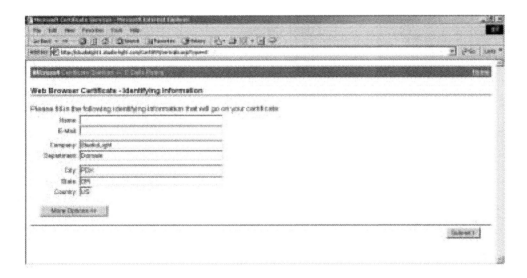

2. From the Microsoft Certificate Services welcome page, choose **Request a certificate**, and then select **Next**.

3. Choose **User** certificate request and **User Certificate** in the list box, and then select **Next** (Figure 6.5).

Figure 6.5 User Certificate Identifying Information

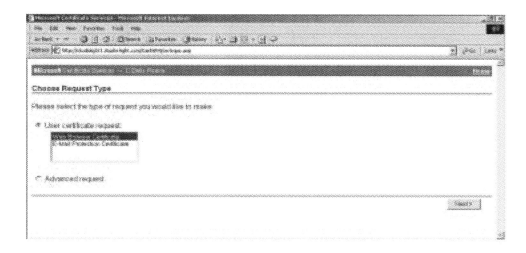

4. A **User Certificate Identifying Information** page displays where connecting to a stand-alone certificate authority. Fill in the online form and select **Next**. If you are connecting to an enterprise CA, the information retrieves from Active Directory and you are prompted to submit your request.

5. Choose **Submit**. The program creates a public/private key pair and a certificate request with the information you provided, and then sends the request to the CA for processing. Select **Install** (Figure 6.6).

Figure 6.6 Installing the Certificate

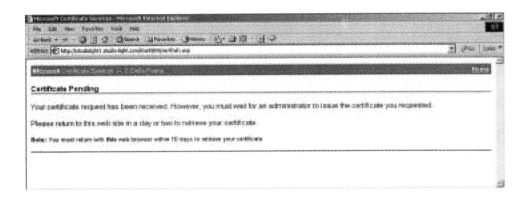

 Note: This procedure assumes that a root certificate is obtained and a CA is set up. It also assumes that the CA is set up to approve the request instantly.

Key material-storing mechanisms depend on the selected CSP. The Microsoft-provided software CSPs (or base CSPs) store key material in an encrypted form on a per-computer or per-user basis. They also support control over public key-pair usage control and exportability. The latter controls private key export from the CSP and the former determines user-notification traits when an application attempts to use the private key. Other CSPs often implement different mechanisms like Smart Card CSPs, which are used to store the public key pair in tamper-proof Smart Card hardware and generally require PIN code entry to access functions involving the private key.

Recalling Keys

Recalling keys suggests constant storage of an entity's private key thus allowing access by authorized individuals without the owning entity's knowledge or consent. This may be required to meet law-enforcement requirements or ensure access to critical business communication. Key-recovery facilities are useful only when applied to keys used in the encryption of constant data, like an entity's key-exchange keys. Archiving the identity of digital-signature private keys is rare because it creates a security risk. Recovery of private keys could enable malignant third parties to impersonate the private key owner information.

To read encrypted e-mail, Microsoft Exchange provides support for the recovery of key exchange. Some third-party CSPs provide general support for key recovery. If you lose your private key, follow these steps:

1.   Request a new security certificate, as described in the previous procedure.

2.   Ask a Recovery Agent to recover your encrypted documents.

Certificate Enrollment

Public key-based technology typically depends on certificates to link public keys to known entities. Windows 2000 PKI supports certificate enrollment to third-party CAs or the Microsoft enterprise CA. Enrollment support is based on public key CS Number 7 responses. The responses consist of two components: the resulting certificate or certificate chain, and the usage of the industry-standard public key CS Number 10 certificate-request messages. Certificates that support Digital Signature Algorithm (DSA) keys and signatures, and Diffie-Hellman keys, and RSA keys and signatures are supported.

A Microsoft-supplied enrollment control mechanism, XENROLL.DLL, can be scripted for Internet-based enrollment or programmatically called to support other transport protocols like Remote Procedure Call (RPC), Distributed Component Object Model (DCOM), and e-mail. XENTROLL.DLL is the support for public key CS Number 10 and public key CS Number 7 messages. This control allows generation of a new key pair, existing key pair and the calling application that specifies the characteristics of the public key CS Number 10 message. Enrollment control is a method for creating an internal association between the certificate, the CSP that created the key pair, the key-pair container name, and the state management to match issued certificates against pending requests. PKI supports multiple enrollment methods including an Enrollment Wizard, Internet-based enrollment, and policy-driven auto-enrollment that occur as part of the logon procedure.

Renewing Certificates

Renewing a certificate, though similar to enrollment, uses the trust relationship in an existing certificate. Renewal assumes that the requestor wants to receive a new certificate with similar attributes as an existing certificate, with, however, extended validity dates. Renewals may use the existing key or require that a new public key be created. Renewal requests process faster than initial requests because it is not necessary to re-verify the existing certificate attributes. Renewal for automatically enrolled certificates is supported in Windows 2000 PKI. For other mechanisms, a renewal is treated as a new enrollment request. The procedure for renewing security certificates and requesting certificates is the same.

Working With Keys and Certificates

The CryptoAPI subsystem manages and stores cryptographic keys and associated certificates. CSPs manage keys. CryptoAPI certificate stores manage certificates. Certificate stores are repositories for certificates and linked properties. The PKI defines these five standard stores:

MY—Holds a computer's certificates or user for which the associated private key is available.

Certificate Authority (CA)—Contains intermediate or issuing certificate authority certificates for use in building certificate-verification chains.

TRUST—Contains Certificate Trust Lists (CTLs) that allow administrators to specify a collection of trusted CAs. They may be transmitted over non-secure links, since they are digitally signed.

ROOT—Contains self-signed certificate authority certificates from trusted root CAs.

UserDS—Gives a logical view of certificate repositories stored in Active Directory as in the user Certificate property of the User object to streamline access to external repositories.

Logical stores present a continual system-wide view of certificates residing on multiple physical media, which allows applications to share certificates and ensure consistent operation for administrative policy. Certificate management functions provide functions to assist in locating specific certificates and supports decoding of X.509 Version 3 certificates.

For simpler application development, the MY store maintains certificate properties that indicate the associated private key's CSP and key-set name. After an application selects a certificate to use, it uses the MY store information to obtain a CSP context for the correct private key.

Recovering Certificates and Public Key Pairs

When certificates and public key pairs are lost because of system failure, replacement may be costly and time-consuming. Windows 2000 PKI enables you to back up and restore both associated key pairs and certificates through certificate management administrative tools.

Specify whether you also want the associated key pair exported when exporting a certificate with Certificate Manager. The information exports as a public key CS Number 12 message that encrypts with a password if you select this option. This message may be imported to another system and used to restore the certificate and keys. To export a certificate and the associated key, follow these steps:

1. From the Certificates MMC snap-in, expand **Certificates**, and then select the certificate you wish to export.

2. Right-click the certificate, choose **All Tasks,** and then select **Export**. The Certificate Export Wizard begins (Figure 6.7).

Figure 6.7 Export Wizard for Certificates

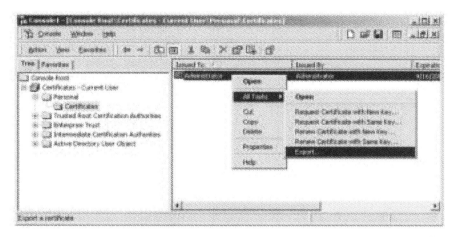

3. Stipulate that the private key is to be exported, then select an export file format and provide a password.

4. Provide the destination file, select **Next, Finish,** and then **OK** (Figure 6.8).

Figure 6.8 Destinations for Certificates

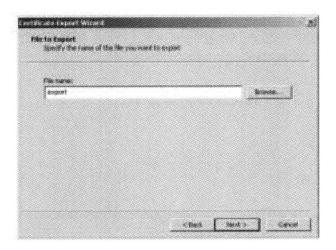

This operation presumes that the key pair is exportable by the CSP. This is true for Microsoft-based CSPs if the CRYPT_EXPORTABLE flag was set at key generation. Since third-party CSPs may or may not support private key export, Smart Card CSPs generally do not support it. Software CSPs with non-exportable keys maintain a complete system-image backup complete with Registry information.

Tip: A key pair is exposed to third-party intervention if it is exportable. There is ongoing discussion concerning the security of exportable keys with Microsoft IE or Outlook Express. A typical discussion document may currently be found at the following site:

http://www.drh-consultancy.demon.co.uk/cexport.html

If the above URL is not available, you might try searching for Crypt-Exportable, Crypt User_Protected, CryptGenKey or CryptimportKey.

Roaming is the process of using the same public key-based applications in the Windows environment on different computers. Windows 2000 PKI supports roaming with the methods following:

Microsoft CSPs—A roaming-profile mechanism supports certificates and roaming keys. When roaming profiles are enabled, this process is transparent to the user.

Hardware token devices like Smart Cards—Roaming is supported with certificate stores. Smart Card CSPs also support roaming.

Integrity of a Certificate

The level of trust associated with certificate verification depends on the trust associated with the CA that initially issues the certificate. The PKI assumes a rooted certificate authority hierarchy whereby control of trust derives from decisions concerning root certificate authority. If the intended certificate usage is consistent with the application context, and a specified end-entity certificate links to a known trusted root certificate authority, the certificate is deemed valid. If neither of these conditions exists, the certificate becomes invalid.

You may make only those trust decisions that relate to your needs within the PKI. You may accomplish this by configuring associated usage restrictions with certificate management administrative tools and installing or deleting trusted root certificate authority. Only experienced users should attempt certificate management. Trust relationships should be established as part of the enterprise policy. They are instantly transmitted to Windows 2000 client computers when established by policy.

Working with Public Key Components and Capabilities

No longer does the presence of users on a network serve as identity verification. Computer networks have advanced to an open architecture, which is more functional, although more challenging for network administrators to control. Today an organization's network could consist of intranets, Internet sites and extranets. All are potentially susceptible to unauthorized access by intruders bent on stealing or falsifying a company's confidential digital data.

Unauthorized access to information on networks is a grave problem. Individuals monitor and alter information streams like e-mail, file transfers, and e-commerce transactions. Employees must have access to certain information resources. However, as users gather a multitude of passwords to remember to access different secure systems, they have tendencies to select less complex or more common passwords for easier recall. This provides hackers with easier passwords to crack and therefore easier access to otherwise secure systems and the data within.

How can system administrators be certain people's identity who want access to information? How can they control which information they access? How does a system administrator securely and easily distribute and manage identification credentials across an enterprise? A well-planned PKI addresses these issues.

A PKI is a system of CAs, digital certificates, and other registration rules that verify and authenticate the identify of each party involved in transactions through the use of public key cryptography. Standards for PKI are still evolving even as they are becoming widely implemented as a necessary element of e-commerce.

Deploying a PKI with Windows 2000 is attractive for the following reasons:

Stronger security—To maintain confidentiality and the integrity of transmitted data on public networks, use Internet Protocol security and the confidentially of stored data with Encrypting File System (EFS). Smart Cards provide strong authentication. Administrator uses security permissions in Windows 2000 to determine what certificates to issue users.

Simplify administration—Organizations distribute certificates instead of passwords. Certificates may be revoked as necessary. You may publish Certificate Revocation Lists (CRLs) and initiate managing trust relationships across enterprises. The integration of Group Policy, Certificate Services, and Active Directory is also very powerful. The ability to map certificates to user accounts in Active Directory and through Internet Information Services is also part of Windows 2000.

New opportunities—Files and secure data may be exchanged over public networks like the Internet. Users may implement secure e-mail with secure Internet connection, Secure Sockets Layer (SSL), Secure Multipurpose Internet Mail Extensions (S/MIME), or Transport Layer Security (TLS). As an important element of e-commerce, users may establish non-repudiation through the use of digital signatures.

Understanding Public Key Applications

Windows 2000 PKI includes the following features:

Certificates—A digital statement issued by an authority that vouches for the identity of the certificate holder is known as a certificate. A certificate ties a public key to the identity of the person, service or computer that holds the matching private key. Certificates are used by various public key security services and applications that provide authentication, data integrity and secure communications across networks like the Internet. Windows 2000 certificate-based processes use the standard certificate format of X.509 v3. An X.509 certificate includes information about the certification authority issuing the certificate, about the certificate itself, and about the person or entity (the subject) to which it is issued. Subject information may include the name, public key, public-key algorithm, and a unique subject ID. Standard extensions for v3 certificates allow for supplementary information related to key identifiers, key usage, certificate policy, alternate names and attributes, certification path constraints, and enhancements for certificate revocation including revocation reasons and CRL partitioning by CA renewal. Certificates MMC console enables you to manage certificates.

Certificate Services on Windows 2000 Server—Use this component to create and manage CAs. CAs are responsible for verifying the identity of certificate holders and establishing them. CAs also revoke certificates if they are not valid, and produces certificate revocation lists for use by certificate verifiers. Simple PKI designs have only one root certificate authority. The majority of organizations deploying a PKI use various certificate verifiers in trusted groups known as certification hierarchies. CA Internet enrollment pages are a separate part of Certificate Services. Internet pages are installed by default when a CA is set up. They allow users to submit certificate requests using Internet browsers. You may also install CA Internet pages on Windows 2000 servers without the CA being installed. Internet pages are used to direct certificate requests to CAs that administrators do not want requesters to access directly. To create custom Internet pages for organizations to access a CA, use the sample Internet pages in Windows. Using the CA MMC console, users may manage Certificate Services.

Smart Card Support—Supports logon through Smart Cards in Windows 2000 and the use of Smart Cards to store certificates for secure e-mail Internet authentication and other public key cryptography-related activities.

Public Key Policies—Use Group Policy to distribute certificates to computers automatically establishing common trusted certification authorities, certificate trusts lists, and managing recovery policies for the Encrypting File System.

Applying Windows 2000 Public Key—Security policies may be applied to Internet sites, OUs, and domains. They affect security of groups of users and computers. PKI security provides a mechanism that defines and manages policy centrally while enforcing it globally.

Trust in root certification authorities is set by policy to create trust in verifying public key certificates. Trusted CAs are configured by Group Policy Editor. They may be configured on a per-computer basis that applies globally to computer users.

To configure a domain to trust an external CA, follow these steps:

1. Select the **Domain Group Policy Properties** box, then edit the Default Domain Policy GPO (Figure 6.9).

Figure 6.9 Domain Policy Group Policy

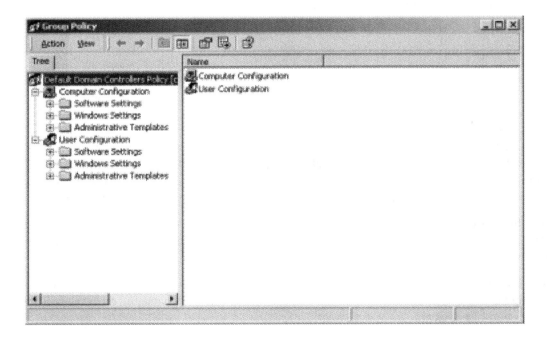

2. Choose **Computer Configuration, Windows Settings, Security Settings,** and then select **Public Key Policy,** then right-click **Trusted Root Certification Authorities** (Figure 6.10).

Figure 6.10 Public Key Policy

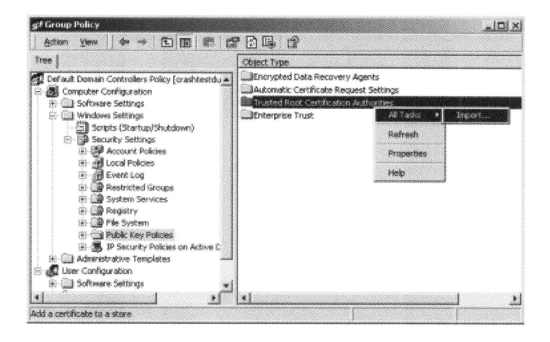

3.   From the context menu, choose **All Tasks**, and then Select **Import**. The Certificate Import Wizard starts.

4.   Select **Next**. In the File name box, either type the name of the file that contains the root certificate you want to import, or use the Browse button to browse to the file. Select **Next** (Figure 6.11).

Figure 6.11 Import File

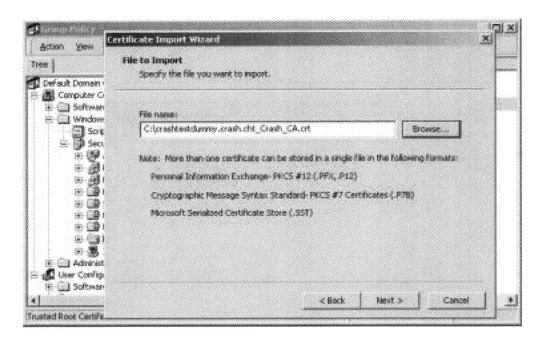

5. Type the password, and choose **Next**. Choose "**Place all certificates in the following store.**" The destination is the Trusted Root Certification Authorities store in the GPO. Select **Next**.

6. Choose **Finish** to import the certificate, **OK** to close the message box, and **OK** to apply the policy to the **GPO**, and then close the MMC (Figure 6.12).

Figure 6.12 Import Certificate

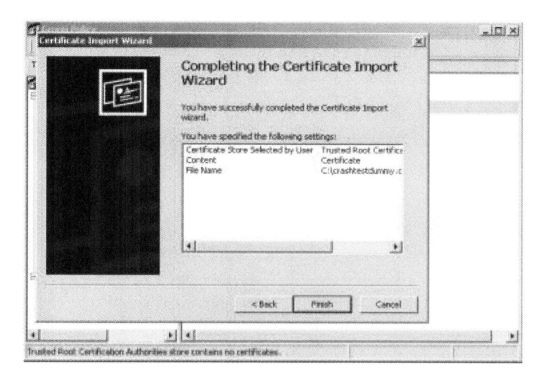

 Note: You can use the same procedure for lower-level GPOs associated with OUs that contain groups of users or computers

Set properties associated with the certificate authority that restrict the purposes for which certificate authority-issued certificates are valid, in addition to establishing a root certificate authority as trusted. These provide a means of restricting use to any combination of the following:

• Server authentication

- Client authentication
- Code signing
- E-mail
- IPSec end system
- IPSec tunnel
- IPSec user
- Time-stamping
- Microsoft Encrypted File System

Certificate types provide a certificate template and associate it with a common name. This template defines elements like naming rules, validity period, allowable CSPs for private key generation, algorithms, and extensions that are embedded in the certificate. Certificate types are logically categorized into computer and user types, and are applied to the policy objects accordingly.

CA services that issue policies are integrated with certificate types. CA services receive, as part of their policy objects, a set of certificate types. These are used by the enterprise policy module to define the types of certificates that the CA is allowed to issue. The CA rejects certificate requests that fail to match these criteria.

Smart Card Logon

Logging on with Smart Cards is easy and straightforward. To log on to a PC with Smart Card logon enabled, follow these steps:

1.   When the sign-on screen reads, Insert card and press Ctrl-Alt-Delete to begin, insert your card in the Smart Card reader.

2.   In the **Log on to Windows** dialog box, type your PIN.

You are now logged on. To lock your workstation without logging off, press Ctrl-Alt-Delete and select **Lock Workstation**. To unlock it with a Smart Card, simply insert your card and type your PIN.

Just like password logons, Smart Card logons can be controlled by policy. Policies are set to enable either Smart Card or password logon, or may be set to enforce Smart Card logon only. While protection against unauthorized access is much better with Smart Cards, you cannot log on if you forget your Smart Card or attempt to use a computer without a Smart Card reader.

To enable the PKI logon feature of Windows 2000, install a Smart Card reader and enable the card to store certificates.

Internet Security With PKI

The Internet has quickly become an important element for creating and deploying solutions for secure, effective information exchanges on a global basis, especially for business. This situation raises the following security issues:

Server authentication—Users need to verify that servers they connect to are what they claim to be.

Client authentication—Servers need to verify a would-be client's identity and control access accordingly.

Confidentiality—Data encryption between server and client foils the interception of information sent over the wire.

The Secure Sockets Layer (SSL) and the Transport Layer Security (TLS) protocols play important roles. SSL and TLS are flexible security protocols that may layer on top of other transport protocols. They depend on public key-based authentication technology that uses public key-based negotiations for creating unique encryption keys for each client server session. They are most commonly associated with Internet-based applications and HTTP protocol (referred to as HTTPS). To set up an SSL enabled Internet site, follow these steps:

1. From the Administrative Tools menu, choose Internet Services Manager (Figure 6.13).

Figure 6.13 Internet Services Manager

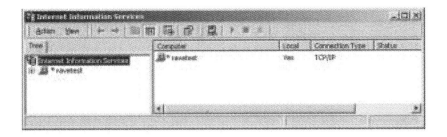

2.   Right-click the **IIS** server name, and if you do not already have a site on which you wish to enable SSL, then select **Add** to add a new site.

3.   Follow the prompts in the Internet Creation Wizard. Do specify a Host Header (Figure 6.14).

Figure 6.14 Internet Creation Wizard

4.   Right-click the new site and select **Properties**.

5.   From the Secure communications section of the **Directory Security** tab, select **Edit**. If this button is inactive (grayed out), select **Server Certificate** and follow the prompts (Figure 6.15).

Figure 6.15 Server Certificate

6.   Select the **Require secure channel (SSL)** box, and specify the encryption and client certificate requirement settings. Select **OK** twice, start the site, and exit from the MMC snap-in (Figure 6.16).

Figure 6.16 Require Secure Channel

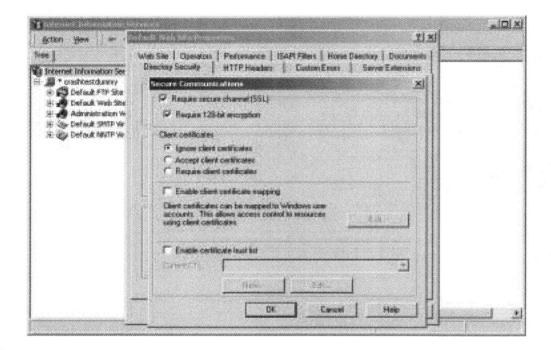

7.   Access the site with **https** rather than **http**.

 Warning: SSL encryption slows site operation and uses a great deal of CPU.

SSL-enabled sites can be used for secure Internet operations, like sending name and credit card numbers.

SSL and TLS are supported by the Secure Channel (SChannel) SSPI provider. For this reason, Microsoft Internet Explorer and Internet information Services both use SChannel. SChannel integrates with Microsoft's SSPI architecture, which makes it available for use with many protocols to support authenticated or encrypted communications.

To benefit fully from SSL and TLS, both client and server must have identification certificates issued by mutually trusted CAs. The certificates allow the parties to authenticate each other. Mutual authentication follows these steps:

1. Each side validates the received certificate.

2. Each side verifies possession of the private key, using the received certificate's public keys.

3. The client uses the server certificate's identifying information to decide whether to conduct business with the server, and the server determines what data the client may access. The server may rely on Active Directory, which can map user certificates on a one-to-one or many-to-one basis against security principals (user objects). Alternatively, SChannel may be set up to automatically synthesize a security token for the client so that the Windows Access Control List (ACL) mechanisms enforce access control to resources. As Windows 2000 public key-infrastructure integrates support for client access decisions, services may use the same access-control mechanism whether the client-authentication mechanism is public key or Kerberos.

4. When the client and server authenticate each other, they negotiate a session key.

5. The client and server begin communicating securely.

SSL and TLS can run in a mode that requires no client authentication. Mutual authentication is recommended in the business environment, however, for the following two reasons:

• Mutual authentication allows the use of Windows-based access-control mechanisms

• PKI simplifies certificate enrollment and management

Implementing and Supporting PKI

PKI infrastructure—the software, policies, laws, and evolving standards that regulate or handle certificates, public keys, and private keys—is being increasingly implemented for the verification and authentication of parties involved in electronic transactions.

Windows 2000 PKI's hierarchical CA model provides scalability, ease of administration, and consistency with CA and commercial products.

Except for the simplest certification hierarchy consisting of a single CA, a hierarchy contains multiple CAs with clearly defined, parent-child relationships. The parent CA certifies that the child subordinate CAs are issued certificates that bind a CA's public key to its identity. A parent CA can also revoke a misbehaving child CA's certificate. The top hierarchical CA is called the root authority or root CA. The child CAs of the root CA are called subordinate CAs.

To trust a root CA in Windows 2000, insert its certificate in your Trusted Root Certification Authorities certificate store. By doing so, you implicitly trust every subordinate CA in the trusted root CA's hierarchy, unless a subordinate CA has an expired or revoked certificate.

Certificate verification requires trust in a small number of root CAs, and the number of certificate-issuing subordinate CAs is flexible.

Reasons to support multiple subordinate CAs include the following:

Usage—Certificates are issued for various purposes, like secure e-mail or network authentication. Since the issuing policy for each use is distinct, it is administratively convenient to have distinct CAs administering distinct policies.

Organizational divisions—Different policies for issuing certificates may arise from an entity's intra-organizational role. You may create subordinate CAs to administer separate departmental policies.

Geographic divisions—Organizations that operate at multiple physical sites may, for inter-site network connectivity purposes, require multiple subordinate CAs, for instance, one for each site.

You can also derive the following administrative benefits from Windows 2000 PKI's CA hierarchy:

Flexible configuration—The hierarchical model enables you to customize your CA security environment, weighing security and usability. For example, your root CA could be surrounded with much greater CA key strength, physical protection, and protection against network attacks, even operating it offline, whereas cost or usability may prevent doing so with subordinate CAs

Frequent update ability—The hierarchical model allows, where key compromise is more likely, more frequent CA key and certificate updates issuance, without having to change established trust relationships.

Turn off ability—The model allows shutting down a portion of the CA hierarchy without affecting the established trust relationships. This may facilitate revoking an issuing CA certificate without affecting other parts of the organization.

Using PKI With E-Mail

Securing e-mail is like inserting a coded letter into a sealed envelope instead of writing plainly on the back of a post card.

To secure your e-mail, follow these steps:

1. Write your message in a public-key-aware messaging application.

2. Obtain the recipient's public key certificate from a trusted security provider.

3. Use your private key with the recipient's public key to digitally sign and encrypt your message.

4. Transmit your message to the recipient over the network (Figure 6.17).

Figure 6.17 Sender's Steps

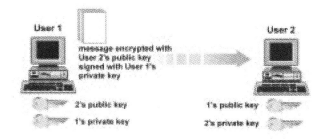

Upon receiving your message, the recipient simply uses his or her own private key to verify and decrypt your message. The recipient's private key compares the data with your public key, to verify that the message really came from you. The recipient's key also analyzes the message received to determine whether it has been tampered with in transit (Figure 6.18).

Figure 6.18 Receiver Verification Steps

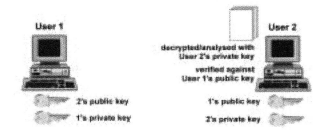

Using Internet Standards With PKI

Secure HTTP (HTTPS) provides an encrypted connection to an authenticated Internet server. When clients try to connect to an URL beginning with **https://** (notice the "s"), the client and server jointly negotiate which security protocol to use, and then exchange authenticating information.

Microsoft Internet Explorer supports the following secure communication protocols for HTTP transactions:

- Transport Layer Security (TLS v1)

- Secure Sockets Layer (SSL Version 2 and Version 3)

- Private Communications Technology (PCT Version 1)

All three protocols provide encryption services to secure the exchanged data, and authentication services for client server mutual identification.

To set up client authentication, follow these steps:

1.   Get a client authentication certificate. Use Microsoft's Certificate Server or VeriSign.

2.   Select the security level.

3.   Visit a URL that uses client authentication.

4. When prompted by the **Client Authentication** dialog box, choose the certificate you want to use, and then select **OK**. To view the contents of individual certificates, select the certificate, and then select **View Certificate** (Figure 6.19).

Figure 6.19 View Certificate

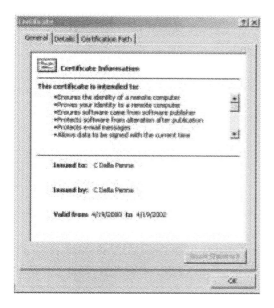

The secure page now displays.

 Note: If you are using a Smart Card for client authentication, a dialog box appears prompting you to insert the card (unless it is already inserted). Insert the card and select **OK**. When prompted for your PIN, type it in and select **OK**.

For additional security for your digital ID, follow these steps:

1.   Check the box for security options.

2.   Select **Accept** on the enrollment form.

3.   On the dialog box, select your security level to protect your private key.

Your private key is the part of your digital ID that is unique to you. Every time you use your digital ID, your private key is accessed. The Medium and High options ensure that no one can access your private key without your permission.

The definitions for the optional security settings are as follows:

High—This setting requires you to type a password to grant access to your private key.

Medium—This setting alerts you and asks for your permission to grant access.

Low—This setting does not add any additional security. Only your system's logon procedure protects your private key.

Achieving Interoperability

The goal of complete interoperability aims at issuing certificates based on a standard certificate-request protocol, which runs without any syntactical or semantic ambiguity, enabling applications to evaluate the certificates in a consistent manner.

The goal has yet to be reached. Digitally signed forms and code signing are still unreliable, and no technical mechanism is able to compare names in two different encodings, because, for example, Unicode encodes accented characters in multiple equivalent forms. On the bright side, SSL/TLS and S/MIME work well with various vendors' products.

Using Internet Standards

Internet standards do not ensure full interoperability yet, but work is in progress. IETF has charged a working group, PUBLIC KEY IX (X.509), with defining the basis for an interoperable PKI. The National Institute of Standards and Technology (NIST) has set up an interoperability workgroup to ensure the workgroup members' implementations of PUBLIC KEY IX Part 1 achieve a minimum interoperability.

Outside the IETF, RSA Laboratories has developed a set of cryptographic message standards (PUBLIC KEY CS). The most relevant to PKI are PUBLIC KEY CS Number 7, *Cryptographic Message Syntax Standard,* and PUBLIC KEY CS Number 10, *Certification Request Syntax Standard.*

Working With PKI-Trusted Domains

The term PKI implies that PKIs themselves may link together. For example, if a division in a company selects Vendor A's PKI model, and the company later selects Vendor B for its mail system, There should be some overlap between the two. It can become more complicated when Company A and Company B choose to join their PKIs into a business-specific extranet. A technical complexity can come from mapping their joined trust relationship and keep track of them over time.

The three following distinct models currently exist for trust relationships:

- Rooted hierarchies (VeriSign, Microsoft, and Netscape)

- Networks (Entrust)

- Internets (PGP)

All three of these trust models do something different in how their trust relationships are created, directly or through an intermediary and in how they are established and maintained. There is no seamless interface between different trust models. Flexibility can be built into the PKI, allowing the users to merge their different trust models in ways that work for their business procedures.

PKI Algorithm and Logons

Table 6.1 describes how the public and private keys in public key cryptography are used.

Table 6.1 Public and Private Keys

Key	Description	Used
Private	Never made known to anyone else	Decryption
Public	Known global	Encryption

In computer security, encryption is takes a plaintext file and processes it so the original data is converted into a new format: ciphertext. The key, is an encryption process that uses an algorithm and a secret value to change the file.

Public key cryptography also is known as asymmetric cryptography. This means different users use different keys to encrypt and decrypt a file. These public key-based algorithms have a very high level of security, however the processing in using them is slow.

Symmetric cryptography uses a single secret key. Data Encryption Standard (DES) is one popular method of symmetric cryptography. DES was defined in 1977 by the National Bureau of Standards for commercial and non-classified use. A team of IBM engineers developed it. They used their Lucifer cipher and input from the National Security Agency. The final result was the DES encryption algorithm with a 56-bit binary number key.

Secret key algorithms are quick. As the DES algorithm key both encrypts and decrypts data, the security design is vulnerable. However, symmetric algorithms are practical for large amounts of data, and they increase security.

Working With PKI Pairs

When a request is generated for a new certificate, information is passed from the requestor to the Microsoft Cryptographic Application Program Interface, (CryptoAPI). CryptoAPI then passes the correct data to the Cryptographic Service Provider (CSP). If the CSP is software-based, it creates a public key and a private key—referred to as a key pair. If the CSP is hardware based, like a Smart Card, CSP tells the hardware to create the key pair.

After the keys are created, a software CSP then encrypts and secures the private key in the Windows 2000 registry. A Smart Card CSP will store the private key on a Smart Card that manages the access to the key. With the certificate requester information, the public key is transmitted to the certification authority. When the CA confirms the certificate request, it will use its own private key in creating a digital signature in the certificate and then issues the certificate to the requester. The requester then has a certificate from the CA and is able to install it in the certificate store (Figure 6.20).

Figure 6.20 PKI Pairs

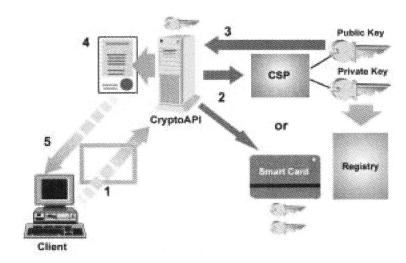

Understanding Public Key Authentication

One of the most critical elements in secure communication is authentication. Users should be able to prove their identity to others and they should be able to verify the identity of others. This becomes complex on a network because the communicating parties do not meet. This can leave room for messages to be intercepted or one user to impersonate another person.

A common credential is the digital certificate. It provides a secure way to verify identity. Because of the lack of physical contact, cryptographic techniques are used by certificates to address the identity problem. These techniques can limit the possibility of anyone intercepting, altering, or counterfeiting messages. Using cryptographic techniques make certificates difficult to modify and difficult for someone to impersonate anyone else.

The data in a certificate includes the public cryptographic key from the certificate subject's public and private key pair. The recipient as authentic by may verify a message signed with the sender's private key with the sender's public key and the Secure Sockets Layer (SSL) Protocol.

Understanding Public Key Interactive Logon

Interactive logon is the usual process whereby you enter your credentials. The public key is found on the sender's certificate. By using a public key to verify a signature from a certificate can prove the signature was produced with the certificate subject's private key. If a sender is careful and has kept the private key secret, the receiver will be confident in the identity of the message sender.

The following scenario shows the process of certificates authentication:

In this scenario, you are authenticating a user on a secure Internet site with the Transport Layer Security (TLS). This is in the form of a username and password shared with other resources requiring Verification for access.

With an interactive public key logon, the process changes drastically. Windows 2000 supports the use of an X.509 v3 Certificate that is stored on the Smart Card with the user's private key. Instead of a username and password, the user inserts the Smart Card into the Smart Card reader and enters a PIN. If the PIN is correct, the user is authenticated.

The user's public key certificate is recovered from the card by a secure process. It is verified as a valid certificate from a trusted provider. During the authentication process, a challenge is issued to the card. This is based on the public key in the certificate. The card verifies it has and can use the private key. The certificate that holds the user identity is checked to the user object stored in Active Directory and, an access token is built for it. The client may then be issued a ticket-granting ticket (TGT).

Vocabulary

Review the following terms in preparation for the certification exam.

Term	Description
CA	A Certificate Authority is responsible for creating and vouching for the validity of the public keys that belong to users or other CAs. The CA can bind public keys to distinguished names through signed certificates and manage certificate serial numbers and revocation.
CryptoAPI	Also called CAPI, CryptoAPI is an Application Programming Interface (API) that is provided as part of Microsoft Windows. It provides a set of functions that allow applications to encrypt or digitally sign data in a flexible manner while providing protection for the user's sensitive private key data. Actual cryptographic operations are performed by independent modules known as Cryptographic Service Providers (CSPs).
cryptography	The processes, art, and science of keeping messages and data secure. Cryptography enables and ensures confidentiality, data integrity, authentication (entity and data origin), and nonrepudiation.
CSP	A Cryptographic Service Provider is code that performs authentication, encoding, and encryption services that Windows-based applications access through the CryptoAPI.
decryption	The process of converting data from encrypted format back to its original format. Once a user has decrypted a file, the file remains decrypted whenever the file is stored on disk.
digital signature	A means for originators of a message, file, or other digitally encoded information to securely bind their identity to the information.

Term	Description
EFS	Encrypting File System is a Windows 2000 file system that allows users to encrypt their files and folders on an NTFS disk to keep them safe from access by others.
encryption	The process of disguising a message or data in such a way as to hide its substance.
GPO	The Group Policy Object is a collection of Group Policy settings. Each Windows 2000 computer has exactly one group of settings stored locally, called the local Group Policy object.
IPSec	IP Security is a suite of cryptography-based protection services and security protocols that requires no changes to applications or protocols for deployment on existing networks.
PGP	Pretty Good Privacy is a standard for e-mail encryption and authentication.
PKI	Public Key Infrastructure describes the laws, policies, standards, and software that regulate or manipulate certificates and public and private keys. It is a system of digital certificates, certification authorities, and other registration authorities that verify and authenticate the validity of each party involved in an electronic transaction.
private key	The secret half of a cryptographic key pair that is used with a public key algorithm. Private keys decrypt symmetric session keys, digitally sign data, or decrypt data encrypted with a corresponding public key.
public key	The nonsecret half of a cryptographic key pair that is used with a public key algorithm. Public keys encrypt a session key, verify a digital signature, or encrypt data decrypted with a corresponding private key.

Term	Description
Smart Card	A credit card-sized device that securely stores public and private keys, passwords, and other types of personal information. It is used with a reader attached to a computer and a PIN number to enable certificate-based authentication and single sign-on to a company system.
symmetric encryption	A fast encryption algorithm that requires the same secret key for encryption and decryption. It's used to encrypt large amounts of data, and is also called secret key encryption.

In Brief

If you want to...	Then do this...
Recover a key	Use the Certificates snap-in to renew a certificate issued from a Windows 2000 enterprise certification authority before or after the end of its validation period, with the Certificate Renewal Wizard.
Validate a certificate	Make certain that the issuer has provided a cryptographically valid signature, confirm there is a binding between the name of the user and the user's public key, and use a source that the issuer trusts.
Use a Smart Card to logon	Insert a Smart Card into the reader on a computer. Give your Smart Card PIN code at the prompt, which controls access to operations with the private key stored on the Smart Card.
Configure a domain to trust a CA	1. From the Domain Group Policy Properties box, edit the Default Domain Policy GPO. 2. Choose Computer Configuration, Windows Settings, Security Settings, and then select Public Key Policy, then right-click Trusted Root Certification Authorities. 3. From the context menu, choose All Tasks, and then Select Import. The Certificate Import Wizard starts. 4. Choose Next. From File name, either type the name of the file that contains the root certificate you want to import, or use the Browse button to browse to the file. Select Next. 5. Type the password, choose Next. Choose "Place all certificates in the following store." The destination is the Trusted Root Certification Authorities store in the GPO. Select Next. 6. Choose Finish to import the certificate, OK to close the message box, and OK to apply the policy to the GPO, and then close the MMC.
Set Internet security	Set up an SSL enabled Internet site.

If you want to...	Then do this...
Create key pairs	Apply for a new certificate. The information will pass from the requesting program to the Microsoft Cryptographic Application Program Interface (CryptoAPI). The CryptoAPI passes the correct data to the Cryptographic Service Provider (CSP). The CSP will create a key pair (public and a private key), if it is software based. If hardware based, such as a Smart Card, the CSP instructs the hardware to create the essential pair.
Make a secret key agreement	Use public key cryptography.
Encrypt data without shared secrets	Public key cryptography can also be used to encrypt bulk data, without establishing shared secrets first. You do this by selecting a key encryption algorithm and generating a random session key. If User 2 is sending the message, the session key is encrypted with User 1's public key. The resulting ciphertext key is sent to User 1, along with the encrypted data. With the private key, User 1 can retrieve the session key and use it to decrypt the data.

Lesson 6 Activities

Complete the following activities to better prepare you for the certification exam.

1. Describe a digital signature.

2. List a number of ways certificates can be used to provide authentication.

3. Explain a number of uses for certificates.

4. Describe how the EFS works.

5. Explain how to logon with a Smart Card.

6. Describe how a domain client requests a certificate.

7. Explain how to export a certificate.

8. Describe how to set up an SSL enabled Internet site.

9. Explain certification hierarchy.

10. Describe the security levels available for Digital Identification.

Answers to Lesson 6 Activities

1. The data in a certificate contains the public key from the certificate subject's public and private key pair. The message's recipient can verify it as authentic by its sender's private key included with the sender's public key. This key can be found on a copy of the sender's certificate. Using a public key from a certificate to confirm a signature, proves the signature was produced with the certificate subject's private key. If the sender has kept the private key secret, the receiver can be confident of the identity of the message sender.

2. Following is a list of ways that certificates provide authentication:

    *   Authentication of a user to a secure Internet site through the Transport Security Layer or the Secure Sockets Layer Protocol.

    *   Authentication of a server to a user through TLS

    *   Logging on to a Windows 2000 domain

    *   Only the owner of the private key could have created the digital signature

    *   Anyone with access to the corresponding public key may verify the signature

    *   Any modification of the signed data invalidates the signature

3. There are a number of uses for certificates. Certificates can provide a means of establishing confidence in the connection between a public key and the owner of the matching private key. Certificates are digitally signed statements for a particular public key. The issuer holds another pair of private and public keys and signs the certificate. Certificates can contain other information connected to the subject public key—like identity information, for the individual who has access to the matching private key. The certificate issuer can ensure the authenticity of the binding between the public key and the identity information.

4. EFS creates a random key for each file that is encrypted. The user's EFS public key then is used to encrypt the key and associates it with the file. A copy of the secret key is encrypted with each of the recovery agent's EFS public keys associated with the file. No plaintext copy of the secret key is ever stored in the system.

    When recovering this file, EFS uses the user's private key to unwrap the copy of the secret key that has been encrypted with the user's public key. This can be used to decrypt the file in real-time —during file read and write operations. A recovery agent can decrypt the file with the private key to access the secret key.

5. Windows 2000 will recognizes a Smart Card as an equivalent to the Ctrl+Alt+Delete sequence for logon. Then the user is prompted for the Smart Card PIN code. The PIN controls the access with the private key stored on the Smart Card. The Smart Card also holds a copy of the user's certificate (issued by an enterprise certificate authority). With this, the user can roam within the domain.

6. If the domain client needs to request a certificate, follow this procedure:

    1. Open the browser, and connect to http://ServerName/ **CertSRV** (where ServerName is the name of the certificate authority server).

    2. On the Microsoft Certificate Services welcome page, select **Request a certificate**. Select **Next**.

    3. Choose **User certificate request** and highlight **User Certificate** in the list box. Select **Next**.

    4. If you are connecting to a standalone certificate authority, you will see a **User Certificate Identifying Information** page. Fill in the online form and select **Next**. Conversely, if you are connecting to a Typeprise certificate authority, the information will be retrieved from Active Directory and you will be prompted to submit your request.

    5. Choose **Submit**. The program creates a public/private key pair and a certificate request with the information provided. Send the request to the certificate authority for processing. Select **Install**.

7. To export a certificate and its related key, follows these steps:

    1. In the **Certificates MMC** snap-in, expand **Certificates** and choose the certificate you wish to export.

    2. Right-click on the certificate, Select **All Tasks** and select **Export**. The Certificate Export wizard begins.

    3. Specify the private key should be exported, select an export file format, and supply a password.

    4. Specify the destination file, Select **Next**, Select **Finish**, then select **OK**

8. To set up an SSL enabled Internet site, perform the following steps:

    1. In the Administrative Tools menu, select **Internet Services Manager.**

    2. Right-click the **IIS** server name and add the new site (unless you already have a site on which you wish to enable SSL).

    3. Follow the prompts in the **Internet Creation Wizard**. Specify a Host Header.

    4. Right-click the new site and select **Properties**.

5. In the Secure communications section of the Directory Security tab, choose the **Edit** button. (if Edit is disabled, choose **Server Certificate** and follow the prompts.)

6. Check **Require secure channel (SSL)**, and specify encryption and client certificate requirement settings. Select **OK**, select **OK** again, start the site, and exit from the MMC snap-in

7. Access the site with https rather than http.

9. The simplest certification hierarchy consists of a single certificate authority. Usually a hierarchy will contain multiple certificate authorities each with clearly defined relationships. In this model, the parent certificate authority certifies the child certification authorities, the issued certificates bind a certification authority's public key to its identity. The certificate authority at the top of a hierarchy called the root authority or the root certificate authority. The child certificate authorities are called subordinate certification authorities.

10. The security levels available for Digital Identification are:

    High—This setting requires you to type a password to grant access to your private key.

    Medium—This setting alerts you and ask for your permission to access your private key.

    Low—This setting does not add any additional security. Only your system's logon procedure protects your private key.

Lesson 6 Quiz

These questions test your knowledge of features, vocabulary, procedures, and syntax.

1.   Which of the following are ways certificates are used for authentication?

    A. TSL

    B. SSL

    C. TLS

    D. Windows 2000 domain

2.   What are the parameters of digital signature authentication?

    A. Only the owner of the private key could have created the digital signature

    B. An agreement between both parties may alter the private key

    C. Anyone with access to the corresponding public key may verify the signature

    D. Any modification of the signed data invalidates the signature

3.   Which of the following are common forms of certificate authorities?

    A. PGP

    B. X.509

    C. VeriSign

    D. PKI

4.   Which of the following are required properties for trust in a public key?

    A. The issuer swears fearsome oaths

    B. The issuer has provided a cryptographically valid signature

    C. It confirms a binding between the name and named entity's public key

    D. It is issued by a trusted source

5.   What are the major features of EFS?

    A. You may encrypt folders or individual files

    B. EFS uses PKI to support bulk encryption without prior shared secrets

    C. EFS creates a random key for each file to be encrypted

D. EFS uses the private key to unwrap the secret key encrypted in the public key

6. Which enrollment protocols are supported by the Windows 2000 PKI?

A. CS Number 10 certificate request

B. CS Number 7 response

C. DSA keys

D. Diffie-Hellman keys

7. With which of the following items does the Windows 2000 PKI support roaming?

A. Digital cell phones

B. Microsoft CSPs

C. Hardware token devices

D. Smart Cards

8. Which of the following are main functions of a certification authority?

A. Establish and vouch for the identity of certificate holders

B. Revoke invalid certificates

C. Publish certificate revocation lists

D. Control certification hierarchies

9. What are some advantages of trusted root authority?

A. Flexible configuration of the certificate authority

B. Frequent updates for issuing certificates

C. May alter the hierarchy without damaging trust relationships

D. Easier Verification to third parties

10. Which Internet security protocols does Microsoft Internet Explorer support?

A. Transport Layer Security (TLS Version 1)

B. Digital ID

C. Secure Sockets Layer (SSL Versions 2 and 3)

D. Private Communications Technology (PCT Version 1)

Answers to Lesson 6 Quiz

1. Answers A, B, C, and D are correct. Transport Security Layer (TSL) and TLS are the same. They, as well as Secure Sockets Layer (SSL) and Windows 2000 domain, are all avenues for authentication.

2. Answers A, C, and D are correct. The owner of the private key is the only one who may create the digital signature. Anyone with the corresponding public key may verify the signature. If the signed data is changed, the signature is invalidated.

    Answer B is incorrect. Once a private key is created it may not be altered, only replaced.

3. Answers A, C, and D are correct. Pretty Good Privacy (PGP), VeriSign and Windows 2000 PKI (PKI) are all certification authorities.

    Answer B is incorrect. X.509 is an Internet standard, not a certification authority.

4. Answers B, C, and D are correct. Valid signatures, confirmation of the connection between the named entity and their public key and origination from a trusted source are all required parts of trust relationship.

    Answer A is incorrect. Even the most binding of oaths does not prove the authenticity of a source.

5. Answer A is correct. You can encrypt folders and individual files. Applications that have access to a user's encrypted files, the same way they do with unencrypted files. However applications cannot decrypt other user's encrypted files.

    Answer B is correct. EFS uses the PKI to support bulk encryption without prior shared secrets. Each EFS user creates a public key pair and obtains an EFS certificate from a enterprise certificate authority.

    Answer C is correct. EFS creates a random key for each file to be encrypted. The user's EFS public key is then used to encrypt this key and associate it with the file.

    Answer D is correct. EFS uses the private key to unwrap the secret key encrypted in the public key. This is used to decrypt the file during read and write operations.

6. Answer A, B, C, and D are correct. CS Number 10 certificate requests and CS Number 7 responses are industry standards that govern certificates and certificate chains. Digital Signature Algorithm (DSA) keys and Diffie-Hellman keys are internally supported protocols.

7.   Answers B, C, and D are correct. Microsoft Cryptographic Service Providers and hardware token devices, like Smart Cards, support PKI roaming.

Answer A is incorrect. Digital cell phones have their own security systems, not connected with Microsoft.

8.   Answers A, B, and C are correct. The main duties of the certification authority are to establish the identity of certificate holders, revoke invalid certificates and publish lists of revoked certificates.

Answer D is incorrect. Certification authorities are members of certification hierarchies. They do not control the hierarchies established by the network administrator.

9.   Answers A, B, and C are correct. You can use the flexible configuration of the certificate authority security environment, to tailor the balance between security and usability, such certificate authority key strength, physical protection, and protection against network attacks.

Answer B is correct. Use of frequent updates for issuing certificate authority keys and certificates, which are most often exposed to compromise, without requiring a change to established trust relationships.

Answer C is correct. The ability to turn off a specific portion of the certificate authority hierarchy without affecting the established trust relationships. For example, you can shut down and revoke an issuing certificate authority certificate associated with a specific geographic site and it will not affect other parts of the organization.

Answer D is incorrect. Verification to or from third parties is unaffected by the internal hierarchical relationships.

10. Answers A, C, and D are correct. Transport Layer Security (TLS version 1), Secure Sockets Layer (SSL Versions 2 and 3), and Private Communications Technology (PCT Version 1) are recognized Microsoft Internet Explorer security protocols.

Answer B is incorrect. The Digital ID is an individual identifier, not an Internet Security Protocol.

Certificate Services

Certificate Services provide convenient and customizable tools used to create, issue, and manage security certificates employed in systems that utilize public key security technology.

The Certificate Services of Windows 2000 can be used to create Certificate Authorities that handle all the functions needed to effectively maintain security certificates. These functions include the reception of certificate requests, verification of the request and the requestor, the issuance of certificates, revocation of certificates, and the creation of a Certificate Revocation List (CRL).

After completing this lesson, you should have a better understanding of the following topics:

- Certificate Authorities (CAs)
- Certificate Mapping
- Enterprise Certificates
- Certificate Service Web Pages
- Advanced Certificates
- External Certificates
- Automatic Certificate Requests
- Certificate Services
- Certificate Services Log and Database
- Certificate Revocation List

Certificate Authorities (CAs)

Certificate Authorities (CAs) are trusted services designed to issue and verify the validity of security certificates. A CA issues certificates to individual users, computers, or organizations that are able to provide proof of identity fulfilling the requirements of the CA's policy. A CA that has verified the request and identity of a requester uses a private key to apply a digital signature the certificate, making the certificate a valid security credential within a Public Key Infrastructure (PKI). CAs are also responsible for revoking certificates and the creation of Certificate Revocation Lists (CRLs).

A CA can either be a local resource created by Windows 2000 Certificate Services, or a remote third-party service, such as Keywitness Canada or VeriSign. Every CA has specific proof-of-identity requirements for the validation of certificates. These requirements can range from driver's license information or employee ID information to the physical address of a computer used to request a certificate. Organizations that require such validation of their employees or users can be well served by a local Windows 2000 based CA.

In Windows 2000, an enterprise CA uses user account credentials to verify the identity of a certificate requester. If a user is logged on within a Windows 2000 domain, and requires the issuance of a certificate, the enterprise CA uses the Active Directory services to ascertain and verify the identity of the user.

CAs are also required to verify their own identity. Each CA has an identity certificate issued by another trusted CA, or, in the case of the root CA, by itself. Anyone can create a CA, but the CA is of little use unless a parent or root CA trusts it and its policies.

Root and Subordinate CAs

Root CAs are the most trusted type of CA in a hierarchical PKI. The certificate issuance policy of the root CA is the most rigorous of any of the CAs in the system. Since the root CA validates Subordinate CAs, which subsequently validate other CAs, a compromised root CA endangers the security offered by every CA within a system. If a root CA dispenses an unauthorized certificate, the certificate can compromise the security of any CA that granted authorization by the root CA. Although root CAs can issue certificates to individual users, they should only be used to issue certificates to subordinate CAs.

Subordinate CAs are certified by other CAs. Subordinate CAs usually issue certificates directly to individual users for specific purposes, such as Smart Card authentication, secure Web-based transactions, or secure e-mail. Subordinate CAs also issue certificates to additional subordinate CAs. Root CAs form the base of a hierarchical PKI, with subordinate CAs making up the branches, and additional CAs that are subordinate to the subordinate CAs forming the smallest end branches.

Windows 2000 Server offers two standard types of CAs—enterprise CAs and stand-alone CAs. The differences between these two types of CAs are discussed in the next section.

Enterprise CAs

Enterprise CAs require the Active Directory service. You can use the Certificate Request Wizard (started from the Certificates snap-in of the Microsoft Management Console) and Internet Explorer (through the use of the CA Web pages) to request certificates from an enterprise CA.

You configure enterprise CAs to offer different types of certificates based upon the certificates it is granted and the security permissions of the user who requests a certificate. By using the Active Directory service, a CA is able to verify a requestor's security permissions and can post its CRL to both a shared directory and the Active Directory.

Stand-Alone CAs

Since stand-alone CAs are not interfaced with the Active Directory services, they are less automated than enterprise CAs.

As shipped, stand-alone CAs can only honor certificate requests made via its Web pages. Stand-alone CAs without access to Active Directory services are unable to automatically verify the identity of requestors and often require extensive identifying information to be provided before the issuance of a certificate. Stand-alone CAs create CRLs in a shard directory or through Active Directory if it is available.

 Note: Windows 2000 allows administrators to create CAs with policy modules that differ from the default ones shipped with Windows 2000. CAs with custom policies are not technically considered stand-alone or enterprise CAs, and may have characteristics of one or the other. The administrator of a custom CA can provide further information on its configuration and usage.

Understanding Certificate Hierarchies

Certificate Hierarchies are structures that define which CAs trust which CAs through the creation of root-subordinate or parent-child CA relationships.

By default, the Public Key Infrastructure provided with Windows 2000 presumes the existence of a hierarchical CA structure. This type of hierarchical structure provides many advantages, including easy administration, scalability, and cohesion with many third-party CA products.

Although a certification hierarchy could consist of a solitary CA, most systems are made up of multiple CAs with obvious parent-child relationships. In this hierarchical structure, child or subordinate CAs are certified with certificates issued by their parent CAs. These certificates bind a CA's public key to its identity. The CA without a parent, which resides at the top of the hierarchy, is known as the root CA or root authority. Subordinate, or child CAs, provide subordinate certification authorities.

If a root CA is listed as trusted, by having its certificate in the trusted root certification authority's certificate store, every subordinate CA within the hierarchy is also trusted, with the exception of CAs with revoked or expired certificates. This makes root CAs security sensitive, as they are likely to be the most important element of trust within an organization. Root CAs should be treated in a very security-minded way. Since the hierarchical structure of the PKI in Windows 2000 allows for subordinate trusts, only a small number of root certification authority trusts need exist. This hierarchical structure also allows for flexibility in the quantity of certificate issuing subordinate CAs.

The following are several common-sense reasons for utilizing multiple subordinate CAs:

Physical divisions—Systems that span large areas often require multiple subordinate CAs to simplify usage procedures as well as administration.

Group divisions—Organizations often are made up of many different entities, and each group usually requires different policies for the issuance of security certificates. The use of subordinate CAs greatly simplifies the task of administering the policies in place within each group.

Usage—By utilizing subordinate CAs, a basis for the administration of certificate issuance is created. Subordinate CAs can issue certificates for secure e-mail, network authentication, or other tasks, and can be administered accordingly.

The use of a certificate hierarchy can also yield the following administrative benefits:

Lockout faculties—A CA hierarchy offers the ability to disable parts of a system without affecting its operation as a whole. For example, a CA in control of a specific physical realm can have its certificate revoked or be shut down, thereby stopping access from that location without adversely affecting the trusts in force throughout the rest of the system.

Ease of updates—Frequent changes can be applied to subordinate CAs and their certificates, which can sometimes be compromised. These changes have no effect on existing trust relationships, making the administrator's job easier.

Configuration Flexibility—The design of the certificate hierarchy allow easy changes to the security environment. This allows for simple fine-tuning of items like key strength and physical security, and allows one to produce a balance between usability and security. The root CA can run in a physically secure area with special cryptographic hardware, while subordinate CAs can run in less restrictive environs, without compromising network security or usability.

Installing Certificate Authorities

To setup a stand-alone root certification authority, follow these steps:

1. Log on to the system as an Administrator, or if you have View Definition, log on to the system as a Domain Administrator.

2. From the Start Menu, choose **Settings**, and then select **Control Panel**.

3. Choose **Add/Remove Programs**, and then select **Add/Remove Windows Components**.

Figure 7.1 Add/Remove Windows Components

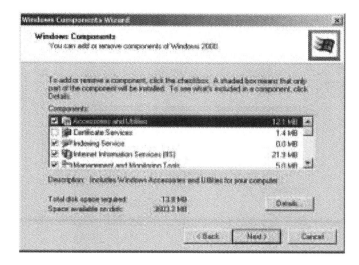

4. In the Windows Components Wizard window, choose the **Certificate Services** check box. A dialog box appears to inform you that the computer cannot be renamed, and the computer cannot join or be removed from a domain after Certificate Services is installed. Select **Yes** and then select **Next**.

5. Choose **Stand-alone root CA** (Figure 7.2).

Figure 7.2 Stand-Alone Root CA

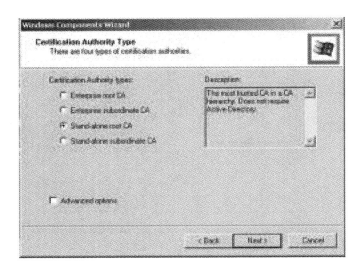

6.   (Optional) Choose the **Advanced options** check box to specify the following. Table 7.1 provides a listing of advanced options.

Table 7.1 Advanced Options

Advanced Option	Comment
Cryptographic Service Provider	This option allows the selection of an alternate CSP. The default selection is the Microsoft Base Cryptographic Provider. Please refer to the documentation for the third party CSP when using this option.
Hash Algorithm	The default is SHA-1.
Existing keys	This option allows the use of pre-existing public and private key pairs, which can be useful when replacing or recreating a pre-existing CA.

Advanced Option	Comment
Key length	Although the Microsoft Base Cryptographic Provider defaults to 512 bits, the default key length for other CSPs may be different. Longer key lengths generally yield more secure certificates, so the root CA should utilize a key with a length no less than 2,048 bits. Note that this option is not available if you use pre-existing keys.

7.   When finished, choose **Next** (Figure 7.3).

Figure 7.3 Advanced Options

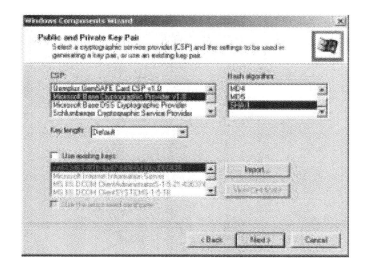

8.   Enter the name of the certification authority and other necessary details. Once the certificate authority setup is completed, any information entered here becomes permanent and cannot be changed

9.   In **Validity duration,** specify the validity duration for the root CA, and then select **Next** (Figure 7.4).

Warning: Be careful setting the validity duration—once the time expires, the CA is no longer valid.

Figure 7.4 Validity Duration

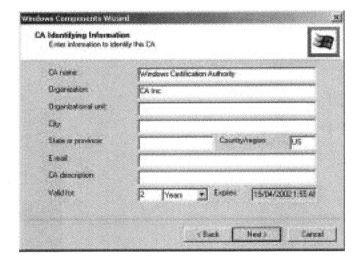

10. Specify the file storage paths for the certificate database, the certificate database log, and the shared folder, and then select **Next**.

11. If the World Wide Web Publishing Service is running, you will be asked to stop the service before completing the installation. Choose **OK** (Figure 7.5)

Figure 7.5 Stop Service Request

If prompted, enter the path of the Certificate Services installation files.

 Note: As long as Active Directory is enabled and write permissions are available, you do not need to specify the shared folder for the CAs.

Requesting a Certificate

Certificate requests require that the service, computer, or user that makes the request have the private key that is associated with the public key that is part of the certificate. Computers and services may request certificates without any user intervention if the public key policies of your system are configured to allow such actions. Additionally, you can configure your system to request Smart Card certificates and Smart Card user certificates at logon time on the behalf of other users by employing their enrollment agent certificate.

A user can explicitly request certificates in Windows 2000 through one of two methods. The user can utilize the Certificate Request Wizard, or access the Web pages for the CA in question. Both of these methods are discussed in the next section.

The Certificate Request Wizard

The Certificate Request Wizard, located in the Certificates snap-in, is used to request certificates from a Windows 2000 enterprise certification authority. This wizard simplifies the following steps:

Selecting the CA to which you will submit the request—Unless an enterprise CA is available within your Windows domain, it cannot issue you a certificate through this wizard.

Selecting the appropriate certificate template to use for the new certificate—Certificate templates listed here are pre-made configurations representative of the most common settings for a certificate request, and include brief descriptions of their intended purpose and usage. The selection of certificates that are listed depends on both the users access rights to the various available templates as well as the type of certificates the CA in question is allowed to issue.

Selecting the CSP—This is optional and only necessary when using a non-default Cryptographic Service Provider (CSP), and can be selected through the advanced options screen.

Private key availability—Only two certificates have their private keys marked as exportable: the Basic Encrypting File System (EFS) certificate, and the EFS Recovery Agent certificate. To export the private key of other certificates to a PKCS Number 12 file when requesting them, you must utilize the advanced request page from the Windows 2000 Certificate Services Web page.

New certificates—The Certificate Request Wizard can also be used to request a new certificate from an enterprise certificate authority with a key pair currently associated with a different certificate.

Request Certificates Using Windows 2000

If you choose not to use the Certificate Request Wizard, or you can not use it on the CA from which you wish to request a certificate, make requests from Web pages that reside on the CA server. The default location of these pages is http://*caservername*/certsrv, where *caservername* is the name of the Windows 2000 server on which the CA runs.

If you want to request certificates from a stand-alone Windows 2000 CA, you must access the Web pages of that CA. Using the Certificate Services Web pages is also useful when requesting a certificate from an enterprise CA if you would like to set optional request features not selectable from the Certificate Request Wizard. For example, if you want to export a key, select an alternate Hash algorithm, or set a custom key length, you would use the Certificate Services Web pages.

Completing a Certificate Request

On a Windows 2000 enterprise CA, certificate requests are immediately processed. Requests are instantly granted or denied, and if granted, a certificate is issued and the user is prompted to download and install it.

Certificate requests sent to a stand-alone Windows 2000 CA can be immediately processed if possible, or, by default, be marked as pending and wait for administrator approval or disapproval. Users who request certificates from a stand-alone CA that are pending can check the status of their request by revisiting the appropriate Web page.

Verifying a Certificate Request

You can use the Certificate Authority tool or Internet Explorer to view or verify your certificate.

To use Internet Explorer 5 to view your certificate, follow these steps:

1.   From the **Tools** menu, choose **Internet Options** (Figure 7.6).

Figure 7.6 IE 5 Internet Options

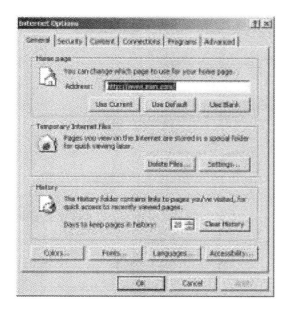

2.   Choose the Content property page.

3.   Choose **Certificates** (Figure 7.7).

Figure 7.7 Certificates

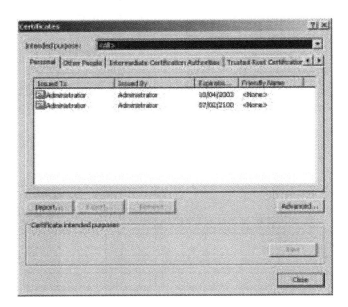

4. Find the certificate that you downloaded and select it to see the details (if the certificate is not listed, then the download failed). You may choose the General, Details, or Certification Path pages.

To use the CA to view your certificate, follow these steps:

1. Log on to the system as an **Administrator**.

2. From the Start Menu, choose Programs, Administrative Tools, and then select **Certification Authority** (Figure 7.8).

Figure 7.8 Certification Authority

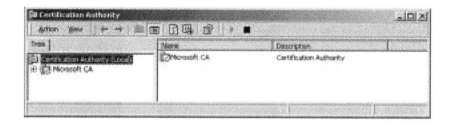

3.   In the console tree, choose the name of the CA.

4.   From the **Action** menu, choose **Properties**.

5.   On the General property page, choose **View Certificate Authority Certificate** (Figure 7.9).

Figure 7.9 View Certificate Authority Certificate

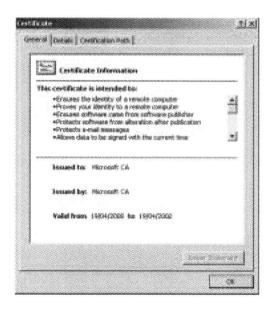

Revoking Certificates

From the CA, you can both revoke issued certificates and unrevoke certificates once revoked. Both tasks are outlined below.

To revoke an issued certificate, follow these steps:

1. Log on to the system as an **Administrator**.

2. Open **Certification Authority** (Figure 7.10).

Figure 7.10 Certification Authority

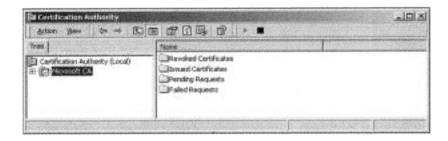

3. In the console tree, select **Issued Certificates**.

4. In the Details pane, select the certificate you want to revoke.

5. From the Action menu, choose **All Tasks**, and then select **Revoke Certificate** (Figure 7.11).

Figure 7.11 Revoke Certificate

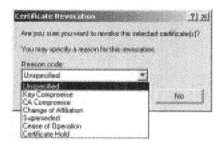

6.   Choose the reason for revoking the certificate and select **Yes**.

The certificate you choose is immediately revoked and moved to the Revoked Certificates folder. The certificate does not appear in the CRL until the next time it is published.

Certificates marked with a revocation reason of Certificate Hold are the only kind of revoked certificates whose status can be changed. However, certificates marked as such can be unrevoked, have their reason code changed, or be left to expire. The use of the Certificate Hold reason indicator is convenient for the administrator who wants to disable suspect certificates without irrevocable removing them.

If you want to unrevoke a certificate marked with a reason code of Certificate Hold, enter the following line at the command prompt of the CA:

```
certutil -revoke certificateserialnumber unrevoke
```

To obtain the certificateserialnumber, choose the revoked certificate in the Details pane of the Revoked Certificates folder and then select details.

To modify the reason code of a certificate once marked with a code of Certificate Hold enter a suitable command line from Table 7.2 at the command prompt of the CA.

Table 7.2 Codes and Commands

New Reason Code for Revoking Certificate on Certificate Hold	Command
Unspecified	Certutil -revoke certificateserialnumber 0
Key Compromise	certutil -revoke certificateserialnumber 1
CA Compromise	certutil -revoke certificateserialnumber 2
Affiliation Changed	certutil -revoke certificateserialnumber 3
Superseded	certutil -revoke certificateserialnumber 4
Cessation of Operation	certutil -revoke certificateserialnumber 5

Certificate Mapping

Certificate mapping allows certificates issued to a user to be mapped to the user's account. Server applications can use the Windows NT PKI and these mappings to authenticate the user in much the same way as if the user provided a logon ID and password. Certificate mapping offers many administrative advantages, including increased flexibility and ease of manageability.

Up until recently, most computer systems utilized central account databases to keep track of users, their permission sets, and their access controls. This type of user structure is well understood and has been in use for many years, but becomes gregariously inefficient and unwieldy as systems grow beyond a few hundred users. Some modern systems support tens of thousands of users, and certificate mapping techniques solve many of the problems inherent in a centralized form of user accounting. Tasks like user administration and account verification are greatly simplified and expedited by using certificate mapping.

Public key certificates, with certificate mapping, alleviate many of the problems presented by older system in large user environments. You can issue certificates by multiple CAs, distribute them widely, and verify them without referring to a central database. Unfortunately, existing operating systems do not utilize this type of user verification, and rely upon centralized accounting. Certificate mapping presents a solution that allows existing operating systems to continue to use their central user accounts while linking those accounts with system wide certificates.

The certificate mapping model allows a user to present a certificate anywhere on the network, have the system examine the certificate, determine to proper mapping of the certificate to an individual user account, and log on that user using the mapped account.

Do not confuse this with Smart Card mapping. Windows 2000 supports automatic logon using Smart Cards with mapped accounts, but through a different mechanism.

Mapping a Certificate to User Accounts

You can control certificate mapping under Windows 2000 by two mechanisms: the Windows 2000 Active Directory service, or the Microsoft Internet Information Services (IIS).

To use the Active Directory to map certificates to user accounts, log on as Administrator and follow these steps:

1. Open Active Directory Users and Computers.

2. Choose **Active Directory Users and Computers**. From the View menu, select **Advanced Features** to put a check mark next to it if it is not already checked (Figure 7.12).

Figure 7.12 Advanced Features

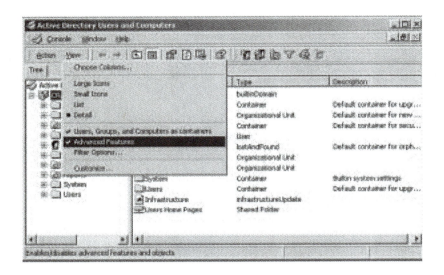

3.   Choose the domain name in the console tree.

4.   Either choose **Users**, or select the container where the user account is held.

5.   In the Details pane, choose the user account to which you wish to map a certificate.

6.   From the **Action** menu, choose **Name Mappings**. On the X.509 Certificates page in the Security Identity Mapping window select **Add** (Figure 7.13).

Figure 7.13 Name Mappings

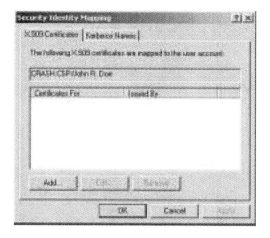

7.   Enter the name and path of the .CER file that contains the certificate you want to map to the user account, then choose **Open**.

8.   Follow one of the procedures defined below in Table 7.3 regarding mapping types. The different types of mapping are also explained below.

Table 7.3 Mapping Certificates

If you want to...	Do this
Map the certificate to one account (one-to-one mapping).	Ensure that the Use Issuer for alternate security identity and the Use Subject of alternate security check boxes are selected.
Map any certificate that has the same subject to the user account, regardless of the issuer of the certificate (many-to-one mapping).	Ensure the Use Issuer for alternate security identity check box is cleared and that the Use Subject of alternate security identity check box is selected.
Map any certificate to that has the same issuer to the user account, regardless of the subject of the certificate (many-to-one mapping).	Ensure that the Use Issuer for alternate security identity check box is selected and that the Use Subject of alternate security identity check box is cleared.

 Note: Certificates mapped to user accounts must be in DER or Base64 encoded binary format. Also, unless Advanced Features are enabled from the View menu, Name Mappings will not appear in the Action menu.

Mapping Types

Usually, certificates map to user accounts in on of two ways. An account can be mapped to a single certificate, or an account can be mapped to multiple certificates. The former type of mapping is called one-to-one mapping and the latter called many-to-one mapping.

User Principal Name Mapping

User principal name mapping is a special case of one-to-one mapping. Active Directory is required to use it, as it uses the user principal name to find the user's account in the Active Directory. User principal names look similar to e-mail addresses and are unique within Windows 2000 domains. The user principal name is inserted into the user's security certificate by enterprise CAs. As a result, Smart Card logins and secure IIS server accesses are automatically verified and the user is logged on.

One-to-One Mapping

One-to-one mapping joins a Windows 2000 user account to a user certificate. This is a good way of providing users with a secure resource that has to be hosted over the Internet. By using certificate mapping, users can log on normally and then utilize Web pages that use the Secure Sockets Layer (SSL) or Transport Layer Security (TLS) from any workstation with no additional hassle. Their identity has been verified by the certificate mapped to their user account.

Many-to-One Mapping

Many-to-one mapping joins a Windows 2000 user account to multiple security certificates. For example, if a specific user had to administer a Web resource accessed by many individual users, a CA policy could be developed that would map all certificates issued by the CA for individual users to the administrative user as well, allowing complete access to the Web-based resource while still retaining pre-existing permissions and user account.

Enterprise Certificates

When a certificate is presented to a system, service, or user with the intent of showing identity of the presenter, the certificate is only useful if the presenter trusts the original issuer of the certificate.

When trusting a CA, a number of assumptions are made about the validity of the CA and its actions. It is taken for granted that the CA has the proper policies in place when evaluating certificate requests, denies certificates to entities that do not meet policy requirements, and revokes certificates that are no longer valid, and publishes an up to date CRL.

Windows 2000 services, computers, and users have trust in a CA when a copy of the root certificate is kept in the trusted root certification authorities store. A valid certification path must also exist. In other words, no certificates between the entity and the root in the hierarchy can be revoked. If a subordinate of a subordinate to the root has a valid root certificate in its store, but the certificate for the first subordinate is revoked, the certification path is broken and the root trust is no longer valid.

If Active Directory is enabled and active, CAs should automatically establish trusts, based on settings made by the system administrator, unless the administrator configures the CAs not to automatically establish trusts.

It is important to understand the concept of certificate store inheritance. If a root CA certificate is in a computer's trusted root certification authorities store or enterprise trust store, every user who uses that computer can view that certificate as if it was in their own certification store. This is a one way street, however, and does not work the other way around. The computer does not inherit trusts in the user's certificate store.

Using an Enterprise CA

To configure automatic certificate allocation from an enterprise CA, follow these steps:

1.   Open Active Directory Users and Computers.

2.   In the console tree, choose **Active Directory Users and Computers**, right-click the domain name in which your certificate authority resides, and then choose **Properties**.

3.   On the Group Policy page, choose **Default Domain Policy**, and then select **Edit** (Figure 7.14).

Figure 7.14 Default Domain Policy

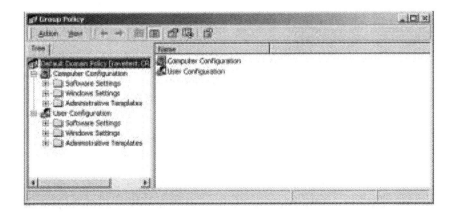

4.   In the console tree, choose **Automatic Certificate Request Settings**.

5.   Right-click **Automatic Certificate Request Settings**, choose **New**, and then select **Automatic Certificate Request** (Figure 7.15).

Figure 7.15 Automatic Certificate Request

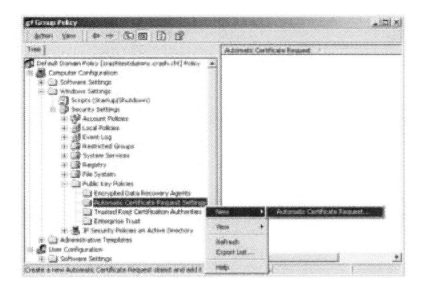

6.   The Automatic Certificate Request Wizard appears. Choose **Next**.

7.   In Certificate templates, choose **Computer**, and then select **Next** (Figure 7.16).

Figure 7.16 Automatic Certificate Request Wizard

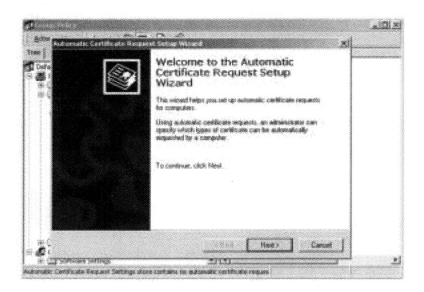

8.   Your enterprise root CA appears on the list.

9.   Choose the CA, select **Next**, and then select **Finish**.

To create a computer certificate for the CA computer, enter the following command at a Windows 2000 command prompt:

```
secedit /refreshpolicy machine_policy
```

Certificate Service Web Pages

By default, every Windows 2000 server that hosts a CA has a Web page available to administrators and users that they can use to perform a number of security certificate related tasks. This Web page is accessible with the URL http://servername/certsrv, where server name is the name of the Windows 2000 server in which the CA resides.

Since stand-alone CAs are unable to use Active Directory services, Web services are the only way certificate requests can be handled. Although enterprise CAs routinely use Active Directory services, the CA's Web page can also be used.

If you have the correct access permissions, you can complete the following tasks from these Web pages:

- Request a basic certificate

- Request a certificate with advanced options

Some user-selectable options available from the advanced certificate request include:

- Cryptographic Service Provider (CSP) options. These options include the name of the CSP, the key size (512, 1,024, 2,048, and so on), the Hash algorithm (SHA/RSA, SHA/DSA, MD2, MD5), and the key specification (exchange or signature).

- Key generation options. These options allow for the creation of a new key set or the use of an existing key set, marking the keys as exportable, enabling strong key protection, and using the local computer store to generate the key.

You may save the request to a PKCS Number 10 file or add any specific attributes you want to add to the certificate.

Checking a Pending Certificate Request

Stand-alone CAs are usually unable to grant a certificate request without the intervention of an administrator. Consequently, anyone who makes a Web request for a certificate from a stand-alone CA must check the status of the request to find out if the certificate has been granted. If the certificate has been issued, the user can download and install it.

The following are some of your options:

- Retrieve the CA's certificate to place in your trusted root store

- Retrieve the current certificate revocation list

- Submit a certificate request using a PKCS Number 10 file or a PKCS Number 7 file

- Request a certificate for a Smart Card on behalf of another user (for administrators only)

Setting Security on Web Pages

The Windows 2000 Certificate Services Web pages allow users to complete many CA related tasks. Users can request CA certificates, process Smart Card enrollment files, and many other procedures.

The Windows 2000 Certificate Services Web pages work somewhat differently on enterprise and stand-alone CAs. On enterprise CAs, the Web page requires the user to log on. The user can choose a pre-defined certificate template, and based upon user information stored in the Active Directory, issues an appropriate certificate if possible.

A stand-alone CA does not ask for a logon ID. Rather, based upon the certificate request information provided, the CA attempts to issue a certificate. Usually, a stand-alone CA cannot immediately issue a certificate, as the certificate request usually needs to be approved by an administrator before issuance, unless the administrator configures the stand-alone CA to immediately issue certificates. This is why users must check the Web page two times, once to request the certificate, and once again to obtain the certificate if they have been approved.

All of the procedures provided in the next section assume that the Microsoft Certificate Service is installed, and that the Web pages are located in the default location, at the following address:

http://ServerName/CertSrv, where *ServerName* is the name of the CA server.

Tip: If you encounter errors when you try to connect to the Certificate Services Web pages, the pages may not be installed. If IIS was never installed, or installed after the certificate service, you will have to reinstall certificate services, and may have to reinstall IIS as well.

Confirming the Web Page Settings

When using enterprise CAs, it is important to verify that security is set correctly on the Web pages. Stand-alone CAs need not have their security permissions set. Enterprise CAs require the certificate requestor to be authenticated so that the Web page is able to place to correct information on the issued certificate.

To confirm the security settings, follow these steps:

1. From the Start Menu, choose programs, Administrative Tools, and then select **Internet Service Manager** (Figure 7.17).

Figure 7.17 Internet Service Manager

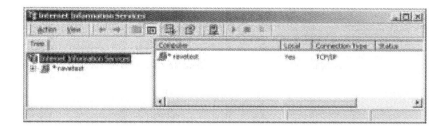

2. Expand the Default Web site and find the CertSrv virtual directory. If you are unable to find CertSrv, make sure that the Certificate Service is installed, and reinstall it if necessary.

3. Right-click **CertSrv** and choose **Properties**.

4. Choose the **Directory Security** page (Figure 7.18).

Figure 7.18 Directory Security

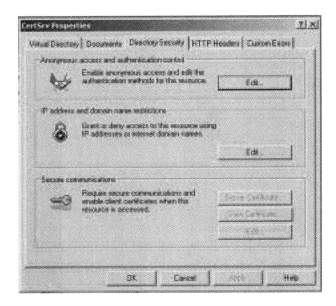

5. From **Anonymous access and authentication control,** choose **Edit.**

6. Make sure the Integrated Windows authentication checkbox is selected and all others are cleared.

7. Choose **OK** and close all dialog boxes.

 Warning: You may be required to uninstall and reinstall the Certificate Service to make virtual directory appear.

Advanced Certificates

You can use the Advanced Certificate Request Web page to set the following options for each certificate request:

Certificate template—Indicates which applications can use the public key in the certificate.

Cryptographic Service Provider (CSP)—Indicates what CSPs are responsible for cryptographic operations, including the creation, destruction, and usage of keys.

Key size—Determines the length, in bits, of the public key on the certificate. Usually, longer keys tend to be more secure and harder to compromise.

Hash algorithm—Determines which Hash algorithm is used for the key. Well-designed Hash algorithms produce very different outputs for even very similar inputs. Typical Hash algorithms include MD2, MD4, MD5, and SHA-1. A hash algorithm is also called a hash function.

Key usage—Determines how the private key is used. Exchange means that the private key can be used in the exchange of sensitive information. Signature means that the private key can only be used to create a digital signature. Both means the key can be used for both exchange and signature functions.

Create a new key set or use an existing key set—Allows the use of an existing public and private key pair stored on your computer or for the creation of a new public and private key pair for a certificate.

Enable strong private key protection—Forces the user to enter a password whenever the private key is needed, to enable strong private key protection.

Mark keys as exportable—Saves the public and private key set to a PKCS Number 12 file when selected. This is useful if a user transits between computers and wants to move the key pair or if a user wants to remove the key pair and secure them on another computer.

Use the local machine store—Selecting this option allows the issue of a certificate and private key to a computer's security store and not an individual user. This allows for multiple users using the same machine to access the same resources.

Save the request to PKCS Number 10 file—Useful if the CA is unavailable for processing certificate requests online at the time of the request.

Requesting an Advanced Certificate

To submit an advanced certificate request via a Web browser, follow these steps:

1. Open Internet Explorer.

2. In Internet Explorer, open http://servername/certsrv, where servername is the name of the Windows 2000 Web server where the CA you want to access is located.

3. Choose **Request a certificate**, and then select **Next** (Figure 7.19).

Figure 7.19 Request a Certificate

4. Choose **Advanced request**, and select **Next**.

5. Choose **Submit a certificate request to this certificate**, and then select **Next** (Figure 7.20).

Figure 7.20 Submit a Certificate Request

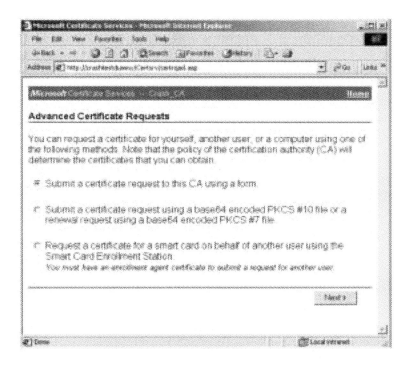

6. Provide any identifying information requested and any other options required.

7. Choose **Submit** and select one of the following processes:

• If you see the Certificate Pending Web page, you must check back later to see if the stand-alone CA has honored your request

• If you see the Certificate Issued Web page, choose Install this certificate

• If you are finished using the Certificate Services Web pages, exit Internet Explorer

External Certificates

External user certificates are a way of verifying a sender's identity without the use of a Security Identifier (SID). External certificates are guaranteed by the CA that issued them. The Message Queuing service on the recipient's compute validates the digital signature of a received message, but not the certificate itself. The receiving application is responsible for validating an external certificate before acting upon the message.

External certificates are necessary when sending authenticated messages to environments other than Windows 2000. When using external certificates between Windows 2000 equipped computers, the certificate needs to be registered in the Active Directory only if the sender authenticates the message with a SID as well.

If an external certificate is registered in the Active Directory, messages can be sent to restricted access queues since the Message Queuing service verifies the sender's SID. Although optional, registering an external certificate adds an additional level of authentication that can be utilized by the receiving application.

Other reasons you may want to utilize external certificates include the following:

- The ability to control who can send authenticated messages through the control of certificates, bypassing the internal certificates created at installation time by Message Queuing

- The ability to send authenticated messages to users without access to Active Directory services

- The ability to function from within a computer workgroup

One method of obtaining external certificates is to use Microsoft Internet Explorer Version 5 or later to request an external certificate from a CA. The following companies are CA vendors:

- AT&T

- InternetMCI Mail

- Keywitness Canada

- VeriSign Commercial Software Publishers

Not all external certificates offer the same security features. Some do not prove identity, but only that the sender is the same user every time the message transmits. While this may be sufficient for subscription-based applications, other more advanced external certificates are often better choices.

Server Authentication

Clients utilize server authentication when the Message Queuing servers receive queries. Clients verify that the query response has not been damaged or tampered with and that they were sent to the correct message cueing server. When in a mixed-mode domain environment, the procedure that a client uses to authenticate a server depends on which version of the Message Queuing service and operating system are running on the client and server. Table 7.4 shows the relationship between method of authentication and Message Queuing versions.

Table 7.4 Server Authentication

Client	Server	Server Authentication Method
Message Queuing client on Windows 2000	Message Queuing server on Windows 2000	Kerberos 5
Message Queuing client on Windows 2000	MSMQ 1.0 controller server on Windows NT 4.0	Windows NTLM (using a server certificate)
MSMQ 1.0 client on Windows NT 4.0, Windows 95, or Windows 98	Message Queuing server on Windows 2000	Windows NTLM (using a server certificate)

Server certificates need only be issued and registered for Message Queuing servers that service MSMQ 1.0 clients that utilize Active Directory under Windows 98, Windows 98, or Windows NT 4.0. Windows 2000 based Message Queuing clients utilize Kerberos 5 for server authentication.

If a Message Queuing client running on Windows 2000 exchanges data with a Windows NT 4.0 bases MSMQ 1.0 controller server, the server must be manually authenticated.

The server certificates employed to authenticate Message Queuing servers have to be installed separately from user or client certificates. Regardless, if your systems are configured properly, the certificate used for Message Queuing authentication can also be used to authenticate IIS servers used to create secure Web (HTTPS) connections.

When upgrading MSMQ 1.0 controller servers, it is important to first create a backup of the existing server key certificate from Windows NT 4.0, and then export this backup. Do this before upgrading the operating system to Windows 2000. You need to do this only once for every server you wish to upgrade that replies to Active Directory queries from MSMQ 1.0 clients.

Trusting an External Certificate Authority

When setting up a trust of an external CA, you must set the Windows 2000 domain to trust an external authority, like VeriSign, or a Microsoft CA from another domain. This procedure assumes you have already obtained a root certificate from the external authority and saved the certificate file.

To set up this process of trusting, follow these tasks:

1. Open the Domain Group Policy Properties box and edit the Default Domain Policy GPO (Figure 7.21).

Figure 7.21 Domain Group Policy Properties

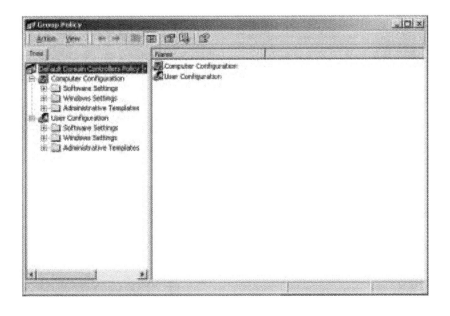

2. Expand Computer Configuration, Windows Settings, Security Settings, Public Key Policies, and right-click **Trusted Root Certification Authorities** (Figure 7.22).

Figure 7.22 Trusted Root Certification Authorities

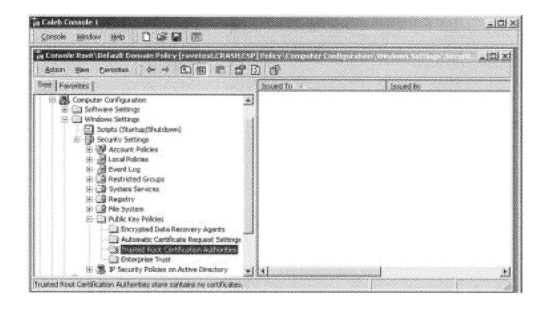

3. From the Context menu, choose **All Tasks** and then select **Import**. The Certificate Import Wizard begins.

4. Choose **Next**. In the File name box, enter the name of the file that contains the root certificate you wish to import or use the Browse button to browse for the file. Select **Next**. Enter a password and select **Next**.

5. Choose **Place all certificates in the following store**. The destination is the Trusted Root Certification Authorities store in the GPO. Select **Next** (Figure 7.23).

Figure 7.23 Placing Certificates in Store

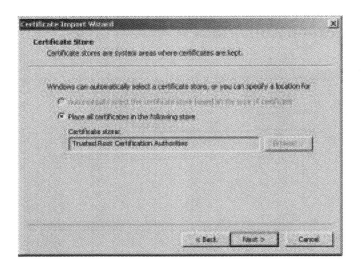

6. Choose **Finish** to import the certificate. Select **OK** to close the message box. Select **OK** to apply the policy to the GPO, and then close the MMC.

Automatic Certificate Requests

Automatic certificate requests allow an administrator to request certificates from a Windows 2000 CA running an enterprise policy for all computers within a specified domain, with the use of only one computer. To proceed with this procedure, you must have a Windows 2000 CA with enterprise policies in your domain and access to the domain controller.

To make an automatic certificate request, follow these steps:

1. Edit the Default Domain Policy GPO.

2. Expand Computer Configuration, Windows Settings, Security Settings, Public Key Policies, and right-click **Automatic Certificate Request Settings** (Figure 7.24).

Figure 7.24 Automatic Certificate Request Settings

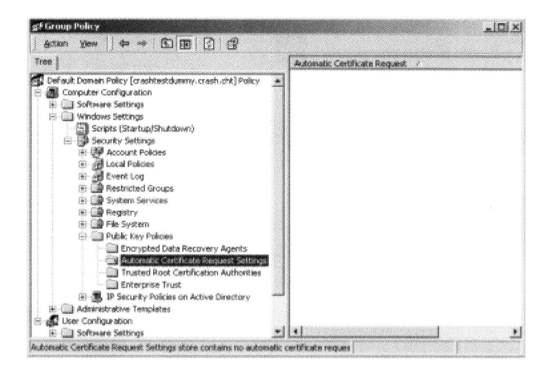

3. From the Context menu, choose New and choose **Automatic Certificate Request**. This opens the Automatic Certificate Request Setup Wizard. Select **Next**.

4. A dialog box appears. This allows you to choose the certificate template to use in the request. Select **Computer** and select **Next** (Figure 7.25).

Figure 7.25 Automatic Certificate Request Dialog Box

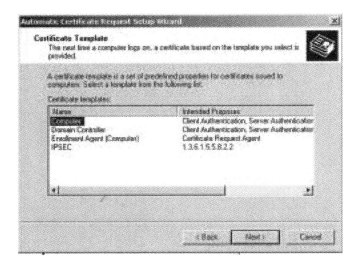

5.   Choose the CA in your Windows 2000 domain to which you want to send the certificate request. Usually, there is only one CA is available on the domain, but an enterprise may have multiple CAs. Note that CAs not running stand-alone or custom policy do not appear on this list. Select **Next**.

6.   Choose **Finish** to create the automatic certificate request. Select **OK** to edit the   Default Domain Policy GPO. The request for the certificate will occur when the GPO is refreshed on the client.

Creating Automatic Requests

To set the default action upon receipt of a certificate request, follow these steps:

1.   Log on to the system as an Administrator.

2.   Open Certification Authority (Figure 7.26).

Figure 7.26 Certification Authority

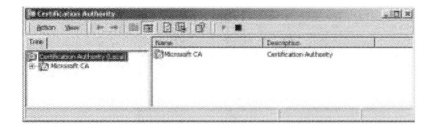

3. In the console tree, choose the name of the CA.

4. From the **Action** menu, choose **Properties.**

5. On the Policy Module property page, choose **Configure** (Figure 7.27). Consult Table 7.5 for settings for certificate requests. Table 7.5 provides a choice of actions for your intended results.

Figure 7.27 Policy Module Configure

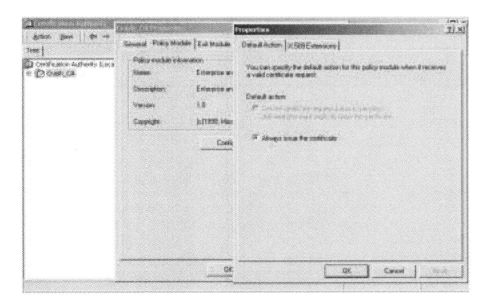

Table 7.5 Certificate Requests

To do this...	Do the following
Have the CA administrator review every certificate request before issuing a certificate.	Choose Set the certificate request status to pending.
Have the CA automatically issue a certificate upon receiving a certificate request.	Choose Always issue the certificate.

6.   Stop and restart the Certificate Services service.

 Warning: To avoid compromising system security, stand-alone CAs should mark all incoming certificate requests as pending. Stand-alone CAs do not have access to Active Directory services to verify the identity of the certificate requester. It is the administrator's responsibility to make sure certificates are issued only to reliable parties.

 Note: To open Certification Authority, choose Start, Programs, Administrative Tools, and then select Certification Authority.

This procedure applies only to stand-alone CAs. The default action of enterprise CAs upon the receipt of a certificate request cannot be changed.
Remember, even if you set a CA to Always issue the certificate, it will only issue certificates for requests made after the change in configuration is made. Certificates pending approval remain pending until the administrator approves or denies the pending certificate requests.

Certificate Services

You can customize Certificate Services to issue and manage certificates in software security systems utilizing a PKI.

You can use Certificate Services to create CAs that receive certificate requests, verify the validity of the requests, verify the identity of the requester, issue certificates, revoke certificates, and publish CRLs.

Certificate Services are also used to accomplish the following:

- Make use of either Web or Certificate management snap-in software to provide users with certificates form the CA

- Provide users with certificates based upon easy to choose security certificate templates

- Make use of Active Directory when publishing trusted root certificates, issued certificates, and CRLs

- Provide services that allow users to log on to a Windows domain using a Smart Card

Understanding Policy Modules

Policy modules create sets of rules and conditions that CAs use when issuing certificates, processing certificate requests, revoking certificates, and publishing CRLs.

When configuring Certificate Services for the first time, you have the choice between two different CA policies, stand-alone and enterprise. These policies are not related to the Windows 2000 Group Policies, and are used to determine the behavior of the CA within your PKI.

CAs using enterprise policy are referred to as enterprise CAs; CAs using stand-alone policy are referred to as stand-alone CAs. The policy is chosen when Certificate Services are installed. If a CA is configured with a stand-alone policy, the policy can be replaced with a customized policy.

Processing Certificate Requests

Users can request certificates from enterprise or stand-alone CAs through the use of an Internet Web browser, such as Microsoft Internet Explorer Version 3.0 or later. Users who wish to receive certificates from an enterprise CA may also use the Certificates snap-in for MMC to make their requests.

Usually, when a user makes a certificate request, a CSP on the local computer generates a private and public key pair for the user. The public key is used to relay important information regarding the user's identity to the CA, and if the information is acceptable, the CA issues a certificate that the client application receives and stores on the local machine.

Security Considerations for CAs

CAs are important to the security of your system, and should be well protected from a security standpoint. There are a number of special security considerations to consider when working with CAs.

Physical protection—CAs are very important to the security of the systems in which they reside, and, unless precautions are taken, can be easily compromised by physical tampering. Physical isolation of CA servers in an area open only to administrators and trusted parties greatly diminishes the chances of such physical attacks.

Restoration—CAs, just like any other computer on a network, can suffer hardware failures at any time. If a CA goes down, it can have dangerous implications for the security of a network, including the possible inability to revoke certain certificates. It is important to have a recent backup of your CAs on hand, and in the case of very important or root CAs, you may want to invest in redundant hardware or backup servers.

Key management—A CA's keys are its most important possession. If the keys of a CA are compromised, many trusts that the CA is involved with become insecure. For CAs working with sensitive data, the purchase of third-party hardware cryptographic modules decreases the possibility that the keys of the CAs become compromised. Certificate Services supports the use of third-party CSPs, although the Windows 2000 documentation is limited to the coverage of the included software CSPs that ship with Windows 20000.

Customizing Certificate Services—Certificate Services were designed with customization in mind. Support is included for additional network transports, formats, extended certificate properties, and custom policies. Implementing custom service can increase the level of security in your system. The Microsoft Platform Software Development Kit includes information about modifying Certificate Services to your needs.

Starting and Stopping a Certificate Service

To start or stop the CA service, follow these steps:

1. Log on to the system as an Administrator.

2. Open Certification Authority (Figure 7.28).

Figure 7.28 Certification Authority

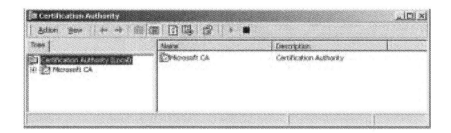

3. In the console tree, choose the name of the CA.

4. From the **Action** menu, choose **All Tasks**, and then select **Start Service** to start the service, or select **Stop Service** to stop the service (Figure 7.29).

Figure 7.29 Stop Service

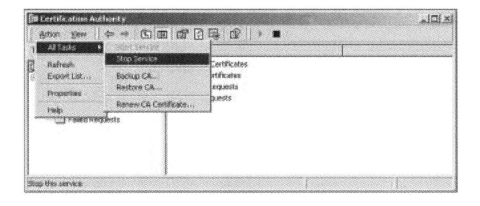

Note: Certificate Services can also be stopped or started from the Computer Management window. In Computer Management, choose **Services and Applications**, and then select **Services**. In the Details pane, select **Certificate Services**. From the **Action** menu, choose **Start** or **Stop**.

Understanding Backup Routines for Certificate Services

To back up a CA, follow these steps:

1.   Log on to the system as an Administrator or Backup Operator.

2.   Open Certification Authority (Figure 7.30).

Figure 7.30 Certification Authority

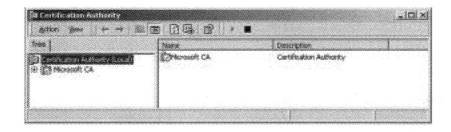

3.   In the console tree, choose the name of the CA.

4.   From the Action menu, choose All Tasks, and then select Backup CA   (Figure 7.31).

Figure 7.31 Certification Authority Backup Wizard

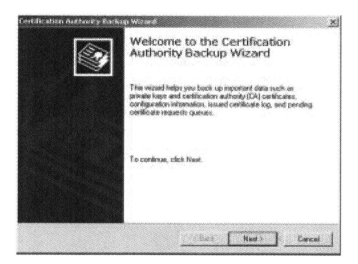

5. Follow the instructions in the Certification Authority Backup Wizard.

Under normal circumstances, you should use the Windows 2000 Backup and Restoration tools to maintain a backup of the CA as well as the server.

Certificate Services Log and Database

It is very important to be able to examine the Certificate Services Log and Database. The log and database contain valuable information that you will find useful when auditing queued requests, issued certificates, and when identifying certificates that may need to be revoked. You can look at the log and database by using the Certificate Services Manager MMC snap-in. This snap-in also allows for customized output, so that you can highlight important or suspicious activities.

Note: If you want to try out the display-filtering faculties of the CA tool, first create a few certificates with a cut-off date and time. This allows you to easily filter out any certificates issued before the ones you created were issued. It also makes it much easier to revoke some or all of the certificates you issued before the ones you created.

Displaying the Database and Log

To display the log, follow these steps:

1.   Open the Certification Authority tool and expand the CN of the Certification Authority.

2.   Choose **Issued Certificates** (Figure 7.32).

Figure 7.32 Issued Certificates

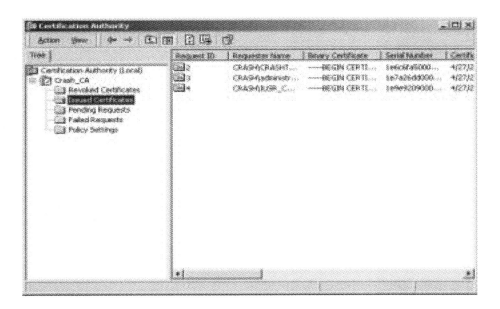

3. Right-click **Issued Certificates**, choose **View**, and then select **Select Columns**.

4. Choose the fields you wish to view. The Request ID field must be selected (mandatory selection). Serial Number, Certificate Effective Date, Certificate Expiration Date, and Issued Common Name are examples of other fields you could select. Select **OK** (Figure 7.33).

Figure 7.33 Select Fields

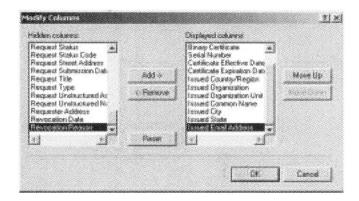

5. Adjust the widths of the column to fit your screen by placing the mouse pointer over the column boundaries and click-dragging (just as you would do in a spreadsheet).

6. To change the order of the columns displayed, right-click the **Issued Certificates** container, choose View, and then select **Choose Columns** (as in Step 3). You could, for example, select **Issued Common Name** and select the **Move up** button. Notice that the Request ID is always the first column that displays.

7. Choose **OK**, and then select the **Refresh** button. You may be required to readjust the column widths.

8. Selecting the **Issued Common Name** column heading lets you sort the records in descending or ascending order by Issued Common Name.

9. To apply a filter on the database, right-click **Issued Certificates**, choose **View**, and then select **Filter** (Figure 7.34).

Figure 7.34 Select Filter

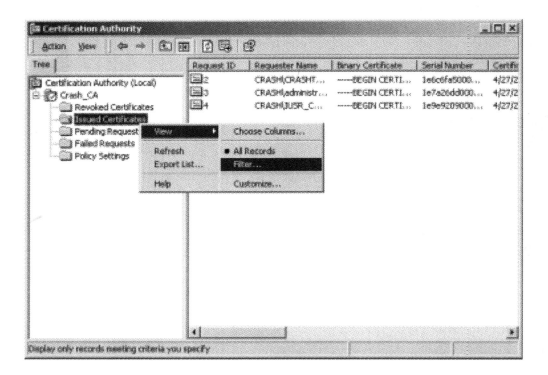

10.   Choose **Add**, and then set the restrictions you require.

11.   Choose **OK**, then select **OK** again.

Certificate Revocation List (CRL)

The CA snap in can be used to revoke certificates, administer CRL publication, and to specify the CRL Distribution Points (CDPs). CDPs are published in every certificate issued by the CA.

Creating and Viewing a CRL

To manually create and publish the certificate revocation list, follow these steps:

1. Log on to the system as an Administrator.

2. Open Certification Authority (Figure 7.35).

Figure 7.35 Certification Authority

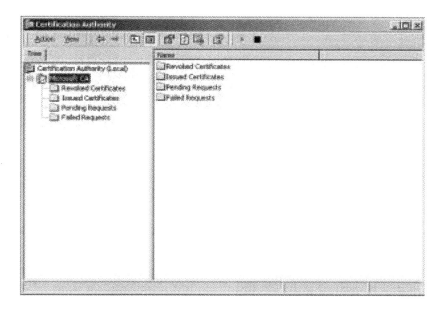

3. In the console tree, choose **Revoked Certificates**.

4. From the **Action** menu, choose **All Tasks**, and select **Publish** (Figure 7.36).

Figure 7.36 Publish Certificate Revocation List

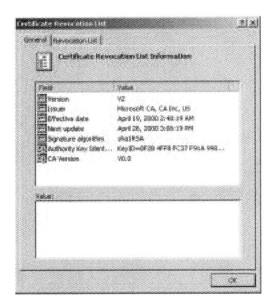

5.   Choose **Yes** to overwrite the previously published CRL.

 Note: Clients that have a cached copy of a CRL that has not yet expired are not affected by the creation and publishing of a new CRL. The new CRL does not replace the older cached copies until they expire.

On the server on which the CA is installed, the CRL publishes in the following path:

`Systemroot\system32\CertSrv\CertEnroll\`

If Active Directory is available, the CRL also publishes to Active Directory.

To view the certificate revocation list, follow the following steps:

1. Log on to the system as an Administrator.

2. Open Certification Authority (Figure 7.37).

Figure 7.37 Certification Authority

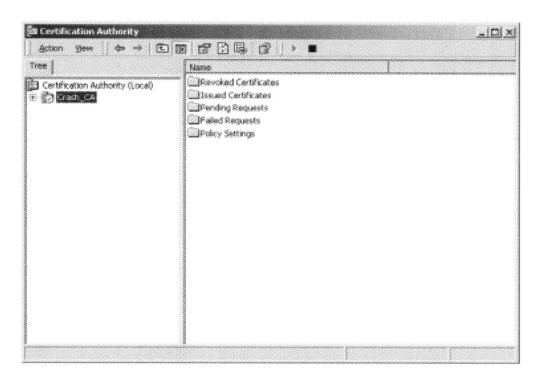

3. In the console tree, choose **Revoked Certificates**.

4. From the **Action** menu, choose **Properties**.

5. Choose **View Current CRL** (Figure 7.38).

Figure 7.38 View Current CRL

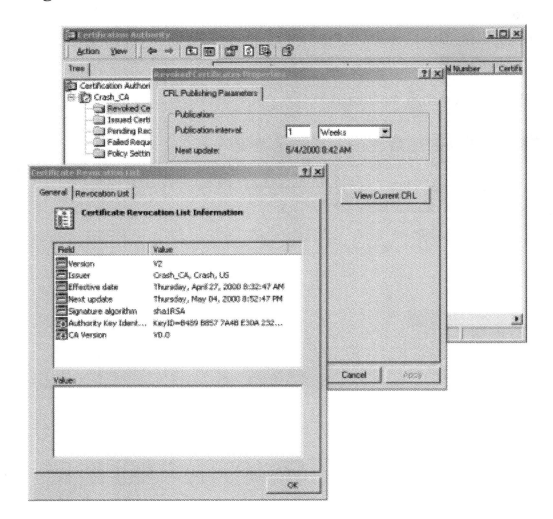

6.   Choose the **Revocation List** property page.

Publishing a CRL

Every CA automatically creates and publishes a CRL after a period of time specified by the CA's administrator. This span of time is called the CRL publish period. By default, the CRL publish period is one week. The administrator can modify this publish period by using the procedure schedule function of the CA snap-in.

It is important to remember that the CRL validity period and the CRL publish period are not the same thing. The validity period determines how long a cached copy of the CRL is deemed trustworthy. Remember that even if a new CRL has been published, it does not displace cached copies of the CRL until their validity period expires.

Although the administrator chooses the publish period of a CA's CRL, the validity period is extended from the publish period, mainly to allow time for Active Directory duplication. Certificate Services extends the validity period by 10%, up to a maximum of 12 hours, by default. If a CA is configured to create a new CRL every 18 hours, the validity period becomes 19.8 hours.

Since there are often variances between the clocks of various computers, a clock skew variance is built into the calculation of the validity period. 10 minutes are allowed on either side of the publish period, so that a CRL would appear to be valid up to 10 minutes (local time) before it's publish period.

The only way to modify the values used to calculate clock skew variances is to change the values of certain system registry entries. The Windows 2000 Resource Kits contain information on using the Registry editor and which values control the clock skew values.

Publishing a CRL Before the Next Scheduled Publish Period

If you wish to obtain an updated CRL, you can publish a new one on demand. The CRL Publishing Wizard allows you to create a new CRL without affecting the next scheduled automatic CRL generation and publication.

Remember that clients often have cached copies of the CRL, and until that CRL expires, it does not update, even if a newer CRL has been published. If you manually publish a new CRL, it does not affect the valid cached copies of the CRL that have yet to expire, but only makes a new copy of the CRL available to systems without a cached copy of it.

Revoking Certificates

If a user associated with a security certificate leaves the organization, or if the private key of a certificate becomes compromised, a certificate should be revoked. Revoking certificates of questionable security helps to maintain the overall security of the PKI. After a certificate is revoked, it is added to that CA's CRL.

Vocabulary

Review the following terms in preparation for the certification exam.

Term	Description
CA	A Certificate Authority is a trusted service responsible for the creation of public keys and the verification of the validity of the public keys of other CAs, users, and computers. CAs link public keys to identities with signed digital certificates, keep track of certificate serial numbers, and manage certificate revocation.
certificate hierarchy	Certificate hierarchies are structures that determine CA trust relationships through the creation of root-subordinate or parent-child CA relationships.
certificate mapping	Certificate mapping is a method where one or more issued certificates are associated with a user account. Servers can then use the private keys of those certificates to authenticate the user or perform secure tasks.
Certificate Services Web pages	These are Web pages that provide, through the use of a CA, authentication support, Web-based authentication, Smart Card authentication, and secure e-mail services.
CRL	A Certification Revocation List is an automatically generated list of invalid and revoked certificates that is periodically generated by a CA.
CSP	A Cryptographic Service Provider is used in all CA based systems to maintain, create, and destroy keys. CSPs also perform many different cryptographic functions and each one uses it's own custom version of the CryptoAPI. Some rely on cryptographic hardware, while others use varying strengths of software ciphers.

Term	Description
Enterprise CA	An enterprise Certificate Authority utilizes Active Directory to automate many tasks and allow for automatic selection of appropriate certificates. The enterprise CA uses Active directory to confirm a requesters identity, the validity of his request, and to determine which kind of certificate to grant based upon the different types of certificates available from an enterprise CA and the information store on the Active Directory about the requester. The enterprise CA also uses the Active Directory, along with a shared directory, to create and publish a CRL.
external certificates	External user certificates are used by CAs to verify a sender's computer's identity instead of the systems SID. External certificates can be used to relay authenticated messages to Windows NT and other non-Windows 2000 environments.
Hash algorithm	An algorithm that creates a hash value from an input, such as a session key or message. Good Hash methods produce vastly different outputs even when only small changes are made to the input. This makes Hash coding an excellent tool to detect any changes in sizeable data objects, like messages. Properly designed Hash algorithms will never create the same Hash code output from different inputs. Common Hash algorithms include MD2, MD4, MD5, and SHA-1. Hash algorithms are also known as hash functions.
message queuing	A message queuing and routing system for Windows 2000 designed to allow distributed applications not running concurrently to pass messages between each other and to queue messages for systems that may be offline or are not responding. Message Queuing, formerly known as MSMQ, can be used in heterogeneous networks and provides a number of important services, including guaranteed message delivery, efficient routing, priority-bases message queuing, and security features.

Term	Description
stand-alone CA	A stand-alone Certificate Authority is a CA that does not depend on Active Directory and, consequently, is less automated than an enterprise CA. Stand-alone CAs handle user requests via a Web interface.
trusted root	A branch of a PKI in which every member inherits all of the trust relationships from the root CA.

In Brief

If you want to...	Then do this...
Use enterprise CAs	Install and enable Active Directory on the server.
Generate a secure key for a root server	Use a key with a minimum length of 2,048 bits.
View your certificate	Use the CA.
Map certificates to user accounts	Use Active Directory to edit Name Mappings, enter the name/path of the certificate, and select Open.
Use store inheritance	Place a root certificate in the computer's enterprise trust store.
Confirm security settings	Locate the CertServ virtual directory on the Internet Service manager system and choose the Directory Security tab to display anonymous access and authentication control.
Get an Advanced Certificate	Use Internet Explorer to access the certsrv directory of the CA, then select the submission form for the Advanced Certificate.
Use an external trusted authority	Open the Domain Group Policy Properties box and modify the Default Domain Policy GPO. Expand Computer Configuration, Windows Settings, Security Settings, Public Key Policies, and right-click **Trusted Root Certification Authorities**. In the context menu, choose **All Tasks** and then choose **Import**. The Certificate Import Wizard will appear.

If you want to...	Then do this...
	Choose **Next**. In the File name box use the Browse button to find and select the appropriate file. Select **Next**. Specify a password and select **Next**. Choose **Place all certificates in the following store**. The destination is the Trusted Root Certification Authorities store in the GPO. Select **Next**.
To start or stop a Certificate Authority Service	Log on to the system as an Administrator. Open Certification Authority. In the console tree, expand the name of the CA. On the **Action** menu, choose **All Tasks**, and select **Start Service** to start the service or select **Stop Service** to stop the service.

Lesson 7 Activities

Complete the following activities to better prepare you for the certification exam.

1. Explain how a CA operates.

2. List the Advanced Options for the stand-alone root CA.

3. Explain the circumstances in which a revoked certificate may have its status changed.

4. Describe the different types of mapping.

5. Name some user-selectable options in advanced certificate request.

6. Describe the procedures for setting Web security.

7. What are the options for requested certificates on a Web page?

8. List some reasons for using external certificates.

9. Define policy modules.

10. What are the procedures to display the log?

Answers to Lesson 7 Activities

1. CAs create and issue certificates to computers, services, or users. These certificates are used to verify the identity and other characteristics of the requester. After a CA receives a request for a certificate, it confirms the identity and appropriateness of the requester, and then applies a digital signature to a certificate using its private key. The CA will then issue the certificate, so that it can be used as a security credential within the public key infrastructure. CAs can also revoke certificates and create lists of currently invalid certificates.

2. Cryptographic Service Provider

    Hash Algorithms

    Existing keys

    Key length

3. A revoked certificate may only have its status changed if its current revocation status is Certificate Hold. A certificate can be unrevoked, left unchanged until its expiry date, or have its revocation status code changed.

4. There are two primary types of mapping: One-to-one mapping and many-to-one mapping. Many-to-one mapping is used when a user requires the permissions provided by more than one security certificate; it allows multiple certificates to be attached to a single user account. One-to-one mapping is used when the permissions of only one security certificate are required. Only one security certificate is attached to single user account.

    User principal mapping a special kind of one-to-one mapping. It is used only for user accounts when Active Directory is available. It uses a single security certificate to identify a user through the Active Directory and to then log that user onto the network.

5. Cryptographic Service Provider (CSP) options include:

    The name of the cryptographic service provider, the key size (512, 1,024, 2,048, etc.), the type of hash algorithm (SHA/RSA, SHA/DSA, MD2, MD5) and the key specification (exchange or signature).

    Key generation options include:

    Create a new key set or use an existing key set, mark the keys as exportable, enable strong key protection, and use the local computer store to generate the key.

6. To configure certificates via the Web interface on a stand-alone CA, the user makes two visits to the applicable Web pages. First, the user requests a certificate. Then, if the administrator approves the request, the user may visit the Web page for a second time and download the new certificate.

    On Enterprise CAs, the process does not require administrator response. A user will visit the applicable Web page, and provides his or her network user ID. The user then selects a certificate template, and based upon the template selection and information stored in the Active Directory, the CA will create an appropriate certificate and issue it to the user.

7. Certificate template, cryptographic service provider, key size, hash algorithm, key usage, create a new key set or use an existing key set, mark keys as exportable, use the local machine store, save the request to PKCS number 10 file.

8. External certificates can be useful when users are part of workgroups and not domains, or do not have access to an Active Directory service. External certificates are also useful in situations where some users need to be allowed to send authenticated messages to privileged parties, as the installation of Message Queuing creates internal certificates that allow everyone to read messages not created with external certificates.

9. Policy modules are sets of conditions or rules that CAs use when committing all certificate transactions, including requests, issuances, revocations, and CRL publishing.

10. Start the Certification Authority tool and expand the certificate name of the Certification Authority.

    Right-click **Issued Certificates**, choose **View**, and then select **Choose Columns**.

    Now define your search, or the fields you wish to see. Choose only the fields you need to observe or work with. Selecting Request ID is mandatory, although all other fields are optional. When finished, choose **OK**.

    Selecting the **Issued Common Name** collumn allows you to list the results of the search in ascending or descending order.

    If you wish to apply a filter to the results, right-click on **Issued Certificates**, choose **View** from the context menu, and then choose **Filter**. In the new window, choose **Add**. Set the parameters as required.

Lesson 7 Quiz

These questions test your knowledge of features, vocabulary, procedures, and syntax.

1. What are some types of certification authorities?

    A. Root and subordinate certification authorities

    B. Branch and leaf certification authorities

    C. Enterprise certification authority

    D. Stand-alone certification authority

2. Which certificates are exportable from the Certificate Request Wizard?

    A. EFS Recovery Agent

    B. CSP

    C. Basic EFS

    D. Key pair

3. Which of the following are reason codes for changing the status of a revoked certificate?

    A. Unspecified

    B. Key Compromise

    C. Certificate authority Compromise

    D. Affiliation Changed

4. How can a certificate be mapped to a user account?

    A. Use a Smart Card

    B. Use Active Directory

    C. Use a hosts file

    D. Use the central database

5. Identify the valid mapping types.

    A. Principal name mapping

    B. One-to-one mapping

    C. Geostationary mapping

    D. Many-to-one mapping

6.   What do the Certificate Service Web pages provide?

A. Requesting the certificate authority certificate

B. Requesting certificates from a CA

C. Processing a certificate request file

D. Process a Smart Card enrollment file

7.   What are some options of Advanced Certificates?

A. Mark keys as exportable

B. Use the local machine store

C. Enable strong private key protection

D. Save the request to PKCS Number 10 file

8.   Which of the following are Certificate Authority vendors?

A. America On-Line

B. Yellowknife Telecom

C. Keywitness Canada

D. VeriSign Commercial Software Publishers

9.   What are some uses for Certificate Services?

A. Create a Certification Authority

B. Enroll users for certificates

C. Create certificate templates

D. Placing orders online

10.   What is the maximum time that Certificate Services will extend a validity period?

A. 24 hours

B. 12 hours

C. 20 minutes

D. 12 hours, 20 minutes

Answers to Lesson 7 Quiz

1. Answers A, C, and D are correct. Root and subordinate certification authorities, Enterprise certification authority, and Stand-alone certification authority are all valid types of certification authorities.

    Answer B is incorrect. Branch and leaf certification is the responsibility of the root Certificate Authority.

2. Answers A and C are correct. By default, only Basic EFS and EFS Recovery Agent certificates have their private keys marked as available for export.

    Answers B and D are incorrect. Neither answer encapsulates a security certificate. The advanced options window of the Certificate Request wizard allows a specific CSP for a key pair to be selected. To export the private key of other certificate types, use the advanced request page to create a PKCS Number 12 export file.

3. All answers are correct. All choices are valid reason codes for changing the status of a revoked certificate on Certificate Hold.

4. Answer B is correct. The Active Directory service is the only valid manner of mapping certificates to user accounts listed.

    Answers A, C, and D are incorrect. Smart Cards can support automatic log on but are not involved with mapping accounts. Hosts files are not used with any certificate service. The central database cannot be used to map certificates to user accounts.

5. Answers A, B, and D are correct. Principal name mapping is a special case of one-to-one mapping, One-to-one mapping maps a single user certificate to a single Windows 2000 user account. Many-to-one mapping maps multiple certificates to a single user account.

    Answer C is incorrect. While important to many branches of science, geostationary mapping has nothing to do with the mapping of certificate trusts.

6. All answers are correct. Windows 2000 Certificate Services provides Web pages that enable the user to request a CA certificate, request certificates from a CA, process a certificate request file, or process a Smart Card enrollment file. The enterprise certificate authority requires the user to log on to the Web pages using the user's ID, unlike stand-alone CAs. The user can then request a certificate base by selecting a certificate template. The certificate authority finds the account via

the Active Directory service and generates a certificate based on information from the Active Directory and from the selected template.

7. All answers are correct.

    When keys are marked as exportable, you can save the public and private key to a PKCS Number 12 file. You can use the local machine store. This option is used to associate a computer to a private key, regardless of the currently logged on user. Choose this option when requesting certificates that are intended to be issued to computers like Web servers instead of certificates issued to people.

    You can also Enable strong private key protection. This forces the password associated with a private key to be requested every time the key is utilized. Finally, you can save the request to PKCS Number 10 file. If the certification authority is unavailable for processing certificate requests online, this can be used to store requests to process at a later date.

8. Answers C and D are correct. Keywitness Canada and VeriSign Commercial Software Publishers are both valid certification authority vendors.

    Answers A and B are incorrect. Neither America On-Line nor Yellowknife Telecom is a certification authority vendor.

9. Answers A, B, and C are correct. All three functions are available from Certificate Services.

    Answer D is incorrect. Online ordering is properly served by Internet server tools, and not network security certificates.

10. Answer D is correct. Certificate Services will extend the validity period to 12 hours and 20 minutes. This figure comes from a maximum limit of 12 hours, and an added + or – 10 minute clock skew.

    Answers A, B, and C are incorrect. 20 minutes is only the total maximum time allocated for clock skew, 12 hours is the maximum time extension that can be applied to a validity period, as well as the default without taking clock skew into account. 24 hours can be added to the validity period if desired but not automatically by certificate services.

Encryption and Authentication

Microsoft's Encrypting File System (EFS) resides in the operating system kernel and relies on public key encryption, which in turn relies on the Cryptographic Application Program Interface (CryptoAPI) architecture. EFS encrypts each file with a randomly generated key that does not depend on the user's public/private keypair. The encryption algorithm is Data Encryption Standard (DES), specified in 1977 by the National Bureau of Standards for non-classified and commercial use. Alternate encryption schemes are planned for the future.

EFS can encrypt and decrypt files located on remote file servers. However, EFS only encrypts data on disk, and does not encrypt data transferred over a network. Network data encryption is provided by Windows 2000 Server's network protocols, such as Secure Sockets Layer/Private Communication Technology (SSL/PCT).

EFS and NTFS are tightly integrated. EFS encrypts the temporary copies of encrypted originals stored on an NTFS volume. Since EFS resides in the operating system kernel, it stores file encryption keys in non-paged memory, ensuring that they never appear in the paging file.

Tip: For more information on DES, obtain the definitive Federal Information Processing Standards Publication IPS PUB 46-2 at www.cryptosoff.com/html/fips46-2htm. The U.S. Department of Commerce controls DES. Export restrictions on 128-bit security are currently in force.

After completing this lesson, you should have a better understanding of the following topics:

• Encrypting File System (EFS)

- Cipher Command Line Utility
- File and Folder Encryption
- File Decryption
- Backup Routines for Encrypted Files and Folders
- Certificate and Private Key Encryption Backup
- Default Recovery Key
- Recovery Agents

Encrypting File System (EFS)

Windows 2000 EFS is a complete encrypting and decrypting system that is simple to use and provides a higher degree of file protection than available in Windows NT 4.0.

This section provides the following information:

- An overview of EFS's features and restrictions
- Recommendations for an encryption strategy
- An introduction to data recovery and user interaction with EFS
- Technical explanations of the key pair, the FEK algorithm, and the EFS components
- Descriptions of how to set data recovery policies and how to disable EFS

Understanding the Main Features of EFS

EFS provides the following advantages:

- Easy and permanent encryption of a file.
- Quick and transparent access to encrypted data without need to decrypt and see it in plain text.
- Updated data automatically re-encrypts, and the process is completely invisible.
- The ability to actively and permanently decrypt a file.

- The ability to recover data encrypted by another user, ensuring data is recoverable if the user who encrypted the data is no longer available, or if the user's private key has been lost or misplaced.

- Use of EFS on systems that are temporarily offline, such as portable computers.

EFS provides the technology used to store encrypted files on NTFS file system volumes. You can work with your encrypted files or folders just as you do with any other files and folders. You do not have to decrypt a file before using it. You simply open, change, and save the file as usual. However, no one else can access your encrypted files. An intruder trying to open, copy, move, or rename your encrypted file or folder receives an Access Denied message.

Understanding EFS Restrictions

The following restrictions apply to using EFS:

- You cannot encrypt system files or compressed files.

- You can encrypt only files and folders stored on NTFS volumes.

- Only the user who encrypted a file can open it.

- You cannot share encrypted files.

- You must copy and paste encrypted files to retain encryption when moving files into an encrypted folder.

 Warning: Encrypted files can become decrypted when copied or moved to a non-NTFS volume.

- Moving files by dragging and dropping does not automatically encrypt them in the new folder. To ensure the retention of encryption, copy and paste files.

- Encryption does not protect against deletion because anyone with delete permission can delete encrypted folders or files.

- Temporary files, created by programs when documents are edited, encrypt if all the files are in an encrypted folder on an NTFS volume.

- You can encrypt or decrypt files and folders stored on a remote computer only if it has been enabled for remote encryption.

- Files are not EFS-encrypted during data transfers over a network and you must use protocols such as SSL/PCT or Internet Protocol Security (IPSec) to encrypt the data for transfer.

 Warning: When attempting to use EFS on any Windows NT partition, Windows 2000 performs a check disk operation that changes the partition to Windows 2000 format.

Creating an EFS Encryption Strategy

When deciding what to encrypt, consider the following recommendations:

- Have your personal documents encrypted by default—encrypt your My Documents folder.

- Automatically have all temporary files created by programs encrypted—encrypt all the Temp folders on your system.

- Create a Temp folder if it does not already exist and encrypt it—some applications may use such a folder.

- Encrypt folders instead of individual files—if a program creates temporary files during editing, these encrypt as well.

Understanding Data Recovery

Data recovery consists of decrypting a file without having the private key of the user who encrypted the file. Data recovery is an essential solution if encryption keys are lost, when businesses need to recover data encrypted by former employees, or if a law enforcement agency makes a decryption request.

The first time a user encrypts a file or folder, EFS automatically implements a recovery policy. Should any users lose their file encryption certificates and associated private keys, the recovery policy enables them to decrypt their files through having recourse to a recovery agent.

The recovery agent must export the data recovery certificate (as described later in this lesson), store it in a safe place, and delete the data recovery certificate from the system's hard disk. This process ensures that the only person who can recover data for the system is the one who has physical access to the data recovery certificate.

If the need for data recovery arises, the recovery agent can retrieve the data recovery certificate from its safe location and import the certificate into the system from which it originally came. Once the data recovery certificate is back on the system, the recovery agent can recover the user's encrypted files. After recovering the data, the recovery agent must delete the data recovery certificate from the system.

 Note: You need not re-export the certificate; you can import the certificate as often as required.

Understanding User Interaction With EFS

Users do not need to perform any administrative tasks to start encrypting their files. EFS automatically generates a public key pair for file encryption for every user (if one does not already exist). Users encrypt and decrypt files on a per-file or per-folder basis. All the files created in an encryption-enabled folder are automatically encrypted. Each file has a unique encryption key that remains encrypted if it is moved from an encrypted folder to an unencrypted folder on the same volume. You can access encryption and decryption from both Windows Explorer and a command-line tool. An administrative interface is also available.

Data transparently encrypts and decrypts as it transmits to and from a disk. Therefore, you do not need to decrypt a file before use. EFS automatically detects whether a file is encrypted. It then retrieves the user's key from the system's key store. As key storage is based on CryptoAPI, users can store keys on Smart Cards and other such secure devices.

Generating a Public Key Pair

A request for a new certificate is passed to the Microsoft CryptoAPI. CryptoAPI then passes the data to a Cryptographic Service Provider (CSP) on your computer or on a device accessible to your computer. A software-based CSP generates a key pair (a public key and a private key) on your computer. A hardware-based CSP (like a Smart Card CSP) instructs some hardware to generate the key pair.

After generating the keys, a software CSP encrypts the private key and secures it in the computer's Registry. A Smart Card CSP stores the private key on a Smart Card, which restricts access to the key. The public key and the certificate requester information are sent to the Certificate Authority (CA). The CA verifies the certificate request according to its policies, and, using its own private key, creates a digital signature in the certificate and issues it to the requester. The certificate requester, upon receiving the certificate from the CA, has the option to store it in the relevant certificate store on the computer or hardware device.

Setting a Data Recovery Policy at the Domain Level

A domain controller defines a recovery policy and enforces it on all of the domain's computers. Domain administrators control the policy and can delegate their control to data security administrator accounts, and withdraw their delegated authority from any such account if the need arises. In a home environment, EPS automatically generates recovery keys and saves them as machine keys when no Windows domain is found.

The Group Policy snap-in defines data recovery policies for domain member, stand-alone, or workgroup servers. You can either export and import your recovery certificates, or request a recovery certificate.

If recovery is necessary, you want to have alternate recovery agents. Administration of the recovery policy can be delegated to an administrator.

 Note: You should limit the number of people authorized to recover encrypted data.

File encryption only happens if the system is configured with at least one recovery key. EFS enables recovery agents to configure public keys used to enable data recovery. The recovery key gives access to only the file's randomly generated encryption key, not the user's private key. This prevents the accidental release of private information to the recovery agent.

Setting a Data Recovery Policy at the Local Computer Level

Before you can add or create a recovery agent, the Group Policy snap-in and its Public Key Policies extension must be installed on your computer. To change the recovery policy for a local computer or add a new one, follow these steps:

1. From the **Start** menu, choose **Run**, type **mmc /a** (Figure 8.1), and then click **OK**.

Figure 8.1 MMC

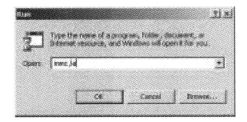

2. From the **Console** menu, choose **Add/Remove Snap-in**, then select **Add**.

3. Under Snap-in, choose **Group Policy** (Figure 8.2), then select **Add**.

Figure 8.2 Add Group Policy

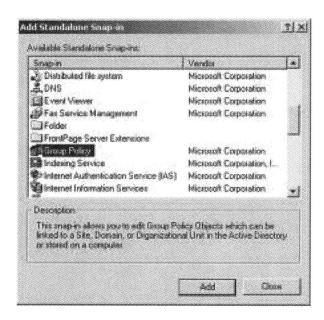

4. In the **Group Policy Object** dialog box, ensure the Local Computer displays, choose **Finish**, select **Close**, and click **OK**.

5. Under **Local Computer Policy**, open **Computer Configuration**, **Windows Settings**, and **Security Settings**, and then select **Public Key Policies** (Figure 8.3).

Figure 8.3 Public Key Policies Selected

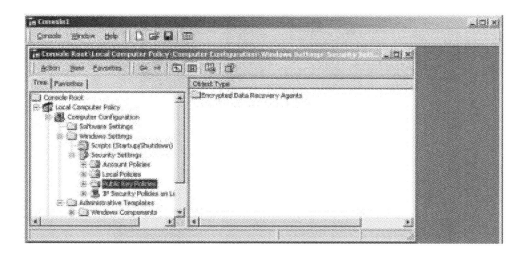

6.   In the right pane, right-click **Encrypted Data Recovery Agents**, and choose one of the following options:

Add—Select this option to designate a user as an additional recovery agent. Using the Add Recovery Agent Wizard (Figure 8.4), either provide the name for a user with a published recovery certificate, or browse for the files that contain information about the recovery agent you are adding. Adding a recovery agent from a file identifies the user as USER_UNKNOWN.

Figure 8.4 Add Recovery Agent Wizard

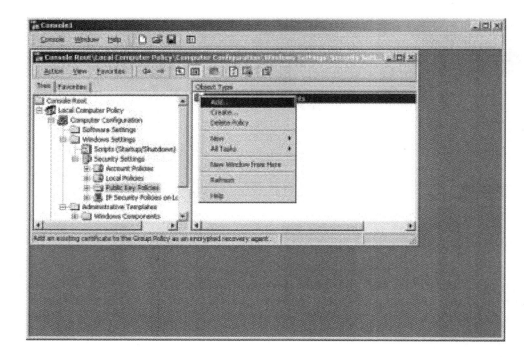

Create—Choose this option (Figure 8.5) to request a new File Recovery certificate using the Certificate Request Wizard. You must have the required permissions to request the certificate, and the CA must be configured to issue this type of certificate.

Figure 8.5 Create Policy Selected

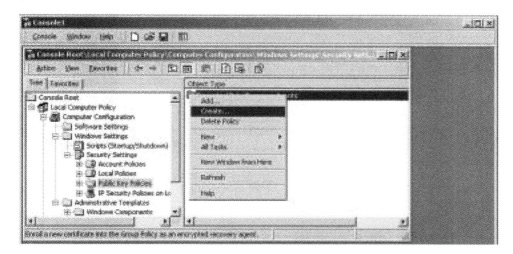

Delete Policy—Choose this option (Figure 8.6) to delete the EFS policy and all recovery agents. The selection ensures that no one will be able to encrypt files on this computer.

Figure 8.6 Delete Policy Selected

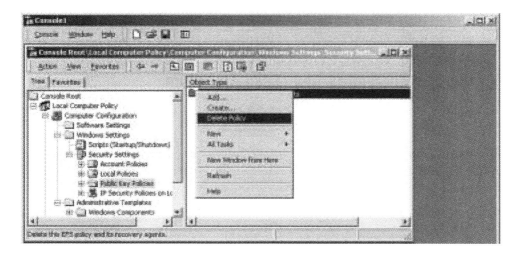

Note: To complete this procedure, you must be logged on as an administrator or a member of the Administrators group. If your computer is connected to a network, network policy settings can prevent you from performing this procedure.

By default, the computer issues a self-signed certificate. This designates the local administrator as the recovery agent. If no other policy is in place and you delete this certificate, the computer will have an empty recovery policy. With this process, no one is a recovery agent. EFS is turned off, and users will not be able to encrypt files on the computer.

Before changing the recovery policy at all, you should back up the recovery keys to another storage media, such as a floppy disk.

At the same time the first domain controller is set up, a recovery policy is set for a domain. A self-signed certificate is issued to the domain administrator, who is thereby designated as the recovery agent. To change a domain's default recovery policy, you must log on to the first domain controller as an administrator.

You can change a File Recovery certificate by right-clicking it and choosing **Properties**. For example, you can rename the certificate and enter a text description.

Understanding the File Encryption Key (FEK) Algorithm

Users do not need to understand the process of data encryption and decryption because it is transparent to them. They need only specify which file to encrypt or decrypt.

However, administrators may find it useful to know that EFS does not encrypt the actual folders or subfolders, it encrypts only the contents of the files within a folder. Folders and subfolders are simply marked to indicate that they contain encrypted file data.

Files encryption has the following characteristics:

• Each file has a unique file encryption key that decrypts that file.

- The file encryption key is encrypted and protected by the user's public key corresponding to the user's EFS certificate.

- The public key of an authorized recovery agent protects the file encryption key.

Files decryption has the following characteristics:

- The file encryption key must be decrypted. This takes place when the user has a private key that matches the public key or when a recovery agent's private key is used.

- A user or recovery agent can use a decrypted encryption key to decrypt the data in the file.

 Note: Private keys are kept in a protective key store. They are not held in the Security Account Manager (SAM) or in a separate directory.

EFS uses a public-key scheme to implement data encryption and decryption. Encryption uses a fast symmetric algorithm with a File Encryption Key (FEK) randomly generated at runtime and unique to the file being encrypted. The FEK currently used in EFS is a 56-bit key for international users. North American users can use 128-bit DES encryption. 128-bit DES encryption cannot be exported abroad except by some specific users, such as large international banks.

Using one or more key encryption public keys, EFS encrypts the FEK to produce a list of encrypted FEKs. This list stores with the encrypted file in the Data Decryption Field (DDF), a special EFS attribute. The private portion of the user's key pair is used during decryption.

EFS encrypts the FEK a second time, using one or more recovery key encryption public keys. The list of encrypted FEKs is stored with the file in the Data Recovery Field (DRF), another special EFS attribute. Since recovery is normally required only when users lose keys or leave organizations, recovery agents can store the private portions of the keys on Smart Cards or other secure storage devices.

Understanding the EFS Components

EFS has the following four main components:

EFS driver—Requests file encryption keys, DDFs, DRFs, and other key-management services from the EFS service and passes the received information to the EFS File System Runtime Library (FSRTL). This process opens, reads, writes, and appends transparently.

EFS FSRTS—Implements NTFS callouts to handle reads, writes, and opens on encrypted files and folders. This component handles data encryption, decryption, and recovery when data is written to or read from disk. File control mechanisms require writing the EFS attribute data (DDF and DRF) as file attributes and passing the FEK computed in the EFS service to FSRTL so that it can be set up in the open file context. The file context is then used for transparent encryption and decryption when data is written or read.

EFS service—EFS service is part of the security system and communicates with the EFS driver through the existing LPC communication port between the Local Security Authority (LSA) and the kernel-mode security reference monitor. In user mode, EFS service interfaces with CryptoAPI to provide file encryption keys and generate DDFs and DRFs. EFS service also supports Win32 APIs for encryption, decryption, recovery, importing, and exporting.

Win32 APIs—Programming interfaces encrypts plaintext files, decrypts or recovers ciphertext files, and imports and exports encrypted files without decrypting them first. These APIs are supported in ADVAPI32.DLL, a standard system Dynamic Link Library (DLL).

The following are two methods to encrypt or decrypt a folder or file:

- Set the encryption property for that folder and file, just as you would any other attribute, such as read-only or hidden.

- Use the command-line function CIPHER.EXE.

If you encrypt a folder, all files and subfolders created in that folder are automatically encrypted.

Tip: It is recommended that you encrypt folders rather than individual files.

Disabling EFS

You may need to disable EFS on a computer. To do so, set up an empty recovery policy. To disable EFS locally on a computer, use the local Group Policy Editor. To disable EFS at the Organizational Unit level (OU), define a Group Policy Object (GPO) at that level with an empty recovery policy. A GPO is a collection of group policy settings.

 Note: An empty policy is not the same as no policy. In Active Directory, the actual policy is an accumulation of Group Policy Objects (GPOs) defined at various directory tree levels. GPOs are collections of group policy settings. If a higher-level node has no policy, the lower-level policies take effect. If a higher-level node has an empty recovery policy, EFS disables because the higher-level node provides no recovery certificates.

Cipher Command-Line Utility

The cipher command-line utility enables you to encrypt and decrypt files from a command prompt.

Using the Cipher Command-Line Utility

Used without parameters, Cipher displays the encryption state of the current folder and any files it contains.

For example, to determine whether the Shakespeare folder is encrypted enter the following:

cipher shakespeare

To determine which files in the StanleyCup folder are encrypted, enter the following:

cipher stanleycup*

The **cipher** command supports the following options:

[/e | /d] [/s:dir] [/a] [/i] [/f] [/q] [/h] [/k] [pathname [...]]

These parameters have the following meanings:

/E—Encrypts the specified files or folders. Folders are marked so that added files are encrypted.

/D—Decrypts the specified files or folders. Folders are marked so that files added are encrypted.

/S—Performs the specified operation on the given folder and all subfolders. By default, /s is followed by 'dir', the current folder.

/A—Performs the specified operation on files and folders. A file could become decrypted if it is modified and the folder that stores it is not encrypted.

/I—Ignores errors and continues performing the specified operation.

/F—Forces encryption on all specified files, even those already encrypted. This switch ensures that files marked as encrypted are, in fact, encrypted. If a hardware failure occurs during the encryption process, a file can be marked as encrypted even though it is not actually encrypted.

/Q—(Quiet mode). Reports only the most essential information.

/H—Specifies files with hidden or system attributes.

 Warning: Do not encrypt system files because the computer may not boot up.

/K—Creates a new file encryption key for the user running **cipher.** If this option is specified, cipher ignores all other options.

pathname—Specifies a pattern, folder, or file. You may use multiple file names and wildcards. Use spaces between multiple parameters.

Encrypting a File or Folder With Cipher

The following examples show how you can combine the /e switch with other switches to encrypt files or folders.

Note: The examples in this section assume you have a Security Certificate from Windows 2000 Certificate Server, Exchange Key Manager, or a commercial provider such as VeriSign.

To encrypt a subfolder named 2004 in a folder named Budget, enter the following command:

```
cipher /e budget\2004
```

To encrypt the Budget folder and all its subfolders enter the following:

```
cipher /e /s:budget
```

To encrypt only the CAPITALASSETS.XLS file in the 2004 subfolder enter the following:

```
cipher /e /a budget\2004\capitalassets.xls
```

To encrypt all the .DOC files of authors beginning with the letter a in the EnglishLiterature folder, type:

```
cipher /e /a englishliterature\a*.doc
```

Decrypting a File or Folder with Cipher

 Note: The examples in this procedure assume you have a Security Certificate from Windows 2000 Certificate Server, Exchange Key Manager, or a commercial provider such as VeriSign.

The following example shows how you can combine the /d switch with other switches to decrypt files or folders.

To decrypt the folder Z:\financial reports, enter the following:

```
cipher /d /s:"Z:\financialreports"
```

Because the /a flag is not used, files currently encrypted in the folder and subfolders remain encrypted. However, any new files created in the folder or subfolders, do not encrypt.

To decrypt the folder Expansion and all the encrypted files inside, enter the following:

```
cipher /d /a expansion
```

File and Folder Encryption

File and folder encryption is a necessary component of a well-planned strategy for providing tight data security because preventing physical access to a computer is not always successful, and New Technology File System (NTFS) security can be bypassed by means of available tools. Although there are other file encryption systems, there are several problems, including the following:

- Most application-level file encryption products have limitations and do not offer full security as they use password-derived keys.

- Systems deriving encryption keys from passwords are subject to dictionary attacks.

- Systems offering password-based data recovery enable the data thief who knows the recovery password to plunder encrypted files.

- This section describes the following:

- How to encrypt a file or folder with Microsoft Windows Explorer.

- How copying, moving, or renaming encrypted files and folders affects the encryption status of files.

Encrypting a File or Folder with Windows Explorer

To encrypt a file or folder with Microsoft Windows Explorer, follow these steps:

1.   Start Windows Explorer.

2.   Right-click the folder or file name and then choose **Properties** (Figure 8.7).

Figure 8.7 Windows Explorer's Properties Option

3. From the **General** property page, choose **Advanced**.

4. In the **Advanced Attributes** dialog box, put a check mark into the **Encrypt contents to secure data** checkbox (Figure 8.8), and choose **OK**.

Figure 8.8 Advanced Attributes Encrypt Option

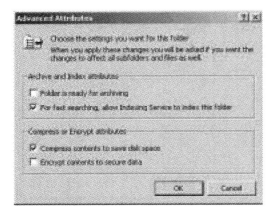

5.   On the **General** page of **Properties**, choose **Apply** or **OK** to effect the encryption change.

6.   In the **Confirm Attribute Changes** dialog box (Figure 8.9), choose the desired level of encryption and select **OK**.

Figure 8.9 Confirm Attribute Changes Screen for Encryption

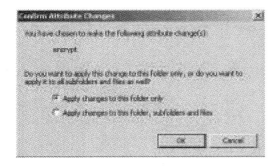

File Encryption

All reads from an encrypted file decrypt transparently, and all writes also encrypt transparently. The only way User A knows whether a file is encrypted is by checking the file properties. Any other user trying to open User A's encrypted files receives an Access Denied error, because that user does not have User A's file decryption key.

Microsoft's EFS enables you to do the following:

- Encrypt files

- Access encrypted files

- Move, copy, or rename encrypted files

- Decrypt encrypted files

By default, the EFS is configured so that users can begin encrypting files immediately without engaging in any administrative procedures. EFS automatically generates an encryption key pair for a user if one does not exist.

EFS uses the expanded Data Encryption Standard (DESX) as the encryption algorithm.

Encryption services are available from both Windows Explorer and the command-line function cipher.

Accessing Encrypted Data

You can access your own encrypted files in the same way as any unencrypted files. EFS transparently decrypts and displays the data. When you update the file and store it on disk again, EFS again transparently encrypts the file.

You are the only one who can access a file that you encrypted. This is ensured because users have private keys that allow them access to their own encrypted files. If any other user tries to access an encrypted file, that user receives an Access Denied message.

Copying, Moving, and Renaming Encrypted Files and Folders

You can copy, move, and rename encrypted files in exactly the same way as unencrypted files. You can modify the encryption status of files by copying or moving files because Windows 2000 does not apply the same encryption rules to file copying and file moving. To avoid jeopardizing your encrypted files, it is important to understand the differences when you copy, move, or rename encrypted folders or files on the same volume, from one volume to another, or from one computer to another. Renaming encrypted files and folders does not affect their encrypted status.

 Note: You can only copy encrypted files and folders that you have encrypted. If you try to copy someone else's encrypted files, or if another user tries to copy your encrypted files, an Access Denied message appears.

 Warning: Windows 2000 does not apply the same encryption rules to file copying and file moving.

Encryption Rules for Copying Files

When you copy files or folders from a Windows 2000 NTFS location to another Windows 2000 New Technology File System (NTFS) location, encryption always takes precedence. For example, when copying an unencrypted file or folder to an encrypted folder, EFS automatically encrypts the file or folder. When copying an encrypted file or folder to an unencrypted folder, the file or folder remains encrypted.

Additionally, when you copy encrypted files or folders from a Windows 2000 NTFS volume to a non-Windows 2000 NTFS volume, a File Allocation Table (FAT) file format volume or a Windows NT 4.0 NTFS (NT File System) volume, the encryption is lost and the copy appears in clear text because the destination file system does not support encryption.

Warning: A floppy disk is always formatted using the FAT filing system—floppies are inherently non-secure.

When you copy encrypted files or folders from a Windows 2000 NTFS location on your computer to a Windows 2000 location on a different computer, the copy may or may not be encrypted. This status depends upon whether the remote computer allows you to encrypt files or refuses to allow encryption. You must trust the remote computer for delegation. In a domain environment, remote encryption is not enabled as the default.

 Note: If your original file was encrypted, Microsoft recommends that you use the Properties, Advanced option in Windows Explorer to confirm the status of the destination file.

Moving Encrypted Files

Moving a file or folder between volumes is actually a copying operation, followed by a delete. When you move an encrypted file within the same Windows 2000 NTFS volume, you do not alter its encrypted status. When you move an encrypted file to another folder, the file remains encrypted, even if the destination folder is unencrypted.

Moving Unencrypted Files to Encrypted Folders

When you move an unencrypted file to an encrypted folder, the file remains unencrypted.

Deleting an Encrypted Folder or File

If you have access to delete the file or folder, you can delete an encrypted file as you would an unencrypted file.

File and Folder Decryption

You normally do not need to decrypt files or folders because EFS provides completely transparent decryption during data reads. However, you need to use decryption in order to share an encrypted file with other users or transmit it over a network.

Once decrypted, the file remains decrypted until you encrypt the file again. You can decrypt files and mark folders as unencrypted by using the cipher command, as described earlier, or by using Windows Explorer.

EFS encryption uses standard 56-bit encryption, by default. North American users desiring the additional security of 128-bit encryption can order the Enhanced CryptoPAK from Microsoft. You cannot decrypt, access, or recover by 56-bit encryption EFS those files encrypted with 128-bit encryption.

Decrypting a File or Folder with Windows Explorer

To decrypt a file or folder with Microsoft Windows Explorer, follow these steps:

1.   Start Windows Explorer.

2.   Right-click the encrypted file or folder, and then choose **Properties** (Figure 8.10).

Figure 8.10 Windows Explorer's Properties Option

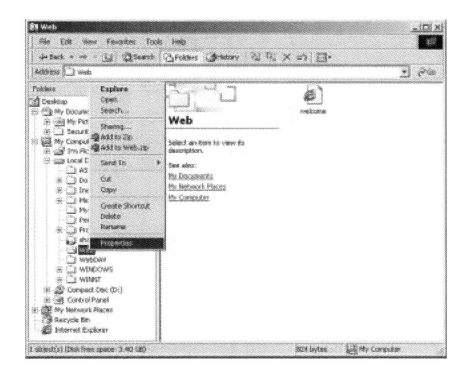

3.   On the **General** property page, choose **Advanced**.

4.   In the **Advanced Attributes** dialog box, remove the check mark from the **Encrypt contents to secure data** check box (Figure 8.11), and choose OK.

Figure 8.11 Advanced Attributes Cleared Encrypt Checkbox

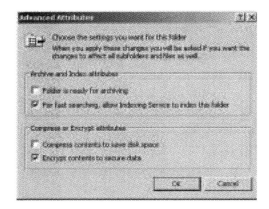

5.   In the **Confirm Attribute Changes** dialog box, choose the desired level of decryption (Figure 8.12) and select **OK**.

Figure 8.12 Confirm Attribute Changes Screen for Decryption

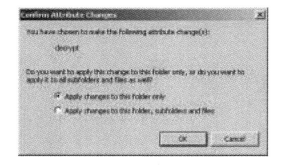

Note: If you choose to decrypt only the folder, all encrypted files and folders within that folder remain encrypted, but all new files and folders that you create after you decrypt the folder will be unencrypted.

Backup Routines for Encrypted Files and Folders

To protect the encrypted status of your files, do not use the command line **copy** command or the **Copy** menu selection in Windows Explorer to back up your encrypted files, as they may end up with no encryption. Instead, you should back them up using any backup utility that supports Windows 2000 features, such as Windows 2000 Backup.

 Warning: Your encrypted files may be decrypted if you back them up with the command line **copy** command or Windows Explorer's **Copy** menu selection.

Windows 2000 Backup maintains file encryption, and runs without access to private keys. Backup backs up the entire encrypted file, folder, or drive to the backup location you choose. You can copy this file to FAT media, such as floppy disks, and remain secure, because the contents remain encrypted.

To use Windows 2000 Backup to back up encrypted files and folders, follow these steps:

1.   From the Start Menu, choose **Accessories**, **System Tools,** and then select **Backup** (Figure 8.13).

Figure 8.13 Windows 2000 Backup's Welcome Property Page

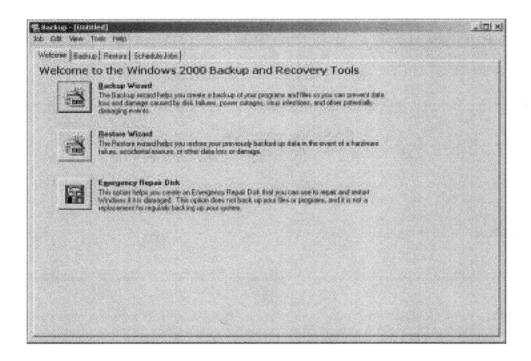

2.   Choose the **Backup** tab.

3.   Check the drive, files, or folders that you wish to back up (Figure 8.14).

Figure 8.14 Windows 2000 Backup's Backup

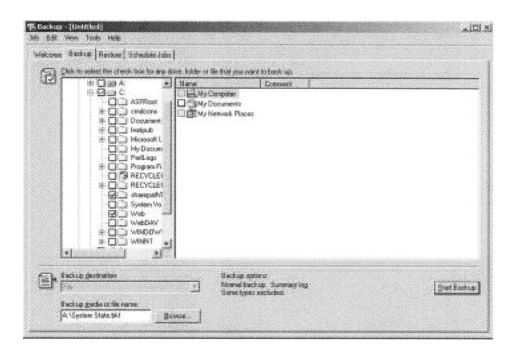

4. Choose the backup media or file name. To locate a pre-existing backup file, select **Browse**.

Note: When you back up encrypted files or folders, the Backup destination drop-down box is grayed out, since you are only able to backup encrypted files and folders to a .BKF file.

5. Choose **Start Backup**.

6. In the **Backup Job Information** dialog box (Figure 8.15), choose the options you require and then select **Start Backup**.

Figure 8.15 Backup Job Information Dialog Box

7. To cancel the backup job while in progress, choose **Cancel** in the **Backup Progress** dialog box (Figure 8.16). Otherwise, the backup finishes.

Figure 8.16 Backup Progress Screen

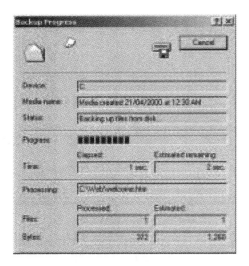

Restoring Encrypted Files and Folders

You can restore 56-bit EFS-encrypted files and folders to the original computer on which they were backed up, or to any other computer set up for EFS encryption. 128-bit EFS-encrypted data must be restored to a system running 128-bit EFS encryption. Perform the restoration with any backup program designed for Windows 2000, such as Windows 2000 Backup.

When you restore encrypted files and folders to a different computer, you need your encryption certificate and private key on that computer; otherwise, you cannot access those files or folders.

If your roaming user profile gives you access to the second computer, your file encryption certificate and private key is available to you on that computer, and transparent decryption enables.

If you cannot access the second computer through your roaming user profile, export your encryption certificate and private key in a .PFX file format from the first computer to a floppy disk, and then import it from the floppy disk to the second computer.

Certificate and Private Key Encryption Backup

You have the option to back up a certificate and private key by exporting it to a .PFX file. This process is accomplished through the Microsoft Management Console snap-ins. You also have the option to decide on which computer to restore the .PFX file. This section shows you how to create a .PFX file and to restore an encrypted certificate. The Certificate Import and Certificate Export wizards facilitate these processes.

Backing Up Encrypted Certificates and Private Keys

You can back up your encryption certificate and private key as a .PFX file that can be restored to the same computer or transferred to a different computer.

To create a .PFX file, follow these steps:

1. Start the Microsoft Management Console (MMC) and add the **Certificates** standalone snap-in (Figure 8.17).

2. When prompted, choose **My user account**, **Finish**, **Close**, and then select **OK**.

Figure 8.17 Certificates Snap-In

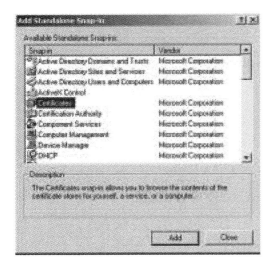

3.   Choose **Certificates - Current User, Personal,** and then **Certificates**   (Figure 8.18).

Figure 8.18 Certificates

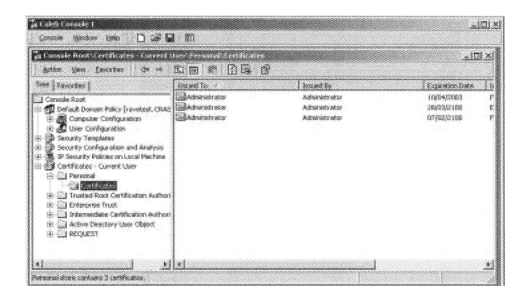

4. For each certificate that you wish to export, right-click the certificate, choose **All Tasks,** and select **Export** (Fig. 8.19).

Figure 8.19 Ready to Export a Certificate

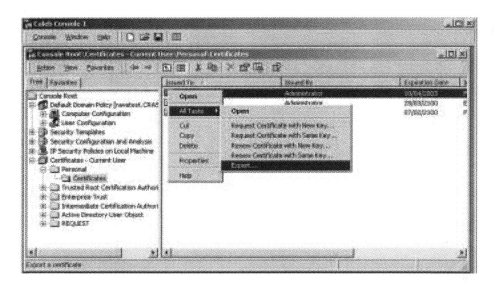

5.   When the **Certificate Export Wizard** appears (Figure 8.20), choose **Next**.

Figure 8.20 Certificate Export Wizard

6. Choose **Yes, export the private key**, and then select **Next**.

7. The **Export File Format** dialog box appears (Figure 8.21). The default export format is Personal Information Exchange-PKCS Number 12 (.PFX), with strong protection enabled. Choose **Next**.

Figure 8.21 Export File Format

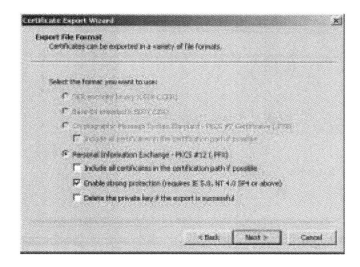

8. Provide a password to protect the PFX data, and choose **Next**.

9. In the **File to Export** dialog box (Figure 8.22), provide the hard-disk path and file name where the PFX data is to be stored (for example, F:\encrypted_docs\data.pfx). Choose **Next**.

Figure 8.22 File to Export

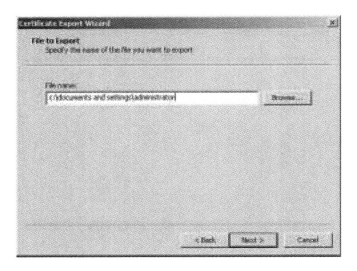

10. When a list of settings displays, choose **Finish** to confirm.

11. Choose **OK** to close the wizard.

Tip: Since your encryption certificate and private key are extremely valuable items, make sure you store the backup disk securely, even though it is encrypted.

Restoring Encrypted Certificates and Private Keys

You can import a .PFX file that contains an encrypted certificate and private key to the same computer from which it was originally exported, or to any other computer set up to support EFS encryption. Installing the .PFX file restores the encrypted certificate and private key.

You can use either MMC or Windows Explorer to start the **Certificate Import Wizard**, which enables you to restore a .PFX file.

To restore an encrypted certificate by using MMC and the **Certificate Import Wizard**, follow these steps:

1. From the **Start** menu, choose **Run**, type **mmc /a** (Figure 8.1), and then select **OK**.

2. Open a console that contains certificates.

3. In the console tree, choose **Certificates—[Certificate Holder]**, **Personal**, and then select **Certificates**.

4. Right-click any file that contains an exported certificate, choose **All Tasks,** and then select **Import**.

5. In the **Certificate Import Wizard**, choose the file that contains the certificates you wish to import.

6. Type the password used to encrypt the private key into the .PFX file.

7. Choose the appropriate check box(es): whether the private key is to be exportable, whether strong private key protection is to be enabled, and whether to automatically place the certificate in a certificate store based on the type of certificate, or to let you specify where the certificate is stored.

8. Choose **Finish**.

Although you can import a certificate into any logical store, usually you import a certificate for your own use into your personal store. If it is a root CA certificate, you import it into the trusted root CA store.

Strong private key protection prompts you for a password every time the private key is used. This ensures that the private key is not used without your knowledge.

To use Windows Explorer to start the **Certificate Import Wizard**, follow these steps:

1. Right-click the .PFX file.

2. Choose **Install PFX**.

Default Recovery Policy

A recovery policy is the policy that users in your computing environment follow to recover encrypted data. The ability to recover data is so essential that no one should encrypt files until a recovery policy is in place. Therefore, the installation of Windows 2000 Server automatically implements a recovery policy for the domain when the administrator first logs on and the first domain controller is set up. A self-signed certificate is issued to the domain administrator, designating the domain administrator as the recovery agent.

Administrators can define one of the following three kinds of recovery policies:

Recovery-agent policy—By adding one or more recovery agents, an administrator automatically puts a recovery-agent policy in effect. These agents are responsible for recovering any encrypted data within their scope of administration. This is the most common type of recovery policy.

Empty recovery policy—By deleting all recovery agents and their public key certificates, an administrator automatically creates an empty recovery policy. As a result, no one is a recovery agent and users cannot encrypt data on the computers under the influence of the empty recovery policy. Setting up an empty recovery policy effectively completely turns off EFS.

No-recovery policy—By deleting the group recovery policy, an administrator creates a no-recovery policy. The lack of group recovery policy turns on, by default, the local policy on individual computers for data recovery. A no-recovery policy at a higher-level node effectively empowers local administrators to control the recovery of data on their computers.

Changing the Default Recovery Policy

To change a domain's default recovery policy, you must log on to the first domain controller as an Administrator. Using the Active Directory Users and Computers snap-in, you must invoke Group Policy, choose **Security Settings**, **Public Key Policies**, and then select **Encrypted Data.**

For stand-alone computers, you configure the default recovery policy locally. For computers in a network, you configure the recovery policy at the domain, OU, or individual computer level, and this policy applies to all Windows 2000-based computers within that domain or OU. A CA issues the recovery certificates, which are managed using Certificates in the Microsoft Management Console (MMC).

A network's recovery policy is set up by a domain administrator or recovery agent who controls the recovery keys for all computers that fall under the influence of the policy.

Recovery Agents

A recovery agent is an administrator authorized to decrypt data encrypted by another user. Before you can add a recovery agent for a domain, you must ensure that each recovery agent has been issued an

X.509 Version 3 certificate. To add recovery agents for a domain, add their certificates to the existing recovery policy. You do this in the procedure described in the above section "Setting a Data Recovery Policy at the Local Computer Level."

The recovery agent has a special certificate and associated private key that enable data recovery within the scope of influence of the recovery policy.

Recovering Encrypted Data

As an essential precaution for possible future data recovery, a recovery agent must secure a copy of the user's certificate and private key. Then, if data recovery is required, the recovery agent can use the certificate and key to recover the data.

To secure a copy of the user's certificate and private key, the recovery agent follows these steps:

1. Exports the recovery certificate and associated private key.

2. Stores the recovery certificate and associated private key in a physically secure location.

3. Deletes the recovery certificate from the computer, using **Certificates** in MMC.

To recover data on the same computer, the recovery agent follows these steps:

1. Restores the recovery certificate and associated private key to the computer.

2. Decrypts the desired files using Windows Explorer or the EFS cipher command.

3. Deletes the recovery certificate.

 Note: The export process does not need to be repeated.

To recover the encrypted data onto another computer, the recovery agent follows these steps:

1. Backs up the encrypted files from the original computer.

2. Restores the backup copies to a secure system.

3.   Imports the user's recovery certificate and private key on the second system.

4.   Restores the backup files on the second system.

5.   Decrypts the files using Windows Explorer or the EFS cipher command.

6.   Deletes the recovery certificate.

Vocabulary

Review the following terms in preparation for the certification exam.

Term	Description
Cipher	A Windows 2000 utility enabling users to encrypt files from the command prompt.
CSP	A Cryptographic Service Provider creates keys, destroys them, and uses them for various cryptographic operations. Some CSPs provide stronger cryptographic algorithms; others contain hardware components, such as Smart Cards.
DESX	A modified Data Encryption Standard (DES) algorithm.
EFS	Windows 2000 Encrypting File System enables users to encrypt files and folders on an NTFS volume disk to keep them safe from unauthorized access.
Enhanced CryptoPAK	A 128-bit encryption system.
FEK	A File Encryption Key is a randomly generated string of bits used by the encryption algorithm to encrypt and decrypt files.
NTFS	Windows 2000 New Technology File System (not to be confused with Windows NT File System).
recovery agent	An administrator who is issued a public key certificate in order to recover EFS-encrypted data.
SAM	A Security Account Manager is a Windows 2000 service used during logon. SAM maintains user account information, including the groups that the user belongs to.

In Brief

If you want to...	Then do this...
Follow EFS best practices	Encrypt the My Documents folder, all Temp and Tmp folders, and encrypt folders rather than files.
Disable the EFS	Set an empty recovery policy.
Copy encrypted folder/files	Make sure the destination is Windows 2000 NTFS formatted.
Permanently decrypt a file	Clear the Encryption check box on the file's Properties dialog box.
Decrypt a 128-bit encrypted file	Make sure the computer is running 128-bit (not 56-bit) encryption.
Backup encrypted files	Use a Windows-2000 compliant backup program that can back up the files in encrypted form.
Recover encrypted files	Ask a recovery agent.
Change the default recovery policy	Use Active Directory and Group Policy.
Add Recovery Agents to the domain	Add their certificates to the existing recovery policy.

Lesson 8 Activities

Complete the following activities to better prepare you for the certification exam.

1. List some important restrictions when working with EFS.

2. Describe what happens when Windows 2000 attempts to use EFS on a Windows NT partition.

3. Explain what happens when you request a new certificate.

4. What are the options for Encrypted Data Recovery Agents?

5. Describe how the FEK works.

6. Discuss the features of using EFS.

7. Discuss the differences between an empty policy and no policy in Active Directory.

8. Explain how to set up your encryption certificate and private key onto another computer.

9. Explain how to recover an encrypted file without a certificate.

10. Name the three kinds of recovery policy.

Answers to Lesson 8 Activities

1. You can only encrypt files and folders stored on NTFS volumes.

    Only the user who encrypted a file can open it.

    You cannot share encrypted files.

    Encrypted files can become decrypted when copied or moved to a non-NTFS volume.

2. When attempting to use EFS on any Windows NT partition, Windows 2000 performs a check-disk operation, which changes the partition to Windows 2000 format.

3. The request is passed to the CryptoAPI. CryptoAPI then passes the data to a CSP on your computer or on a device accessible to your computer. A software-based CSP generates a key pair (a public key and a private key) on your computer. A hardware-based CSP (like a Smart Card CSP) instructs some hardware to generate the key pair.

4. **Add** designates a user as an additional recovery agent using the Add Recovery Agent Wizard.

    Create requests a new File Recovery certificate using the Certificate Request wizard. To complete this procedure, you must have the required permissions to request the certificate, and the Certificate Authority (CA) must be configured to issue this type of certificate.

    Delete Policy deletes this EFS policy and all recovery agents. The result of this deletion is that no one will not be able to encrypt files on this computer.

5. Each file has a unique file encryption key that used to decrypt that file.

    The file encryption key is encrypted, and is protected by the user's public key that corresponds to the user's EFS certificate.

    The public key of an authorized recovery agent also protects the file encryption key.

6. You can easily encrypt your files when storing them on disk.

    You can access your encrypted data quickly and easily. You see your data in plain text.

    Your data are automatically encrypted, and the process is completely transparent to you.

    You can actively and permanently decrypt a file by clearing the Encryption check box on the file's Properties dialog box.

Administrators can recover data encrypted by another user.

EFS encrypts data only when it is stored on disk.

To encrypt data for transport over a TCP/IP network—you can use Internet Protocol Security (IPSec) or PPTP encryption.

7. In Active Directory, the actual policy is an accumulation of Group Policy Objects (GPOs) defined at various directory tree levels. If a higher-level node has no policy, the lower-level policies take effect. If a higher-level node has an empty recovery policy. However, EFS disables because the higher-level node provides no recovery certificates.

8. First export your encryption certificate and private key in a .PFX file format to a floppy disk. To do this, use the Export command from Certificates in Microsoft Management Console (MMC). Then, on the second computer, use the Import command from Certificates in MMC to import the .PFX file from the floppy disk into the Personal store.

9. Ask the recovery agent to recover the data on your machine.

10. **Recovery-agent policy**—By adding one or more recovery agents, an administrator automatically puts a recovery agent policy in effect. These agents are responsible for recovering any encrypted data within their scope of administration. This is the most common type of recovery policy.

    Empty recovery policy—By deleting all recovery agents and their public key certificates, an administrator automatically creates an empty recovery policy. As a result, no one is a recovery agent and users cannot encrypt data on the computers under the influence of the empty recovery policy. Setting up an empty recovery policy effectively turns off EFS altogether.

    No-recovery policy—By deleting the group recovery policy, an administrator creates a no-recovery policy. The lack of group recovery policy turns on, by default, the local policy on individual computers for data recovery. A no-recovery policy at a higher-level node effectively empowers local administrators to control the recovery of data on their computers.

Lesson 8 Quiz

These questions test your knowledge of features, vocabulary, procedures, and syntax.

1.   What files formats does EFS work with?

A. FAT

B. HPFS

C. NTFS

D. FAT-32

2.   What are the recommended practices for file encryption?

A. Encrypt the My Documents folder

B. Encrypt the Temp folder

C. Encrypt the system folder

D. Encrypt folders, not files

3.   How are the files in an encrypted folder protected?

A. The folder itself is encrypted

B. Each file has a unique encryption key

C. Each key is, itself, encrypted

D. The corresponding public key protects the file

4.   Which of the following are features of EFS?

A. Users can encrypt their files

B. Encryption of data is accomplished automatically.

C. Users can actively decrypt a file

D. EFS only encrypts data when it is stored on disk

5.   Which of the following is/are false?

A. Encryption works on compressed or uncompressed files.

B. Encryption works on most disk filing systems

C. Once you encrypt a file you can share it with anyone

D. Once a file is encrypted it is safe from harm

6. Which of the following is not a cipher command line switch?

   A. /E

   B. /A

   C. /Y

   D. /Q

7. When do you have to decrypt a previously encrypted file?

   A. When you reboot the computer

   B. When you copy the file to a non-NTFS volume

   C. When you want to share the file

   D. When you want to edit the file

8. Which of the following is not a legitimate policy?

   A. Recovery agent policy

   B. Empty recovery policy

   C. Check-cashing policy

   D. No-recovery policy

9. Administrators can configure public keys using which of the following?

   A. EFS

   B. DESX

   C. Certificates snap-in

   D. cipher

10. In a Windows 2000 system, which of the following is correct?

    A. Encrypted files copied to unencrypted folders remain encrypted

    B. Unencrypted files copied to encrypted folders remain unencrypted

    C. Encrypted files copied to FAT file format folders remain encrypted

    D. Encrypted files copied to remote location encrypted folders remain encrypted

Answers to Lesson 8 Quiz

1. Answer A is correct. Only files and folders on NTFS volumes can be encrypted.

    Answers B, C, and D are incorrect. FAT and FAT-32 do not support EFS. HPFS is also not supported by EFS.

2. Answers A, B, and D are correct. The My Documents folder and Temp folder should both be encrypted. Generally it is better to encrypt folders (and hence everything in them) rather than single files.

    Answer C is incorrect. If you encrypt your system folder your computer will not reboot.

3. Answers B, C, and D are correct. Each file has a unique encryption key.

    Answer A is incorrect. The folder itself is not actually encrypted, just marked to indicate that the files therein are encrypted, each key is encrypted and the corresponding public key protects the file.

4. All answers are correct. Users can encrypt their files when storing them on disk. Users see their data in plain text when accessing the data from disk. Encryption of data is completely transparent to the user. EFS only encrypts data when it is stored on disk. To encrypt data as it is transported over a TCP/IP network use IPSec or PPTP.

5. All answers are false. Encryption does not work on compressed files. Encryption also works only in the NTFS filing system, if you copy a file onto a FAT volume, you will lose the encryption. Only the person who encrypts the file can open it. Even though a file or folder has been encrypted, it can still be damaged or deleted.

6. Answers A, B, and D are correct. /E — Encrypts the specified files or folders. /A — Performs the specified operation on files as well as folders. /Q — Reports only the most essential information (quiet mode).

    Answer C is incorrect. There is no /Y switch for the cipher command line utility.

7. Answer C is correct. You must decrypt the file if you want to share it with others.

    Answers A, B, and D are incorrect. Booting has no effect on file encryption. When you copy the file to a non-NTFS volume files automatically lose their encryption. You can edit a file without having to decrypt it.

8.   Answers A, B and D are correct. Recovery agent, no-recovery and empty recovery are all valid recovery policies.

     Answer C is incorrect. Check cashing policies vary, but usually require identification.

9.   Answer C is correct. The MMC Certificates snap-in may be used by administrators to configure the public key.

     Answers A, B, and D are incorrect. The default configuration of the EFS requires no administrative effort. EFS uses the expanded Data Encryption Standard (DESX) as the encryption algorithm. Users may use cipher to encrypt a file or folder.

10. Answers A and D are correct. Encrypted files copied to unencrypted folders remain encrypted in a Windows 2000 system. Encrypted files copied to remote location encrypted folders remain encrypted if the remote location allows you to encrypt files and if it is trusted for delegation.

     Answers B and C are incorrect. Unencrypted files copied to encrypted folders are automatically encrypted. Encrypted files copied to FAT file format folders lose their encryption and are copied in clear text.

Smart Cards

For tasks such as client authentication, logging on to a Windows 2000 domain, code signing and securing e-mail, Smart Cards are a tamper-resistant and portable way to provide security solutions. Support for cryptographic Smart Cards is a key feature of the Public Key Infrastructure (PKI) that Microsoft has integrated into Windows 2000.

After completing this lesson, you should have a better understanding of the following topics:

- What Is a Smart Card?

- Smart Card Security

- Types of Smart Cards

- Smart Card Readers

- Smart Card Troubleshooting

- Smart Card APIs

What is a Smart Card?

Smart Cards are a part of the Public Key Infrastructure (PKI), important to the Windows 2000 security system. You can use Smart Cards during logon, client authentication and remote logon. They are a tamper resistant storage for protecting private keys and other forms of personal information, and they separate secure operations, such as private key validation, from other system functions. One of the best features of Smart Cards is their portability. A Smart Card user has an uncomplicated, safe, and convenient and safe way of transporting logon credentials and other information between.

Applying Windows 2000 Public Key Security

A Smart Card looks likes a standard credit or debit card except it is missing the magnetic strip and holds more data. It is similar to a miniature computer embedded in a flat plastic card. The circuitry in the Smart Card gets its power from the Smart Card reader. The reader and its associated device drive manage the communication between a Smart Card and an application or service on a computer is through a serial interface.

The following are types of Smart Cards:

- A stored value card

- A contactless card

- An Integrated Circuit Card (ICC)

Windows 2000 uses the ICC format. This format can carry out sophisticated procedures, such as digital signature key exchange. Instead of entering a user account name and password, you log on by inserting the Smart Card into the reader and keying in your Personal Identification Number (PIN) exactly as you would using an ATM card.

Contact Smart Cards have a small gold plate embedded in the front of the card, known as the contact plate or *module*. This plate has eight contacts and acts as a connector between the integrated circuit chip in the card and the Smart Card reader.

Eurocard, Masterplay, and Visa (EMV) defined an industry specific Smart Card specification—adopted the ISO 7816 standards in 1996. This ISO defines additional data types and encoding rules for the financial services industry. Consequently, the

European telecommunications industry chose to accept the ISO 7816 standards for its Global System for Mobile Communications (GSM) Smart Card specification for enabling the identification and authentication of mobile phone users.

Although these specifications (ISO 7816, EMV, and GSM) were steps in the right direction, each was either too low level or application specific to gain broad industry support. In addition, application interoperability issues, such as device independent Application Programming Interfaces (APIs), development tools, and resource sharing are not addressed by any of these specifications.

The PC/SC Workgroup

The Personal Computer/Smart Card (PC/SC) workgroup was formed in May 1996 by several major computer and Smart Card companies. The workgroup was formed to focus on the limitations in the existing standards complicating the integration of ICC devices with personal computers and did not address interoperability between products from multiple vendors.

Workgroup members saw the need for a standard interface designed to connect Interface Devices (IFDs) as well as specific common PC programming interfaces and control mechanisms. The workgroup also recognized their efforts should comply with existing products and applications as much as possible to develop solutions to meet the needs of the industry at large. From the beginning, the group has tackled issues from a broad perspective and with the intention to make the results of the workgroup efforts available on a royalty-free basis.

Currently the membership of the PC/SC includes Bull, Gemplus, Hewlett-Packard, IBM, Microsoft, Schlumberger, Siemens, Nixdorf Information Systems, Sun Microsystems, and Toshiba. Each member brings expertise in relevant technologies –PC software, PC hardware and ICC systems development—to the workgroup.

 Note: The current PC/SC specifications are based on the ISO 7816 standards and are compatible with both the EMV and GSM specifications. These specifications have industry-wide support.

Smart Card Security

You can set up your own public key infrastructure using certificate services and the certificate management tools in Windows 2000.Through a public key infrastructure, you can implement standards-based technologies such as Smart Card logon capabilities, client authentication (through Secure Sockets Layer (SSL) and Transport Layer Security (TLS)), secure e-mail, digital signatures and secure connectivity (using Internet Protocol Security).

Understanding the Functions of a Smart Card

Table 9.1 describes some of the functions of Smart Cards.

Table 9.1 Functions of Smart Cards

Function	Description
Tamper-resistant storage	Protects private keys and other forms of personal information.
Isolation of security critical computations	Keeps security critical computations—particularly those used for authentication like digital signatures and key exchange—from other parts of the organization that do not have a need to know.
Portability	Allows easy transfer of credentials and other private information between computers at work, home, or on the road.

Using a Smart Card to log onto a network gives you a clear form of authentication because it uses cryptography-based identification and proof of possession when authenticating a user to a domain.

For example, passwords are open to attack as often people choose passwords that are easy to remember. If a malicious person acquires a user's password, that individual can assume the user's identity on the network simply through use of the password. However, if a Smart Card were used, that same malicious person would have to obtain both the user's Smart Card and the PIN to impersonate the user.

Using Smart Cards is more difficult to attack because it requires an additional layer of information to impersonate a user. An added benefit of using Smart Cards is that after a limited number of unsuccessful PIN numbers have been entered on the card, the Smart Card locks. This makes a dictionary attack against a Smart Card extremely difficult. Figure 9.1 shows how Smart Cards improve security.

 Tip: A PIN does not have to be a series of numbers. It can also use other alphanumeric characters.

Figure 9.1 System Securities

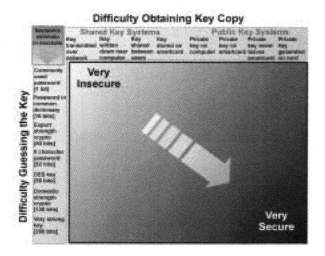

You can see by Figure 9.1 that the system security increases as you move to the lower right of the chart. Smart Cards help along both axes of the figure. They help along the left axis, as they allow you to store long keys that would be difficult to remember. They help along the top axis as they give you more control over the location of the keys.

You can help your users keep their data secure by making design choices, which place the system towards the lower right of the chart.

Understanding Interoperability

Interoperability among various vendors' products is necessary for consumers to accept Smart Cards. To prevent incompatibility between applications, cards and readers, a universally accepted set of standards is essential. Thus, Smart Card standards are based on the ISO 7816 standards for integrated circuit cards with contacts. These specifications focus on interoperability at the physical, electrical, and data link protocol levels.

Understanding Smart Card Access

The need for security has been increasing as electronic forms of identification replace face-to-face and paper based identification. The expansion through the Internet and many corporate networks to include access for customers and suppliers from outside their firewalls has accelerated the demand for answers based on public-key technology. Smart Cards are an integral part of the public-key infrastructure that Microsoft has integrated into Windows 2000. Smart Cards add to software solutions, such as user authentication, logon, and secure e-mail. Smart Cards are a point of convergence for public-key certificates and associated keys.

OpenCard Framework (OCF)

The OpenCard Consortium is the group that specifies the standards and drives the software framework for the OpenCard Framework (OCF). This framework for Smart Card access is object–oriented, meaning it supports the use of objects. The OpenCard Consortium was founded by Bull, Dallas Semiconductors, First Access, Gemplus, International Business Machines Corp., Network Computer Inc., Schlumberger, SCM Microsystems, Sun Microsystems, UbiQ, and Visa International.

OCF is considered complimentary to PC/SC and provides a structured model for the two following major categories of providers within the Smart Card industry:

• Application and service developers

• Card and terminal providers

OCF specifies the following two interfaces:

High-level API—Masks the characteristics of a particular provider, specific types of Smart Cards or Smart Card terminals from the application and service developers.

Common API—Enables the seamless integration of Smart Card building blocks from the different vendors.

OCF recognizes the following standards:

• PKCS Number 11 (Cryptoki)

• EMV

• The Committee European Normalization standard CEN EN726

• ISO 7816

- PC/SC

EMV and CEN726 detail card-level characteristics. PKCS Number 11 is a standard for application information security. OCF provides Card Services as a PKCS Number 11 API so applications can add hardware tokens into a variety of digital security schemes.

PC/SC is not necessary to OCF, but when it exists, the Smart Card reader OCF APIs can use it. OCF and PC/SC continue to work together toward harmonization with regard to the Smart Card itself. OCF can provide solutions to many of the problems faced by Smart Card developers and providers.

Requesting Smart Card Logon Certificates

A user cannot get a Smart Card logon certificate that is authentication or a Smart Card user certificate that is authentication plus secure e-mail, unless an administrator has given access rights to the certificate template stored in Active Directory. Smart Card certificates should be limited like employee badges.

The Smart Card enrollment station is the recommended method for enrolling users for Smart Card based certificates and keys. This integrates with Certificate Services in Windows 2000 Server and Windows 2000 Advanced Server.

When an enterprise CA is installed, it includes the Smart Card enrollment station. This situation allows an administrator to request and install a Smart Card Logon certificate or Smart Card User certificate onto a user's Smart Card. However, before using the Smart Card enrollment station, the issuer must obtain a signing certificate based on the enrollment agent certificate template. You use the signing certificate to sign the certificate request generated for the Smart Card recipient as shown in Figure 9.2.

Figure 9.2 Smart Card Certificate

Only a domain administrator has permission to request a certificate based on the enrollment agent template. Other users obtain permission to apply for an enrollment agent certificate through Active Directory Sites and Services.

 Warning: Someone with an enrollment agent certificate can enroll for a certificate and generate a Smart Card on behalf of anyone in the organization. This individual could then use the obtained Smart Card to log on to the network and impersonate the real user.

The enrollment agent certificate has powerful capabilities. It is very important to maintain strong security policies over those in your organization who have one. To minimize risk of enrollment agent misuse, have one secondary CA with very tight administrative controls to use only for issuing enrollment agent certificates. After the initial enrollment agent certificates are issued, the CA administrator can disable the issuing of enrollment agent certificates until future need. Through limiting the administrators who can carry out the CA service on the subordinate CA, the service can be kept online for the initiation and distribution of CRLs. However, it is still possible that other CAs in the hierarchy could still issue enrollment agent certificates with a change of policy settings. Check the Issued Certificates log for each CA on a regular basis to determine if improper enrollment agent certificates have been issued.

 Note: Creating a file structure or setting the PIN are card specific functions that can be done using specialized software provided by the Smart Card manufacturer.

Using a Smart Card to Log On

To log on to a computer using a Smart Card, follow these steps:

1. Log on to the computer as an enrollment agent for the domain where the user's account is located.

 Note: Anyone in the domain who has an enrollment agent certificate and has security permissions to issue Smart Card certificates is considered an enrollment agent.

2. From Internet Explorer, in the **Address** box, enter the address of the Certificate Authority (CA) that issues Smart Card logon certificates, and select **Enter**.

The address of the certification server is the name of the server followed by /Certsrv. For example, to connect to the CA on a server named SmartcardCA, you would enter the following:

http://SmartcardCA/Certsrv

Be sure to use the name of the server upon which the CA is installed, not the CA name itself. In many cases, these names are different (Figure 9.3).

Figure 9.3 Certificate Authority Address

3. Choose **Request a certificate** (Figure 9.4).

Figure 9.4 Smart Card Request Certificate

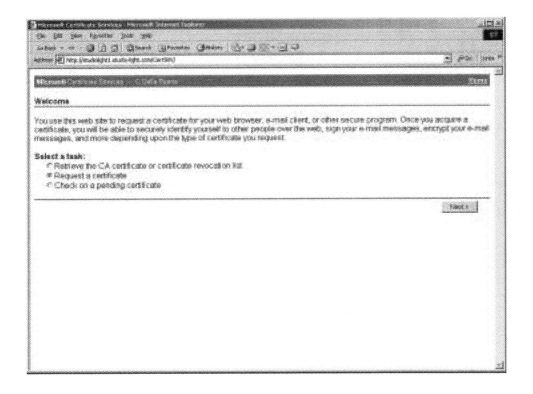

4.   Choose **Next**, **Advanced request** (Figure 9.5), and then select **Next**.

Figure 9.5 Smart Card Advanced Request

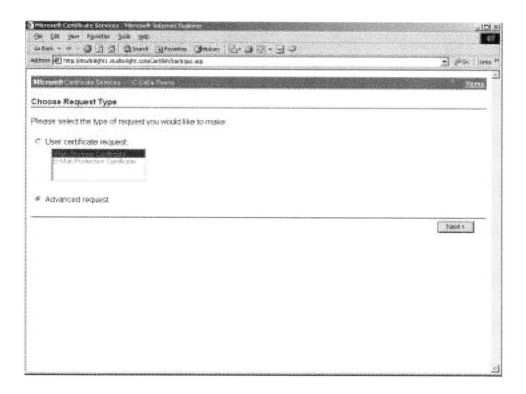

5.   Choose **Request a certificate for a smart card on behalf of another user using the Smart Card Enrollment Station**, and then select **Next**. If the system prompts you to accept the Smart Card signing certificate, select **Yes** (Figure 9.6).

Figure 9.6 Smart Card Certificate Request for Another User

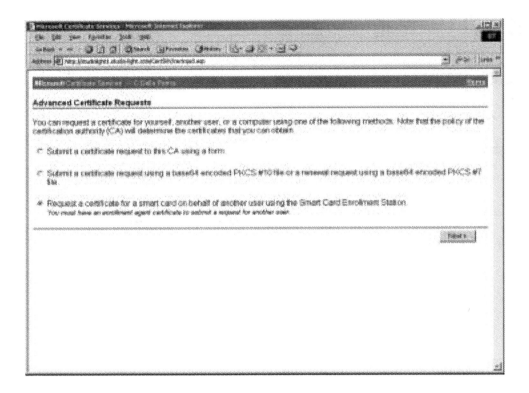

6.   On the **Smart Card Enrollment Station** Web page, in Certificate Template, and perform either of the next two steps, as shown in Figure 9.7.

7.   Choose Smart card Logon if you want to use the Smart Card for logging on to Windows only.

Or:

8.   Choose **Smart card User** if you want to use the Smart Card for secure email as well as logging on to Windows.

Figure 9.7 Smart Card Certificate Choices

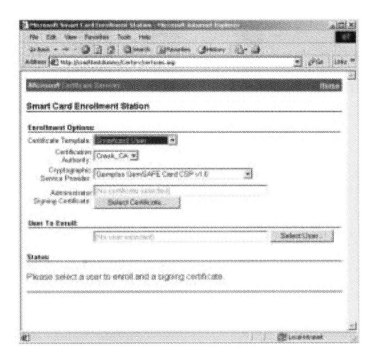

9. From **Certification Authority**, choose the name of the CA you want to issue the Smart Card certificate.

10. From **Cryptographic Service Provider**, choose the Cryptographic Service Provider (CSP) of the Smart Card's manufacturer (Figure 9.8).

Figure 9.8 Smart Card Certificate CSP Provider

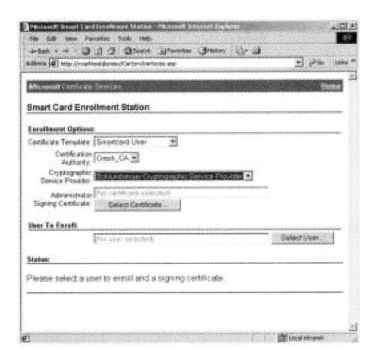

11. From **Administrator Signing Certificate**, choose the enrollment agent certificate to sign the enrollment request (Figure 9.9).

Figure 9.9 Smart Card Admin Signing Certificate

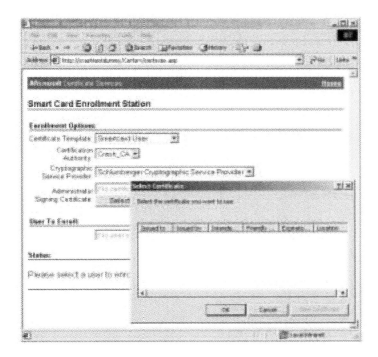

12. From **Enter User Name**, choose the appropriate user account, and then press **Submit Certificate Request**.

13. After the system prompts you, insert the Smart Card into the Smart Card reader on your computer. Choose **OK**. When the system prompts you, enter the PIN for the Smart Card.

14. This step is optional. If the Smart Card you are setting up has a previously installed certificate on it, a message appears asking if you want to replace the existing credentials on the card. Choose **Yes**.

From the CA Web page, and after you have installed the certificate on the Smart Card, you have the option of viewing the certificate you just installed or to begin a new Smart Card certificate request.

Authenticating to a Windows 2000 Domain

The most effective form of authentication in Windows 2000 comes from using Smart Cards. With remote access VPN connections, you use the Extensible Authentication Protocol (EAP) in conjunction with the Smart Card or other certificate Transport Level Security (TLS) EAP type, also known as EAP-TLS). A computer running Windows 2000 Server and the Routing and Remote Access service is identified as the Windows 2000 remote access router.

To use Smart Cards for remote access VPN authentication, follow these steps:

1.   Configure remote access on the remote access router.

2.   Install a computer certificate on the remote access router.

3.   Enable a Smart Card logon process for the domain.

4.   Enable the Extensible Authentication Protocol (EAP), and configure the Smart Card or other certificate (TLS) EAP type on the remote access router computer.

5.   Enable Smart Card authentication on the VPN connection on the remote access client computer

Understanding the Client Logon Process

To log on to a computer with a Smart Card, follow these steps:

1.   From the Windows logon screen, insert your Smart Card in the Smart Card reader.

2.   When prompted by your compter, enter your PIN for the Smart Card.

If your PIN is correct, you are able to log on to the computer and to the Windows domain. Your access is based on the permissions assigned to your user account by the domain administrator.

If you enter the incorrect PIN for a Smart Card several times in a row, the Smart Card locks, and you are unable to log on to the computer using that Smart Card.

Note: The number of Smart Card allowable invalid log on attempts varies according to the manufacturer. Users must contact their administrator for a replacement card.

Logging on to a Remote Computer

To log on to a remote computer, follow these steps:

1. From Routing and Remote Access (Figure 9.10), and right-click the name of the remote access server.

Figure 9.10 Routing and Remote Access

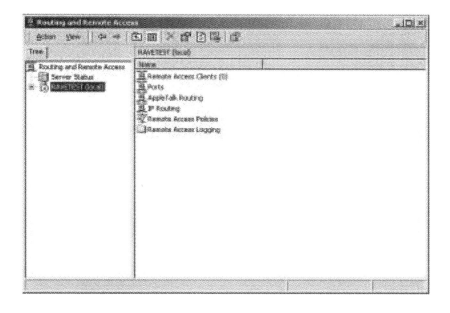

2.   From the remote access server, then choose **Properties** (Figure 9.11.)

Figure 9.11 Remote Access Server

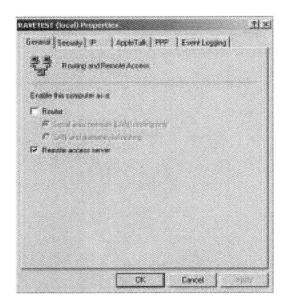

3.   From the **Security** property page, choose **Authentication** (Figure 9.12).

Figure 9.12 Remote Access Server Authentication

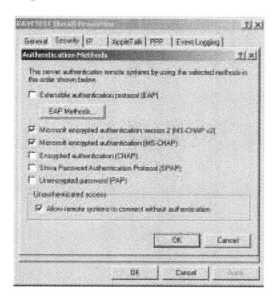

4. From **Authentication Methods**, choose the **Extensible authentication protocol (EAP)** check box, select **OK**, and then **OK** again (Figure 9.13).

Figure 9.13 EAP

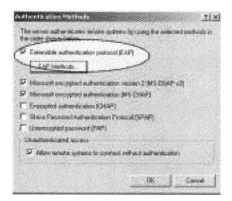

5. From the console tree, double-click the name of the remote access router name to enable and open then select **Remote Access Policies** (Figure 9.14).

Figure 9.14 Remote Access Policies

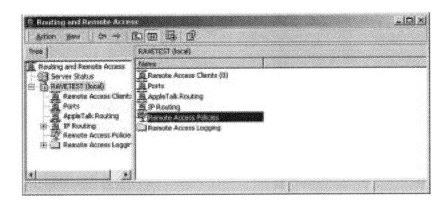

6. From the **Details** pane, right-click the remote access policy you have chosen for your Smart Card remote access clients to use. Select **Properties**, and then choose **Edit Profile** (Figure 9.15).

Figure 9.15 Remote Access Edit Profile

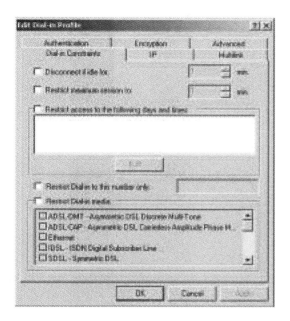

7.   From the **Authentication** property page, enable the **Extensible Authentication Protocol** check box. Select **Smart Card or Other Certificate (TLS)**, and then select **Configure** (Figure 9.16).

Figure 9.16 Remote Access EAP Configuration

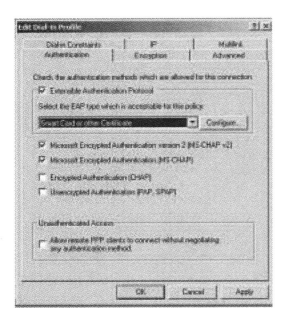

8. From **Smart Card or Other Certificate (TLS) Properties**, choose the machine certificate you will be using and select **OK**

9. Choose **OK** to save the settings of the profile, and then select **OK** again to save the settings of the policy.

 Note: To open **Routing and Remote Access**, choose Start, Programs, Administrative Tools, and then select Routing and Remote Access.

Types of Smart Cards

Windows 2000 does not work directly with the operating system (OS) on the Smart Card itself. It is designed to accommodate any card OS. Therefore, it works with any Smart Card with the appropriate card service provider installed.

When you install Windows 2000, the support for the Gemplus GemSAFE and Schlumberger Cryptoflex Smart Cards is included in the default installation. You do not need to configure the client or server to use these cards.

While the files required to support these cards are included in Windows 2000, other RSA-based cryptographic Smart Cards work with Windows 2000, if the card vendor has developed a CSP for the card using CryptoAPI and the Smart Card Software Developer's Kit.

 Warning: You can change the Smart Card PINs anytime the CSP displays the private key PIN dialog box. Windows 2000 does not manage PINs that are the responsibility of the Smart Card CSP and the administrator.

Exploring Java Cards

Java Cards Smart Cards run the Java Card byte code as defined in the Java Card API 2.1 specification from Sun Microsystems' JavaSoft division. Using Java Cards, application developers can use object-oriented Write Once, Run Anywhere Java technology. The Java Card API 2.1 was developed in collaboration with the industry, including Smart Card manufacturers, card issuers, and Smart Card associations. The Companies that have endorsed Java Cards include Bull, Citicorp, de la Rue, First Union, Gemplus, Giesecke & Devrient, Hitachi, IBM Corporation, Mitsubishi Electric, Mondex, Off, NTT Data Corporation, Motorola, Schlumberger, Texas Instruments, Toshiba, VeriFone, and Visa.

Understanding Windows 2000 Smart Card Support

With interactive logon, you authenticate a user to a network using a form of shared credential like an encrypted hashed password. Windows 2000 supports public key interactive logon using a certificate stored on a Smart Card along with the private key. Instead of a password, the user enters a PIN.

The user's public key certificate is retrieved from the card and is verified to be valid and from a trusted issuer. During this authentication procedure, a challenge based on the public key contained in the certificate is asked of the card to verify that the card is in possession and can use the private key. After the verification is successful, the user's identity contained in the certificate is used to reference the user object stored in the Active Directory. Once this process is complete, the user is logged on to the system.

Issuing Smart Cards

Smart Cards are a trusted ID that can be compared to an employee badge. Many businesses could integrate Smart Cards with employee badges rather than issue a second card and ID. In most situations, obtaining an employee badge usually requires a visit to the company security office for the employee to provide proof of identification. The new smart badge could contain a Smart Card certificate issued by the corporation. The administrator in the security section can then act as the registration authority, perform an enroll-on-behalf operation, and install a certificate on the employee's Smart Card badge.

Tip: The CA service in Windows 2000 Server and Windows 2000 Advanced Server supports integrating Smart Cards with employee badges as part of its Web enrollment interface.

Smart Card Readers

Because Windows 2000 is a Plug and Play (PnP) operating system, Smart Card readers that are not PnP-compliant are not recommended on computers running Windows 2000. If you want to use or have an existing Smart Card reader that is not PnP, you need to obtain installation instructions and associated device driver software directly from the manufacturer of the Smart Card reader.

Windows 2000 supports those Smart Card readers described in table 9.2. Their drivers are installed only when Windows 2000 detects the PnP Smart Card reader hardware.

Table 9.2 Smart Card Manufacturers

Manufacturer	Smart Card Reader	Interface	Device Driver
Bull CP8	Smart TLP3	RS-232	Bulltlp3.sys
Gemplus	GCR410P	RS-232	Gcr410p.sys
Gemplus	GPR400	PCMCIA	Gpr400.sys
Litronic	220P	RS-232	Lit220p.sys
Rainbow Technologies	3531	RS-232	Rnbo3531.sys
SCM Microsystems	SwapSmart	RS-232	Scmstcs.sys
SCM Microsystems	SwapSmart	PCMCIA	Pscr.sys

Warning: Microsoft recommends only Smart Card readers tested by the Microsoft Windows Hardware Quality Lab and the Windows compatible logo be installed on Windows 2000 computers.

Installing a Smart Card Reader

 Tip: Smart Card readers come with setup instructions from the manufacturer. If your reader comes with instructions, you should use them.

If your Smart Card reader does not come with setup instructions from the manufacturer, to install a Smart Card reader, follow these general steps:

1. Shut down and turn off the computer you will be connecting the Smart Card reader to.

2. Connect the reader to an available serial port or insert the PC card reader into an available PCM-CIA Type II slot. This depends on the type of reader you are installing.

3. Restart the computer and log on as an administrator.

4. If the device driver for the connected reader is in the DRIVER.CAB file, the Smart Card reader installs automatically. (The DRIVER.CAB file installs as part of the Windows 2000 installation.) This process can take several minutes. The Unplug or Eject Hardware icon appears in the tool-bar. Open the Unplug or Eject Hardware dialog box and confirm the reader you have just installed is in the list of hardware devices. This confirms your installation was successful.

5. If the device driver software for the connected Smart Card reader is not available in the DRI-VER.CAB file, the Add/Remove Hardware Wizard starts. Follow the directions to install the device driver software for your card reader. The Add/Remove Hardware Wizard may ask you for the media (such as a CD-ROM or floppy disk) from the manufacturer containing the device driver.

 Note: If the Smart Card reader does not install or the Add/Remove Hardware Wizard does not start automatically, your Smart Card reader may not be Plug and Play-compliant. Contact the Smart Card reader manufacturer for the device driver and the instructions on how to install and configure the device.

Connecting a Smart Card Reader

Usually your Smart Card reader has a complete set of instructions for setup and connection. If these are missing, follow these steps:

1. Shut down and turn off the computer you will be connecting the Smart Card reader to.

2. Connect the reader to an available serial port or insert the PC card reader into an available PCM-CIA Type II slot.

3. Some Smart Card readers have a supplemental PS2 connector. connect your keyboard and mouse to the reader andplug it into the keyboard or mouse port. Most Smart Card readers take power from the keyboard or mouse ports as it is not generally avaiable from the RS-232 port.

4. Restart your computer and log on as an administrator.

Smart Card Troubleshooting

Windows 2000 supports an account policy that requires a Smart Card for a user to log on. When the administrator has set this policy on an account, the user cannot use a password to logon to the account either interactively or from a command line. The policy does not apply to remote access logon as remote access logon uses a different policy configured on the remote access server. Although the administrator may not set the Smart Card required for interactive logon for every account in an enterprise, it should be set for ordinary users who are using Smart Cards to logon to a Windows 2000 domain.

Tip: You should not set an account policy that requires Smart Card for user log on to Administrators and the Power Users groups as some higher-level tasks can require password-authenticated logon.

On Smart Card Removal Policy

Security policies for each organization are dependant upon the business practices of that organization. In a highly secure environment, a user who leaves a computer during an active logon session should either log off or lock the computer through setting the lock or having a screen saver lock. If the user fails to do this, the network may be open for an attack by a malicious insider who can access the unlocked computer with all of the first user's rights and identity. A more common situation in organizations with more users than computers is that an innocent second user sits at the computer and amends the first user's files, thinking they are working on their own.

The Smart Card removal policy is administered on a per-machine basis, rather than on a per-user-account basis. You can implement this policy in circumstances where people use computers in an open floor or kiosk environment, such as in a college or school where there a computer is not available to each student. Where individual users have a dedicated computer or multiple computers that only they use, it may not be necessary to implement this policy.

Managing User-Related Issues

Issues with Smart Cards are probably as numerous as Smart Card users—only the most common are described in this section. There are fewer problems with user error because of the prevalence of ATMs and card-based banking, making people familiar with plastic cards and PINs.

The Forgotten Card

The following are the two most common ways of dealing with a forgotten Smart Card:

1. Set up your user accounts so they are also accessible using passwords. Share the password with the user only when the situation arises. Reset the password after the user has had to use it. If you decide to use this method, you should not set the logon policy called, Smart Card required for interactive.

2. Issue a temporary Smart Card that has a certificate with a short expiration time, most often one day.

Lost PIN

There is no working around the predicament of a lost PIN. You need to enroll the user for another Smart Card certificate and have the user enter a new PIN on a new Smart Card. You also need to be sure that you place the user's old Smart Card certificate on the CRL. In the future, more and more

Smart Cards will use biometrics—the PIN identification method will be replaced by fingerprints, a retina scan, hand geometry, or a voiceprint.

Duplicate Pin

Because both the card and the PIN are required to break into a Smart Card system, a malicious person obtaining a user's PIN is less of a threat to security than the same person obtaining a password. However, a malicious person who has both becomes a real security threat. No short-term answer exists to this situation, other than ensuring no one has more rights or permissions than required. For the long term, biometrics may provide the solution.

Incorrect Pin Entered

Passwords are the area where a security system breaks down, especially when users choose easy-to-remember passwords. It is best to have users avoid PINs, such as 1111 or 1234. However, an easy-to-remember PIN is less of a problem for the following reasons:

- A Smart Card is predefined to lock when too many consecutive wrong PIN inputs are entered

- The PIN does not transmit in any form across the network

- A replay attack is very complicated because it requires possession of the card

- Smart Cards are not open to classic dictionary attacks

The design of Smart Cards makes frequent PIN changes unnecessary. A user cannot change their PIN with the same ease or as often as a password. You can only change a PIN when a private key operation is performed and an administrator is enrolls for a Smart Card certificate on behalf of the user because there is a lack of standards in PIN management across card operating systems.

As discussed previously, PINs will probably become obsolete in the future. Developments in biometrics can provide authentication techniques based on the user's physical characteristics, such as fingerprint, hand geometry, retina scan, or voice print. However, the cost factor is presently quite high for development of this technology.

Smart Card APIs

Microsoft's Smart Card Software Development Kit (SDK) and the Microsoft Platform SDK are integrated products. The Platform SDK contains the tools and APIs to develop Smart Card-enabled and Smart Card aware Windows software applications. To download the Platform SDK, follow these steps:

1. Open your browser and access http://msdn.microsoft.com/developer/sdk/platform.asp.

2. Carefully read the contents list on the Web page. For more information on any of the compoents you can select the appropriate link.

3. Choose **Platform SDK Setup** (Figure 9.17).

Figure 9.17 Platform SDK

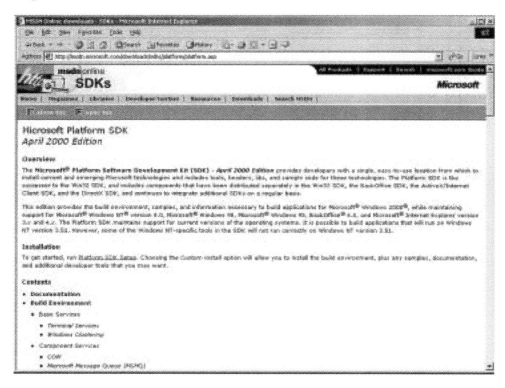

4.   Choose the **Custom Install** option. You can now install the build environment, including any samples, documentation, and additional developer tools you require (Figure 9.18).

Figure 9.18 Custom Install

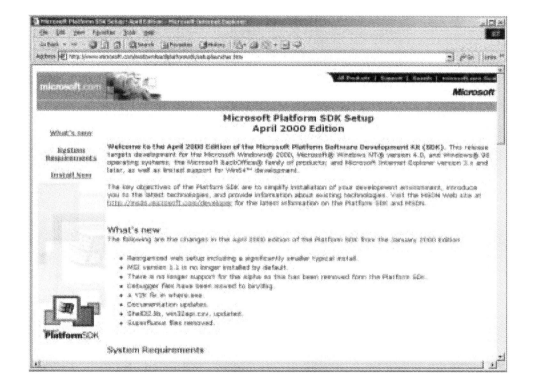

Tip: You can get more information about Smart Cards, a Frequently Asked Questions (FAQ) page, and developers information from:

http://www.microsoft.com/security/tech/smartcards/

Table 9.3 describes the Component Object Models (COM) interfaces that the Smart Card SDK provides.

 Note: The Smart Card user interface is a common dialog box that lets a user connect to a Smart Card and use it in an application. The user can use the dialog box to specify a specific card, or to search for the Smart Card to open.

Table 9.3 Component Object Models (COM)

COM	Function
IbyteBuffer	Reads, writes, and manages stream objects. This object is a wrapper for the IStream object. There are no defined procedures for using IbyteBuffer.
ISCard	Used to open and manage a connection to a Smart Card. Each connection to a card requires a single, corresponding instance of the ISCard interface. The Smart Card Resource Manager must be available whenever an instance of ISCard is created or the interface will fail. You use the ISCard interface to connect to the Smart Card, submit a transaction, and release the Smart Card. These procedures are as follows: 1. Create an ISCard interface. 2. Connect to a Smart Card by specifying a Smart Card reader or by using a previously established, valid handle. 3. Create transaction commands with the ISCardCmd and ISCardIS07816 Smart Card interfaces. 4. Use ISCard to submit the transaction commands for processing by the Smart Card.

COM	Function
	5. Use ISCard to release the Smart Card. 6. Release the ISCard interface.
ISCardAuth	Used to access authentication services such as, application authentication, Smart Card authentication, and user authentication. The ISCardAuth interface is used as follows: 1. Create an ISCardAuth interface through the corresponding ISCardManage interface method. 2. Call the appropriate ISCardAuth method (APP_Auth, GetChallenge, ICC_Auth, or User_Auth). 3. Release the ISCardAuth interface.
ISCardCmd	Used to construct and manage a Smart Card Application Protocol Data Unit (APDU). The interface uses two buffers: The APDU buffer, which contains the command sequence to be sent to the card and the APDU Reply buffer, which contains data returned from the card after execution of the APDU command. This data is also referred to as the return APDU. To create an ISCardCmd interface: 1. Build a Smart Card APDU command by using the ISCardISO7816 interface or one of ISCardCmd's build methods. 2. Execute the command on the Smart Card by calling the appropriate ISCard interface method. 3. Evaluate the returned response. 4. Repeat the procedure, as required. 5. Release the ISCardCmd interface and any others called by the procedure.

COM	Function
ISCardDatabase	Carries out the Smart Card Resource Manager's database operations including: listing known Smart Cards, readers, and reader groups, retrieving the interfaces supported by a Smart Card and its primary service provider. To create an ISCardDatabase interface: 1. Call ListCards to retrieve all the known Smart Cards based on their ATR strings or their supported interfaces. 2. Release the ISCardDatabase interface.
ISCardFileAccess	This process gives a high-level interface to a card based file system, through an underlying card file system based on the structure defined in ISO/IEC 7816-4. It provides means for locating specific files and performing common actions, such as selecting, reading, writing, creating, and deleting. The interface summarizes and conceals much of the low-level detail in performing these actions at the card level. To create ISCardAccess: 1. Call ISCardManage, CreateFileAccess to build an ISCardFileAccess interface. 2. Call Open to select and open the file. 3. Call Write. 4. Call Close. 5. Release the ISCardFileAccess interface.
ISCardIS07816	Implements ISO 7816-4 functionality, the interface creates an APDU command that is summarized in an ISCardCmd object. The following shows how the ISCardIS07816 interface is used to build an APDU command to submit a transaction to a specific card:

COM	Function
	1. Create an ISCardISO7816 interface and an ISCardCmd interface. The ISCardCmd interface is used to encapsulate the APDU. 2. Call the ISCardISO7816 interface, that passes the required parameters and the ISCardCmd interface pointer. 3. The ISO 78164 APDU command will be built and encapsulated in the ISCardCmd interface. 4. Release the ISCardISO7816 and ISCardCmd interfaces. The exception to this is the ISCardISO7816:SetDefaultClassId
ISCardLocate	Uses the Smart Card's name to locate it. If necessary, it can display the Smart Card user interface. To build an APDU to locate a specific card using its name: 1. Create an ISCardLocate interface. 2. Call ConfigureCardNameSearch to search for a Smart Card name. 3. Call FindCard to search for the Smart Card. 4. Interpret the results. 5. Release the ISCardLocate interface.
ISCardManage	Connects to a specific Smart Card or reader to create other interfaces that can perform specific Smart Card functions. It can also lock a specific Smart Card for exclusive use and determine the status of a Smart Card or reader. These services preserve the context where an application can communicate with a Smart Card or a Smart Card reader. The use of the ISCardManage interface within an application is mandatory. The following process describes how the ISCardManage interface is used to connect to a Smart Card:

COM	Function
	1. Create the ISCardManage interface associated with the card. 2. Connect to a Smart Card by connecting to a specific Smart Card reader (AttachByIFD) or by using a previously acquired handle (AttachByHandle). 3. Create other interfaces to perform Smart Card operations using CreateAuth, CreateFileAccess, CreateVerify, or CreateInterface. 4. Release the card (Detach). 5. Release the ISCardManage interface and any others called by the procedure.
ISCard TypeConv	The ISCardTypeConv interface provides the methods needed to support the users of the other Smart Card COM interfaces. Beginning with Microsoft Windows 2000, this interface is provided for backwards compatibility only and should no longer be used.
ISCard Vertfy	Used to set CHV code and to verify the user. The ISCardVerify class is defined for those applications that implement an application specific CHV policy, and have a detailed knowledge of the Smart Card's internal implementation. The following procedure describes how the ISCardVerify interface can be used to change the CHV code of a Smart Card: 1. Create an ISCardVerify interface using the corresponding ISCardManage interface method. 2. Call ChangeCode. Provide new code, and specify whether it's local or global and whether it's enabled or disabled. 3. Release the ISCardVerify interface.

More information about the above Smart Card interfaces can be found at the following site:

http://msdn.microsoft.com/isapi/msdnlib.idc?theURL=/library/psdk/scard/scint2_88th.htm

Note: The ISO 7816-4 specification defines the standard commands available on Smart Cards. This specification also defines how a Smart Card APDU command should be constructed and sent to the Smart Card for execution. The ISCardISO7816 interface automates the building process.

Tip: When you download the Microsoft Platform SDK, you also receive sample code in a variety of development languages. With these tools, you can learn how to program Smart Card applications. It is recommended you spend some time on the debug code provided.

APIs

From the software developer's perspective, there are three different APIs for accessing the services supported by a Smart Card. These are CryptoAPI, the Microsoft Win32 API, and SCard COM. The method selected depends on the type of application and the capabilities of a specific Smart Card.

Using CryptoAPI

CryptoAPI is also called CAPI. CryptoAPI is the cryptographic API for writing a CSP and requires a separate development kit, available from Microsoft. CryptoAPI gives you a set of functions that allow applications to encrypt or digitally sign data in an adaptable manner. It also provides protection for the user's sensitive private key data. Actual cryptographic operations are performed by independent modules known as CSPs. The CSPs are the codes that performs authentication, encoding, and encryption services that Windows-based applications access through the CryptoAPI. A CSP is responsible for creating keys, destroying them, and using them to perform a variety of cryptographic operations. Each CSP works with the CryptoAPI differently, providing different functionality. Some use stronger cryptographic algorithms, while others contain hardware components, such as Smart Cards.

Using CryptoAPI has several significant benefits. Developers use the cryptographic features integrated into Windows operating systems without having to know cryptography or how a particular cryptographic algorithm works. For example, a Smart Card CSP would use an existing CSP, such as Microsoft Base Provider, to perform all public key operations and use the Smart Card itself to perform all private key operations.

Using Scard COM

Scard COM is a non-cryptographic interface for Smart Cards for accessing generic Smart-Card-based services from applications written in different programming languages, such as C, Java, and Microsoft Visual Basic. It is made up of a collection of COM interface objects that can be used to build a set of interfaces for use by Windows applications. The software developer can use standard application development tools, such as C and Visual Basic, to develop applications that are Smart Card enabled and Smart Card aware.

The software application developer does not need to know how a particular Smart Card functions to access its services through COM. This speeds up Windows application development and saves both time and development costs. It also protects the application from obsolescence caused by future changes to a Smart Card's design.

Using Microsoft Win32 API

The Win32 APIs are base-level APIs for accessing Smart Cards that require a more in-depth understanding of the Windows operating system and Smart Cards to be used effectively. Win 32 APIs also provide the most flexibility for the software application to control Smart Cards and Smart Card readers. Developers use the Win32 APIs for applications that need maximum control over Smart Cards. This extension to the base Win32 API provides the required interfaces for managing interactions with smart-card devices.

The Smart Card SDK integrates with the Microsoft Platform SDK. The Platform SDK contains the necessary tools and APIs to develop Smart Card enabled and Smart Card aware Windows based applications.

To download the Platform SDK, follow these steps:

1. Access http://msdn.microsoft.com/developer/sdk/platform.asp.

2. Read the contents list on the Web page. You can obtain details about any of the components by clicking the appropriate link.

3. Choose Platform SDK Setup.

4. Choose the Custom Install option. This enables you to install the build environment, plus any samples, documentation, and additional developer tools that you require.

Using The Java Card API 2.1

A Java-based Smart Card is capable of running programs written in the Java language. You can load these applets or Java programs onto the card after it is issued. The Java Card API 2.1 specifies a particular subset of the full Java language specifically tailored for use on limited memory machines.

The Java Card API 2.1 was developed by leading members of the Smart Card industry, and has been adopted by most of the manufacturers in the industry. It is a virtual machine, meaning that it is a software layer that sits on top of the native operating system and executes the Java byte code. This conceals the complex and proprietary Smart Card hardware technology from the programmer and provides a standardized set of APIs for developing Java Card applications.

You can obtain the Java Card 2.1 Platform specification and implementation software by following these steps:

1. Access http://java.sun.com/products/javacard.

2. Choose the Java Card 2.1 Specification link.

3. Download the following specifications:

   Java Card 2.1 Runtime Environment (JCRE) Specification

   Java Card 2.1 Virtual Machine (JCVM) Specification

   JCVM Specification Release Notes

   Java Card 2.1 API Specification (Figure 9.19)

Figure 9.19 Java Card SDK

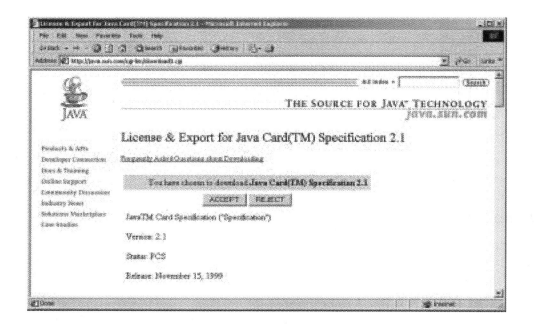

Tip: You can also view the entire Java Card 2.1 Platform specification online at the following site:

http://javasun.com/products/javacard/htmidoc/index.html.

Vocabulary

Review the following terms in preparation for the certification exam.

Term	Description
COM	Component Object Model is a set of integrated services and tools used for software development.
CSP	Cryptographic Service Provider is the code that performs authentication, encoding, and encryption services that Windows applications access through the CryptoAPI. A CSP is responsible for creating keys, destroying them, and using them to perform a variety of cryptographic operations. Each CSP provides a different implementation of the CryptoAPI. Some of these provide stronger cryptographic algorithms, while others contain hardware components, such as Smart Cards.
EAP-TLS	Extensible Authentication Protocol-Transport Level Security is an extension of the Point-to-Point Protocol (PPP) that provides remote access user authentication by means of other security devices. Support for a number of authentication schemes may be added. These schemes include token cards, dial-up, the Kerberos Version 5 protocol, one-time passwords, and public key authentication using Smart Cards, certificates, and others. EAP works with dial-up, PPTP, and L2TP clients. It is an important component for secure Virtual Private Networks (VPNs) because it offers more security against brute force or dictionary attacks (where all possible combinations of characters are attempted), and password guessing than other authentication methods.
enrollment agent	The enrollment agent certificate template generates signing certificates used to sign the certificate request generated for a Smart Card recipient.

Term	Description
Java Card	Java Cards are Smart Cards that run the Java Card byte code following the Java Card API 2.1 specification from Sun Microsystems' JavaSoft division. Smart Card application developers can benefit from object oriented Write-Once, Run Anywhere technology and from Java application development tools.
OCF	The OpenCard Framework is an object-oriented software framework for Smart Card access. The Open Card Consortium is the group that specifies the standards and drives the software framework.
PC/SC	The Personal Computer/Smart Card workgroup was formed in May 1996 by major computer and Smart Card companies. This group works to provide Smart Card standards.
PCMCIA	Personal Computer Memory Card International Association devices are removable devices, approximately the size of a credit card, which can be plugged into a PCMCIA slot in a portable computer. PCMCIA devices can include modems, network cards, and hard disk drives.
PIN	A Personal Identification Number is a number that the user can have placed onto their Smart Card for identification.
SDKs	Software Development Kits provide developers with all the necessary tools and documentation to program applications using libraries of functions that make up an SDK.
Smart Card	A credit card-sized device used to securely store public and private keys, passwords, and other types of personal information. To use a Smart Card, you need a Smart Card reader connected to the computer and a personal PIN number for the Smart Card. In Windows 2000, Smart Cards can be used for certificate-based authentication and single sign-on to the enterprise.

In Brief

If you want to...	Then do this...
Change a PIN	Smart Card personal identification numbers (PINs) can be changed any time the cryptographic service provider displays the private key PIN dialog box.
Combine security with identification	Issue Smart Cardsmart cards as ID badges.
Control security on accounts	Use Windows 2000 per-user account policy that requires a Smart Card to use an interactive logon.
Deal with forgotten cards	Issue temporary cards or set up user accounts so they are also password-accessible.
Develop a Java Card	Java Card developers can choose from any number of off-the-shelf, integrated Java development tools from leading vendors, such as Borland, IBM, Microsoft, Sun, and Symantec.
For remote VPN authorization	Enable the EAP and configure the Smart Cardsmart card on the remote access router computer.
Have secured roaming access	Use a Smart Card system.
Request Smart Cardsmart card certificates	Use the Smart Card enrollment station.
View a recently installed certificate	Use the Certificate Authority's Web page to view the certificates.

Lesson 9 Activities

Complete the following activities to better prepare you for the certification exam.

1. Describe Smart Cards.

2. Explain the functions of the OFC.

3. Explain the process of installing a logon certificate on a user's Smart Card.

4. Describe Java Cards.

5. Explicate a typical Smart Card issuing scenario.

6. List the groups exempted from Smart Card controlled per-user logon.

7. Explain On Smart Card Removal Policy.

8.   Describe the procedure for recovering a lost PIN.

9. Explain the significance of CryptoAPI.

10. Explain the significance of Microsoft's Smart Card Software Development Kit.

Answers to Lesson 9 Activities

1. A Smart Card is a miniature computer embedded in a flat plastic card that looks just like a standard credit or debit card, except for the missing magnetic stripe and it holds more data.

    The circuitry in a Smart Card receives its power from the Smart Card reader.

    Communication between a Smart Card and an application or service on a computer is done through a serial interface, managed by the reader and its associated device driver.

2. The OpenCard Framework (OCF) is an object-oriented software framework for Smart Card access. The OpenCard Consortium is the group that specifies the standards and drives the software framework. OCF is complimentary to PC/SC, and provides a structured model for two major categories of providers within the Smart Card industry: Application and service developers and Card and terminal providers.

3. When an enterprise Certificate Authority (CA) is installed, it includes the Smart Card enrollment station. This allows an administrator to request and install a Smart Card Logon certificate or Smart Card User certificate on a user's Smart Card.

    Before using the Smart Card enrollment station, the issuer must obtain a signing certificate based on the enrollment agent certificate template. The signing certificate is used to sign the certificate request generated for the Smart Card recipient.

4. Java Cards are Smart Cards which run the Java Card byte code following the Java Card API 2.1 specifications from Sun Microsystems' JavaSoft division.

    Using Java Cards, Smart Card application developers benefit from object oriented Write-Once, Run Anywhere technology and from Java application development tools.

5. Typically, the security office or the administrative user in the security section acts as the registration authority, performing an enroll-on-behalf operation and install a certificate on the employee's Smart Card based badge. The CA service that is installed with Windows 2000 Server and Windows 2000 Advanced Server supports this operation as part of its Web enrollment interface.

6. The policy would not be applied to members of the Administrators and Power Users groups because they require password-authenticated logon to perform high-level tasks.

7. The on Smart Card removal policy is a local computer policy administered on a per-machine basis (unlike the Smart Card required for interactive logon policy on a per-user-account basis). In

situations where users use computers in an open floor or kiosk environment, in a college, or school where there is not one computer for each student, this policy option is appropriate.

8.   This problem has no workaround. You have to enroll the user for another Smart Card certificate and have the user enter a new PIN on a new Smart Card. Be sure you place the user's old Smart Card certificate on the Certificate Revocation List (CRL).

9.   An Application Programming Interface (API) is provided as part of Microsoft Windows. CryptoAPI includes functions that enable applications to encrypt or digitally sign data in and provide protection for users sensitive private key data.

Actual cryptographic operations are performed by autonomous modules known as Cryptographic Service Providers (CSPs).

CryptoAPI is also called CAPI.

10. Microsoft's Smart Card Software Development Kit (SDK) is integrated with the Microsoft Platform SDK.

The Platform SDK contains the necessary tools and APIs to develop Smart Card enabled and Smart Card aware Windows applications.

Lesson 9 Quiz

These questions test your knowledge of features, vocabulary, procedures, and syntax.

1. Which of the following are the different types of Smart Cards?

    A. Stored-value

    B. ICCs

    C. contactless

    D. Eurocard

2. What are some features of Smart Cards?

    A. Tamper-resistance

    B. Isolation

    C. Portability

    D. PIN

3. Which of the following certificates does the Smart Card provide?

    A. Logon certificate

    B. Transfer certificate

    C. User certificate

    D. Download certificate

4. In order to use Smart Cards for remote access VPN authentication which of the following steps must be done?

    A. Configure remote access on the remote access router

    B. Install a computer certificate on the remote access router

    C. Enable a Smart Card logon process for the domain

    D. Enable the (EAP) and configure the Smartcard on the remote access router computer

5. Which Smart Cards does Windows 2000 support?

    A. Any RSA-based card using CryptoAPI and SmartCard SDK

    B. Java Cards

    C. GemSafe

    D. Cryptoflex

6.   Which of the following may occur when you are installing a Smart Card reader?

A. The installation of the driver will take place without any prompting

B. Confirm that the installation has taken place by the appearance of the Unplug or Eject Hardware icon in the toolbar

C. If the device driver software for the Smart Card reader is not available in the DRIVER.CAB file, the Add/Remove Hardware Wizard starts

D. Nothing, your Smart Card reader may not be Plug and Play-compliant

7.   What are the most common complications arising from Smart Card usage?

A. Forgotten Cards

B. Lost PINs

C. Biometrics

D. Incorrect PIN entered

8.   What are the major elements of Microsoft's approach to Smart Card extensions?

A. A standard model for interfacing Smart Card readers and cards with computers

B. Device-independent APIs for enabling Smart Card-aware applications

C. Familiar tools for software development

D. Integration with all Windows platforms

9.   Which of the following interfaces does the Smart Card SDK support?

A. SCard COM

B. Win32 API

C. Java Card API 2.1

D. Netscape

10.   What are the situations where Smart Cards are recommended?

A. Roaming

B. Combined security and identification

C. ATMs

D. Per-account security

Answers to Lesson 9 Quiz

1.   Answers A, B, and C are correct. Stored-value and contactless cards are synonymous, ICC is an integrated circuit card.

     Answer D is incorrect. Eurocard is a company that helped to define the Smart Card specification.

2.   Answers A, B, C, and D are correct. Tamper resistance helps protect private information. Isolation: Smart Cards help to wall off critical data. Portability of credentials and the Personal Identification Number are other features of the Smart Card.

3.   Answers A and C are correct. Logon and user certificates can be issued for Smart Cards.

     Answers B and D are incorrect. Transfer and download privileges are inherent in logon and user certificates.

4.   Answers A, B, C, and D are correct. You must configure remote access on the remote access router, install a computer certificate on the remote access router, enable a Smart Card logon process for the domain and Enable the (EAP), and configure the Smartcard on the remote access router computer.

     However, But there is still another step: Enable Smart Card authentication on the VPN connection on the remote access client computer

5.   Answers A, B, C, and D are correct. GemSafe, Cryptoflex, any RSA-based card using CryptoAPI and SmartCard SDK and Java Cards are all supported under Windows 2000.

6.   Answers A, B, C, and D are correct. Any of these events may happen:

     11. The installation of the driver will take place without any prompting

     12. You may have to confirm that the installation has taken place by the appearance of the Unplug or Eject Hardware icon in the toolbar

     13. If the device driver software for the Smart Card reader is not available in the DRIVER.CAB file, the Add/Remove Hardware wizard will start

     14. Nothing, your Smart Card reader may not be Plug and Play compliant

7.   Answers A, B, and D are correct. Forgotten Cards, Lost PINs, and Incorrect PIONB entries are the most common complications of Smart Card usage.

Answer C is incorrect. Biometrics will replace PINs as identifiers but they are not now a complication for Smart Cards.

8.   Answers A, B, C, and D are correct. Having a standard model for how readers and cards interface with a computer enforces interoperability among cards and readers from different manufacturers. Device independent APIs insulate application developers from differences between current and future implementations. Device independence also reduces software development costs by avoiding application obsolescence due to underlying hardware changes

9.   Answers A, B, and C are correct. Scard COM and the Win32 API are both Microsoft developed products and the Java Card API 2.1 is supported by the Smart Card SDK.

Answer D is incorrect. Netscape is an Internet browser.

10.   Answers A, B, and D are correct. Roaming, Combined security and identification and per-account security are all part of Smart Cards.

Answer C is incorrect. Smart Cards have no connection with ATMs.

Lesson 10

Virtual Private Networks (VPNs)

You use a A Virtual Private Network (VPN) to emulates a point-to-point private link network connection over shared or public networks such as the Internet. You can securely send data between two computers with a VPN connection. The act of creating and configuring a VPN is called virtual private networking.

After completing this lesson, you should have a better understanding of the following topics:

* VPN Overview
* VPN Strategy
* VPN Server Set Up
* VPN Server Configuration
* VPN Client Set Up
* Remote Access User Accounts
* Tunneling
* Authentication
* Tunneled Data and Tunnel Maintenance
* Remote Authentication
* Mutual Authentication
* RADIUS server

VPN Overview

To allow the data to traverse the shared or public network over the emulated point-to-point link and reach its endpoint, the data encapsulates, or wraps, with a header that provides routing information. The data encrypts for confidentiality and is indecipherable without encryption keys. This type of link is a VPN connection. Figure 10.1 illustrates these concepts.

Figure 10.1 Packets on the Network

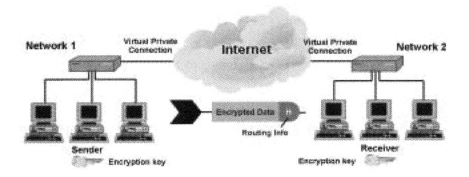

Users working at home or on the road can employ VPN connections to establish a remote access connection linking that links their computer, (the VPN client,) to an organization server (the VPN server). These connections use a public network such as the Internet. From the user's perspective, the VPN is a direct point-to-point connection, and the traversal of the infrastructure of the shared or public network traversed infrastructure is irrelevant. It logically appears to the user logically as if the data transmits over a dedicated private link.

VPN connections are also used by organizations to establish routed connections with geographically separate offices or other organizations. VPN routed connections allow the organization to maintain secure communications over a public network such as the Internet. A routed VPN Internet connection logically operates like a dedicated Wide Area Network (WAN) link.

Organizations use VPN remote access and routed connections to replace long-distance dial-up or leased line connections to a local Internet Service Provider (ISP).

Windows 2000 provides two types of VPN technology:

Point-to-Point Tunneling Protocol (PPTP)—PPTP uses user-level Point-to-Point Protocol (PPP) authentication methods. PPTP data encryption can be done with Microsoft Point-to-Point Encryption (MPPE).

Layer Two Tunneling Protocol (L2TP) with Internet Protocol Security (IPSec)—Like PPTP, L2TP uses user-level PPP authentication methods. However, L2TP uses machine-level certificates with Internet Protocol Security (IPSec) for data encryption.

Virtual private networking under Windows 2000 includes the following components:

Virtual Private Network (VPN) servers—The VPN server can be configured to restrict access to just the resources of the VPN server or to provide access to an entire network.

VPN clients—Clients can be any of the following:

- Individual users who obtain a remote access VPN connection

- Routers that obtain a router-to-router VPN connection

- A non-Microsoft Point-to-Point Tunneling Protocol (PPTP) client

- A Layer Two Tunneling Protocol (L2TP) client that uses Internet Protocol security (IPSec).

A remote access server running Windows 2000 that acts as a VPN server can be accessed by remote access VPN connections created by Windows NT 4.0 and later versions, Windows 95, and Windows 98 VPN clients.

Router-to-router VPN connections can be created by computers running

Windows 2000 Server or Windows NT Server 4.0 and the Routing and Remote Access Service (RRAS). Some of the connection protocols and options are as follows:

LAN and remote access protocols—Application programs transporting information use LAN protocols such as TCP/IP, IPX, AppleTalk, and NetBEUI. These protocols enable access to Internet, UNIX, Apple Macintosh, and Novell NetWare resources. Windows 2000 remote access supports the PPP remote access protocol for VPN connections, WAN links connection negotiation and LAN protocol data framing are performed by the remote access protocols.

Tunneling protocols—Tunneling protocols are used by VPN clients to create secure connections to a VPN server. The PPTP and L2TP tunneling protocols are included in Windows 2000.

WAN options—VPN servers use permanent WAN connections, such as T1 or Frame Relay, to connect to the Internet. VPN clients can connect to the Internet by using permanent WAN connections or by dialing in to a local ISP using standard telephone lines or an Integrated Services Digital Network (ISDN) connection. Figure 10.2 illustrates the WAN options.

Figure 10.2 WAN Options

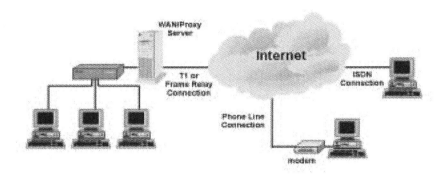

Security options available are as follows:

Internet support—Windows 2000 virtual private networking provides complete services for VPNs on the Internet. A computer running Windows 2000 Server can be configured as a VPN server that provides secured connections to either remote access clients or to demand-dial routers.

Security options—Secure network access for VPN clients are provided by the following features:

- Windows 2000 logon and domain security

- Support for security hosts

- Data encryption

- Remote Authentication Dial-In User Service (RADIUS)

- Smart Cards

- IP packet filtering

- Caller ID

VPN Strategy

This section describes some common scenarios for setting up and using VPNs through illustration with a fictional company. Your network configuration probably differs from the one described, but the basic concepts still apply.

Creating a VPN Strategy for an Organization

 Note: A Windows 2000 remote access router is a computer running Windows 2000 Server and the Routing and Remote Access Service (RRAS).

Widget, Inc. is a printed circuit board design and manufacturing company. The main corporate campus of Widget, Inc. is in New York. Widget, Inc. has branch offices and distribution business partners throughout the United States. Consequently, Widget, Inc. has decided to implement a VPN solution using Windows 2000 that connects remote access users, branch offices, and business partners.

The VPN server at the Widget, Inc. corporate office provides the following:

- Remote access
- Router-to-router PPTP and L2TP VPN connections
- Routing of packets to intranet and Internet locations

VPN Server Set Up

Windows 2000 Server administrators use Routing and Remote Access to perform the following tasks:

- Configure a VPN server
- View connected users
- Monitor remote access traffic

A Windows 2000 server that provides VPN access from the Internet typically has a permanent connection to the Internet. If an ISP supports demand-dial connections, a nonpermanent connection to the Internet is possible. In this uncommon configuration, the connection creates when traffic is delivered to the VPN server.

You can configure the VPN server to provide access to a network. If the VPN server provides access to a network, you must install and connect a separate network adapter that attaches to the provided network.

After the Routing and Remote Access Wizard runs, you can configure remote access servers. You must specify the protocols to use on the LAN (IPX, TCP/IP, AppleTalk, and NetBEUI). You must also specify whether or not a protocol provides access to the entire network or to just the remote access server. In addition, you need to select both the authentication and encryption options.

VPN Server Configuration

Prior to configuringBefore you configure a VPN server, you need to make an analysis of the current state of the network, determine the remote user needs, and establish any future migration plans. After these matters have been consideredconsideration, you are ready to make informed decisions regarding about the implementation of a VPN server.

Configuring a VPN Server

In this scenario, pPrior to deploying a VPN solution, the network administrator for Widget, Inc. performs an analysis of the corporate need for VPN and makes design decisions regarding the following:

• Network configuration

• Remote access policy configuration

• Domain configuration

• Security configuration

The Widget, Inc. corporate intranet uses two private networks of 153.68.0.0 and 192.168.0.0. The subnet mask of the corporate campus 153.68.0.0 network segments is 255.240.0.0. The subnet mask of the 192.168.0.0 network the branch offices use is 255.255.0.0.

Using a DS-3 (also known as a T-3) dedicated WAN link, The VPN server computer is directly attached to the Internet. The corporate campus is shown in Figure 10.3.

Figure 10.3 Corporate Campus

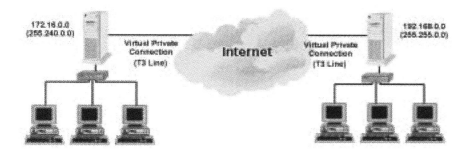

The ISP for Widget, Inc. allocates the IP address of 207.46.130.1 for the WAN adapter on the Internet. This IP address is referred to on the Internet by the domain name vpn.widget.com.

The computer used as the VPN server is directly attached to an intranet network segment that contains the following:

• A RADIUS server

• A file and Web server for business partner access

• A router that connects to the rest of the Widget, Inc. corporate campus intranet

The intranet network segment has an IP network address of 153.45.0.0 with a subnet mask of 255.255.0.0.

The Widget, Inc. VPN server is configured with a static pool of IP addresses. These addresses are allocated to remote access clients and calling routers. The VPN server computer of the Widget, Inc. corporate campus intranet is configured based on the Widget, Inc. network configuration as follows:

1. Install the VPN server hardware.

   Install the network adapter that connects to the intranet segment and its drivers according to the adapter manufacturer's instructions.

   Install the WAN adapter that connects to the Internet and its drivers according to the adapter manufacturer's instructions. Once the adapters and their drivers are functioning, both adapters appear as local area connections in the Network and Dial-Up Connections folder (Figure 10.4).

2.   Configure TCP/IP on the LAN and WAN adapters.

Figure 10.4 Network Adapter in Network and Dial-Up Connections Folder

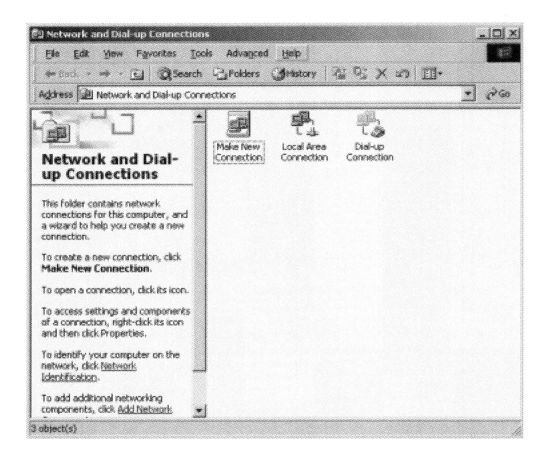

3.   The IP address of 172.31.0.1 with a subnet mask 255.255.0.0 is configured for the LAN adapter. The IP address of 207.46.130.1 with a subnet mask 255.255.255.255 is configured for the WAN

adapter. Neither adapter is configured for a default gateway. Also configured are DNS and WINS server addresses.

4. Routing and Remote Access service is installed.

    Remote access and LAN and WAN routing are enabled using the Routing and Remote Access Installation Wizard. Using the wizard, all ports are enabled for both routing and remote access. IPSec encryption is required for any L2TP connections. Also using the wizard, a static IP address pool with a base IP address of 172.31.255.0 and a mask of 255.255.255.0 is configured to create a static address pool for up to 253 VPN clients.

5. Enable the EAP authentication method.

    The network administrator enables the Extensible Authentication Protocol (EAP) on the VPN server to enable the use of Smart Card-based remote access VPN clients as well as certificate-based calling routers (Figure 10.5).

6. Configure static routes to reach intranet and Internet locations.

Figure 10.5 Enabling the EAP

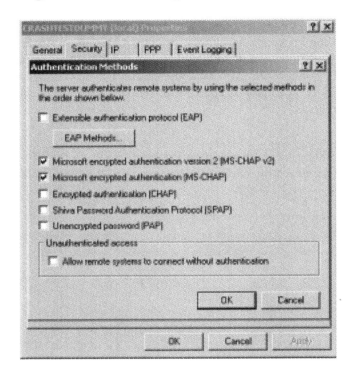

A static route is configured to reach intranet locations with the following settings:

- Interface: The LAN adapter attached to the intranet

- Destination: 153.68.0.0

- Network mask: 255.240.0.0

- Gateway: 172.31.0.2

- Metric: 1

A static route is configured to reach Internet locations with the following settings:

- Interface: The WAN adapter attached to the Internet

- Destination: 0.0.0.0

- Network mask: 0.0.0.0

- Gateway: 0.0.0.0

- Metric: 1

 Note: 0.0.0.0 is the unspecified IP address. You can enter any address for the gateway because the WAN adapter creates a PPP connection to the ISP. The gateway address of 0.0.0.0 is used as an example.

7.   Increase the number of PPTP and L2TP ports.

Only five L2TP ports and five PPTP ports are enabled for VPN connections by default. The Widget Inc. Network administrator increases the number of L2TP and PPTP ports to 253 (Figure 10.6).

Figure 10.6 Increasing Port Connections

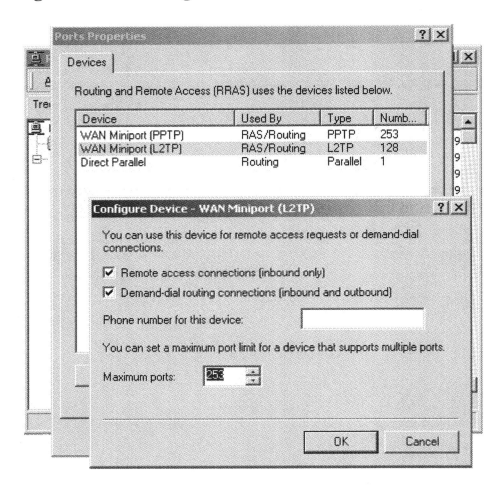

8.   Configure PPTP and L2TP over IPSec packet filters.

The combination of L2TP and IPSec is known as L2TP over IPSec. PPTP is configured on the WAN adapter that connects to the Internet. Also configured on the adapter is L2TP over IPSec packet filters.

The Remote Access Policy Configuration

You can use an access-by-user administrative model to ease the transition from a Windows NT 4.0 environment. Setting the dial-in permission of individual user accounts to either Allow access or Deny access controls remote access. You use remote access policies based on group membership to apply different VPN connection settings.

The Domain Configuration

Widget, Inc. has a mixed-mode domain. One of the Windows 2000 servers in the domain is assigned as the VPN server. The VPN server has the ability to apply different connection settings to different types of VPN connections. To take advantage of this, the Widget Inc. network administrator creates several Windows 2000 groups. The group "VPN_Users" is created for remote access VPN connections. The group "VPN_Routers" is created for router-to-router VPN connections originating from Widget, Inc. branch offices. The group "VPN_Partners" is used for router-to-router VPN connections from the business partners of Widget, Inc. (Figure 10.7).

Figure 10.7 Widget, Inc. VPN Groups

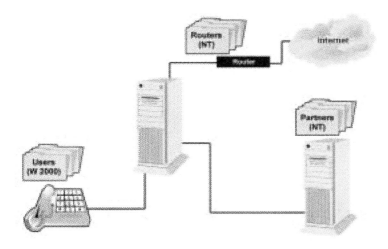

The Security Configuration

The Widget, Inc. domain is configured to auto-enroll machine certificates to all domain members which enables the following:

- L2TP over IPSec connections
- Use of Smart Cards by remote access clients
- Use of the Extensible Authentication Protocol-Transport Level Security (EAP-TLS) by routers

VPN Client Set Up

You must configure a VPN server before a client can connect with it. This section describes how to configure the VPN client.

Configuring a VPN Client

VPN clients that connect to remote access servers running Windows 2000 can run the following operating systems:

- Windows NT 4.0 and later
- Windows 95
- Windows 98

Because the client must be able to send TCP/IP packets to the remote access server, one of the following connection types is required:

- A network adapter
- A modem with an analog telephone line
- A WAN connection

Microsoft VPN Client Tunneling Protocols

Microsoft VPN client support for tunneling protocols PPTP and L2TP is defined in Figure 10.8 and outlined in Table 10.1.

Figure 10.8 OS/Tunneling Protocols

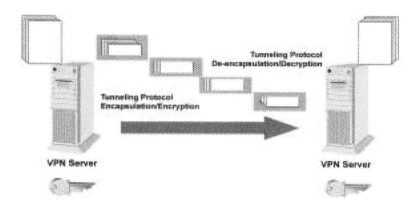

Table 10.1 VPN Client Tunneling Protocols

VPN Client	Supported Protocols	Unsupported Protocols
Windows 2000	PPT PL2TP	None
Windows NT version 4.0	PPTP	L2TP
Windows 98	PPTP	L2TP
Windows 95	PPTP (requires the Windows Dial-Up Networking 1.3 Performance and Security Upgrade for Windows 95)	L2TP

Note: PPTP or L2TP are not supported by Windows NT Version 3.5x.

Authentication for Microsoft VPN Clients

Microsoft VPN clients support the following authentication protocols:

- Microsoft Challenge Handshake Authentication Protocol (MS-CHAP)

- Challenge Handshake Authentication Protocol (CHAP)

- Shiva Password Authentication Protocol (SPAP)

- Password Authentication Protocol (PAP)

- MS-CHAP Version 2 (MS-CHAP Version 2)

- Extensible Authentication Protocol (EAP)

Microsoft VPN client support for authentication protocols is outlined in Table 10.2.

Table 10.2 VPN Authentication Protocols

VPN Client	Supported Authentication Protocols	Unsupported Authentication Protocols
Windows 2000	MS-CHAP, CHAP, SPAP, PAP, MS-CHAP V2, and EAP	None

VPN Client	Supported Authentication Protocols	Unsupported Authentication Protocols
Windows NT version 4.0 with the Windows NT 4.0 Service Pack 4 and later	MS-CHAP, CHAP, SPAP, PAP, and MS-CHAP V2	EAP
Windows 98 with the Windows 98 Service Pack 1 and later	MS-CHAP, CHAP, SPAP, PAP, and MS-CHAP V2	EAP
Windows 95 with the Windows Dial-Up Networking 1.3 Performance & Security Upgrade for Windows 95	MS-CHAP, CHAP, SPAP, PAP, and MS-CHAP V2	EAP

 Note: Windows 95 provides support for MS-CHAP Version 2 over VPN connections with the Windows Dial-Up Networking 1.3 Performance & Security Upgrade for Windows 95. The upgrade does not provide support for MS-CHAP Version 2 over dial-up connections.

Non-Microsoft VPN Clients

Non-Microsoft VPN clients can access a remote access server. These clients can access a server running Windows NT 4.0 only using PPTP. However, clients can access a server running Windows 2000 using either PPTP or L2TP with Internet Protocol Security (IPSec).

Non-Microsoft VPN clients do not require any special configuration of the remote access server. If you want to secure VPN connections from a non-Microsoft VPN client, you must make sure that the non-Microsoft VPN client supports the proper encryption. If you use PPTP, then Microsoft Point-to-Point Encryption (MPPE) must be supported. For L2TP clients, IPSec encryption must be supported.

Remote Access User Accounts

Remote or mobile workers connect to their organization's network through Windows 2000 Server remote access. This allows traveling or off-site users to work as if their computers were physically connected to the LAN. Remote access is part of the integrated Routing and Remote Access service that Windows 2000 provides.

A computer running Windows 2000 Server and the Routing and Remote Access service is a remote access server. The remote access server authenticates users and provides the user with session services until the session is terminated by the user or by the network administrator. Remote access connections are the means by which the services typically available to a LAN-connected user are enabled. These services include file and print sharing, messaging, and Web server access.

Remote users can initiate a connection to the remote access server by running remote access software. These remote access clients use standard tools to access network resources. Remote access full supports drive letters and Universal Naming Convention (UNC) names. Additionally, most commercial and custom network access applications work without modification. For example, clients on a computer running Windows 2000 can use Windows Explorer to connect to printers and to make drive connections. These connections are continuous, and do not require re-establishment during future remote sessions.

A Windows 2000 remote access server provides the following two different types of remote access connectivity:

- Dial-up networking
- VPN

Dial-up networking—A remote access client using the service of a telecommunications provider making a nonpermanent connection to a remote access server is called dial-up networking. For example, a dial-up networking client dials the phone number whose receiving modem connects to one of the ports of a remote access server.

A connection to a physical port on the remote access server can be made with various mediums that include the following:

- Analog phone

- ISDN

- X.25

An analog phone or ISDN line makes a direct physical connection between the dial-up networking server and the dial-up networking client. If desired, you can encrypt data sent over the direct physical connection. However, data encryption is not required.

VPN—The creation of secured, point-to-point connections across a private network or a public network such as the Internet is called virtual private networking. A Virtual Private Network (VPN) is created using tunneling protocols, which are special TCP/IP-based protocols. Using tunneling protocols, a virtual call is made by the VPN client to a virtual port on a VPN server. For example, a VPN client uses the Internet to make a VPN connection to a remote access server. The remote access server then performs the following actions:

- Answers the virtual call

- Authenticates the caller

- Transfers data between the virtual private networking client and the corporate network

VPNs always consist of an indirect logical connection between the VPN client and the VPN server. Because the connection can be made over public networks, you must encrypt data sent over the connection to ensure privacy.

Creating Remote Access User Accounts

Widget, Inc. employees who require remote access do so by using remote access VPN connections across the Internet. These remote access VPN connections are based on the settings configured for the VPN server as described above and the following additional settings:

- Domain configuration

- Remote access policy configuration

- PPTP-based remote access client configuration

- L2TP-based remote access client configuration

Domain Configuration

To configure VPN access for a user, follow these steps:

1.   Set the remote access permission to **Allow access** on the dial-in properties of the user account.

2.   Add the user account to the VPN_Users Windows 2000 group (Figure 10.9).

Figure 10.9 Employee Configuration

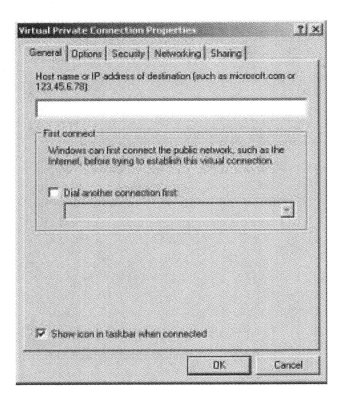

Remote Access Policy Configuration

A remote access policy is created to define the authentication and encryption settings for remote access VPN clients. The policy for Widget, Inc. is defined in this section.

The policy name is Remote Access VPN Clients. Permission on the policy is set to **Grant remote access permission.** The settings for the conditions for the remote access permissions policy are listed in Table 10.3.

Table 10.3 Remote Access Permissions

Condition	Setting
NAS-Port-Type	Virtual (VPN)
Windows-Groups	VPN_Users
Called-Station-ID	207.46.130.1

The profile settings for the policy are set using the following tabs:

Authentication tab—Smart Card or other certificate (TLS) is configured to use the installed machine certificate. In addition, the following are enabled:

• Extensible Authentication Protocol

• Microsoft Encrypted Authentication version 2 (MS-CHAP Version2)

• Microsoft Encrypted Authentication (MS-CHAP)

Encryption tab—The only option that is selected under the encryption tab is **Strongest.**

The Widget, Inc. network administrator sets the **Called-Station-ID** condition to the IP address of the Internet interface to the VPN server. Only Internet initiated tunnels are allowed. Widget, Inc. intranet initiated tunnels are not permitted. Widget, Inc. users on the Widget, Inc. intranet that require Internet access must go through the Widget, Inc. proxy server. The proxy server is where Internet access is controlled and monitored.

Note: The remote access policy remote access permission has no effect on granting remote access permission when using the access-by-user administrative model.

To ease the transition to an access-by-policy administrative model in a native mode domain, the network administrator for Widget, Inc. sets the remote access permission on the policy to **Grant remote access permission.** When the upgrade to native mode is accomplished, the transition does not require changing all the remote access permission settings on all of the remote access policies that have been configured.

PPTP-Based Remote Access Client Configuration

To create a new VPN connection, use the **Make New Connection Wizard**. The network administrator for Widget, Inc. sets the host name or IP address to: **vpn.widget.com** .

L2TP-Based Remote Access Client Configuration

When a remote access computer logs on to the Widget, Inc. domain, it receives a certificate through auto-enrollment. The **Make New Connection Wizard** then creates a VPN connection with the host name or of IP address of **vpn.widget.com**. On the **Networking** page, the option for **Type of dial-up server I am calling** is set to **Layer-2 Tunneling Protocol (L2TP).**

Creating Remote Access Policies

You can create a policy that requires remote access VPN connections to use a specific authentication method by using remote access policies. You can also set the desired encryption strength.

For example, the network administrator for Widget, Inc. creates a new Windows 2000 group called VPN Users. The group's members are the user accounts of the users that create remote access VPN connections across the Internet. The network administrator then creates a policy with the following two conditions:

- NAS-Port-Type is set to **Virtual (VPN)**
- Windows-Group is set to **VPN Users**

Finally, the network administrator for Widget, Inc. configures the profile for the policy to select a specific authentication method, encryption method, and encryption strength.

Using an IAS Server

You may have more than one Windows 2000 VPN server. If so, then you need to configure remote access policies and logging for each of the VPN servers. You may want to take advantage of centralized remote access policies and logging. To do so, configure a Remote Authentication Dial-In User Service (RADIUS) server running Windows 2000 and the Internet Authentication Service (IAS). Then configure the VPN servers as clients to the RADIUS server as illustrated in Figure 10.10.

Figure 10.10 RADIUS

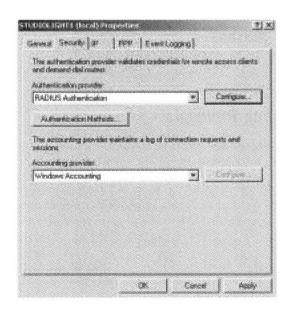

If you have VPN servers running Windows NT 4.0 with the Routing and Remote Access Service (RRAS), then you should also use an IAS server if you want to take advantage of Windows 2000

remote access policies. You cannot configure servers running Windows NT 4.0 as RADIUS clients. You must upgrade a VPN server running Windows NT 4.0 to a VPN server running Windows NT 4.0 and RRAS.

Using Connection Manager

If you have the need for many remote access VPN connections, you can provide a custom dialer with pre-configured VPN connections to all remote access clients by using the Connection Manager and the Connection Manager Administration Kit.

Tunneling

Under a tunneling protocol, a packet is hidden or encapsulated inside a new packet. The new encapsulating packet provides routing information that enables the packet to travel through transit Internetworks to its destination without revealing the true final destination that is stored in the original packet header. The transit internetwork could be a private intranet or the Internet. Once the encapsulated packet reaches its destination, the encapsulation header removes and the original packet header routes the packet to its final destination. The process of tunneling includes the encapsulation, routing, and final de-encapsulation of the packet.

Understanding the Windows 2000 Tunneling Protocols

There are voluntary and compulsory tunnel types. IAS can control access to compulsory tunnels. On behalf of the user, IAS can tell the Network Access Server (NAS) to initiate the tunnels.

You can control user access to tunnels based on the Windows 2000 group users belong to. You configure this control using IAS and the Remote Access Policies feature. Doing so provides more control granularity and power than found in static tunneling or in realm-based tunneling. Static tunneling requires a dedicated NAS. Realm-based tunneling requires that all users in a given realm be given the same access privileges.

Voluntary Tunneling

You have several options for creating tunnels, but the two major types are voluntary tunneling and compulsory tunneling. Both of these are defined here.

Voluntary tunneling occurs when a virtual connection to the target tunnel server creates by a workstation or routing server that uses tunneling client software. A user or a client computer issues a VPN request to configure and create a voluntary tunnel. The user's computer acts as the tunnel client and is a tunnel endpoint. To accomplish this, the appropriate tunneling protocol must be installed on the client computer. You authenticate users and control access to voluntary tunnels with IAS.

Compulsory Tunneling

In compulsory tunneling the NAS sends an authentication requests to IAS. IAS then returns attributes that tell the NAS to initiate a tunnel to a destination VPN server. The VPN server at which the tunnel is terminated is the tunnel-endpoint. The tunnel-endpoint can be changed based on conditions in a remote access policy. The following are examples of parameters that change the tunnel-endpoint:

- User credentials

- Groups to which the user belongs

- Dialed Number Identification Service (DNIS)

- Automatic Number Identification (ANI) Service, (Caller ID)

RADIUS Attributes With Compulsory Tunneling

RADIUS Attributes are used to carry tunneling information from the IAS server to the NAS. Figure 10.11 outlines this concept. The following sections list the attributes by their types:

- Attributes used in authorization only

- Attributes Used in authorization and accounting

- Attributes Used for accounting only

Attributes used in authorization only include the following:

- Tunnel-Private-Group-Id

- Tunnel-Assignment-Id

- Tunnel-Preference

- Tunnel-Password

Note: The Tunnel Password is not for use with proxies.

Attributes Used in authorization and accounting include the following:

- Tunnel-Type (for example, PPTP or L2TP)
- Tunnel-Medium-Type (for example, X.25, ATM, Frame Relay, or IP)
- Tunnel-Client-Endpoint
- Tunnel-Server-Endpoint

The following attribute is used for accounting only:

- Acct-Tunnel-Connection

Figure 10.11 RADIUS Attributes

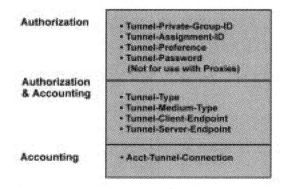

Tunnel Example

An example of the RADIUS attributes for a remote access profile that enables compulsory tunneling is listed in Table 10.4. The attributes in the profile are sent to the NAS that initiates the tunnel.

Table 10.4 Tunneling Attributes

Attribute	Value
Framed-Protocol	PPP
Service-Type	Outbound-User
Tunnel-Medium-Type	IP (IP version 4)
Tunnel-Password	1234
Tunnel-Server-Endpt	10.10.10.10
Tunnel-Type	L2TP

The VPN server terminating the tunnel is where the tunnel password should be configured. This server is the L2TP Network server (LNS). You can send tunnel attributes describing multiple tunnels by using a RADIUS Access-Accept packet. The current implementation, however, returns information only for a single tunnel.

 Note: Internet Authentication Service (IAS) supports one compulsory tunnel per dial-in profile.

Creating Tunnels

Tunneling is a means by which data for one network can be safely transferred over a second, intermediate network. The data transferred is divided into data packets or frames. The tunneling protocol encapsulates each frame or packet in an additional header. The encapsulating header provides routing information so that the encapsulated data can traverse the intermediate network. After the encapsulated data reaches the tunnel endpoint on the intermediate network, the information de-encapsulates, its true destination address is determined and the data forwarded to its final destination. Tunneling encompasses the entire process of encapsulation, transmission, and de-encapsulation. Figure 10.12 shows tunnel creation.

Figure 10.12 Creating Tunnels

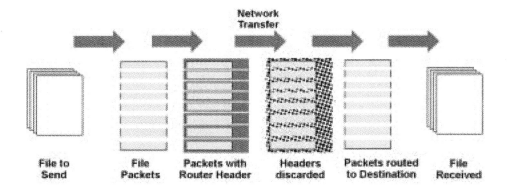

A frame consists of the following parts:

- A header associated with a specific protocol

- The frame data

- A Cyclic Redundancy Check (CRC) or checksum

A packet can contain several related frames.

Note: Data Link Layer (Layer 2) tunneling protocols encapsulate frames. Transport Layer (Layer 3) tunneling protocols encapsulate packets.

Voluntary Tunnels

As mentioned, there are voluntary tunnels and compulsory tunnels. This section describes each type.

A voluntary tunnel configures and creates in response to a VPN request issued by a client (Figure 10.13). Remember that the client computer is a tunnel endpoint. The roaming remote user creates a voluntary tunnel when connecting to a central office.

Figure 10.13 Voluntary Tunnels

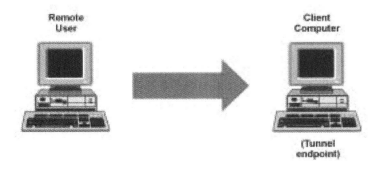

Compulsory Tunnels

A compulsory tunnel creates and configures by a VPN-capable dial-up access server. In this case the user's computer isn't a tunnel endpoint. Widget, Inc. typically creates compulsory tunnels between its branch offices and its central office.

The Open Systems Interconnection (OSI) model Data Link Layer (Layer 2) and the Network Layer (Layer 3) tunneling protocols provide the foundation for tunneling. If Layer 2 protocols are used, a tunnel must be created, maintained, and then terminated. However, Layer 3 protocols assume that all the configuration issues have been handled elsewhere. Layer 3 protocols provide network level security that is transparent to the user. Typically, these protocols have no tunnel maintenance phase. An exception to this rule is the Internet Protocol Security-Internet Security Association and Key Management Protocol (IPSec ISAKMP) negotiation. This protocol provides mutual authentication of the tunnel endpoints. Windows 2000 supports the following protocols:

- Point-To-Point Tunneling Protocol (PPTP)

- Layer 2 Tunneling Protocol (L2TP)

- IPSec tunnel Mode

Point-To-Point Tunneling Protocol (PPTP)

PPTP is a Layer 2 protocol that allows Internet Protocol (IP), Internet work Packet Exchange (IPX), or Network Basic Input/Output System Enhanced User Interface (NetBEUI) traffic to be encrypted and encapsulated in an IP header and then sent across an IP network, such as the Internet.

Layer 2 Tunneling Protocol (L2TP)

L2TP is a Layer 2 protocol that allows IP, IPX, or NetBEUI traffic to be encrypted and sent over any medium that supports point-to-point datagram delivery. Examples of mediums that support point-to-point datagram delivery include IP, X.25, Frame Relay, and Asynchronous Transfer Mode (ATM).

IPSec Tunnel Mode

IPSec is a Layer 3 protocol that allows IP payloads to be encrypted and encapsulated in an IP header and then sent across an IP network, such as the Internet.

Warning: IPSec, by itself, supports only computer-based certificates. This means that any user with access to a tunnel endpoint computer has access to the tunnel.

Windows 2000 uses L2TP over IPSec by default. This overcomes the potential security weakness inherent in using just IPSec on its own.

A combination of Layer 3 and Layer 2 protocols is typically used as a tunneling strategy. Using protocols from both layers provides both network-level protection and tunnel maintenance. The PPTP and L2TP protocols are based on the Point-To-Point Protocol (PPP) and provide the following features:

User authentication—The user authentication schemes of PPP are inherited by PPTP and L2TP. This includes the Extensible Authentication Protocol (EAP) methods. A wide variety of authentication methods can be supported by these protocols including one-time passwords, cryptographic calculators, and Smart Cards.

 Note: Layer 3 tunneling protocols also supports user authentication. For example, IPSec's ISAKMP/Oakley negotiation defines public key certificate authentication.

Dynamic address assignment—Dynamic assignment of client addresses is supported by the PPTP and L2TP protocols based on the Network Control Protocol (NCP) negotiation mechanism.

Data compression—Microsoft Point-To-Point Compression (MPPC) is used in Microsoft implementations of both the PPTP and L2TP protocols.

Data encryption—Microsoft Point-To-Point Encryption (MPPE) is based on the Rivest-Shamir-Adleman (RSA) RC4 encryption algorithm. Use of MMPE is an option in The Microsoft implementation of PPTP. IPSec encryption is used in the Microsoft implementation of the L2TP protocol to protect the data stream.

Key management—The initial key generated during user authentication is employed by MPPE. MPPE refreshes the key periodically. During an ISAKMP exchange, IPSec explicitly negotiates a common key and also refreshes it periodically.

Multiple protocol support— Multiple protocols are supported by PPTP and L2TP. However, PPTP requires the TCP/IP protocol. Only target networks that use the IP protocol are supported by IPSec Tunnel Mode.

Note: IPSec is still under development. In the future IPSec may support many of the features currently implemented by PPTP and L2TP.

Choosing a Data Link Layer or a Tunneling Protocol

The tunneling protocols provided by Windows 2000 for creating router-to-router VPN connections are PPTP and L2TP described in detail in this section.

PPTP

PPTP was first supported in Windows NT 4.0. PPTP is a de facto industry standard tunneling protocol that leverages the authentication, compression, and encryption mechanisms of PPP. PPTP is an extension of the PPP.

PPTP is installed with the Routing and Remote Access service. By default PPTP is configured for five PPTP ports (Figure 10.14). You can use Routing and Remote Access to increase the number of PPTP ports as needed. You use the Routing and Remote Access Wizard to enable PPTP ports for inbound remote access and for demand-dial routing connections. You can also enable PPTP ports for routing after the wizard runs by using Routing and Remote Access.

Figure 10.14 Increasing the Number of PPTP Ports

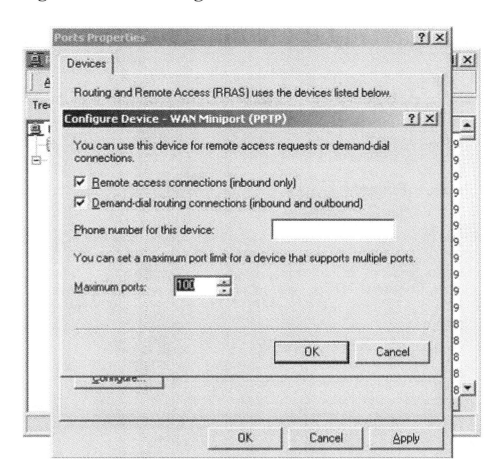

The two primary services of VPN, encapsulation and encryption are defined as follows:

Encapsulation—A PPP frame can contain either an IP datagram or an IPX datagram. The PPP frame is wrapped with both a Generic Routing Encapsulation (GRE) header and an IP header. The source and destination IP address that correspond to the VPN client and VPN server are found in the IP header.

Encryption—The PPTP protocol does not provide encryption services. PPTP merely encapsulates a PPP frame that has already been encrypted. MPPE encrypts the PPP frame using encryption keys generated from the MS-CHAP or EAP-TLS authentication process. In order to encrypt PPP payloads, VPN clients must use either the MS-CHAP or EAP-TLS authentication protocol. It is possible to have a non-encrypted PPTP connection where the PPP payload is sent in plaintext.

 Note: A non-encrypted PPTP connection is not secure and not recommended for VPN connections over the Internet.

L2TP

L2TP is a draft Request For Comment (RFC)-based tunneling protocol. It appears that L2TP is destined to become the industry standard. L2TP leverages the authentication and compression mechanisms of PPP. L2TP in Windows 2000 does not utilize MPPE to encrypt PPP frames. For encryption services L2TP relies on IPSec.

L2TP-based VPN connections are a combination of L2TP and IPSec. Both VPN routers must support L2TP and IPSec. Use the Routing and Remote Access service to install L2TP. By default, L2TP configures for five L2TP ports. Using the Routing and Remote Access Wizard, L2TP ports can be enabled for inbound remote access and for demand-dial routing connections.

The two primary services of VPN are encapsulation and encryption. The following two layers of encapsulation are employed in L2TP over IPSec encapsulation of packets:

L2TP encapsulation—A PPP frame that contains either an IP datagram or an IPX datagram wraps with a L2TP header and a User Datagram Protocol (UDP) header.

IPSec encapsulation—The resulting L2TP message encapsulates with the following trailers and header:

• An IPSec Encapsulating Security Payload (ESP) header and trailer

• An IPSec Authentication trailer

• A final IP header

The IPSec Authentication trailer provides message integrity and authentication. The source and destination IP address that correspond to the VPN client and VPN server are found in the final IP header.

The L2TP message is then encrypted with IPSec encryption mechanisms using encryption keys generated from the IPSec authentication process. Figure 10.15 outlines encapsulation.

Figure 10.15 IPSec Encapsulation

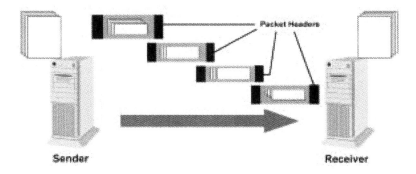

Authentication

Authentication is the process of verifying the identity of a user or computer that is attempting access to the network. In this section we discuss authentication methods implemented on the Data Link Layer (Layer 2) of the OSI model.

Using Data Link Layer Authentication Methods

Authentication for VPN connections at the Data Link Layer takes the following three different forms:

- User-level authentication using PPP authentication
- Machine-level authentication using ISAKMP

- Data authentication and integrity

User-Level Authentication Using PPP Authentication

Prior to establishing a VPN connection, a VPN server authenticates the VPN client that is attempting the connection. This is done by using the PPP user-level authentication method. The VPN server also verifies that the VPN client has the appropriate permissions. In the case where mutual authentication is employed, the VPN client also authenticates the VPN server. Mutual authentication provides protection against masquerading VPN servers.

Machine-Level Authentication Using ISAKMP

Before any exchange of data in a secure environment, a Security Association (SA) must be established between the VPN client and VPN server. To establish an IPSec SA, the VPN client and the VPN server use machine certificates and the ISAKMP. The Oakley key generation protocol generates and manages authentication keys.

Data Authentication and Integrity

Data transmitted over a VPN contains a cryptographic checksum based on an encryption key known only to the sender and the receiver. The checksum verifies that the data sent on the VPN connection was not modified in transit and that it actually originated at the other end of the connection. Only L2TP over IPSec connections can provide data authentication and integrity.

Data Encryption

Data that transmits is encrypted by the data transmitter and decrypted by the data receiver. Both the sender and the receiver use a common encryption key. This ensures the confidentiality of the data as it traverses the shared or public transit internetwork. The encryption and decryption processes depend on the shared encryption key.

Packets Intercepted while traversing the transit internetwork are unintelligible to anyone who does not have the common encryption key. An important security parameter is the length of the encryption key. Computational techniques are used to determine the encryption key. However, as the encryption keys become larger, such techniques require more computing power and more computational time. To ensure data confidentiality, it is important to use the largest possible key size.

Tunneled Data and Tunnel Maintenance

Tunnels are created using tunneling protocols that are special TCP/IP-based protocols. To understand tunneling protocols, it is first necessary to understand Transmission Control Protocol (TCP) connections.

Understanding the TCP Connections

The TCP standard is defined in RFC793 entitled Transmission Control Protocol (TCP). TCP provides a reliable, connection-oriented packet delivery service. TCP performs the following services:

- Guarantees delivery of IP datagrams

- Provides segmentation and reassembly of large blocks of data sent by programs

- Ensures proper sequencing and ordered delivery of segmented data

- Checks on the integrity of transmitted data by using checksum calculations

- Sends positive acknowledgement of received data

- Transmits the positive data receipt message to the data sender if the data was received successfully. Negative acknowledgments for data not received are also sent when using selective acknowledgments. TCP offers the preferred method of transport for programs that must use reliable session-based data transmission. Examples of such programs are client/server database applications and e-mail programs.

How TCP Works

Point-to-point communication between two network hosts provides the foundations for TCP. Programs provide TCP with data. TCP then processes this data as a stream of bytes that are grouped into segments that TCP numbers and sequences for delivery (Figure 10.16).

Figure 10.16 TCP

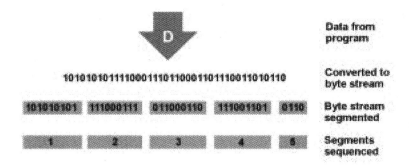

The two TCP hosts must first establish a session with each other before they can exchange any data. A process known as a three-way handshake initializes the TCP session (Figure 10.17). This process synchronizes the sequence numbers and provides the control information needed to establish the virtual connection between the two hosts.

Figure 10.17 Three-Way Handshake

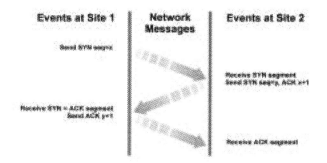

Once the initial three-way handshake completes, a connection establishes between the two TCP hosts. Data segments transmit and are acknowledged between both the sending and receiving hosts in a sequential manner. Before closing a connection, a similar handshake process is used by TCP to verify that both hosts are finished sending and receiving all data (Figure 10.18).

Figure 10.18 Closing Connection

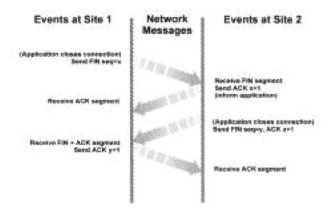

TCP ports—TCP uses a specific program port for delivery of TCP data. TCP ports are more complex than User Datagram Protocol (UDP) ports and also operate differently than UDP ports.

A UDP port operates as a single message queue. The UDP port is the network endpoint for UDP-based communication. Two address/port pairs uniquely identify TCP connections. There is one IP address and one TCP port for each TCP host (Figure 10.19). Each TCP connection can be uniquely identified by its dual endpoints. The final endpoint for all TCP communications is a unique connection. Because the TCP host identifies connections by an IP address/Port pair, each TCP port is capable of offering shared access to multiple connections.

Figure 10.19 TCP Ports

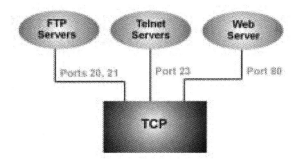

The server side of a program that uses TCP ports will listen for messages arriving on their port number.

 Note: The Internet Assigned Numbers Authority (IANA) has reserved and registered all TCP server port numbers less than 1,024. Some higher numbers are also reserved by IANA.

A partial list of some well-known TCP server ports that are used by standard TCP-based programs are listed with their descriptions in Table 10.5.

Table 10.5 TCP Port Numbers

TCP Port Number	Description
20	FTP server (data channel)
21	FTP server (control channel)
23	Telnet server
53	DNS zone transfers
80	Web server (HTTP)
139	NetBIOS session service

Understanding the Difference between PPTP and L2TP

PPTP requires the use of an IP network. L2TP does not require the IP connectivity that PPTP does between the client workstation and the server. L2TP requires only that packet-oriented point-to-point connectivity provided by the tunnel medium. The L2TP protocol can be used over media such as ATM, Frame Relay, and X.25.

PPTP utilizes MPPE to encrypt PPP datagrams and L2TP in Windows 2000 does not. L2TP relies on IPSec for encryption services.

PPTP only supports a single tunnel between endpoints. L2TP provides multiple tunnel use. PPTP does not provide tunnel authentication where L2TP does. If either protocol is used over IPSec, then IPSec provides tunnel authentication. Finally, when header compression is enabled, PPTP uses 6 bytes of overhead while L2TP uses only 4 bytes.

Remote Authentication

The Remote Authentication Dial-In User Service (RADIUS) performs remote authentication. RADIUS is a client/server UDP-based security authentication protocol widely used by ISPs on non-Microsoft remote servers. RADIUS is also the most popular means of authenticating dial-up and tunneled network users.

Using a Dial-In User Service

The network administrator for Widget, Inc. finds that in addition to VPN-based remote access, there is a need to provide modem-based dial-up remote access for employees of the Los Angeles office. A Windows 2000 group called LA_Employees contains all employees of the Los Angeles office. A separate Windows 2000 remote access server at the phone number 555-1234 provides dial-up remote access. The Widget, Inc. network administrator configures a computer running Windows 2000 with the IAS as a RADIUS server. The administrator does this rather than separately administer the remote access policies of both the VPN server and the remote access server. The IAS server has an IP address of 172.31.0.9 on the Widget, Inc. extranet. The IAS server also provides centralized remote access authentication, authorization, and accounting for both the remote access server and the VPN server.

Mutual Authentication

Mutual authentication means that both the client and the server must prove their identities when a connection establishes. You can achieve Mutual authentication using MS-CHAP Version 2. MS-CHAP Version 2 is a one-way encrypted password, mutual authentication process.

When a client attempts to connect, the authenticator, which is either the remote access server or the IAS server, sends a challenge to the remote access client. The challenge consists of a session identifier and an arbitrary challenge string.

The remote access client responds to the challenge by sending a response that contains the user name, an arbitrary peer challenge string, and a one-way encryption of the received challenge string, the peer challenge string, the session identifier, and the user's password.

The authenticator then checks the client's response and sends back a further response containing an indication of the success or failure of the connection attempt and an authenticated response based on the sent challenge string, the peer challenge string, the encrypted response of the client, and the user's password. Figure 10.20 illustrates this concept.

The remote access client then verifies the authentication response and, if the response is correct, uses the connection. If the authentication response is not correct, the remote access client terminates the connection.

Figure 10.20 Mutual Authentication

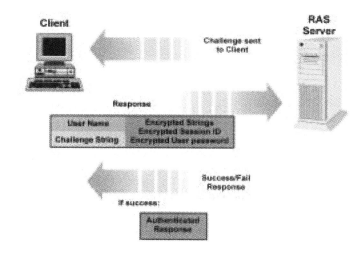

Creating Two-Way Connections

To enable MS-CHAP Version 2-based authentication, you must perform the following tasks:

1. Ensure that MS-CHAP Version 2 is enabled as an authentication protocol on the remote access server (MS-CHAP Version 2 enables by default).

2. Ensure that MS-CHAP Version 2 is enabled on the appropriate remote access policy (MS-CHAP Version 2 is enabled by default).

3. Enable MS-CHAP Version 2 on the remote access client running Windows 2000.

 Note: Before you enable MS-CHAP Version 2 on a remote access policy on an IAS server, make sure your Network Access Server (NAS) supports it.

RADIUS Server

As described previously, the RADIUS server is a popular remote authentication server used by many ISPs. RADIUS is also the most popular means of authenticating dial-up and tunneled network users

Setting Up a RADIUS Server

A RADIUS server is a computer running Windows 2000 with the IAS configured for RADIUS clients. You must install the IAS networking component. You must also configure the IAS for two RADIUS clients, the VPN server and the remote access server. To set up a RADIUS Server, perform the following tasks configure the domain and configure the remote access policies.

Configuring the Domain

The remote access permission for the dial-in properties for each employee that is allowed dial-up access is set to **Allow access**.

Configure the Remote Access Policies

The following two tasks are required to configure remote access policies on the IAS server:

Copy existing remote access policies—Any existing remote access policies that have been configured on the Windows 2000 VPN server must be copied to the IAS server. These policies are no longer used once the VPN server configures to use RADIUS authentication. The remote access policies stored on the IAS server are used instead.

New remote access policy—You need to create a new remote access policy for dial-up remote access clients on the IAS server. This policy should define the authentication and encryption settings for dial-up connections by remote users. The example remote access policy for Widget, Inc. was described earlier in this lesson.

RADIUS Configuration

The network administrator for Widget, Inc. needs to configure RADIUS authentication and accounting. The administrator configures the following:

1.   Register a remote access RADIUS client on the IAS server with a shared secret for each the VPN server and the remote access server.

2.   Configure the Windows 2000 remote access server running to use RADIUS authentication and accounting at the IP address of the IAS server.

3.   Configure the Windows 2000 VPN server running to use RADIUS authentication and accounting at the IP address of the IAS server.

Dial-Up Remote Access Client Configuration

The network administrator for Widget, Inc. uses the Make New Connection Wizard on the client computer to create a dial-up connection with the following setting:

Phone number: 555-1234

Vocabulary

Review the following terms in preparation for the certification exam.

Term	Description
IAS	Internet Authentication Service is used to manage, at one time and from one place, all the remote access servers used by a network.
IPSec	Internet Protocol Security is a suite of cryptography-based protection services and security protocols. Because it requires no changes to applications or protocols it can easily be deployed for existing networks.
ISAKMP	Internet Security Association and Key Management Protocol is a protocol used by a Windows 2000 IP Security filter to start setting up a secure environment for a packet to travel in.
L2TP	Layer 2 funneling Protocol allows IP, IPX, or NetBEUI traffic to be encrypted and then sent over any medium that supports point-to-point datagram delivery, such as IP, X.25, Frame Relay, or Asynchronous Transfer Mode (ATM). L2TP is a Layer 2 protocol
MS-CHAP Version 2	MS-CHAP Version 2 is a one-way encrypted password, mutual authentication process.
PPTP	Point-To-Point Tunneling Protocol allows IP, IPX, or NetBEUI traffic to be encrypted, encapsulated in an IP header, and sent across an IP network, such as the Internet. PPTP is a Layer 2 protocol.
RADIUS	Remote Authentication Dial-In User Service.

Term	Description
RRAS	Routing and Remote Access Service is a software router and an open platform for routing and internetworking.
TCP	TCP is based on point-to-point communication between two network hosts. TCP receives data from programs and processes this data as a stream of bytes. Bytes are grouped into segments that TCP then numbers and sequences for delivery
tunneling	Tunneling is the entire process of encapsulation, transmission, and de-encapsulation of data transmissions.
VPN	A Virtual Private Network is a private network on a PPP connection that is formed upon a public system that allows its restricted users to communicate through encryption.

In Brief

If you want to...	Then do this...
Set up a VPN with remote access and router-to-router connections	Use the VPN server.
Configure remote servers after a Wizard has run	Specify the protocols to use on the LAN (IPX, TCP/IP, AppleTalk, or NetBEUI), and whether access by using that protocol is to the entire network or to the remote access server only.
Configuration Remote access policy	Control remote access by setting the dial-in permission of individual user accounts to either **Allow access** or **Deny access**. Remote access policies are used to apply different VPN connection settings based on group membership. The default remote access policy named **Allow access if dial-in permission is enabled** is deleted.
Configure RADIUS	The remote access server running Windows 2000 is configured to use RADIUS authentication and accounting at the IP address of the IAS server. The VPN server running Windows 2000 is configured to use RADIUS authentication and accounting at the IP address of the IAS server.

Lesson 10 Activities

Complete the following activities to better prepare you for the certification exam.

1.   List the types of VPN technology in Windows 2000.

2.   Describe the components of Virtual Private Networking.

3.   List what is involved in configuring a VPN.

4.   Describe a sample domain configuration.

5.   List supported protocols for Windows 2000 remote access authentication protocols.

6.   Describe how to create a remote access policy.

7.   Explain how to configure the system for multiple VPN servers.

8.   Explain tunneling.

9.   Describe the differences between voluntary and compulsory tunneling

10. Explain the differences between PPTP and L2TP.

Answers to Lesson 10 Activities

1.   The types of VPN technology in Windows 2000 include:

Point-to-Point Tunneling Protocol (PPTP) uses user-level Point-to-Point Protocol (PPP) authentication methods and Microsoft Point-to-Point Encryption (MPPE) for data encryption.

Layer Two Tunneling Protocol (L2TP) uses user-level PPP authentication methods and machine-level certificates with IPSec for data encryption.

2.   Virtual private networks include:

Virtual private network (VPN) servers

You can configure the VPN server to provide access to an entire network or to restrict access to just the resources of the VPN server.

VPN clients

VPN clients are either individual users who obtain a remote access VPN connection or routers that obtain a router-to-router VPN connection.

LAN and remote access protocols

Application programs transporting information use LAN protocols.

Tunneling protocols

VPN clients use tunneling protocols to create secured connections to a VPN server.

WAN options

VPN servers are connected to the Internet by using permanent WAN connections.

3.   The following activities are required to configure a VPN:

The network configuration

The remote access policy configuration

The domain configuration

The security configuration

4. A sample domain configuration includes:

    VPN_Users—Used for remote access VPN connections.

    VPN_Routers—Used for router-to-router VPN connections from Widget, Inc. branch offices.

    VPN_Partners—Used for router-to-router VPN connections from Widget, Inc. business partners.

5. Supported protocols for Windows 2000 remote access authentication include:

    Microsoft Challenge Handshake Authentication Protocol (MS-CHAP), Challenge Handshake Authentication Protocol (CHAP),

    Shiva Password Authentication Protocol (SPAP),

    Password Authentication Protocol (PAP),

    MS-CHAP version 2 (MS-CHAP Version 2), and

    Extensible Authentication Protocol (EAP).

6. A remote access policy is created with a Windows 2000 group called VPN Users. The VPN Users group is created, whose members are the user accounts of the those users that will be creating remote access VPN connections across the Internet. You then create a policy with two conditions on the policy: The condition **NAS-Port-Type** is set to Virtual (VPN) and the condition **Windows-Group** is set to VPN Users. Finally, configure the profile for the policy to select a specific authentication method, encryption method, and encryption strength.

7. If there are multiple VPN servers running Windows 2000, you will need to configure remote access policies and logging for each of the VPN servers. You can configure the VPN servers as Remote Authentication Dial-In User Service (RADIUS) clients if you want to take advantage of centralized remote access policies and logging.

8. During the process of tunneling, the original packet is hidden (encapsulated) inside a new packet. The encapsulating packet provides routing information that enables the packet to travel through transit internetworks. The new packet does so without revealing the final destination stored in the original packet header. The transit internetwork could be a private intranet or the Internet. Once the encapsulating packets reach their destination, the encapsulation header is removed. The original packet header routes the packet to its final destination.

9. A user or client computer can configure and create a voluntary tunnel by issuing a VPN request. The user's computer acts as the tunnel client and is a tunnel endpoint. When a workstation or routing server uses tunneling client software to create a virtual connection to the target tunnel

server voluntary tunneling occurs. The appropriate tunneling protocol must be installed on the client computer. In the case of compulsory tunneling, the Network Access Server (NAS) sends an authentication requests to IAS. IAS then returns attributes that tell the NAS to initiate a tunnel to a destination VPN server that acts as a tunnel-endpoint. The VPN server at which the tunnel is terminated could be changed based on conditions in a remote access policy.

10. The Point-to-Point Tunneling Protocol (PPTP) requires the use of an IP network. Layer Two Tunneling Protocol (L2TP) does not.

PPTP utilizes Microsoft Point-to-Point Encryption (MPPE) to encrypt PPP datagrams; L2TP in Windows 2000 does not. L2TP relies on Internet Protocol security (IPSec) for encryption services.

PPTP can only support a single tunnel between endpoints. L2TP provides multiple tunnel use.

PPTP does not provide tunnel authentication where L2TP does.

When header compression is enabled, PPTP uses 6 bytes of overhead while L2TP uses only 4 bytes.

Lesson 10 Quiz

These questions test your knowledge of features, vocabulary, procedures, and syntax.

1. Which of the below are VPN technologies supported by Windows 2000?

   A. PPTP

   B. EFS

   C. L2TP

   D. ISP

2. What are the components of a Windows 2000 VPN?

   A. Virtual private network (VPN) servers

   B. VPN clients

   C. LAN and remote access protocols

   D. Tunneling protocols

3. What are some of the key concerns when configuring a VPN?

   A. The network configuration

   B. The remote access policy configuration

   C. The domain configuration

   D. The security configuration

4. What is the default number of ports for PPTP and L2TP?

   A. 20

   B. 253

   C. 5

   D. 100

5. What domain groups were created by the Widget, Inc. network administrator for the Windows 2000 VPN?

   A. VPN_Users

   B. VPN_Routers

C. VPN_Partners

D. VPN

6. Which remote access authentication protocols does Windows 2000 support?

A. MS-CHAP

B. SPAP

C. EAP

D. MS-CHAP Version 2

7. What are the types of tunnels?

A. Staggered

B. Voluntary

C. Compulsory

D. Parallel

8. Which of the following are RADIUS attributes?

A. Tunnel-Type (PPTP, L2TP)

B. Tunnel-Medium-Type (X.25, ATM, Frame Relay, IP)

C. Tunnel-Client-Endpoint

D. Tunnel-Server-Endpoint

9. Which OSI layers are employed in Windows 2000 tunneling?

A. Data Link Layer

B. Presentation Layer

C. Network Layer

D. Session Layer

10. What are some of the key IPSec operations?

A. Dynamic address assignment

B. Data compression

C. Data encryption

D. Key management

Answers to Lesson 10 Quiz

1. Answers A and C are correct. PPTP and L2TP are the two types of VPN technology supported by Windows 2000.

   Answers B and D are incorrect. Neither EFS nor ISP are VPN technologies.

2. Answers A, B, C, and D are correct. All the items listed are VPN technologies used by humans. But there are missing items: WAN options. Internet support. Security options.

3. Answers A, B, C, and D are correct. Network, remote access policy, domain and security are all key considerations.

4. Answer C is correct, both protocols default to 5 ports.

   Answers A, B and D are incorrect. They are made up numbers.

5. Answers A, B, and C are correct. Users, routers and Partners are all domain configurations.

   Answer D is incorrect. VPN, by itself, is not a domain configuration.

6. Answers A, B, C and D are correct. MS-CHAP, SPAP, EAP, and MS-CHAP Version 2 are all protocols supported by Windows 2000.

7. Answers B and C are correct. Voluntary, where a user or client makes the VPN request, and compulsory where the server makes the VPN request.

   Answers A and D are incorrect. Staggered and Parallel mean nothing as far as VPN tunneling is concerned.

8. All answers are correct. They are used in authorization and accounting.

9. Answers A and C are correct. The Data Link Layer (Layer 2) and the network layer (Layer 3) are the layers employed in standard tunneling protocols.

   Answers Band D are incorrect. They have no connection with tunneling.

10. All answers are correct.

    Dynamic address assignment—PPTP and L2TP support dynamic assignment of client addresses based on the Network Control Protocol (NCP) negotiation mechanism.

Data compression—Microsoft implementations of both PPTP and L2TP use Microsoft Point-To-Point Compression (MPPC).

Data encryption—The Microsoft implementation of PPTP optionally uses Microsoft Point-To-Point Encryption (MPPE), based on the RSA/RC4 algorithm. The Microsoft implementation of the L2TP protocol uses IPSec encryption to encrypt the data stream.

Key management—MPPE employs and periodically refreshes the initial key generated during user authentication. IPSec explicitly negotiates a common key during the ISAKMP exchange and refreshes it periodically.

GLOSSARY

Term	Description
account lockout policy	A Windows 2000 security feature that locks a user's account when a number of failed logon attempts have occurred in a specific period of time, based on policy settings. Locked accounts cannot log on.
ACE	An Access Control Entry identifies permissions for a group or user object.
ACEs	Access Control Entries are entries in a Discretionary Access Control List (DACL) that identify security groups or individual user accounts, and their permissions.
ACL	Access Control List is a list of entries in the Active Directory object's security descriptor. It grants or denies access rights to individuals or groups.
Active Directory	A directory service based on central policies that manages authorization and authentication services, remote network administration and security features.
ADSI	Active Directory Service Interfaces is a simple, powerful, object-oriented interface to Active Directory.
API	Application Programming Interface is a set of routines that an application uses to request and carry out services performed by a computer's operating system. These routines are used for maintenance tasks such as managing files and displaying information.
AS Exchange	Authentication Service Exchange is used when the KDC gives the client a logon session key and a TGT.
audit policy	Determines which security events are reported to the administrator.

Term	Description
authentication	A screening process during access to a network resource where a person's identity is verified with a username and password.
CA	Certificate Authority is a trusted third-party organization or company that issues digital certificates that create digital signatures and public-private key pairs. The role of the CA in this process is to guarantee that the individual granted the unique certificate is, in fact, whom they claim to be. CAs are a significant component in data security because they guarantee that the two parties exchanging information are really who they claim to be.
CA	A Certificate Authority is a trusted service responsible for the creation of public keys and the verification of the validity of the public keys of other CAs, users, and computers. CAs link public keys to identities with signed digital certificates, keep track of certificate serial numbers, and manage certificate revocation. The CA can bind public keys to distinguished names through signed certificates.
CAPI	Crypto Application Programming Interface, also known as CryptoAPI, provides functions that allow applications to encrypt or digitally sign data, and provide protection for sensitive private key data.
certificate hierarchy	Certificate hierarchies are structures that determine CA trust relationships through the creation of root-subordinate or parent-child CA relationships.
certificate mapping	Certificate mapping is a method where one or more issued certificates are associated with a user account. Servers can then use the private keys of those certificates to authenticate the user or perform secure tasks.
Certificate Services Web pages	These are Web pages that provide, through the use of a CA, authentication support, Web-based authentication, Smart Card authentication, and secure e-mail services.

Term	Description
Certificate Template	A Windows 2000 function that pre-specifies format and content for certificates based on their intended use. When requesting a certificate from a CA, certificate requestors are able to choose from a variety of certificate types based on certificate templates, such as "User" and "Secure Signing."
Cipher	A Windows 2000 utility enabling users to encrypt files from the command prompt.
COM	Component Object Model is a set of integrated services and tools used for software development.
container object	An object that contains other objects, such as a folder that holds files.
CRL	A Certification Revocation List is an automatically generated list of invalid and revoked certificates that is periodically generated by a CA.
CryptoAPI	Also called CAPI, CryptoAPI is an Application Programming Interface (API) that is provided as part of Microsoft Windows. It provides a set of functions that allow applications to encrypt or digitally sign data in a flexible manner while providing protection for the user's sensitive private key data. Actual cryptographic operations are performed by independent modules known as Cryptographic Service Providers (CSPs).
cryptography	The processes, art, and science of keeping messages and data secure. Cryptography enables and ensures confidentiality, data integrity, authentication (entity and data origin), and non-repudiation.
CS Exchange	Client/Server Exchange is used when the client presents the session ticket for admission to a service.
CSP	Cryptographic Service Provider is the code that performs authentication, encoding, and encryption services that Windows applications access through the CryptoAPI.

Term	Description
	A CSP is responsible for creating keys, destroying them, and using them to perform a variety of cryptographic operations. Each CSP provides a different implementation of the CryptoAPI. Some of these provide stronger cryptographic algorithms, while others contain hardware components, such as Smart Cards.
DACL	Discretionary Access Control Lists define security groups, user accounts, and associated permissions, and enforces resource security and access levels for each list member. Discretionary Access Control Lists define object permissions and impose resource security for each list entry. DACLs are security group, user account, and associated permissions lists.
DCE-RPC	Distributed Computing Environment Remote Procedure Call.
decryption	The process of converting data from encrypted format back to its original format. Once a user has decrypted a file, the file remains decrypted whenever the file is stored on disk.
DES-CBC	Data Encryption Standard-Cipher Block Chaining is a secret key algorithm for confidentiality. A random number generates for use with the secret key to encrypt the data.
DESX	A modified Data Encryption Standard (DES) algorithm.
Diffie-Hellman	Diffie-Hellman groups determine the length of the base prime numbers for use during the key exchange.
digital signature	A means for originators of a message, file, or other digitally encoded information to securely bind their identity to the information.
DNS	Domain Name Service is a network server service that translates domain names into IP addresses.
domain	A group of computers on a network that share a common directory database, with a unique name, organized in levels, and administered as a unit with common rules and procedures.

Term	Description
EAP-TLS	Extensible Authentication Protocol-Transport Level Security is an extension of the Point-to-Point Protocol (PPP) that provides remote access user authentication by means of other security devices. Support for a number of authentication schemes may be added. These schemes include token cards, dial-up, the Kerberos Version 5 protocol, one-time passwords, and public key authentication using Smart Cards, certificates, and others. EAP works with dial-up, PPTP, and L2TP clients. It is an important component for secure Virtual Private Networks (VPNs) because it offers more security against brute force or dictionary attacks (where all possible combinations of characters are attempted), and password guessing than other authentication methods.
EFS	Windows 2000 Encrypting File System enables users to encrypt files and folders on an NTFS volume disk to keep them safe from unauthorized access.
encryption	The process of disguising a message or data in such a way as to hide its substance.
Enhanced CryptoPAK	A 128-bit encryption system.
enrollment agent	The enrollment agent certificate template generates signing certificates used to sign the certificate request generated for a Smart Card recipient.
Enterprise CA	An enterprise Certificate Authority utilizes Active Directory to automate many tasks and allow for automatic selection of appropriate certificates. The enterprise CA uses Active directory to confirm a requesters identity, the validity of his request, and to determine which kind of certificate to grant based upon the different types of certificates available from an enterprise CA and the information store on the Active Directory about the requester. The enterprise CA also uses the Active Directory, along with a shared directory, to create and publish a CRL.
ESE	Extensible Storage Engine is the database engine for Active Directory. ESE (ESENT.DLL) is a better version of the Jet

Term	Description
	database used in Microsoft Exchange Server Versions 4.x and 5.5. The ESE uses log files to make sure committed transactions are safe (transacted database system).
ESP	IPSec's Encapsulated Security Payload protocol is referred to as a Virtual Private Network (VPN).
Event Log	Event Logs record audit entries when specific events happen. Events include services starting and stopping and users logging on, off, and accessing resources. The Event Viewer is used to review the events.
explicit domain trusts	Trust relationships manually created by the administrator.
external certificates	External user certificates are used by CAs to verify a sender's computer's identity instead of the systems SID. External certificates can be used to relay authenticated messages to Windows NT and other non-Windows 2000 environments.
external trusts	Trusts relationships to domains outside the forest.
FEK	A File Encryption Key is a randomly generated string of bits used by the encryption algorithm to encrypt and decrypt files.
forest	A collection of one or more Windows 2000 domains that share a common schema, configuration, and global catalog and are linked with two-way transitive trusts.
FQDN	The Fully Qualified Domain Name for the computer is its primary (or default) name.
GINA	Graphical Identification and Authentication is a Dynamic Link Library (DLL), MSGINA.DLL.
GPO	Group Policy Object is a virtual collection of policies, defining access, configuration and usage settings for accounts and resources. These policies are given unique names, such as a Globally Unique Identifier (GUID). GPOs store the policy settings in two locations: a Group Policy Container (GPC) and a Group Policy Template.

Term	Description
Group Policy	Group Policy allows administrative settings and applies management policies to Active Directory OUs.
Hash algorithm	An algorithm that creates a hash value from an input, such as a session key or message. Good Hash methods produce vastly different outputs even when only small changes are made to the input. This makes Hash coding an excellent tool to detect any changes in sizeable data objects, like messages. Properly designed Hash algorithms will never create the same Hash code output from different inputs. Common Hash algorithms include MD2, MD4, MD5, and SHA-1. Hash algorithms are also known as hash functions.
HMAC	Hash Message Authentication Code is a mechanism for message authentication using cryptographic hash functions.
I2O	Intelligent Input/Output architecture allows for higher I/O performance on servers by offloading certain I/O operations to a secondary processor.
IAS	Internet Authentication Service is used to manage, at one time and from one place, all the remote access servers used by a network.
IEAK 5	The Internet Explorer Administration Kit 5.
IPSec	Internet Protocol Security is a suite of cryptography-based protection services and security protocols. Because it requires no changes to applications or protocols it can easily be deployed for existing networks. IPSec Security protocols provide data and identity protection for each IP packet. Windows 2000 IPSec uses the Authentication Header and Encapsulating Security Payload to provide these services.
ISAKMP	Internet Security Association and Key Management Protocol is a protocol used by a Windows 2000 IP Security filter to start setting up a secure environment for a packet to travel in.

Term	Description
Java Card	Java Cards are Smart Cards that run the Java Card byte code following the Java Card API 2.1 specification from Sun Microsystems' JavaSoft division. Smart Card application developers can benefit from object oriented Write-Once, Run Anywhere technology and from Java application development tools.
KDC	Key Distribution Center runs on each domain controller as part of Active Directory, storing all client passwords and other account information.
Kerberos	An authentication system developed at the Massachusetts Institute of Technology (MIT), Kerberos is designed so two parties can exchange private information across an open network. It works by assigning a unique key, called a ticket, to each user that logs on to the network. The ticket is embedded in messages to identify the sender of the message.
L2TP	Layer 2 funneling Protocol allows IP, IPX, or NetBEUI traffic to be encrypted and then sent over any medium that supports point-to-point datagram delivery, such as IP, X.25, Frame Relay, or Asynchronous Transfer Mode (ATM). L2TP is a Layer 2 protocol
LDAP	Lightweight Directory Access Protocol, a communications protocol designed for use on TCP/IP networks, defines how a directory client accesses directory servers, performs directory operations and shares directory data.
MAPI	Messaging Application Programming Interface is used by Active Directory to support backward compatibility with Microsoft Exchange applications.
message queuing	A message queuing and routing system for Windows 2000 designed to allow distributed applications not running concurrently to pass messages between each other and to queue messages for systems that may be offline or are not responding. Message Queuing, formerly known as MSMQ, can be used in heterogeneous networks and provides a number of important services, including guaranteed message delivery, efficient routing, priority-bases message queuing, and security features.

Term	Description
MS-CHAP Version 2	MS-CHAP Version 2 is a one-way encrypted password, mutual authentication process.
NDS	Novell Network Directory Services is a distributed database that maintains information about every resource on the network and provides access to, and control of, these resources.
NTFS	Windows 2000 New Technology File System (not to be confused with Windows NT File System).
Oakley	Oakley is a key determination protocol that uses the Diffie-Hellman key exchange algorithm.
object	An entity such as a file, folder, shared folder, printer, in the Active Directory object.
object permission	Authorization or restriction assignment made by the network system administrator to a user or user group regarding access to functions or resources.
OCF	The OpenCard Framework is an object-oriented software framework for Smart Card access. The Open Card Consortium is the group that specifies the standards and drives the software framework.
OU	An Organizational Unit is an entity or entity group logically organized by the system administrator according to business or system functions or policies. Organizational Units are Active Directory containers for users, groups, computers, and other OUs. An OU cannot contain objects from other domains.
password policy	Passwords restrict logon names to user accounts and computer systems and resources. The policy determines the settings for the passwords on a specific system.
PC/SC	The Personal Computer/Smart Card workgroup was formed in May 1996 by major computer and Smart Card companies. This group works to provide Smart Card standards.

Term	Description
PCMCIA	Personal Computer Memory Card International Association devices are removable devices, approximately the size of a credit card, which can be plugged into a PCMCIA slot in a portable computer. PCMCIA devices can include modems, network cards, and hard disk drives.
permission inheritance	When objects within a container or OU automatically inherit that container's permissions.
PGP	Pretty Good Privacy is a standard for e-mail encryption and authentication.
PIN	A Personal Identification Number is a number that the user can have placed onto their Smart Card for identification.
PKI	Public Key Infrastructure describes the laws, policies, standards, and software that regulate or manipulate certificates and public and private keys. It is a system of digital certificates, certification authorities, and other registration authorities that verify and authenticate the validity of each party involved in an electronic transaction.
policy engine	The policy engine implements at decision points to perform policy selection, evaluate conditions, and decide what actions must be performed.
PPP	Point-to-Point Protocol is a set of industry-standard framing and authentication protocols that is part of Windows 2000 remote access to ensure interoperability with other remote access software. PPP negotiates configuration parameters for networking protocols such as TCP/IP, IPX, and AppleTalk.
PPTP	Point-To-Point Tunneling Protocol networking technology supports multi-protocol VPNs, enabling remote users to access corporate networks securely across the Internet or other networks by dialing into an Internet service provider (ISP) or by connecting directly to the Internet. The Point-to-Point Tunneling Protocol (PPTP) tunnels, or encapsulates, IP, IPX, or NetBEUI traffic inside of IP packets. This means that users can remotely run applications that are dependent upon particular network protocols.

Term	Description
predefined security templates	A physical representation of a security configuration, it is a file where a group of settings store, making it easier to administer.
private key	The secret half of a cryptographic key pair that is used with a public key algorithm. Private keys decrypt symmetric session keys, digitally sign data, or decrypt data encrypted with a corresponding public key.
public key	The nonsecret half of a cryptographic key pair that is used with a public key algorithm. Public keys encrypt a session key, verify a digital signature, or encrypt data decrypted with a corresponding private key.
RADIUS	Remote Authentication Dial-In User Service.
recovery agent	An administrator who is issued a public key certificate in order to recover EFS-encrypted data.
Restricted Groups	A Windows 2000 security feature that acts as a governor for group membership. Restricted Groups automatically provide security membership for default groups that have pre-defined capabilities. This includes administrators, Power Users, and so forth. Any groups that are sensitive or privileged can be added to the Restricted Groups.
RFC	A Request for Comments is an evolving series of reports, proposals for protocols, and protocol standards that describe the internal workings of TCP/IP and the Internet.
RRAS	Routing and Remote Access Service is a software router and an open platform for routing and internetworking.
SA	A Security Association is a combination of a policy and keys that defines the common security services, mechanisms, and keys used to protect the communication from end to end.
SAM	A Security Account Manager is a Windows 2000 service used during logon. SAM maintains user account information, including the groups that the user belongs to.

Term	Description
SDKs	Software Development Kits provide developers with all the necessary tools and documentation to program applications using libraries of functions that make up an SDK.
SECEDIT.EXE	A command-line form of the Security Configuration and Analysis snap-in that enables security configuration and analysis without a Graphical User Interface (GUI).
security options	Enables or disables security settings for the computer, such as digital signing of data, Administrator and Guest account names, floppy drive and CD-ROM access, driver installation, and logon prompts.
security settings	Defines the security-relevant behavior of the system. Through use of GPOs in the Active Directory, administrators can centrally apply the security levels required to protect enterprise systems.
Security Templates	Security Templates do not introduce new security parameters, but organize existing security attributes into one place to ease security administration. A physical depiction of a security configuration, this is a file that contains a group of security settings. Windows 2000 includes a set of security templates, each based on the role of a computer, from low-security domain clients to highly-secure domain controllers. These templates can be used as provided, modified, or serve as a basis for creating custom security templates.
shortcut trusts	Shortcut trusts are Windows 2000-computed trust paths between the domain controllers for two domains in a forest.
SIDs	A Security Identifier enables the operating system to uniquely identify each group and each user who is logged on to the system. Security Identifiers are part of Access Control Entry (ACE). Each ACE contains a SID that identifies the user or group to whom the ACE applies, and information on what type of access the ACE grants or denies.
Smart Card	A credit card-sized device used to securely store public and private keys, passwords, and other types of personal information.

Term	Description
	To use a Smart Card, you need a Smart Card reader connected to the computer and a personal PIN number for the Smart Card. In Windows 2000, Smart Cards can be used for certificate-based authentication and single sign-on to the enterprise.
snap-in	Snap-ins are control modules that conform to and *snap-in* to the Microsoft Management Console (MMC) user interface.
SSPI	The Security Support Provider Interface defines the security APIs for network authentication
stand-alone CA	A stand-alone Certificate Authority is a CA that does not depend on Active Directory and, consequently, is less automated than an enterprise CA. Stand-alone CAs handle user requests via a Web interface.
symmetric encryption	A fast encryption algorithm that requires the same secret key for encryption and decryption. It's used to encrypt large amounts of data, and is also called secret key encryption.
TCO	Total Cost of Ownership in networked systems is the cost to an organization for all the phases of setup and maintenance of computer systems.
TCP	TCP is based on point-to-point communication between two network hosts. TCP receives data from programs and processes this data as a stream of bytes. Bytes are grouped into segments that TCP then numbers and sequences for delivery
TCP/IP	Transmission Control Protocol/Internet Protocol is a set of networking protocols used on the Internet that provides communications across interconnected networks made up of computers with diverse hardware architectures and various operating systems. TCP/IP includes standards for how computers communicate and conventions for connecting networks and routing traffic.
TGS Exchange	Ticket Granting Service Exchange is used when the KDC distributes a service session key and a session ticket for the service.

Term	Description
TGT	Ticket Granting Tickets is used by the Kerberos Key Distribution Center for securing network authentication in a domain.
transitive trusts	Transitive trusts are two-way relationships. They are a series of trusts between parent and child domains in a domain tree, and among root domains of domain trees in a forest. They allow all domains in a forest to trust each other for authentication purposes.
trusted root	A branch of a PKI in which every member inherits all of the trust relationships from the root CA.
tunneling	Tunneling is the entire process of encapsulation, transmission, and de-encapsulation of data transmissions.
VPN	A Virtual Private Network is a private network on a PPP connection that is formed upon a public system that allows its restricted users to communicate through encryption.
WinInet	An application protocol interface designed to support Internet security protocols, such as Secure Sockets Layer (SSL).

INDEX

www.ingramcontent.com/pod-product-compliance
Lightning Source LLC
Chambersburg PA
CBHW080129060326
40689CB00018B/3728